Talking Back

Talking Back

Images of Jewish Women in American Popular Culture

Edited by Joyce Antler

Brandeis University Press

Published by University Press of New England

Hanover and London

Brandeis University Press
Published by University Press of New England, Hanover, NH 03755
Printed in the United States of America
5 4 3 2 1
CIP data appear at the end of the book

This book was published with the help of the Lucius N. Littauer Foundation, Inc.

For Lauren and Rachel

Contents

Joyce Antler
Epilogue: Jewish Women on Television:
Too Jewish or Not Enough?

Acknowledgments

I would like to express my gratitude to Shulamit Reinharz, director of the Brandeis University Women's Studies Program; Sylvia Barack Fishman and Jonathan Sarna of the Department of Near Eastern and Judaic Studies at Brandeis; Stephen Whitfield of the Department of American Studies; Sherry Israel of the Hornstein Program; Sylvia Fuks Fried of the Tauber Institute; Sharon Pucker Rivo, Executive Director of the National Jewish Film Center; Michael Feldberg, Executive Director of the American Jewish Historical Society; and Richelle Budd, for helping to conceive and implement the conference "Developing Images: Representation of Jewish Women in American Culture," which was held at Brandeis University in March 1993. The conference took place despite what was hailed as the blizzard of the century, and became the starting point of this volume.

Series editors Jonathan Sarna and Sylvia Barack Fishman provided insightful comments on the essays, and Phyllis Deutsch of the University Press of New England was a dream editor whose contributions aided the volume enormously. I am extremely grateful for her input. Ann Kraybill and Mary Crittendon of the University Press of New England skillfully saw the manuscript through the production process. John Hose, representing Brandeis University Press, offered valuable support.

Many students and colleagues helped sharpen my thinking. I owe a special thanks to Marjorie Feld and Felicia Herman of Brandeis University for superb research assistance. I would also like to thank my colleagues in the American Studies Department for their encouragement—especially Tom Doherty, for his helpful suggestions regarding film photos—as well as my colleagues in the Women's Studies program. Angie Simeone provided generous and expert assistance at every stage of this process. The librarians at Brandeis University offered invaluable guidance concerning new technological resources available to cultural historians.

As usual, my family became deeply involved in my work and helped me track down sources and flesh out ideas. I thank my husband, Stephen Antler, for his abundant and useful suggestions, and my daughters, Lauren and Rachel, for enriching my understanding and appreciation of popular culture.

My greatest debt is to the contributors to this volume, who reacted with enthusiasm and diligence to every request I made. In "talking back," they improved the product immeasurably.

Talking Back

Joyce Antler

Introduction

For generations, American Jewish women have been in the forefront of political, social, and cultural life, playing dynamic roles in many of the leading social movements of the twentieth century and in the creation of popular culture. Through their activism and their contributions to literature, cinema, vaudeville, drama, comedy, journalism, radio, and television, they have helped to shape the main currents of modern and postmodern life.

Our understanding of these past experiences derives not only from historical accounts, which are few, but from a series of compelling images that circulate in the mass media, in narrative and stories, and in other arenas of popular culture. The Yiddishe Mama, the Jewish Mother, and the Jewish American Princess (JAP) are only a few of the most powerful and durable of these images.

The essays in this book analyze these various and multiple representations. Together they construct a dialogue about the ways in which popular images and stereotypes of American Jewish women complement and interact with each other to both distort and reflect reality. Documenting a conflicting and often disturbing record of representations, essayists expose manifold images of Jewish women as victims and resisters, onlookers and activists, homemakers and paid workers, exotic "dark ladies" or clumsy "losers." They are at once self-reliant, assertive, and risk-taking, proud of the multiple poles of their identity; and doubtful, envious, and self-hating, ashamed of their heritage, their bodies, and their intellects. Such contradictory images of Jewish women—domineering and vulnerable, manipulative and quiescent, alluring and unattractive—highlight the impressive yet threatening aspects of Jewish women's roles and their power.

These paradoxical images emerge in a variety of media throughout the course of the twentieth century. Beginning with the immigrant period and continuing through the events of midcentury and the contemporary era, essayists focus on representations of Jewish women in popular and "high" fiction; silent films and talkies; autobiographies and diaries; vaudeville, comedy, satire, and

I

drama; Passover Haggadot and children's Bible stories; they also probe the interplay between images of Jewish women and the material, social, and cultural changes of the twentieth century.

The essays highlight the role of pivotal events—immigration, the Depression, the world wars, the Holocaust, and the feminist movement—at the same time that they show how the major images of Jewish women were constantly developing; that is, they became self-reflective and interactive over several generations. As they developed from generation to generation, text to text, medium to medium, a repository of images with enormous power was created.

As analyzed by scholars from the many disciplines included in this book, the images of American Jewish women in the twentieth century reflect two parallel developments in American ethnic culture. The first documents the creation of the multiple paradigms, models, and representations by which Jewish women were named, viewed, and placed—by both Jews and non-Jews, men and women—within their times. Such representations called forth a variety of responses: the experience of self-hatred, the drive to "pass" as non-Jewish, and the pervasive internalization of "otherness" coupled with resistance to such categorizations and the creation of a store of alternative images.

The second development is synonymous with becoming American: the creators of images of Jewish women used the tools of American culture to carve out an identity among the multiple ethnic and racial groups of the United States while simultaneously giving to the dominant Anglo-American society symbols, images, and narratives that enriched the collective American consciousness. In different ways the essays in this book examine how American Jews used American media to establish their own legitimacy while at the same time contributing a uniquely Jewish—and uniquely female—aspect of cultural identity to the nation's developing sense of its potential. In imagining Jewish women in a variety of roles, even in those that stereotyped them and constructed false mythologies, American Jews helped establish their own cultural autonomy and became "true" Americans. In this way images of Jewish women served as reference points for projections of the fears and dreams of American Jews over the course of the twentieth century.

The tensions between these constructed images and the realities of the lives of American Jewish women is a continuous thread in these essays. Women responded to the images in a variety of ways. They could internalize negative presentations, leading them to hope to "pass" as Gentile, often accompanied by paroxysms of self-hatred. Another response was to create a dialogue with the image makers, "talking back" to them, as Riv-Ellen Prell suggests was the case for women novelists of the 1970s who rejected and, through their work, subverted the damaging JAP stereotype that such male novelists as Herman Wouk and Philip Roth had made into national currency in the 1950s and 1960s.

As this collection shows, Jewish women talked back in a variety of ways to ideas, images, and roles that they felt constrained them. As immigrant mothers and daughters they challenged the narrowness of ideals framed by the popular culture as well as stereotypes created about immigrants themselves. During the middle decades of the century, as members of the so-called lost generation of American Jews who seemingly sacrificed ethnic and religious identification in order to assimilate into American life, they chronicled both the fears and the achievements of women who led the way into a more American future. In the latter part of the century, whether as professional novelists, screenwriters, dramatists, and entertainers or as members of grass-roots women's groups seeking to expand the representations of women in literature, history, and ritual, they created new possibilities for the expression of women's voices.

The images of Jewish women portrayed in popular culture were never a mimesis of reality; indeed, they often protested against both the actual conditions of Jewish women's lives and the false representations of them. As Catharine Stimpson has argued about women writers in general, to create was in some degree "an act of defiance." Female authors (and by extension other female artists and innovators) were cultural rebels who presented their own versions of reality and visions of the future. For Jewish women as well as for other American women, as Stimpson suggests, the history of such image makers may well be a collective biography of subversive self-assertion.[1]

Readers may have in turn transformed reality as they selected certain features of cultural texts and abandoned others. Female readers and audiences may have been especially alert to signals of resistance or tactics of disobedience that appeared in dramas of subordination; from these presentations they took what they needed to reconstruct their world.

In this manner alternative images became tools of rebellious women's consciousness, helping women to claim the truth of their lives and to transform gender and sexual standards. An understanding of these images as they developed across several generations can restore the voices of Jewish women to the cultural record, modifying myths and stereotypes and shaping new meanings.

I. Between Two Worlds: Changing Images of Immigrant Women

Following the assassination of Czar Alexander II in 1881, which called forth a wave of violent pogroms and the passage of laws restricting Jewish settlement, employment, and education opportunities, over two million Jews emigrated from the Russian Empire to the United States in the four decades between 1880 and 1920.

Almost all of the Eastern European Jewish immigrants began life in the United States amid grim circumstances; poverty, dislocation, and discrimination were common. Responding to the bewildering conditions of the New World, they created multiple and often conflicting images of Jews, and of America, in their stories and narratives. The texts they eventually produced bridged the worlds of Europe and the United States, Jews and Gentiles, men and women, mothers and daughters, reality and imagination.

Among the most significant dislocations Jews confronted in the United States involved a reordering of gender roles. In Eastern Europe, wives generally shared the breadwinning role with husbands; if the latter were religious scholars, wives frequently assumed sole economic responsibility for their families. But in America, where cultural ideals did not support married women's work, Jewish women relinquished their marketplace responsibilities as soon as they were able, and the burden shifted more to husbands. Daughters often became breadwinners as well, entering the industrial work force and forever altering family culture and traditional expectations.[2]

Giving voice to the traumatic experiences of their resettlement, an unusual number of immigrant women turned to writing. Through the power of words, they sought to relieve the tremendous cultural and social anxieties of acculturation while shaping their own new identities as American women. Janet Burstein explores the psychic dimension of four immigrant writers' struggles to translate the gendered and ethnic ambiguities of their own experience into usable public forms. In the novels and autobiographies of Mary Antin, Anzia Yezierska, Emma Goldman, and Kate Simon, she finds a series of fluid, emotionally turbulent images etched out in resistance to and sometimes in imitation of matriarchal models. Through storytelling, mothers passed on their own varied and multiple identities to daughters, who wrote of themselves as variable, manifold selves. Burstein's analysis of these multiple modes of self-representation exposes the numerous psychic costs, strategies, and models of becoming American women in the developing culture.

Sharon Pucker Rivo's examination of twenty-six Yiddish and English-language films about Jews, made from the turn of the century through the early 1930s, chronicles a trajectory of changing cinematic images of Jewish women. From images of young women as impoverished victims of the immigrant experience in the early period of Eastern European immigration to the portrayal of stronger, self-reliant women who sought their own independent identities but held fast to their Jewish heritage a decade later, these images incorporate the perspectives of such influential women writers as Yezierska and Fannie Hurst. Rivo highlights the 1920s as a moment in time when unusually positive and realistic images of Jewish women came to dominate artistic expression, albeit briefly. The problematic relationship of these representations to the more naive and often hostile images that came before and after suggests an important nexus for exploring the links between images, image makers, audiences, and the cultural imperatives of assimilation.

II. Assimilating Images: Representations of the "Lost Generation"

Despite a rising tide of anti-Semitism and the crisis of the Depression, American Jews continued their progress into the American mainstream during these decades. Jewish women made rapid advances in education and professional life, attending colleges, universities, and professional schools in numbers disproportionate to their representation in the population; many helped pioneer new careers for women in teaching, law, social work, and civil service.

Jewish women also played a vital role in developing the myriad forms of mass entertainment that flourished in the teens, twenties, thirties as the so-called secular temples of twentieth-century Jewry. From Yiddish theater to vaudeville to musical comedy, nightclubs, radio, film, and television, the new mass culture became a kind of Jewish popular religion, relieving the tensions and fears of the "lost" generation of American Jews—second-generation Jews who abandoned the religious heritage of their immigrant parents—as they journeyed forth to find places in the pluralist world of America.

Images of Jewish women in popular culture serve as a barometer of the acculturation process and of the changing and often contradictory nature of women's attitudes, roles, and achievements during this period. While, as Rivo shows, the films of the 1920s portrayed Jewish women's independence and positive sense of ethnicity, the turmoil, confusion, and rootlessness that others experienced as they set forth on new pathways is captured in Joan Jacobs Brumberg's study of the rare diary of a Jewish adolescent in the 1920s. As Brumberg explains, Jewish girls did not typically keep diaries until the 1950s, when American Jews as a group had attained middle-class status and possessed the leisure to contemplate their "private" thoughts and write them down. When Anne Frank became a staple of American popular culture following the 1952 publication of her diary and the Broadway play and Hollywood film based on it, diary writing among Jewish girls received further impetus. Brumberg uses the contrasting self-images of Jewish girls in 1920s and 1950s diaries to assess the dual processes of assimilation and the growth of mass culture during this period.

Feeling like an outsider both among Christians and among wealthier Jews, her 1920s diarist articulates the intimate aspects of growing up Jewish in the second generation. For many such women, the pain of being different—being Jewish—tempered the rewards of assimilation, even for those women who, like the diarist, were able to attend private, elite women's colleges. Despite her keen sense of her origins, the young writer judged herself in terms of the dominant gender and beauty images that denied the worth of her ethnic background and its distinctiveness. Internalizing the anti-Semitism of her times, she criticized other Jews by the same standards of popular culture and found them—and herself—wanting. By the 1950s, Jewishness had disappeared even more fully from adolescent diaries in favor of concerns about appearance, social life, and sexual identity. Mass culture images of youth and beauty, not religious identity, had become predominant influences in shaping the female self.

While Jewish women's self-images were thus formed by the culture's dominant image of women as gentle, Gentile, and gendered (i.e., performing standard, domestic female functions), a different set of images—of women as rebellious, assertive, sexual, even bawdy—seeped into the popular culture by way of such entertainers as Sophie Tucker and Fannie Brice, vaudeville stars who attracted mass audiences despite their ethnic origins. Using parody, satire, and off-color (some said vulgar) lyrics and jokes, they discussed social problems regarding sexuality, marriage, divorce, and other personal issues. Rather than absorbing images around them, Tucker and Brice challenged normative standards, using humor to probe and upset social expectations.

By offering audiences a series of unconventional images of women that often reversed traditional sex roles, they helped viewers to alter their own sense of self or to contemplate alternative points of view. While they incorporated elements of activist tradition from the past, their routines pointed the way to the future. The images of assertive, backtalking Jewish women developed by Tucker and Brice extended into later generations with the work of Joan Rivers, Bette Midler, and Barbra Streisand. June Sochen argues that these later comic entertainers can be considered reformers as well as performers because their social critiques countered rigid codes of gender behavior as well as of Americanness and inspired audiences to rethink their own values.

Gertrude Berg, the writer, producer, and actor who created the character of Molly Goldberg, leading figure of the hit radio and television show *The Goldbergs*, provided another example of a powerful cultural image that mediated American Jews' rapid integration into the American middle class and offered an assertive, albeit accommodating, figure of Jewish womanhood. According to Donald Weber, Gertrude Berg's influence lay in inscribing the figure of Molly Goldberg as conservative agent of familial and intercultural harmony. Situating Berg's ethnic art within a developing spectrum of Jewish performances extending from vaudeville to the legitimate stage and the new medium of radio, Weber sees Berg's career as a continuing effort to bridge the dual identities of ethnic and American in the middle decades of the twentieth century. A far cry from the literary heroines of immigrant writers or the brash images of vaudeville women like Tucker and Brice, the Molly Goldberg image of lovable Jewish matriarch fostered and represented ideals of interdenominational harmony highly valued by second-generation Jews. Berg's character, Molly, possessed a strength, boldness, and cunning that were widely admired by non-Jews and Jews alike, assuring her status as a popular culture heroine for over three decades.

III. Changing Stereotypes: Jewish Women in Postwar America

According to some commentators, the decades from 1945 to 1964 represented nothing less than a "Golden Age" for American Jewry.[3] Recovering from the exhaustion of World War II and the Holocaust, Jews enjoyed unprecedented economic prosperity and a great increase in opportunities in education, the professions, and business. Anti-Semitism declined precipitously, and religious life, as evidenced by the widespread construction of Jewish synagogues and community centers, apparently enjoyed a sharp revival. The creative outpouring of Jewish writers, in both quality and quantity, and the American public's receptivity to their works was astonishing.[4]

Despite the prominence of Jewish writers, most were reluctant to introduce Jewish themes into their work. When Jews did address Jewish subjects, it was most frequently to turn their razor-sharp wit to the foibles, not the successes, of American Jews as they climbed to higher reaches of American society. Jewish women in particular seemed to stand as symbols—and stereotypes—of the darker side of the Jewish ascension to the American mainstream.[5] Philip Roth's Sophie Portnoy, a "domineering, castrating, enticing, meddling and thoroughly maddening monster," according to critic Marya Mannes, was only the most exaggerated of the all-engulfing, sometimes comic, sometimes venomous Jewish mothers portrayed in postwar novels.[6]

Susanne Klingenstein's essay examines the maternal icon that appears at the center of many narratives about the Holocaust present in postwar American fiction, television, and film. Surprisingly, books and films on the Holocaust did not make an impact until several decades after the war's end. One of the first to reach popular consciousness was Herman Wouk's 1971 novel *Winds of War*, which sold five million copies in the United States. Comparing the maternal figure in the works of such "high" literary stylists as Cynthia Ozick, Norma Rosen, Susan Fromberg Schaeffer, and Rebecca Goldstein to Wouk's clichéd portrayal of Natalie Jastrow, the heroine of the *Winds of War* and its 1978 sequel, *War and Remembrance* (made into the 1983 TV miniseries *The Winds of War*), Klingenstein explores the possibility of popular fiction serving as moral illumination, especially about the catastrophe of the Holocaust.

Klingenstein concludes that there is a fundamental incompatibility between sentimental fiction and "stone-hard history": the high realism of wartime events that Wouk successfully portrays is undermined by the inventedness of his romantic characters. Yet she acknowledges that Natalie occupies a place within the "dark lady" tradition of American romance fiction; even beyond this literary significance is the fact that for millions of Americans during the 1970s, Natalie served as an important and sometimes sole conduit of knowledge about the Holocaust.

As Riv-Ellen Prell points out in her essay, Jewish daughters' representations grew in tandem with those of the Jewish mother. In the works of Philip Roth, Herman Wouk, and Bruce Jay Friedman, daughters appeared as beautiful but excessively concerned with appearances and possessions. To Prell, the multiple images of these spoiled and materialistic young women—commenting on such aspects of domestic life as clothing, sexuality, appetite, and leisure—personified the promise and disappointments of postwar American Jewish life. It was not incidental that at the point at which Jewish economic success and mainstream status became the norm, images of women became the perfect embodiment of a world about which Jews, especially Jewish men, remained ambivalent and often rejecting. Circulating from literary representations to film and the routines of comedians on radio and television to jokebooks and novelty cards, Jewish women's images became crucial components of the construction of American Jewish culture and identity in the postwar period.

Prell finds that in nine popular novels written by Jewish women in mid-1970s, the protagonists' embodied otherness and "grotesque bodies" are means not only of sexual warfare but of cultural definition. In opposition to the images of Marjorie Morningstar and Brenda Patimkin, the sleek, self-assured heroines of Wouk's *Marjorie Morningstar* and Roth's *Goodbye, Columbus*, these 1970s heroines, who call themselves JAPs, are overweight and unattractive. Transitional women, sexually independent and autonomous, they are unable to completely reject cultural norms of physical beauty and domesticity. Disappointed in love, they became objects of their own derision and emerge as comic characters. Yet they remain unwilling to ascribe their own lives according to representations they recognize as false and "talk back" to the male authors' JAP stereotypes.

Bonnie Lyons explores the images of women in the work of the two most distinctive Jewish woman writers to emerge in the postwar period—Cynthia Ozick and Grace Paley. In Lyons's view, their work "fills in the large blank area" of Jewish American fiction left by male writers' failure to create memorable female characters or to probe the world as it appears to women.

Lyons discusses Ruth Puttermesser and Faith Darwin—central characters in much of Ozick's and Paley's fiction—as more intensely realized representations, with much greater intellectual and spiritual depth, than the female characters of Roth, Mailer, Bellow, and Malamud. Distinguishing between the two women's sensibilities both as Jews and as feminists, Lyons sees Ozick's work as emblematic of the "Great Tradition" of formal Jewish law and study of sacred texts, while Paley's derives from the "Little Tradition" of *Yiddishkeyt*, in particular, the validation of the common person, or *mentschlekhkeyt*. Whereas Ozick's feminism centers on notions of androgyny and a universal human ideal, Paley emphasizes sexual difference, female friendship, and a woman-centered world. Lyons's inquiry clarifies the richness of the Jewish tradition and the potential of feminism as sources for imagining Jewish women.

IV. Contemporary Jewish Feminists as Image Makers

The process of creating and shaping images of Jewish women has been in-eluctably and continually transformed by the many changes in contemporary life wrought by the feminist movement over the past twenty-five years. Jewish women have contributed to and benefited from these changes; participating in the leadership and rank and file of the women's movement in numbers dispro-portionate to their representation in the American population, they have been enthusiastic supporters of women's rights and the movement toward egalitari-anism in politics, the workplace, education, and religion.[7]

Essays in the collection illuminate the growing complexity of representa-tions of Jewish women that have accompanied these changes. In fiction, film, and drama, the period marks the emergence of strong women's voices through the presentation of a plethora of female Jewish characters whose world visions are presented with unusual perspicacity.

Focusing on numerous authors and cinematic image makers who, since the 1960s, have provided increasingly nuanced portrayals of Jewish women, Sylvia Barack Fishman scrutinizes the interactions of female characters with other women, arguing that the mixed emotions revealed in such relationships are indicators of the complexity of Jewish women's natures. Fishman analyzes the images of female characters in Herman Wouk's *Marjorie Morningstar* (1955) and the even more "unpleasant" representations of women in Philip Roth's *Goodbye, Columbus* (1969). Even in relatively positive portrayals by male writers—for example, the portraits of family members provided in the memoirs of Alfred Kazin—Jewish women are not seen from the inside and rarely achieve fullness. One exception Fishman examines is Neil Simon's *Brighton Beach Memoirs*.

In exploring the images of women that appear in prose works by Ozick, Vi-vian Gornick, Rebecca Goldstein, Daphne Merkin, Lynne Sharon Schwartz, and Sylvia Rothchild and in the films of Nora Ephron and Joan Micklin Silver, Fishman finds a rich chronicle of contemporary American Jewish women's lives; in these works, women are not "accessories to the internal dramas of male characters." Yet Fishman finds that some of the demons with which Jew-ish women wrestle and that turn them against each other emerge from stereo-types men have promulgated; others are based on the changing emotional and social dynamics of female achievement in the modern world. Probing the com-plicated relationships between mothers, grandmothers, daughters, grand-daughters, sisters, and friends presented in contemporary writings and films by women, Fishman shows that questions of attachment and individuation, be-longing and independence, in the lives of modern American Jewish women touch on complex and interrelated questions of female psychology, Jewish as-similation, and social opportunity.

More than any other filmmaker or performer, Barbra Streisand has created a rich and varying body of cinematic images of Jewish women. In contrast to June Sochen's article in this volume, discussed earlier, Felicia Herman questions whether Streisand should be seen as a reformer critical of the status quo. Focusing on *Funny Girl* (1968), *The Way We Were* (1973), *A Star Is Born* (1976), *The Main Event* (1979), and *Yentl* (1983), Herman suggests that Streisand's intended critique of mainstream culture falls short because of characterizations that show women—however assertive—as longing for romance and marriage. Yet Herman acknowledges that audiences remember Streisand's characters not for their romantic or religious shortcomings (she sees Streisand's Jewish women as expressive of a secular liberalism, not Judaic values). Paying tribute to the staying power of Streisand's representations, she ultimately agrees that the images that remain with audiences are those of "feisty Jews and feisty women"—images that may well allow viewers to imagine alternatives to their own lives. It is a measure of the complexity of Streisand's portrayals that the meaning of her cinematic images of Jewish women have become a matter of scholarly debate even among Jewish feminists.

Sarah Blacher Cohen offers a personal account of her transformation from academic critic to "untamed playwright." As a scholar, Cohen modeled herself on men; her theatrical career began helping to shape Isaac Bashevis Singer's play, *Schlemiel the First*. Tired of serving as "handmaiden" to Singer's creativity, Cohen wrote the drama, "The Ladies Locker Room," loosely based on her experiences as a disabled Jewish woman. She has since written plays about Mollie Picon, Sophie Tucker, Belle Barth, and Totie Fields—"obstreporous sisters" who used humor to counter sexism, anti-Semitism, and ageism. Breaking tradition and flaunting taboos in their own day, these "big mouths" are fitting role models for Cohen's "unkosher" experiments in drama.

V. Recovering Religious Role Models: New Images of Jewish Women in Stories and Song

The women's movement has galvanized a generation of Jewish women, even those who had not been previously committed to Judaism, to return to their religion. By reclaiming Jewish women's history and spirituality, Jewish women in all denominations hoped to enrich their traditions and provide role models for the future. For many, this meant asking rigorous questions about halacha (Jewish law), theology, ritual, and liturgy while also exploring images of women within the Jewish tradition that circulated in the more popular forms of culture, including holidays texts, children's stories, songs, music, and drama.[8]

Gail Reimer draws on a diverse group of popular retellings of the biblical story of Esther (including a libretto by Elizabeth Swados and children's books) to explore shifting representations of biblical women in the work of contemporary feminist writers. Her essay examines the ways in which efforts to exalt Vashti and vilify Esther fail to challenge the traditional polarizations of biblical women into good and bad, whereas they reinforce the tensions women feel between feminism and Judaism. Recent efforts to resolve these tensions have led to some powerfully charged contemporary representations of Esther as a sexually daring "Jewish wonder woman." Such continuing retellings of the Purim story according to changing ideas of women's roles provide further indications of the ferment in popular images of Jewish heroines. The promulgation of such stories reveals that the changes that had begun to be debated among scholars and theologians are now reaching into Sunday school and bedtime stories and are influencing the next generations.

In her essay, Maida Solomon appraises the grass-roots movement that has taken place over the past quarter of a century and has placed women at the center of feminist Passover haggadot. She charts the development of female imagery from innovative lesbian feminist haggadot of the 1970s, used in small, individual, friendship-based seders, to contemporary hagaddot written by committees of established organizations and used in local community seders and even international seders for hundreds of participants. Incorporating biblical heroines—from Miriam and the midwives to the matriarchs, Deborah, and other political and military figures—as well as leading women from centuries of Jewish and world history, including Holocaust resisters and American political activists—the new haggadot offer hundreds of traditional and new images and midrashim (commentary) on female-centered Jewish visions of the exodus and struggle for freedom. The invention and re-creation of such heroines and their placement in the most popular sources of Jewish ceremonial storytelling, a basic aspect of Jewish renewal and commitment, is a measure of the wide reach of contemporary feminist religious transformation.

As seen throughout this collection, the development of Jewish women's images in popular culture over the course of nearly a century has proceeded in tandem with emerging directions of American Jewish socialization and women's lives generally. In identifying and analyzing these multiple representations, the essayists establish Jewish women's contributions to history, literature, art, religion, scholarship, radio, television, film, and performance. Collectively, they provide a valuable contribution to American Jewish history and feminist criticism, demonstrating that American Jewish women's studies is finding a place in the developing gendered, multidisciplinary discourses of the academic world today.

I

Between Two Worlds:
Changing Images of Immigrant Women

Janet Burstein

Translating Immigrant Women
Surfacing the Manifold Self

> We are translations into different dialects
> of a text still being written
> in the original.
> —Adrienne Rich, "Sibling Mysteries"

From where we are, in the last decade of the twentieth century, the Jewish women who came to America from Europe look like heroic beginners. Founders of our families, the matrix that nurtured our mothers and/or grandmothers, they seem to us pioneers: intrepid adventurers who move always forward, setting in motion the long process that produced us. From a less self-centered point of view, however, these women who began Jewish life in America were also part of a much longer process. Caught in a moment of radical change, they were also shaped by ancient influences that resisted change. Thus, they lived at the confluence of powerful forces that moved in different directions. Out of the tensions created by their situation as immigrants, as Jews, and as women, they fashioned a distinctive—if not always heroic—sense of self. And the stories of their daughters not only translate that achievement but also record its effects on their own efforts to become Americans.

Bearing featherbeds and samovars from Eastern Europe to make homelike the New World, Jewish women brought to America an assortment of disparate self-images.[1] As Jews they had all seen themselves reflected in the prejudices of gentile Europe. By reflection in the teachings of traditional Judaism, moreover, they knew themselves as women to be secondary creatures, excluded from authority in communal and religious life and denied the educations enjoyed by their brothers, fathers, and husbands.[2] They were responsible, however, for the sustenance of their families. Husbands and older children might help to earn the bread and maintain the "fundamental religious rituals of private life"[3]; but in a world where most Jews were poor and politically impotent, women's work at home and in the marketplace was acknowledged to be an "essential component of physical and cultural survival"—even though women themselves "were considered inferior to men" within their own communities.[4] Such discordances between their actual accomplishments and their subordinate cultural status were among the givens of gender that they transmitted to their daughters.[5]

In America the work of immigrant mothers remained essential to the survival and acculturation of their families. But the circumstances and scope of their lives changed in ways that further shaped their daughters' perceptions and self-images. As Jews began to "conform to modern, not traditional, understandings about women's roles,"[6] married women withdrew from the marketplace into the home. They were barred not only by pretensions to middle-class status but also by the proprietary sexual protectiveness of their husbands from work in factories and shops—marketplaces of the New World that quickly absorbed their children and husbands. Thus, the social scope of the Jewish mother, whose domestic *and* economic prowess had been widely acknowledged in Europe, whose work had given her "some family authority, a knowledge of the marketplace, and a certain worldliness"[7] seemed to her daughters to be diminished rather than enlarged by her emigration to America. Indeed, when daughters of these women speak to contemporary interviewers, they often stress the hardships and the deprivations of their mothers' lives.[8]

This perceptual shift owed something as well to the changed circumstances of the daughters' lives in America. As the scope of an immigrant mother's social and economic activity contracted, her daughter's expanded. She was freer than her mother to work for and with men, for the sexuality of an unmarried woman escaped ritual notice and male control.[9] As she entered the factories and shops of the American marketplace, she benefited as well from the tradition of women's work in Eastern Europe that had empowered and validated her mother. But according to Sydney Weinberg, immigrant "mothers could not provide role models for their teenage daughters on the Lower East Side of New York any more than they could in the working-class areas of Bialystok or Odessa. Urbanization and industrialization had altered life in both places, and their mothers' homebound lives offered no clues to behavior."[10] In time the daughter's sensitivity to the malaise of the newly sequestered mother and the disjunctions between her life and her mother's distanced these two generations of immigrant women from one another and complicated the development of the Jewish immigrant daughter.

Out of this developmental complexity arose for immigrant daughters an image of a manifold self that owed much to the disparate self-images sustained by their mothers. This complexity is often submerged in historical accounts and oral histories. The reasons for this submergence are multiple. Such complexities often fall beneath the notice of historical accounts that concentrate, necessarily, on achievements rather than the subjective issues that inspire or accompany achievement. Developmental complexities are also muted in oral histories, which, according to Kathryn Anderson and Dana C. Jack,[11] implicitly encourage inexperienced informants toward versions of their experience that suit the scholarly agendas and listening skills of their interviewers. Then too, memory often obscures difficulties unresolved by time—or delivers them transformed by resignation. But the stories of Jewish immigrant women writers surface the complex personal issues these women confronted as they turned themselves into Americans. The stories reveal the emergence of a gendered self in which disjunctions and discordances coexist with the power, ambition, and drive that fuel the achievement of immigrant daughters. Despite the distances between generations of immigrant women, the daughters develop into translations of their mothers.

Mary Antin, Anzia Yezierska, Emma Goldman, and Kate Simon are prominent among the immigrant writers whose stories probe the ethnic, gendered, and developmental complexities that fashion the model of the manifold self. To the disjunctive self-images sustained by their mothers, protagonists in these stories add another layer of complexity that rises from the failure of the immigrant mother as a model of worldliness. To meet both their own and their families' expectations, unmarried fictional protagonists and autobiographical personas need to become active subjects in a public world where their mothers once flourished but from which they have virtually withdrawn. To accomplish that task, immigrant daughters in fictions and memoirs accommodate themselves to the changes in their mothers' lives and to the increasing disjunction between their mothers' experience and their own. Without current maternal models of worldliness, however, some daughters in these stories require—more than ever—fathers who can be for them what psychoanalysts believe fathers always are: the "way into the world" that daughters need and long to enter.[12] Like the disparate self-images sustained by their mothers, however, the disjunction between such needs and their uncertain gratification appears in the stories to further complicate the development of immigrant daughters.

The first fruits of the tension created by these disjunctions are the stories themselves, which translate into the language of America the experience of women born in Europe. Unlike the Jewish women who continued to write in Yiddish after they came to America, these writers departed from the model of their mothers by trying to tell for the first time, in a new language, stories that carried the European past into the American present. Despite the new language, however, and despite the increasing differences between mothers' and daughters' lives, the stories testify to the power of the mothers' images by revealing the emergence into awareness, through storytelling, of an American Jewish woman who, like her mother, knew several disparate versions of herself. This manifold sense of self—and the power to formulate it in stories—

For Mary Antin, duality was a developmental puzzle. Fulfilling
her father's ambitions, she remained her mother's daughter.
(Courtesy American Jewish Archives, Cincinnati Campus,
Hebrew Union College, Jewish Institute of Religion)

may have been one of the immigrant mother's most characteristic legacies to
her American daughter.

No single story represents more clearly than Mary Antin's (1881–1949)
The Promised Land (1912) both the division between mother and daughter and
the daughter's sense of herself as a manifold being: European and American,

child and adult, woman and writer. As a Jew in a non-Jewish culture, as an immigrant among people who were at home in the world, and as a female in a patriarchal religious tradition, this child knew very early what Elaine Showalter has called the dual languages and paradigms of both the "muted" groups to which she belonged and the "dominant" groups within which she had to function.[13] Thus, Antin's writing became a strategy of negotiation, for her memoir presents duality as the developmental puzzle her protagonist must solve as she becomes both an American and a woman. Antin's narrative persona is actually created by the disjunctions and connections she manages to embody. She connects two personas in herself. She is, on one hand, the adult who objectifies as "absolutely other" the child whose story she tells.[14] She is also, however, the child who claims the role of subject as she speaks for herself, demonstrating repeatedly her likeness to the adult narrator.

As Antin's child tells her story, the adult narrator clarifies and confirms her own sense of self by identifying likeness or difference between them. She heightens awareness of difference, for example, by recalling the moment in which she first transgressed a Jewish law to test the wrath of God and then piously kissed a Bible she had dropped to avoid the certain wrath of her grandmother. In this anecdote, Antin first objectifies the child she was, then owns her as a different version of herself. She records this shift in relationship by shifting pronouns: from third to first person. And she highlights the shift by calling attention to it in the text: "How, I wonder, would this Psalm-singing child be enabled by the investigator of her mind? . . . I should say the child was a piteously puzzled little fraud. To return to the honest first person, I *was* something of a fraud."[15] The unstable yet undeniable mode of connection this memoir creates between these disparate personas gradually becomes a metaphor for the self-creating American Jewish woman who was once—and remains, in part—a Russian immigrant child. Thus, the memoir embodies the narrator's validation of two editions of herself: the Russian original and the American translation.

Readers often perceive in this narrator's efforts to differentiate herself from the child she was, the displacement of an immigrant self-image by an American one. Werner Sollors, for example, identifies Antin's "distance from her old self" with her "rebirth" as an American. He describes Antin's treatment of these two "subjects" as evidence of a "conversion" experience.[16] But division within this narrator's self-image appeared long before her American experience began. And the memoir suggests that differences are no more important to Antin than similarities. Among the likenesses that connect these two personas, perhaps the most significant is their identical response to the massive dissonances produced by their experiences: of poverty, of prejudice, of dislocation. Both personas become writers/translators partly in response to the disintegrative power of those experiences. For both, writing/translating services the survival of the self.

For example, by the time she is ten years old, Antin masters potentially dis-integrative anxiety by translating feelings into words. When government agents invade her fatherless, impoverished home in Europe, she retires to a "quiet corner" to "grapple" with the "oppressive fear" that threatens to over-whelm her: "I was not given to weeping," she writes, "but I must think things out in words."[17] She learned even earlier the power of words to overcome sep-aration. Her letters to her father in America and the ones she writes later, from America to an uncle in Europe, not only bind absent ones in far places to one another but also bind past to present and facets of the self to one another. They find their way into this narrative where—in translation—they draw the impres-sions of the child into the narrative of the adult writer.

Characteristically, the text embodies without resolving the tensions created by experiential dualities. The most sustained source of tension for this immi-grant daughter, for example, is created by the ethnic and gendered dichotomies that shaped her parents. Antin's father and mother can and do sustain her work of self-creation. But both ethnicity and gender prevent these immigrant parents from giving Antin what Jessica Benjamin has called the "recognition" she needs to take her place as a subject outside the text, in the world.[18] For Ben-jamin, "recognizing the other" and being recognized as a subject who can de-sire and act independently are essential to individual development. "Recogni-tion," she explains, ". . . allows the self to realize its agency and authorship. . . . but [it] can only come from another whom we, in turn, recognize as a per-son in his or her own right."[19] When both parent and child can recognize one another as capable of acting on their own, apart from the other's control, they confirm one another as subjects. Children learn this interaction as early as eighteen months, Benjamin suspects, but they depend on it as long as they live.[20]

Antin depends for "recognition" chiefly on her father, whose male privilege entitled him to the education and the freedom of movement in the world that her mother longed for but was denied. Antin identifies with him: like him, she would be an intellectual, a doubter of conventional pieties, an adapter to modernity, and an unquestioning believer in the virtues of learning. He affirms these shared characteristics in his daughter. By his unwavering support he con-firms her status as an active subject. In Benjamin's terms, he "recognizes" her as a being like himself.

But her gender keeps her different from him. And her mother and sister cannot provide the "recognition" that only subjects can offer one another. Mother and sister help her to become her father's intellectual daughter partly by releasing her from domestic tasks—unlike them she will neither sew nor cook nor work in their store. But the traditional self-subordination of even a powerful and generous mother like Antin's limits her ability to validate her daughter as the subject of her own life. From her mother Antin inherits not only the image of woman as worker but also, less advantageously, the image of woman as subordinate creature, ruled by parents and husband.[21]

Antin's story reveals fully the context in which this image was formed. After defying unsuccessfully the parents who would rather marry than educate her, Antin's mother not only submitted but also clung for the rest of her life, respectfully and obediently, to the authority of a patriarchal tradition. She became, her daughter says, "one of those women who always obey the highest law they know, even though it leads them to their doom."[22] She followed her husband's orders, painfully divesting herself in America of the "mantle of Orthodox observance . . . that . . . was interwoven with the fabric of her soul."[23] Seeing her mother's pain, Antin praises, half-patronizing, her "native adaptability, the readiness to fall into line, which is one of the most charming traits of her gentle, self-effacing nature."[24] Thus, despite her physical strength, her economic prowess, her resourcefulness, this mother's subjective status is highly qualified by the obedience exacted of her by parents and husband. Antin records as well her mother's acquiescence to the assaults of non-Jews. When her child is abused in Europe by a Gentile peasant boy, this mother teaches passiveness and resignation: "The Gentiles do as they like with us Jews," she says.[25]

Constrained thus by gender and ethnicity, Antin's mother transmits to her daughter her own limitations. Antin rejects them, in part, by denying her likeness to her mother. In her defiant assertions of equality with George Washington, her embarrassingly self-celebratory claims to success as a student, and her insistent refusal of "woman's work" that might liken her to her mother, one hears echoes of that denial. But her defiance betrays the inner uncertainty that makes defiance necessary.[26] Like both parents, who subordinated themselves to the will of the Gentiles, she is a Jew.[27] Like her mother, whose youthful story recalls defiance but whose behavior models obedience, Antin becomes obedient to a fault to the non-Jewish authorities who dominate the world she seeks to enter. As she yields, always gratefully, to the power of multiple mentors in this memoir, she fulfills her intellectual father's ambitions but remains her subordinate mother's daughter. Sustaining the tensions between these personas, the narrative testifies eloquently to the emergence of the manifold self.

Anzia Yezierska (1880–1970) lived and wrote much closer than Mary Antin to the emotional turbulence of self-creation. In her changes of direction one discerns the uncertainties that often divided her against herself and frustrated her development as both a woman and a writer. Marrying twice but unwilling to live with either husband; bearing a daughter whom she could not raise by herself but to whom she was devoted; forging and reforging fictional versions of her own story, whose imperfect untangling kept her at work for nearly a decade on her autobiography; and creating a series of narrator/protagonists whose relationship to their creator defies clarification,[28] Yezierska's life and work, like clouded mirrors, reflect the insecurity of her sense of herself as an active subject in the world and her drive to satisfy her need for "recognition." If, as Thomas Ferraro persuasively argues, Yezierska's *Bread Givers* (1925) chronicles the reinscription of traditional Jewish patriarchy in ethnic American middle-class culture,[29] the novel identifies the Jewish daughter's need for "recognition" by a powerful male figure as one motive force behind that dynamic.

Both parents shape the quest for recognition that dominates Anzia Yezierska's life and work. Her protagonists, like Yezierska herself, are usually driven by longing not only for food or money but for the regard of powerful subjects. The intensity of that longing owes much to the triadic relationship between a daughter, a traditional Jewish patriarch, and an idealizing Jewish mother. The gendered imbalance described by the novel *Bread Givers* is too familiar to need much description here. In the world of this novel the spiritually dependent, traditional mother serves and obeys the patriarch who can study and speak for her before God. She idealizes him because he embodies the agency and desire[30] that subjects possess but that women in this patriarchal culture lack. However angry she may be at his selfish tyrannies, when her husband smiles at her, this mother's anger melts away.[31] One daughter, Sara, defies his control. Like Antin, she demonstrates her likeness to him as an intellectual. But he withholds what Antin's father gives: recognition of her as a subject like himself.[32]

Sara learns from her mother, moreover, the habit of idealizing what Benjamin calls an "other who is what she cannot be"[33] and whose recognition would confirm her as a subject like himself. In *Bread Givers*, Sara's achievements will feel empty to her until her father recognizes them. But in other stories—as in Yezierska's own life—the idealized male "others" whose recognition can confirm the immigrant daughter's sense of self are not usually Orthodox Jewish patriarchs. They possess the patriarch's power to recognize immigrant daughters and thus to confirm them as active subjects in the New World. But these father-surrogates are not socially handicapped in America by Orthodox religious practices or immigrant poverty. In Yezierska's *Salome of the Tenements* (1923), *All I Could Never Be* (1932), and *Red Ribbon on a White Horse* (1950) the lovers/mentors who possess this power are all non-Jews.[34] In their confirming male gaze, as one protagonist says, "I had found some one who saw me, knew me, reassured me that I existed."[35] Like Yezierska herself, one suspects, these protagonists seesaw between rebellion and submission as they seek confirmation of themselves in the regard of powerful men.[36]

Yezierska's brief but intense relationship with John Dewey furnishes the prototypical love affair in which a whole series of her protagonists enjoy, momentarily, the recognition by idealized men that transforms women into subjects of their own lives. Sometimes the transformation has spiritual overtones. More often, the effect of the idealized male gaze upon the woman who lives only to be seen by him is psychological. Fania's mentor/lover in *All I Could Never Be* (1932) specifies exactly this effect: "You desire to be. You are: but you do not yet fully know that you are. And perhaps I can have the happiness of helping you realize that you are and what you are."[37] An earlier protagonist, Sonya in *Salome of the Tenements* (1923), knows the "fire of worship" is "roused" in her by her mentor/lover's "unconscious air of superiority." "It's my worship for him that lifts me out of myself!" she cries.[38] As Yezierska herself was urged into becoming a writer by Dewey's recognition of her talent, Sonya is fired by her lover's regard to create of her shabby self a stylish, silken creature capable of winning and holding a Protestant American millionaire. In her later "memoir," *Red Ribbon on a White Horse* (1950), Yezierska clarifies the source of the father/mentor/lover's power to transform a woman by his gaze into her better self: when she meets the figure called in this work John Manning, she says: "I had found some one who saw me, knew me, reassured me that I existed."[39]

Although several of her protagonists suspect that their inability to become and to sustain themselves as subjects is related to their cultural alienation from family and ghetto, these protagonists—like Yezierska herself, one suspects—actually seek all their lives confirmation of themselves as subjects in the regard of powerful men. Insofar as they idealize these men, they also unconsciously imitate—like Sara Smolinsky—the mothers whose lives they are determined not to repeat. From the tension between rejection and imitation of the subordinated mother, the manifold self of Yezierska's characteristic protagonist emerges: ambitious, creative, driven, vividly self-expressive, and at the same time emotionally dependent on the confirming gaze of a powerful man.

The determination not to repeat the life of one's mother rises, for Yezierska's Sara, out of an unbalanced family in which the mother is diminished and the father correspondingly enlarged—and rejecting of his daughters. That gender imbalance, the determination not to replicate one's mother, and the development of a turbulent self—powerfully self-assertive on one hand yet uncertain of its subjective status on the other hand and thus dependent in part on the regard of a beloved, idealized man—appear as well in the autobiography of Emma Goldman (1869–1940).

Goldman tried both to revise her mother and to repair the conditions that oppressed her. Like other immigrant daughters who connected their own deprivations with their mother's pain,[40] Goldman's autobiographical persona describes her mother and her own childhood self as victims of the same oppressor. Her violent, sexually demanding father frequently beat his daughters and held their mother in an "iron grip."[41] Sexually abused as an adolescent,[42] frequently beaten,[43] and starved for the affection her depressed mother could

In Emma Goldman, the abused, unloved child persisted within the heroic, public persona. (Courtesy Schlesinger Library, Radcliffe College)

never give, Goldman understood her mother's plight through the medium of her own suffering. And she never forgot. As an adult she wrote: "the old-time motherhood to me is the most terrible thing imposed upon woman"; "it has made her so unspeakably helpless and dependent, so self-centered and unso-cial as to fill me with absolute horror."[44]

Resisting that horror in her public career, Goldman opposed conventional marriage, sought to improve children's health and safety, worked as midwife among the poor, and agitated tirelessly for birth control.[45] Privately, however, her own "passionate maternal spirit"[46] led Goldman to "mother" several lovers and a multitude of friends. She also translated her mother's gifts as a storyteller and her mother's eloquence as public advocate on behalf of others[47] into a command of language and feeling that filled large lecture halls.[48] Thus, Goldman created, on one hand, a heroic persona that revised and idealized the maternal image she knew best[49] and also attempted to reshape the circumstances that had constricted her mother's life.

The subtext of her memoir also reveals, however, the child's anger at the mother who failed to protect her from sexual abuse and paternal violence. Anger may well account for some of the ways in which Goldman's adult career pointedly diverged from the pattern of her mother's life. Denying her likeness to the mother who bore many children to a man she did not love, Goldman refused to become a mother herself. And denying her likeness to a mother so depressed by the death of her first husband that she became both emotionally and sexually unresponsive, Goldman lived her life as a sexually and emotionally generous—and demanding—woman. Both denial and identification, then, participate in Goldman's revision of the maternal model.

Her father's role in Goldman's development is similarly complex. As a child, Goldman not only longed for his approval, but her many love affairs translated sexual desire—one of her father's most problematic attributes—into a source of intense personal gratification and transformative social energy and vision. Her tendency to idealize this hated father in later surrogates, however, also helps to explain her passionate devotion to a series of male lovers for whom he was the prototype[50] and who invariably failed to satisfy her emotional needs.[51]

In love, she knew herself to be "weak and dependent, clinging to the man" she loved.[52] Aware of the ways in which successive lovers first obsessed and then disappointed her by their "inability to give what she needed,"[53] Goldman not only "hid her personal failures and pain"[54] but also began to believe that "a personal love is not for one who dedicates himself [*sic*] to an ideal. Somehow it is like serving two Gods."[55] Her use of the masculine pronoun and her periodic lapses into affairs that first confirmed and later subverted her sense of herself suggest that residual uncertainties about her subjective status as a woman sought resolution in the attempt both to identify with and to idealize what she wasn't sure she could ever be.

The persistence within Goldman of the abused, unloved child kept separate her personal and public personas and gave her, as one biographer notes, "something to hide." Personally and politically, moreover, Goldman's passionate devotion to people and to causes that she idealized trapped her in cycles of expectation and disappointment that repeated themselves throughout her life,[56] and sustained the division between the heroic mother she became in public and the child whose passionate need for love dominated her private life. In the shadow of Goldman's public persona, then, as in the textual interstices of Antin's self-celebratory American narrator and Yezierska's rebellious protagonists, the unresolved developmental issues of immigrant daughters and their mothers assert themselves. Handicapped like all immigrants by class and culture, these women experience also the gendered ambiguities of Jewish daughters. Empowered by their mothers' considerable strengths, they are also confused by their mothers' submissiveness to (sometimes oppressive) male authority.

They respond in different ways to this confusion. Antin denies her likeness to her mother by modeling herself on her intellectual father, masking insecurity by self-congratulation. Yezierska's Sara also models herself on her intellectual father, while she and other of Yezierska's protagonists imitate Sara's mother, dramatizing the maternal strategy of seeking ideal lovers to confirm them as subjects. Emma Goldman, however, revises her mother, dividing the fragile self who needs to be loved from the heroic self who fights and gives to others, sustaining in disjunctive private and public lives two versions of herself, neither one of which, alone, can translate fully the abused European child into the powerful American woman. Driven by the need to resolve the gendered ambiguities transmitted by their mothers, through their formidable talent and energy these immigrant daughters develop—as did their mothers before them, one suspects—multiple modes of being themselves as they become productive American women.

Like them, Kate Simon (1912–1990) knew the domestic imbalance of the immigrant Jewish family and the gendered ambiguities of women's status in it. But the narrative persona of Kate Simon's memoirs neither denies, nor imitates, nor revises her mother. She is, instead, maternally groomed to defy her mother's fate, tuned in by her own experience to the adversaries she must overcome and made aware, by her mother's story, of the weapons most effective in a woman's hands. She is empowered in many ways by her mother. But she develops, nevertheless, the manifold sense of self that seems to persist in immigrant daughters.

Power, rather than negotiation, denial, or revision, is the central issue in Simon's memoirs. The earliest and most fruitful sources of power are first revealed to Simon by her mother. Impressed in early childhood by her mother's verbal skill in both argument and anecdote, Simon recalls—like Emma Goldman—her mother's power to give or to withhold sympathy from certain characters.[57] The romantic story of her mother's independent girlhood in Warsaw, replete with a Gentile lover, lends depth and perspective to the maternal image and weight to her lectures on "female independence."[58]

Even in America, Simon's mother demonstrates her power to be an active, self-determining subject in the world. Never an advocate of the "overrated charms of marriage,"[59] this mother doesn't succumb to either domestic responsibilities or her husband's authority. She sings, laughs, and studies, insisting that she would always rather study or work than clean house.[60] Unlike other women in the tenement, she "didn't accept her fate as a forever thing. She began to work during our school hours after her English classes had taught her as much as they could."[61] Simon portrays this mother not only as a creature "so beautiful that I couldn't see her; her radiance blinded me,"[62] but also as a creative person whose work is a source of power and pride to herself. Simon's early financial independence and adventurous, self-sustaining career as a travel writer testify to her early familiarity with work as a source of independence, recognition, and self-realization for her mother.

This mother's most powerful resource, however, is her sexuality. Parental sex is a carefully kept secret in this memoir, a secret that both tantalizes and terrifies this immigrant daughter. But its presence is powerfully felt. Behind the memorable sewing machine, Simon recalls, looms "the dignity of the parental bed,"[63] which guarantees the stability of this family. When Simon discovers that her mother had had thirteen abortions, she concludes that her mother "had enjoyed sex and was fatalistic and stalwart about abortions."[64]

Ultimately, this mother presides over Simon's own transformation into a sexual being, slapping her face when menstruation begins and then surprising her with a "woman's dress"[65] that makes this newly adolescent daughter feel "ready" for sexual combat. Thus, punishment and power are always tangled in Simon's experience of sexuality. Furtively exploited in her girlhood by assorted relatives and neighbors,[66] Simon knows she is a woman when she feels ready "to play, to tease, to amorously accept, to confidently reject" men.[67]

She recognizes in herself a longing for male regard that she associates with her father's long absence in America and with his harshness toward her when they were reunited. Desiring his affection and admiration, she receives from him only punishment, criticism, deflating sarcasm, and a readiness to absorb her in fantasies of his own. Because of him she will, like Emma Goldman, always find it hard to believe that she is lovable.[68] Baby-sitting for another family, she will learn to generalize paternal abuse of daughters and male lust and anger toward the women who serve them.[69] But she will blame her father for not protecting her from sexual exploitation[70] and also for damaging her self-confidence as a woman. Both her mother's readiness for sexual pleasure and her father's rejections and deflations of this immigrant daughter participate in Simon's characteristic acceptance of the many brief sexual adventures that she enters with a shrug and leaves without regret.

Unlike Goldman's autobiography, Simon's memoir embraces her private as well as her public life; her story includes the personal developmental issues that Goldman hid from the public in her letters. But her sense of self remains as bipolar as the narrative persona of Mary Antin, as fluid and driven as the protagonists of Anzia Yezierska, as divided as the heroic persona of Emma Goldman. As an adolescent, driven by guilty self-doubt and courageous self-assertion, Simon creates different versions of herself in every situation. Moreover, within her adventurous adult persona, modeled on her mother's strengths and strategies, her father's critical image of her persists as a "doppelganger companion" who always mocks the "twin me."[71] Because of him she knows in herself an "other" who seeks in many lovers the "father who left" even though she knows the search is futile. She confesses at the end of her memoir that "little more than I knew at seventeen do I surely know who I am at seventy-five."[72]

By the end of her memoirs, however, the writer/persona has become central to her self-image, though she carries within her "an envelope of earlier shapes": the child she "would never again be" as well as all the people who hurt or helped her to become an adult. These other personas are never "altogether lost," for the writer/self translates them into her own story, where they become "immutably mine."[73] Assuming, like her immigrant mother, the storyteller's superior power to mock, to mourn, and to "destroy" other subjects, Simon achieves a public self primarily by re-presenting them—and herself. She shares with Goldman, Yezierska, and Antin, then, the verbal power that allowed them and many lesser immigrant women writers to be recognized, to stand firmly at what Francoise Lionnet called "the confluence of different cultures"[74] and to become there—themselves. In that place, these writers spoke not only for and of themselves but also for those whose voices were not supposed to be heard outside the home and the marketplace and had never reached beyond Yiddish to non-Jewish readers. In their words, moreover, the manifold self of the American immigrant daughter-writer emerged, to be inscribed in all its complexity and strength in her stories. It was stabilized partly, as Patricia Waugh has suggested, by her relations to others[75] and partly by narratives that kept moving her forward. But her stability rested most profoundly, one suspects, on her long familiarity with the stable, though disparate, sense of self modeled for her by her European mother.

Feminist writers who followed these daughters of immigrants developed in striking ways the sense of a manifold self, emphasizing its political as well as personal ramifications. In "Tell Me a Riddle" (1956), for example, Tillie Olsen's Eva, an aging woman who seeks at the end of her life to acknowledge to herself the many personas within her, enrages the large family and husband who have known her only as nurturing mother and wife. As this immigrant mother struggles first to recall and finally to validate the multiple facets of self fashioned in a European shtetl, a Russian prison, and a poor American home, the voices and faces that belong to this manifold self are never synthesized, reconciled, or unified. Instead, they are gathered into a whole—like fragments of mica and silicon in a stone or like disparate sounds that can make either music or noise.

An even later writer, who recognizes herself as a Jew despite her assimilated father's denials and her southern gentile upbringing, surfaces more pointedly the extrafamilial ramifications of the manifold self. Adrienne Rich's autobiographical memoir, "Split at the Root" (1982), describes this self—like Olsen's Eva—in terms of both personal history and political commitments. Thus, Rich recognizes in herself

The middle-class white girl taught to trade obedience for privilege. The Jewish lesbian raised to be a heterosexual gentile. The woman who first heard oppression named and analyzed in the Black civil rights struggle. The woman with three sons, the feminist who hates male violence. The woman limping with a cane, the woman who has stopped bleeding. . . . The poet who knows that beautiful language can lie, that the oppressor's language sometimes sounds beautiful. The woman trying, as part of her resistance, to clean up her act.[76]

All these facets of self coexist for Rich, as for other feminist writers, within a manifold persona. In its political dimension this person recalls the radical European women who became socialists, anarchists, Zionists. Unlike those foremothers, however, many American Jewish feminists of the seventies turned their revolutionary attention not only outward, to the injustices of the larger society, but inward as well, to the imbalances and inequities of their own tradition. Whatever their specific political commitments, these writers have enlarged the capacity of our own generation for imagining oneself as manifold. Thus, the refusal of contemporary American Jewish women to "to sever or choose between different aspects of our identity,"[77] as Judith Plaskow has described it, carries into the vernacular of our own culture the persona of the immigrant mother and the daughter who first translated her into an idiom familiar to American women.

Sharon Pucker Rivo

Projected Images
Portraits of Jewish Women in Early
American Film

Over the past twenty years I have had the unusual opportunity as the director of the National Center for Jewish Film to become acquainted with a growing body of film materials referable to the Jewish experience. Originally a student of political science and then a television producer, my predilection has been to view film as documents of history. I have always had a particular interest in the images of women in the film materials, especially prodded by my two daughters, who helped heighten my awareness and see anew the images that will be examined in this essay. The conference titled "Developing Images: Representations of Jewish Women in American Culture," held at Brandeis University, March 14–15, 1993, provided the immediate stimulus to search the holdings of the Center and to examine the portraits contained in the moving images that have been preserved and are now accessible to scholars[1] and the public.

I discovered a rich body of material, from the earliest narrative films produced in 1903 to the mid 1930s, when strong ethnic images virtually disappear from the American film scene, not to reappear until many decades later. Although it is difficult to make large thematic and analytic statements about the materials, I do hope to demonstrate how the documents relate to their historical context; how the producers, directors, and writers who created the materials played a significant role in shaping the images; and how the materials relate to one another.

This essay is divided into three segments, beginning with the early years, in which the flickering images of the earliest extant American movies portray Jewish immigrant women as sympathetic victims of the immigration experience. Produced between 1903 and 1915 by non-Jewish filmmakers in and around New York City for audiences composed largely of immigrants, these portraits of vulnerable women differ significantly from the images presented in the 1920s feature films produced in Jewish-dominated Hollywood—strong Jewish mothers and daughters guarding their Jewish heritage and sustaining their clans as they struggle to adapt to America—but foreshadow images of Jewish women as victims contained in the Depression era American and Yiddish feature films.

Jewish Women as Vulnerable Immigrants: 1903 to 1915

Although there were large numbers of Jewish immigrants in the 1880s, the first images of Jewish immigrants which were captured on film date back to the turn of the century, the time when motion picture technology came into popular usage. This new medium's growth paralleled the increasing tide of immigration in the early 1900s, enabling America to discover its Jews at about the same time it discovered film.[2] The earliest extant film containing a Jewish character dates from 1903.[3] Lifted directly from the vaudeville stage, the Jew of the early American screen, with his hook nose, bald head, oversize shoes, and round pouch, is clearly recognizable. *Levi and Cohen: The Irish Comedians* (1903) and *Cohen's Advertising Scheme* (1904) feature this stereotypical "shyster." The films duplicate the pattern established in live vaudeville of the times by ridiculing and debasing the Jewish merchant to engender laughter. Interestingly, these films, as well as the written records of films of this era that have not survived, do not contain any comparable characterizations of Jewish women.

The first identifiable image of a Jewish woman in an extant film is that of Cohen's fiancée in *Cohen's Fire Sale* (1907). This early narrative production of the Edison Company, owned by Thomas Alva Edison,[4] contains one of the nastiest depictions of Jews in early American film. Cohen, the film's primary character, burns down his millinery store (by tying a candle to a cat's tail) to collect the insurance. The grotesque portrait of Cohen, which includes a large fake nose, bald head, oversize shoes and belly, is mirrored by that of his fiancée, who is equally unattractive with an exaggerated enlarged nose. She works alongside Cohen in the store and accompanies him on his chase through the streets, scrounging to retrieve hats that have been taken away in the garbage. Obviously intended as a vaudeville slapstick routine, the filmmakers refrain from any sympathetic portrayals. These ugly characterizations are disturbingly anti-Semitic.

Despite such anti-Semitic images presented by Edison, most extant images in early narrative film offer very different portraits. These one- or two-reel short features were made in and around New York City by non-Jewish men (Griffith, Sennett, Porter, McCutcheon), with the exception of Sigmund Lubin, who was Jewish and produced films in the Philadelphia area. Shot on location on the Lower East Side, the films offer rare ethnographic footage of Jewish neighborhoods, including street peddlers, children at play, women shopping, men and women manning pushcarts, boys hawking newspapers, tailor shops, and trolley cars. In these early narrative films about the immigrant experience, Jewish women are consistently presented as victims of the immigrant experience, as objects of charity and symbols of the struggle for survival. None of the films shows religious rites or activities, except Lubin's *The Yiddisher Boy* (1909). The majority of the portrayals are sympathetic, with the exception of those produced by the Edison Company and one Kalem Company film, *A Female Fagin* (1913).

Two 1908 films created by D. W. Griffith sensitively portray Jewish women as victims of cruel immigrant circumstances. In *Old Isaac, the Pawnbroker* (1908), a small girl in the urban slum seeks aid for her sick and starving mother. After the child meets with a bureaucratic brick wall at the official charity organization, she finds a compassionate helping hand from Isaac the elderly pawnbroker. The portraits of both the child and her sick mother convey the cruelty of the immigrant experience. Although the female characters are not fully developed, the producer's publicity bulletin for the film states that "the portrayal of charity is the theme of the Biograph's story, which dissipates the calumnies launched at the Hebrew race."[5] The target audience was clearly the immigrants, who did not need to read or understand English to enjoy the pathos of this film.

In *Romance of a Jewess* (1908), D. W. Griffith borrowed the theme of generational conflict popular in Yiddish theater. The plot is similar to Zalmen Libin's play, *Broken Hearts* (1903).[6] This melodrama was shot on the Lower East Side near the Biograph studio on Fourteenth Street and centers on Ruth, the daughter of a religious immigrant family, who rejects the wealthy suitor her father has arranged for her through a marriage broker. This defiant, liberated act by a second-generation daughter is the ultimate symbol of Americanization. Even though the husband Ruth chooses for herself is Jewish, her father disowns the couple. Ruth becomes a headstrong, independent, hardworking wife and mother. When her husband dies in an accident, she is overwhelmed by the struggle to make it alone in the harsh environment. Undoubtedly aimed at the sympathetic immigrant audience, the reconciliation scene between father and daughter at the film's end probably helped make this Griffith's most successful picture up to that time.[7]

The Yiddisher Boy (1909), Sigmund Lubin's only surviving film with a Jewish theme, presents a realistic depiction of Eastern European Jewish life on the Lower East Side. Lubin, the first American Jewish filmmaker, had firsthand knowledge of the world he illustrates on film. The story of a young boy who repays a childhood friend with good deeds, *The Yiddisher Boy* is remarkable for its authentic treatment of a poor Jewish home. In one particularly poignant scene, the family—a father, mother, and three young children—are shown sewing piecework in the kitchen of their tenement apartment. After the young daughter is sent to deliver some finished needlework, the family puts aside its work and transforms the kitchen for the Sabbath. At a table set with a white cloth and candlesticks, the parents, dressed in their best clothes, place their hands on the heads of the children and offer the traditional Sabbath blessing. This scene presents the most traditional depiction of religious Jewish life in any of the early surviving films.

In *Child of the Ghetto* (1910), Griffith returns to the theme of a Jewish immigrant woman struggling to survive in a hostile urban environment. After her mother dies, Ruth (Dorothy West), now an orphan, finds a job taking home piecework to sew. When this innocent young woman becomes the victim of a scam and is falsely accused of theft, she flees the cold, heartless sidewalks of Rivington Street for the bucolic countryside. She is rescued by an American farmer and his family and is rejuvenated by the fresh country air and their tender care. Ruth develops a romantic relationship with the handsome non-Jewish farmer. *Child of the Ghetto* is the earliest known film to deal with Jewish intermarriage. The lack of conflict surrounding the intermarriage and the loss of Ruth's Jewish heritage is made possible by the absence of other Jewish characters, particularly a traditional Jewish family, to mourn her departure from Judaism.

The only surviving early film to portray a Jewish woman in a role other than that of an innocent girl victimized by the immigrant experience is *Cohen Saves the Flag* (1913), a Mack Sennett farce. A period piece set outside the urban environs of the Lower East Side, the film acknowledges the presence of Jews in the Union Army during the Civil War. Well dressed in a fancy frock and bonnet, *Cohen*'s heroine, Rebecca, is an attractive, literate, clever, and aggressive young woman. She intercedes on behalf of her boyfriend, Cohen, who has saved the Union flag at Gettysburg. The image of Rebecca charging off on a white horse to save her man from the firing squad is a dramatic contrast to that of Ruth as the "child of the ghetto." Inexplicably, as opposed to Rebecca, the male lead, Cohen (Ford Sterling), is depicted in some scenes as a cowardly burlesque "schlemiel" hiding in a pigsty.

The portrait of a Jewish woman as an aggressive criminal in the Kalem Company's *A Female Fagin* (1913) is astonishingly negative. Many films throughout the years have been based on the negative characters of Dickens's Fagin and Shakespeare's Shylock, but this little film is unusually nasty. The setting is the Lower East Side, where the milieu of poverty fostered the criminals. Rosa Rosalsky, who runs a school dedicated to teaching young girls how to steal, is once again a victim of the struggle to survive. While crime was indeed a daily threat to immigrant women and the communities,[8] this depiction is a particularly harsh stereotype; women as petty thieves and criminal instructors do not seem to have been predominant. The two teenage girls who actually do the stealing, Nellie and Jane, do not appear to be Jewish. They are reformed and redeemed, while sinister Rosy gets caught and punished.

Although it is nearly impossible to measure the impact of these images on audiences, they reportedly had a far-reaching effect, especially on the lower-class ethnic immigrants who could enjoy this form of entertainment even though they were illiterate in English.[9] Tenement dwellers were fervent picture fans.[10] It is estimated that, in 1908, 16 million people each week attended motion pictures. By 1910, 26 million Americans, or 20 percent of the population, attended nickelodeon theaters on a weekly basis. The numbers were even higher in New York City, where 25 percent of Manhattan residents frequented the city's 123 film houses, close to a third of which were located on the Lower East Side.[11]

Even though the portraits of the women were generally sympathetic, rendering them harmless and unthreatening, they were amazingly incomplete. They do not reflect the full range and multifacted experiences of early-twentieth-century Jewish women immigrants; there are no film depictions of Jewish women as successful breadwinners, strong matriarchs of large families, or seekers of education and position. The historically important role women played in managing many Jewish-owned businesses while their men studied and prayed is also ignored, as are images of the financially secure or upwardly mobile German Jewish social reformers and social elite. The extant films mirror much of the immigrant experience of first-generation Jewish women and present women in a generally positive light; the non-Jewish filmmakers were careful not to present negative portraits but capitalized on the pathos of immigrant experiences to create box office pleasers.[12]

Jewish Mothers and Daughters as Strong, Capable Women: Post–World War I to 1927

After World War I the image of Jewish women as vulnerable immigrants was transformed to that of capable, strong, and independent mothers and daughters. This change was engendered by a number of converging factors. The locus of moviemaking moved from the independent producers on the East Coast to the big studios in Hollywood, mostly controlled by Jewish men. In 1915 and 1916 the theater owners and the Anti-Defamation League pressured the studios to alter any anti-Semitic bias resulting in the decline of Jewish and other unfavorable stereotypes.[13] During the war years there was a significant decline in Jewish-theme pictures, with only ten titles produced from 1916 to 1919. Most important, many of the immigrants who had arrived at the turn of the century were beginning to share in the economic vitality of the post–World War I years; thus, the depiction of Jewish women in both the American feature films and the nascent independent Yiddish feature film industry, emanating from the Yiddish theater scene in New York, began to reflect these factors.

After 1915, movies began to gain a new respectability. Theaters were built to attract more upscale clientele, stage actors were lured with high salaries, and as Gary Carey has written, "film promoters built bigger, better, safer theaters and changed the tenor of the screen fare to deal increasingly with more sophisticated levels of society. Screen characters became middle-class or better, losing the traces of their national antecedents: they became, simply, Americans."[14] The message and themes of these films were targeted to an increasingly upwardly mobile populace.

Beginning in 1920, New York's Lower East Side emerged as a most popular location for Hollywood productions. Rather than stories of hardship and tenuous survival, these films focus on the tensions between Americanization and acculturation. The characterizations of Jewish women mirrored what was becoming the reality for the majority of immigrant women—identification as new American citizens and successful adjustment to an American way of life. The first generation of immigrant women were now the mothers of American-raised children, and the young women, their daughters, were the second generation, fulfilling their own desires. To no great surprise, their aspirations often conflicted with the values of their more traditional parents. Generational conflict became a popular subject for Hollywood treatment of the immigrant experience.

The images of Jewish women in 1920s films—both in American productions made in Hollywood and in Yiddish-language feature films produced mainly in New York—are those of strongly defined individuals who succeed. The immigrant mothers are hardworking, independent, nurturing figures. The younger generation, the daughters, are often willing to take risk and typically defy the traditional authorities of parents and society, voicing their individuality and espousing American values. These are not images of the Jewish woman as victim but of women who are upwardly mobile, seeking an education, gaining affluence, and becoming independent.

Although much of the critical writing about Jews in American silent film in the 1920s emphasizes the depiction of assimilation and intermarriage, the extant images of Jewish women, including recently restored films, do not project this image. In fact, they project positive images of Jewish women who perpetuate and foster Jewish family values; intermarriage of a Jewish girl occurs in only one film. Many do focus on the tensions arising from the conflict between old- and new-world values and between parents and children, but the dominant theme is acculturation, not assimilation and intermarriage. Interestingly, there are no negative images of Jewish women in the films of this era.

The first full-length silent feature to capture Jewish immigrant life, *Humoresque* (1920), provides a fascinating portrait of a powerful, warmhearted "Jewish Mother" and a liberated, educated young woman.[15] Based on the Fannie Hurst short story with a scenario by one of the important early women writers and directors, Frances Marion, and directed by Italian filmmaker Frank Borzage, the film showcases an indomitable Jewish mother, Mama Kantor (played by Vera Gordon, a veteran of the Yiddish stage), who maintains a household of six children, including a severely retarded child, Mannie. Patricia Erens has noted of the film that finally "the Long Suffering Mother makes her first important appearance."[16] Produced by William Randolph Hearst for his company, Cosmopolitan Pictures, the film was made in New York City at the Harlem River Casino and on the Lower East Side, where vivid documentary footage was shot with concealed cameras.

Unlike so many others, this film presents a warmhearted version of immigrant life. Contrary to the written production notes, the film is not a "melting pot" or an "assimilation" piece, as were many of the later Hollywood films produced under the auspices of the Jewish moguls. *Humoresque* is a poignant tale of a successful and upwardly mobile, yet not materialistic, Jewish family. Although the film was criticized by the prominent critic Potamkin as a "highly extravagant and incorrect study of Jewish Society,"[17] many of the scenes proudly present a range of Jewish rituals. The father puts on a fedora to go outside but wears a yarmulke indoors, the mother lights a Sabbath candelabra with her head covered appropriately, the mother gives thanks before an ark of Torah scrolls, and the family tenderly cares for a retarded child at home. A valuable historical document, the film preserves lively Lower East Side street scenes and captures the integrity of Jewish family life.

A major theme of the story is the altruism and patriotism of Leon, the talented violinist son, who volunteers to fight in World War I for "freedom"; he blames his brother's affliction on the tyranny of "autocracy." Although the mother-son relationship is overly melodramatic, the depiction of the mother is not that of an emasculating, overpowering matriarch like Philip Roth's character, Sophie Portnoy, several decades later, but of an ever-loving, sacrificing immigrant mother who basks in the success of her genius son. The brief portrait of Leon's girlfriend, Gina, presents a sophisticated daughter from a wealthy Jewish family who is educated in Italy. Produced only a decade after Griffith's *Child of the Ghetto*, this film seems to be a millennium apart in terms of realistic characterization. The film provides a clear representation of a financially secure immigrant family that retains its Jewish ethnicity, religious character, and close family relationships.

The producer, William Randolph Hearst, reportedly loathed *Humoresque*, and the distributor, Adolph Zukor, did not want to release the film, commenting that "if you want to show Jews, show Rothschilds, banks and beautiful things. It hurts us Jews—we don't all live in poor houses."[18] Nevertheless, *Humoresque* was a huge success when it opened at the Criterion to rave reviews and one of the longest film runs ever. According to Kevin Brownlow, "the stunning success of *Humoresque* proved that audiences did not want their realism unadulterated, when a little hokum could make even squalor and mental disease acceptable, evoking a tear rather than a grimace."[19] The film's success may also have been due to the audience's preference for the cohesive family and patriotic values depicted and the recognition that immigrant families, like many viewers, had been achieving success in America.

The success of *Humoresque* spawned other Lower East Side dramas. When *Hungry Hearts*, based on Anzia Yezierska's 1920 book of short stories,[20] was pitched to Samuel Goldwyn, he was agreeable to the project but wanted to focus on the subject of Americanization rather than specifically Jewish themes. And that is what he got. The best-selling book was purchased for $10,000 by Goldwyn's Hollywood studio, and the author was brought to Hollywood and paid $200 a week to work on the screenplay. Despite Yezierska's involvement in the early stages of the production, the finished film was radically different from the book. Hollywood's manipulation of the original story, and indeed, the tale behind those alterations, demonstrates how images are created by the studios.

An amalgam of several of Anzia Yezierska's stories, *Hungry Hearts* (1922) focuses on Hannah Levin (played by Rosa Rosanova, a veteran Yiddish stage actress) and her daughter Sara (played by Helen Ferguson, a non-Jew), who is a composite of many of the characters in Yezierska's collection. Hannah is a strong-willed, hardworking woman who battles the Cossacks, moves her brood to America, and labors inside and outside the home to survive. She endures the daily humiliations of poor immigrant life, yet she she scrimps and saves to buy white paint to brighten her dingy and dark tenement kitchen. She steals time from her numerous obligations—her job, the cooking, the house-cleaning, the child rearing—to paint the dingy room a bright white. When the landlord, himself a Jew, sees that she has improved the apartment, he quickly doubles her rent. In a fit of rage, Hannah destroys her beautiful white kitchen with an ax, an act for which she is taken to court.

In Yezierska's short story "The Lost Beautifulness," Hannah loses in court. She reports to her family that the judge has ruled that the landlord has the right to "raise the rent or put us out." She is left a broken woman. This and other Yezierska stories are infused with the pathos, humiliation, and victimization of the immigrant poor; they embody Yezierska's anger against the capitalist, money-driven society. Yet in the film the scenario is dramatically changed. The judge, a dignified non-Jew, shows sympathy and compassion for Hannah. He asks the landlord, "How could you raise this poor woman's rent? You who were once a poor immigrant yourself?" In the film a young Jewish lawyer

The film rendition of *Hungry Hearts* sanitizes the anguish of many of Yezierska's downtrodden characters. Sara (Helen Ferguson) scrubs floors to gain the money necessary to break out of poverty. (Courtesy Samuel Goldwyn Pictures; film preserved and restored by the National Center for Jewish Film at Brandeis University)

courting Sara comes to her aid. By the second summer in America, the daughter has married the lawyer, and the family has moved from the teeming poverty of the Lower East Side to an affluent, flower-bedecked white house in the suburbs.

The film rendition sanitizes the anguish of many of Yezierska's downtrodden characters. In the story "When Lovers Dream," Sara is abandoned by her beloved David because his rich uncle insists that he not be saddled with a family of poor immigrants. In the film, David, who has been sent to school by his money-hungry uncle, refuses to obey him and defends Sara's mother against him in court. Sara is of the new generation—those who scrub floors to gain the money necessary to break out of the poverty. "My heart chokes," she exclaims. "Why should they live and enjoy life while I look on?" She works her way out of the ghetto and into the arms of an upwardly mobile Jewish lawyer.

The transformation of Yezierska's material from the original to the Hollywood version exemplifies the 1920s portraits of Jews set forth on millions of theater screens across the nation and the world. The signature of the Holly-wood studios—the optimistic happy endings—showed Jewish characters suc-cessfully integrated into the American mainstream; most Jewish immigrants strove to achieve this material and social success that many of the Jewish stu-dio heads had already achieved. Yezierska's original tales, as published in *Hungry Hearts*, were filled with pathos, hardship, pain, and poverty. Indeed, the American dream was elusive for most of Yezierska's characters, including her Hannah and Sara, but the Samuel Goldwyn Picture Company's filmed ver-sion transformed these women into symbols of American "success." Sara achieves self-esteem and good wages with a job in a shirt factory; after her marriage to David she does not have to work at all. Hannah improves her lot through hard work and fortitude and receives "justice" in the American court system. Underlying it all is the belief that the American system can be counted on to help the immigrant poor, all the while allowing them to retain their Jew-ish identity and values.

While Samuel Goldwyn was struggling to find a way to transform Yezier-ska's stories for the American film audience, Sidney Goldin, one of the pioneer American Jewish filmmakers, was embarking on the production of feature films in the Yiddish language in far off Vienna. Although the film *East and West* (*Mizrakh un Mayrev* or *Ost und West*, 1923) was made in Europe, it was directed and written by Americans and features an American cast.[21] The cen-tral character, Molly (played by Molly Picon), is the daughter of an unedu-cated, wealthy American immigrant who has returned to his native Poland for a traditional family wedding. Molly is an irreverent, intelligent, educated, and financially secure young woman. She wears boxing gloves and cross-dresses in a symbolic representation of her fight for feminine independence and the ability to control her own destiny. She is a prime example of the typical Yid-dish film characterization of the second-generation daughter in conflict with parental authority, religious tradition, and a male-dominated world. Strict reli-gious observance is mocked, yet an unintended Orthodox marriage is honored by Molly and her father, providing the plot for this irreverent comedy.

None So Blind (1923) is a strange and somewhat convoluted tale of revenge, greed, intermarriage, and reconciliation. The film may have been spawned by the phenomenal success of the 1922 play *Abie's Irish Rose*, the quintessential love story of the Irish girl and Jewish boy of immigrant families on the Lower East Side. *None So Blind* relates the tale of the ill-fated intermarriage of Rachel Abrams to a New York socialite, Russell Mortimer. The film revolves around three intermarriages and contains an unflattering portrait of the Jewish granddfather, Aaron Abrams, as the "the Shylock of Wall Street." The central portrait of Ruth, the Jewish granddaughter of a wealthy man, enjoying a luxu-rious, prosperous life is a sharp contrast to the early portraits of struggling im-migrant women. Ruth's choice—marriage to a non-Jew instead of an arranged

Molly Picon as "Molly" in *East and West*, 1923. (Copyright © 1987 Rutenberg and Everett Yiddish Film Library of the National Center for Jewish Film, Brandeis University, Waltham, Mass.)

marriage with a Jewish suitor, Lewis Cohen—is treated openly, with tolerance and total acceptance. Tom Gunning has noted that "the film's message of tolerance is labeled as a specifically Christian concept . . . not only are the interfaith marriages celebrated, but the former opponents consider a new business partnership."[22] This dramatic feature foreshadows the intermarriage and assimilationist themes of the ethnic comedies of the period, such as *The Cohens and Kellys* (1926), *The Cohens and Kellys in Atlantic City* (1929), *The Cohens and Kellys in Paris* (1928), *Izzy and Lizzy* (1926), and *Kosher Kitty Kelly* (1926).[23]

Two films directed by Edward Sloman for Carl Laemmle at Universal Studios contain some of the strongest Jewish characterizations of any Hollywood productions, including revealing portraits of Jewish women and vivid religious rituals. The daughter in *Surrender* (1927) represents a modern-day Queen Esther.[24] The Jewish mother in *His People* (1925), Rose Cominsky, played by Rosa Rosanova (who played Hannah Levin in *Hungry Hearts*), is depicted as a sympathetic, supportive wife and mother; she is wise yet not domineering. She

performs Sabbath rituals such as lighting candles with a covered head and prepares the Sabbath meals. Although the film, based on Isadore Bernstein's
story, "The Jew," is primarily a vehicle for actor Rudolph Schildkraut in the
role of the father, David Cominsky, the scenario explores the jarring transformation of values between the Old World and the new. The story focuses on the
two sons: Morris, the intellectual "ideal" student who turns out to be a selfish
lawyer, and Sammy, the boxer who lovingly takes care of his aging parents.
The mother passively accepts Morris's selfish and cruel betrayal of his father's
love and sacrifice while unproblematically accepting the other son's Irish girlfriend. Unfortunately, the mother's role is not as fully developed as the male
roles in this sophisticated portrayal of generational conflict and the pain of
Americanization.

Generational conflict and defiance of parental authority take center stage in
both Yiddish and American film portrayals of the immigrant experience during the next few years. *Broken Hearts*, based on the 1903 Libin play, was shot
in the Bronx in early 1926 while the original play of *The Jazz Singer* was being
performed on Broadway. In both vehicles the children of cantors refuse to follow the traditional roles demanded by the fathers, and both are disowned by
the fathers while the mothers look on helplessly.

The renowned actress Lila Lee, who starred with Rudolf Valentino in *Blood
and Sand*, came to New York to co-star with Maurice Schwartz in *Broken
Hearts*, his directing debut. Here she plays Ruth Esterin, a cantor's daughter,
who refuses an arranged marriage to run off with a Russian-Jewish intellectual
and political refugee, Benjamin Resanov (played by Schwartz), whom she has
been tutoring in English. Her religious father, outraged at her intransigence,
disowns her. The couple enjoy a few months of happiness before Resanov
learns that the wife he left in Russia is not dead, as he had believed. He departs
for Russia, leaving Ruth and her newborn child thrust into poverty.

The film begins to mirror the pathos and pain of the original 1903 play as
well as some of the earlier films made on the Lower East Side. Out of despera-
tion, Ruth returns to her family on the eve of Yom Kippur for a reconciliation.[25] The original Libin play and contemporary reviews of the film confirm
that there is a happy ending to this melodrama. After discovering that his first
wife died, Benjamin returns from Russia just as Ruth's father finally accepts
her marriage and the new child. The defiant American daughter triumphs over
the old-world values and rigidity of her father. She rejects money and security
for the love of her intellectual Russian refugee. The generational conflict is
happily resolved, all within the framework of the Jewish family.

The Jazz Singer (1927), based on the 1925 play by Samuel Raphaelson, is
the hallmark of the Hollywood "assimilationist" film. Jakie Rabinowitz, the
son of a cantor, not only rejects the traditional way of life by becoming a vaudeville entertainer but also takes up with a Gentile woman. The film epitomizes

the struggle between past and present, father and son, love and duty, parochialism and freedom. This is not just a generational conflict—it is a clear break with tradition. The only Jewish woman's role is that of the mother, Sara Rabinowitz, who portrays a warm, affectionate, loving mother to her only child. She sides with the son against the stern traditional father, explaining, that "maybe our boy doesn't want to be cantor." But although she weeps for her "lost son," she cannot keep from beaming in the audience at his Broadway success.

The Hollywood studio features and the Yiddish films of the 1920s contain surprisingly similar images of Jewish women. The Hollywood features of the 1920s were aimed at the broadest possible audience, while the early Yiddish films were produced with the hope of reaching the same audiences, even though the audience they did reach was predominantly composed of secular Jewish immigrants. The female images that both types of film project are of liberated, self-reliant, strong characters in search of their own identities; in some cases they present women becoming the breadwinners out of pure necessity. Most of the mothers are strong nurturing figures; the daughters of the immigrant families project images of the new generation, full of confidence, educated or striving to become educated, financially secure or working to become affluent. They are liberated women who challenge tradition and parental authority yet remain within the fold (except for Ruth Abrams in *None So Blind*). Their values are more modern than those of their mothers, but these women are neither victims of the immigrant experience nor do they reject Judaism and intermarry.

Made by Jewish filmmakers in Hollywood and in the New York area for the increasingly upwardly mobile audience, the images flickering on the screen reflect the self-assurance and strong character of the women involved with making the films, both behind the scenes and on the silver screen—Fannie Hurst, Frances Marion, Vera Gordon, Anzia Yezierska, Rosa Rosanova, Molly Picon, and Lila Lee. The vulnerability of the early Jewish immigrant women as reflected in the early films has been replaced by portraits of strong, capable Jewish immigrant mothers of the 1920s, embellished and further strengthened by the depictions of their independent and capable daughters.

Return of Jewish Women as Vulnerable Immigrants: 1928 to 1937

With the advent of motion picture sound and the unprecedented success of *The Jazz Singer*, the Hollywood studios in the late 1920s and early 1930s produced a number of early sound features set in the Jewish immigrant neighborhoods of New York. Although reasonably successful, these Jewish ghetto features were abruptly curtailed after the establishment of the Production Code Administration (Breen Office) in July 1934. The PCA imposed strict self-regulatory codes, including the principle that no offensive references to a character's national origin would be tolerated. Strong ethnic characterizations virtually disappeared from the silver screen: there were only thirty-nine Jewish theme features in that decade, compared to eighty-nine in the previous decade.[26]

Thematically, the films of the 1930s portray the Lower East Side immigrant experience with nostalgia for the "good old days" of family unity and the warmth of traditional family and communal life. The images of the Jewish women frequently mirror those of the male characters: the more virtuous characters are hardworking, sacrificing toilers who shun easy economic and personal gain for family and communal good. Obviously affected by the Depression and the reversal of the economic and social gains that had been attained by some of the early immigrants and by much of the audience, the filmmakers in both the Hollywood studios and the emerging Yiddish cinema arena in New York tried to capitalize on nostalgia for the values of traditional family life, with the women anchoring the family and its economic survival.

The roles of the Jewish women, whether as strong matriarchs, supportive girlfriends, independent daughters, or nurturing mothers, are all portrayed sympathetically. The women embody the pathos and pain of the millions of struggling immigrants in the 1930s yet represent their ability to survive against all odds. The immigrant experience as a whole is viewed through a rose-colored lens; the poverty and difficulties of two decades earlier are more palatable yet evocative enough to produce cathartic tears in the darkened movie theaters.

Although few in number, some important studio productions of this period focus on the plight of the Jewish immigrant: *The Younger Generation* (1928), *Heart of New York* (1932), and *Symphony of Six Million* (1932). These Hollywood productions are specifically Jewish in several aspects: the scripts are sprinkled with Yiddish, the dialogue is heavily accented, the characterizations are almost stereotypically Jewish and played by well-known Jewish actors, and the costumes and sets are evocative of the earlier period. The ethos of unchecked capitalism is beginning to be questioned.

The Younger Generation, which repeats the earlier themes of generational conflict, contains two strong female roles, the mother (Rosa Rosanova) and the daughter, Birdie (Lina Basquette). Based on the Fannie Hurst play *It Is to Laugh* and directed by Frank Capra, this half-talkie melodrama concerns the upwardly mobile ambitions of children of immigrants and their lack of respect for parental authority. The film tells the story of a social-climbing and successful antiques dealer son, Morris Fish (who changed his name from Goldfish); it is infused with the stark reality and the pain and suffering of acculturation. The mother is so infatuated with her darling son that she spoils him: "the big challah is always for Morris." His financial successes lift the family out of the Lower East Side ghetto, and they move to Fifth Avenue, where the father, miserable despite financial security, declares, "Money ain't good for nothing, mama—if it don't buy happiness."[27] The son's success in America has one major drawback—he loses respect for his immigrant roots. In a painful scene (reminiscent of the scene in *His People*) in the lobby of their expensive apartment building, Morris, in the company of his affluent guests, disowns his parents because he is ashamed of them.

During the first half of the picture, Morris's sister Birdie appears as a weepy minor character, but in the second half of the film she emerges as a bold and confident woman. She openly defies her brother's wishes by marrying her Jewish boyfriend, Eddie Lesser, a songwriter still living in the ghetto. Disowned by her brother and in dire poverty, she bravely strikes out on her own, finding work to sustain her and her newborn baby while her husband serves time in jail for petty theft. Birdie ultimately returns to rescue her mother from the sterile Fifth Avenue apartment and takes her home with her to Coney Island. While struggling to make it on her own, Birdie is an example of the second-generation woman who retains a warmth and love for her immigrant family and the values they have brought to America.

The Younger Generation is quite different from Fannie Hurst's *Humoresque*, the film that opened the decade with Hollywood's image of a successful, close-knit Jewish family "making it" together in America. *The Younger Generation* finds turmoil spawned amid newly acquired wealth. The Goldfish family is in conflict, not over intermarriage but over values and money. Nevertheless, in both these Hollywood films the Jewish women characters hold fast and true to their Jewish identity and family values.

The nostalgia for the values of family and community of the Lower East Side that is evoked and applauded in *The Younger Generation* is echoed in two other 1932 Hollywood films: *Heart of New York* (based on the play *Mendel, Inc.* by David Freedman and directed by Mervyn LeRoy for Warner Brothers) and *Symphony of Six Million* (screenplay by Fannie Hurst, directed by Gregory La Cava for RKO with executive producer David O. Selznick). As Patricia Erens points out, "with Jews no longer crowded together in ghettos, it was easier to remember with fondness the sense of community and to make light of physical discomforts."[28]

Although not in leading parts, the women play important roles as cohesive forces in these families. Mama Zelda Marantz in *Heart of New York* is determined to take on the responsibility of being the breadwinner. "A wife's place is in the house in the kitchen over the stove," she proclaims. "I always wanted to be such a wife. I tried, but you wouldn't let me. From now on I'm the father of the family. If you don't want to go to work, I will."[29] She is a strong, determined, self-reliant character.

In *Symphony of Six Million,* the mother, Hannah Klauber, played by Yiddish actress Anna Appel, anchors the family and is its nurturing pillar of strength. Her sacrifice to obtain a microscope for her son Felix is reminiscent of the mother in *Humoresque* buying a violin for her son. But it is the young woman, Jessica, who embodies the real values of the film as she describes Felix's financial success: "What a price he paid for it. . . . When Felix lost the ghetto he lost himself, his ideals. He lost his love of life, of work—real work. He lost his love of people, tender, human people who paid him back with more than money. He lost his soul."

While the Hollywood features sentimentalize life in the ghetto, the Yiddish films of this same era present the raw pain and poverty endured by millions of immigrants. In two of the earliest sound Yiddish features, young women play central roles—Golde in *His Wife's Lover* (1931) and Masha in *Uncle Moses* (1932)—and are once again portrayed as victims of the immigrant experience. In both films the women ultimately prevail, but America is shown not as the golden land of happiness and opportunity but as a place of despair, hardship, and poverty. The New York–based producers of the Yiddish films acutely feel the impact of the Depression, which is embodied in their film productions.

His Wife's Lover, a Yiddish film written by a woman, Sheyne Rokhl Simkoff (based on Molnar's *The Guardsman,* a 1931 Academy Award–winning feature film with Alfred Lunt and Lynn Fontanne), tells the story of an actor, Ludwig Satz, who bets his friend Stein that all women are fickle. The film features Golde Blumberg in the consummate role of a Jewish woman as immigrant victim. "I came alone to these shores in search of happiness," she cries, "but instead I found your cold machines. . . . I would have married anyone to escape my slavery."[30] Although she marries for security and money, the film defends the virtues of women like Golde, who, despite her love for a younger man, remains true to her word and her vows. This first Yiddish talkie opened September 25, 1931, at the Clinton Theatre on Lower East Side to favorable reviews in the Yiddish and English press and then played three theaters in Brownsville and the Bronx, reaching a general audience.

The following year, Maurice Schwartz directed and starred in *Uncle Moses* (1932), a film based on the 1918 Yiddish novel by Sholem Asch. The film became the most successful Yiddish talkie to date. Judith Abarbanell played Masha, the daughter of an immigrant family, who is persuaded by her parents to marry the rich Uncle Moses. Although she is in love with Charlie, a local union organizer, Masha agrees to the arranged marriage with Moses to help her family survive. Both Golde and Masha reflect the women of the transitional generation, who sacrificed themselves for their families.

The most memorable 1930s portrayal of the Jewish immigrant woman as victim is that of Celia Adler, doyenne of the Yiddish stage, in *Where Is My Child?* (1937). The plot, which could have been taken from the real-life stories presented in the "Bintel Brief" column of the *Daily Forward,* focuses on a widow who places her baby in an orphanage while she looks for employment. An unscrupulous doctor sells the child, leaving Adler bereft and wandering in

In *Uncle Moses*, Masha (Judith Abarbanell), daughter of an immigrant family, is persuaded by her parents to marry the rich Uncle Moses (Maurice Schwartz). (Courtesy National Center of Jewish Film; film preserved and restored by the National Center of Jewish Film)

search of her loved one throughout the picture. Set between 1911, the height of the exodus that brought two million Eastern European Jews to the United States, and 1937, when immigration was still fresh in the audience's memory, the film exemplifies the ruptures and betrayals many immigrants experienced.

By the early 1930s, the image of the Jewish female lead as the "victim" of the times and of the immigrant experience had come full circle from the earliest images presented in the one-reel features at the nickelodeons. The strong, self-confident, pre-Depression images of the Hollywood Jewish heroines disappeared from the screen, only to be replaced by the familiar characterization of Jewish women as helpless to control their fate. There is a striking similarity in the images of the early silent films made by non-Jews in the New York area or created by the Hollywood studios and those of the Yiddish filmmakers of the early 1930s—both depict the Jewish woman as victim of the immigrant experience and symbol of survival. Produced to entertain the urban, immigrant audiences in America and to be exported to Yiddish-speaking audiences and general audiences in Europe, the sagas of mass immigration found receptive audiences among those who remembered their days in the urban ghettos, as well as the second-generation upwardly mobile children of the original immigrants.

The omission of the true diversity of Jewish women's experiences is once again almost as notable as the roles that are presented. There are no characters portraying Jewish women as political or union activists; no Zionists, no Emma Goldmans, no Henrietta Szolds. There is also a lack of upper-middle-class society women: affluent reformers, settlement house or welfare patrons, professional women. There are no disapproving images of Jewish women: no vamps or villains.

Surprisingly, the American and Yiddish films of the 1920s project parallel views that differ from both the earlier and the later images of Jewish women as victims. The films contain images of strong-willed, independent mothers and daughters of immigrant families willing to take risks, to defy the traditional authority of parents and society, to voice values of individualism and belief in American pluralism while retaining their Jewish values and traditions. These celluloid images reflect the social and economic situation of a growing percentage of American Jewish women during this period. The creators of the films—Samuel Goldwyn, Fannie Hurst, Anzia Yezierska, Molly Picon, Maurice Schwartz—were themselves the beneficiaries of the American dream.

After the establishment of the Breen Committee in the mid-1930s, images of American Jewish women virtually disappeared from the silver screen. The only Hollywood studio productions containing Jewish characters were historical dramas portraying such figures as Disraeli and Dreyfus, wherein the Jewishness of the characters is sanitized. During the next two decades an occasional Jew shows up in a wartime movie foxhole or in a minor role. Strong, prominent Jewish portraits do not return to the screen until the 1960s, when another generation of filmmakers began to assume prominent roles in the film industry. In the 1970s, Jewish women reappear as Fanny Brice, "Jewish American princesses," and even as the valorous star of *Hester Street.* By the 1980s, with the emergence of Barbra Streisand, Elaine May, Joan Micklin Silver, and others as respected filmmakers, strong, admirable Jewish women increasingly play starring roles in American feature films. The fate of the Yiddish feature films was not so fortunate; with the decimation of the Yiddish-speaking world during World War II the once vibrant Yiddish film industry came to an abrupt end.

This initial examination of portraits of Jewish women contained in moving images in early American cinema brings to our attention a body of material not previously known. Because only a small percentage of the films produced in the early years has survived, the images examined may not be entirely representative of their genres, yet they provide a valuable body of primary documents to help rediscover the world of our grandmothers and great-grandmothers. While there are no glaringly anti-Semitic caricatures in these films, neither are there representations of wealthy German Jewish women, successful professionals, trade unionists, political activists, or any other images that fully reflect the wide range of roles actually performed by Jewish women in this period.

Made as vehicles to entertain and make money, not as "documentary" films, many were shot on location and thereby add important information to our first-hand knowledge of the ethnography and historical data of the period. Equally important, while they do not provide a full range of Jewish types, the representations of Jewish women they project are significant and often belie popular stereotypes of Jewish mothers and Jewish daughters and assimilation. The preserved celluloid images of Jewish women projected onto the silver screen provide fresh insight into the real world of the early decades in America as well as the *reel* world that produced them.

Filmography in Chronological Order

Levi and Cohen: The Irish Comedians. 1903. American Mutoscope and Biograph Company. Photographer: Billy Bitzer.*

Cohen's Advertising Scheme. 1904. Edison Company. Filmmaker: Edwin S. Porter.*

Cohen's Fire Sale. 1907. Edison Company. Filmmaker: Edwin S. Porter.*

Romance of a Jewess. 1908. American Mutoscope and Biograph Company. Director: D. W. Griffith. Photographer: Billy Bitzer.*

Old Isaac, the Pawnbroker. 1908. Biograph. Director: Wallace McCutcheon. Writer: D. W. Griffith.*

The Yiddisher Boy. 1909. Lubin Company.*

Child of the Ghetto. 1910. Biograph. Director: D. W. Griffith. Photographer: Billy Bitzer.*

Cohen Saves the Flag. 1913. Keystone Film Company. Director: Mack Sennett.*

A Female Fagin. 1913. Kalem. (Available only at the British Film Institute, London)

Humoresque. 1920. Paramount. Director: Frank Borzage.

Hungry Hearts. 1922. Goldwyn Picture Co. Director: E. Mason Hopper.*

East and West. 1923. Goldin Films. Director: Sidney Goldin.*

None So Blind. 1923. Arrow Pictures. Director: Burton King.*

His People. 1925. Universal Pictures. Director: Edward Sloman.*

Broken Hearts. 1926. Jaffe Films. Director: Maurice Schwartz.*

The Jazz Singer. 1927. Warner Brothers. Director: Alan Crosland.*

Younger Generation. 1929. Columbia Pictures. Director: Frank Capra.

* Film and/or video copies available from the National Center for Jewish Film, Brandeis University, Lown 102, MS 053, Waltham, MA. 02254. Phone 617 899 7044, fax 617 736 2070, email NCJF@logos.cc.brandeis.edu. Web site: www.brandeis.edu/jewishfilm/index.html

His Wife's Lover. 1931. High Art Pictures. Director: Sidney Goldin.*
Symphony of Six Million. 1932. RKO. Director: Gregory La Cava.
Heart of New York. 1932. Warner Brothers. Director: Mervyn LeRoy.
Uncle Moses. 1932. Yiddish Talking Pictures. Directors: Sidney Goldin, Aubrey Scotto.*
Where Is My Child. 1937. Henry Lynn Prod. Directors: Abraham Leff, Henry Lynn.*

II

Assimilating Images:
Representations of the "Lost Generation"

Joan Jacobs Brumberg

The "Me" of Me
Voices of Jewish Girls in Adolescent Diaries of the 1920s and 1950s

In March 1955, fifteen-year-old Sandra Rubin wrote in her private diary: "Often as I open this book . . . I wonder, what is to become of all this writing? Some is silly, some serious and meaningful. Will it all be on the bottom of an aged cedar chest in the attic? Or will it be read by a few close friends? Or will I become important enough to have it published? Or will it be destroyed in a war? How I wonder and dream about my diaries! They are so meaningful! They show so well the 'me' of me."[1]

Just like many other middle-class Jewish girls in her generation, Sandra regarded her personal diary as her "most treasured possession," and she appreciated its usefulness as an important emotional outlet: "Without you, O my dearest of books, without you as a companion I should be so lonely, so inhibited, so tightly bottled up." Because she understood the ways in which she had inscribed herself on its pages, Sandra Rubin fantasized about threats to the diary and proclaimed her loyalty to it. "I swear that the first thing I will save in any crisis will not be money, nor clothes, nor jewels, but you!" she assured the inanimate little book. Sandra's conviction that her diary captured her true self, what she called "the 'me' of me," suggests a great deal about the continuing emotional needs of girls, needs that transcend time, place, and ethnicity but are also shaped by those same considerations.[2]

But diary keeping was not something that either Sandra's mother or her grandmother did. In the 1950s, for the first time, large numbers of American Jewish girls began to keep diaries, just as their Gentile sisters had done since the nineteenth century.[3] Until the post–World War II era, diaries were, by and large, the expressive vehicle of well-educated white Protestant girls, and the personal voices of Jewish adolescents were muffled and hard to discern. But in

53

the 1950s, Jewish girls found a satisfying vehicle for describing and reflecting on the process of growing up. These diaries now provide historians and psychologists with an opportunity to assess the relationship between popular culture and self-image, particularly the ways in which Jewish girls did (or did not) internalize messages from the mainstream Gentile culture.

Why this expressive form was generally delayed until the 1950s is a complex matter that reflects the changing nature of Jewish life in America. Although I have searched long and hard for the manuscript diaries of ethnic girls, no group—whether African American, Italian American, Asian American, Latino, or Jewish—seems to produce a sizable cohort of adolescent diarists until they are substantially middle-class or at least until they are driven by bourgeois imperatives and expectations for self-expression and personal happiness. Obviously, opportunities to express oneself in adolescence are structured by social class, a reality that makes both the existence and the content of diaries an important barometer of the acculturation process.

By the 1950s, more and more American Jewish families had achieved middle-class status, and as a result, their daughters were emotionally and materially privileged in ways that earlier generations were not.[4] This generation—the grandaughters of immigrants—had the time, space, and inclination to contemplate "private" thoughts and write them down. They lived at home, and they did not work for wages except for occasional jobs that provided them with their own "spending money." Girls like these also had their own rooms, where they wrote in their diaries without parental surveillance, surrounded by clothes, cosmetics, stuffed animals, and phonograph records, all of which were linked to their sense of identity. Diary writing in this generation was further stimulated by the fact that adolescents could purchase, with their weekly allowance, small leatherette volumes embossed in gold and provided with a lock and key.[5]

After the American publication of Anne Frank's diary in June 1952, many adolescent girls, Jewish and Gentile alike, began to think about the value of a private journal.[6] Anne Frank represented all the Jews who were murdered in the Holocaust, but she also epitomized the normal difficulties of adolescent girls, especially anxieties associated with sexual development and learning to assert one's individuality in the context of family life. Anne Frank's diary was an immediate publishing sensation: the first printing was sold out on publication day; by the end of the summer of 1952 it had become a staple on national best-seller lists. By 1957 there was both a Broadway play (starring Susan Strasberg) and a Hollywood film (starring Millie Perkins). By 1959 the diary had sold over 3.5. million copies.[7]

In this way, Anne Frank became a fixture of American popular culture in the 1950s. Middle-class Jewish parents reinforced the idea that Anne was a model of the spirit and resiliency of the youthful Jewish female by giving the diary to their daughters, either as a special gift or simply to read after the adults had finished it. Although few Jewish girls actually cited Anne Frank as the reason for starting a diary, many mentioned that they had read or seen the story of her life in the Secret Annex, and they used this experience to reflect on their own diaries and on the differences in their situations.

In 1959, after seeing the Preminger movie at a Saturday matinee in Queens, New York, thirteen-year-old Ruth Teischmann wrote: "I know I can't make this diary like hers because there's no Hitler (thank G–d), but I'll try. I'd rather there would be no Hitler and a fair diary than Hitler and a great diary." Ruth felt that her life as a teenager was less interesting than Anne's because of the freedom she had as an American Jew, but she reveled in the high emotions generated by the film: "It was fabulous. Every minute [the Franks] thought the Nazis would find them, my heart beat so fast. I thought everyone around me would hear it." Ruth's reading of that awful moment when the Franks were discovered and taken from the Secret Annex demonstrated how Hollywood priorities and adolescent sensibilities combined to turn the story into a romance: "At the end, when the Nazis finally did come I was so sad because Anne and Peter were in love, and they would have to *split up*, but I didn't cry"[8] (my emphasis).

For Lynn Saul, another Jewish teenager growing up in the 1950s, Anne Frank's diary also provoked comparison. "I certainly hope and pray my diary never will serve the purpose hers did. The purpose of my diary is to tell all the happenings of my daily life which I simply would boil over with if I couldn't tell something about them."[9] Lynn Saul clearly regarded her diary as an important outlet in her emotional life, but she also understood that her daily writing—done in the comfort and security of her suburban Pittsburgh bedroom—probably was no testament to history, the way Anne's was. For girls like Ruth and Lynn, reading and thinking about Anne Frank was a way to explore and affirm the value and privilege of being a Jewish girl in a country where it was possible to feel safe and unthreatened.

Despite their familiarity with Anne Frank and the specter of European anti-Semitism, adolescent diarists in the 1950s rarely wrote about their Jewishness as an issue or influence in their personal development. This is not to say that Jewish identity had disappeared among daughters of middle-class Jews in postwar America; these girls went to "services," attended seders, and sometimes reported on the rabbi's sermon. In general, however, religious identity took a backseat to concerns about appearance, social life, and heterosexual identity. In the 1950s the core subject matter of most adolescent diaries was remarkably formulaic, regardless of religion or locale. Driven by powerful protocols for popularity, Protestant, Catholic, and Jewish girls alike filled their diaries with rapturous reports about "sighting" desirable boys, the contents of important telephone conversations, and wistful thoughts about perfect hairdos and prospective dates. Being Jewish gave some structure to these possibilities—usually in terms of whom to date or which parties to go to—but it was rarely mentioned as a factor in defining the self, and it appeared only occasionally as an issue in high school when real dating began. Instead of classic issues of adolescent sturm und drang, girls' diaries in the 1950s seem preoccupied with the trivial.

The personal diaries of the postwar cohort reflected images of women in American popular culture. These girls wanted to be pretty, personable, and, most of all, popular.[10] When they represented themselves to themselves in their private journals, they worried more about their individual social success than they did about patterns of exclusion because they were Jews. In effect, poor grooming or an awkward social style were treated as greater liabilities than being Jewish. Although these girls clearly understood anti-Semitism, it did little to limit their aspirations. Almost all wanted good grades and looked forward to college, an expectation that marked them as a watershed generation in the history of American Jewish women.[11]

The absence of Jewish content in the identity struggles of girls in the 1950s and their concentration on the details of adolescent social life provide a stark contrast to the experience of Jewish girls who came of age in the 1920s. These two generations of adolescents, the 1950s and the 1920s, are linked not only by their common experience of postwar prosperity but also by their familial and emotional relationship to one another: many girls who were adolescent in the 1920s became the mothers of girls who were teens in the 1950s. Because of the exigencies of life during the Great Depression and the fact that many young people did not have jobs, marriages were delayed throughout the 1930s; opportunities for higher education also evaporated, particularly for girls.[12]

Jewish girls who were daughters of immigrants rarely kept diaries, a reality that makes the reconstruction of their experience in the 1920s more difficult than for the prolific and well-documented 1950s. Although I looked persistently for manuscript diaries by adolescents in the second generation, I had little success until I discovered a rare diary that provides a revealing contrast to the "assimilationist" voices of the 1950s. This diary, the personal journal of Helen Labrovitz, provides an invaluable window into the thoughts and experiences of a Jewish girl in the 1920s, one who came of age in a distinctive New England environment that was decidedly different from either the shtetls of the Old World or the urban ghettos of the New World. Being Jewish was inextricably tied to how Helen represented herself, and her words and thoughts on this subject prefigure themes of popular fiction writers of the 1950s, such as Herman Wouk and Philip Roth, who created female characters who saw themselves as forever marked and different because of their Judaism.[13] Helen Labrovitz's diary is a firsthand account of the particular difficulties of being Jewish in the 1920s, but it also evokes the struggle of countless other minority girls who shaped their self-image in a mass culture that did not include representations of their "own kind."

"Sweet Sixteen" parties (like this one in 1924) were a way for Jewish girls, as well as other ethnics, to approximate the debutante parties that characterized the adolescent lives of the daughters of American elites. Just like upper-class debutante balls, the invitation lists were usually constructed to include only young men and women of "one's own kind." (Courtesy American Jewish Historical Society, Waltham, Mass., Greene Family Collection)

.   .   .

Helen Labrovitz was born in 1907 in Amherst, Massachusetts, to Russian immigrant parents; she was the fourth child in a family of eight that included three girls and five boys. Helen had one older sister, Rose, born in 1900, and one younger sister, Edith, born in 1909. Until after World War I, the Labrovitzes were the only Jewish family in Amherst, although there were a growing number of Jewish boys who were students at the area's colleges and universities.[14]

Helen's father, Issac, was apprenticed as a tailor in his native Odessa, and he spent a year in London before his arrival in the "Golden Medina," where he took advantage of every economic opportunity. In short order he moved away from New York's East Side to Northampton, Massachusetts (where he had family), and then to nearby Amherst, where he turned his talents with needle and cloth into a successful collegiate haberdashery business that rented caps, gowns, and tuxedos but also sold clothing geared to the tastes of male students in a flourishing college town. In Amherst the growing Labrovitz family lived above the store, and all the children attended local schools. By the early 1920s, when Helen entered high school, the business was prospering, and its proprietor had changed his name from Labrovitz to Landis, an alteration that he hoped would save his children from discrimination and also make for a shorter, snappier business sign.[15]

Although Helen enjoyed hanging around "the store" because it provided her with an opportunity to flirt with attractive Amherst College freshmen, she was sometimes embarrassed by her father's behavior there. Whether he was Landis or Labrovitz, Papa was less refined than she wanted him to be, a fact that galled Helen in her adolescent years: "Felt how foolish papa was to talk to customers in his absurd manner which is terrible. This isn't the first time I realized [sic] it but I can't believe it." Her father's "absurd manner," which was designed to entertain and sell merchandise, included "telling dirty jokes" and being "abjectible" (sic), both of which did little to win the heart of a teenage girl who was attuned early in life to the politics of Gentiles and gentility in a town dominated by a Congregationalist elite.

In this environment, Helen learned and came to embrace popular distinctions about "good" and "bad" Jews. In the early 1920s, when Harvard publicly announced its intention to impose a Jewish quota, the policy was often justified on the grounds that the university did, after all, accept good ones; it simply had no responsibility for the others: "No one objects to the best Jews coming but the others make much trouble especially in the library." Even the liberal and sympathetic editors at the *Nation*, a magazine that took a strong stand against institutional anti-Semitism, admitted that there were "disagreeable Jews, the product of a race in transition."[16]

Distinctions between good and bad Jews were operative for Helen because they were useful in establishing her own identity in adolescence, but they also explain some of her impatience with her father. Although she did not mind that her parents sometimes spoke privately to one another in Yiddish, when she was mad at Papa, she was not above casting him as old-fashioned and uncouth. And when she saw the 1922 silent film *A Five Dollar Baby*, about an orphaned Irish waif adopted by a kindly Jewish pawnbroker named Ben Shapinsky, she was pleased that it was about "good Jews." Helen developed early an acute sensitivity not only to how her "own kind" were portrayed but also to how they behaved.

Because her mother was so busy with younger siblings, Helen's older sister, Rose, became her guide to what was right in American clothing, education, and social behavior. As in many large families, the Landis siblings grouped themselves into older and younger cohorts, and Helen forged a special relationship with Rose, the second oldest child, who was a home economics major at the

State Agricultural College in Amherst when Helen began keeping her diary in 1922 at the age of fifteen. By this time, Rose was living in a nearby dormitory, where Helen could drop in to chat and even spend the night with her sister. As a result of her enthusiasm for her older sister's collegiate life, Helen had little patience for younger sister Edith, the only other girl at home. They had frequent disagreements, which Rose tried to mediate from afar but with little effect. "Fight with Edith," Helen noted summarily in October 1922. "How terrible I am. For that I get another pimple."

Because she was the oldest girl at home, Helen had a considerable amount of domestic work throughout her high school years. As a fifteen-year-old she regularly cleaned the house, ironed clothes, did the dishes, and cared for her younger brothers but not without resentment. "I washed the floors, like a good little girl," Helen reported sarcastically. On the other hand, Helen clearly understood her role in the family economy, and she worked hard at a number of menial jobs that many middle-class girls would not do by the 1920s: she cleaned regularly at the Ginsburgs' boardinghouse, and in the summer of 1922 she joined Rose in the White Mountains of New Hampshire, where they both worked as waitresses at the Crawford Notch House. It was hard serving and clearing three meals a day when you were just fifteen, and there were some unhappy moments when Helen overheard nasty comments at her tables "about Jews and the oatmeal." Still, it was extremely lucrative, and she made enough money to send most of it home to her parents in the form of money orders written at the local post office. When she returned to Amherst, she had another job, providing child care for the son of an Amherst College faculty member. A significant portion of Helen's earnings was set aside for college tuition.

For Helen and for her entire family the educational institutions in and around Amherst were a natural stimulus to think about higher education. The Landis boys swam in the Amherst College pool and belonged to the Boys Club led by college students; the girls attended basketball games at the State Agricultural College, now the University of Massachusetts, and went to lectures. Although they were well aware that "Aggies" lacked the social status of Amherst or Smith students, the elder Landis children were quick to take advantage of the free tuition at the state college. When Edward went there to study horticulture and Rose to major in home economics, the family made an important step into the middle class.

In this collegiate environment, both Rose and Helen developed tastes and aspirations for the life-style of middle-class, educated New England women. Their mother, Sarah, supported the Yankee ambitions of her girls: as early as her sophomore year in high school, Helen was encouraged by her mother to think about Smith (rather than "Aggie" or one of the state normal schools) despite its hefty tuition and upper-class ambiance. When Helen actually saw the Smith campus for the first time, she wrote: "It's wonderful. I'd like to be rich and go there." When sister Rose graduated from "Aggie" and went off to Cornell University to study for an advanced degree in dietetics, she urged her little sister to follow her to Ithaca. Neither Smith nor Cornell was exactly a plebeian place in the 1920s, and neither attracted many girls who still ate kreplach, borscht, and gefülte fish in their homes, as Rose and Helen Landis did.

At Amherst High School, where there were only a few other Jewish students, Helen worked hard to achieve academic and social success. Like any adolescent girl, regardless of religion or race, Helen wanted to be well liked and popular, and she assumed that if she did well and also looked good, friends would come her way. Her diary reveals a young woman who was constantly concerned about receiving high grades and who often prayed for assistance in that realm: "Had English exam which I hope God will help me through with an A." But when Helen made the honor roll, she proudly linked that achievement to her Jewish identity: "Mr. Brown read my name on the [sophomore] honor roll . . . Edith and I were the only Jewish kids. Was happy because [I] deserved it after hard work. Even Emily Lockwood congratulated me."

Helen's blonde, blue-eyed good looks and petite figure also won her numerous compliments, which she recorded in great detail: "Mr. Novick thinks I am pretty. I wonder who else does." And "Ade Henry said I was the best looking girl in the sophomore class and Maxie [her brother] said I was beautiful but selfish." At fifteen, Helen was attractive enough to generate constant compliments even from Gentiles, but she was just as often confused as she was exhilarated by this admiration: "[Steven] Witt told me I was pretty. Can it be true?"

Despite all the compliments and her solid school record, Helen remained convinced that being Jewish had a negative effect on her status at Amherst High. In her mind, Judaism was a burden that inhibited her popularity. On a number of different occasions she told her diary what she told some of her teachers and a few of her peers: "the girls do not like me because I am a Jew." When she announced this in English class, she got a negative reaction and came home frustrated: "now they hate me worse." Although she spoke to one of her teachers about her feelings, the issue was never resolved, and Helen remained on edge about it, sometimes turning to her closest friend, Sadie Ginsburg, for empathy and long "chats about [our] Jewishness." These conversations were clearly about social identity, not about religion, however. The Landis family owned no Bible, Helen knew no Hebrew, and she attended a synagogue for the first time in her life when she was fifteen.[17]

Yet being Jewish clearly defined the shape of Helen's adolescence: although she mixed with Protestant and Catholic youngsters in school, extensive interactions with non-Jewish boys were discouraged if not prohibited. In October 1922, when she had an interest in a Gentile boy from Amherst, Helen wrote: "Saw McLead—Dear boy is lucky [that I like him] but he is not Jewish." Discrimination based on religion was an operative principle in the 1920s, and family names, such as Labrovitz or even McLead, were often a basic impediment to acceptance by mainline Protestant groups. When a college student told Helen about the systematic exclusion of both Catholics and Jews in Theta Chi fraternity, she responded: "Ah what a world that a nation should be held in shame for their names."

Like many girls, Helen worried about peer acceptance, but her concerns were intensified by an undercurrent of anti-Semitism, which gave normal adolescent anxieties an even more painful edge. Although she never used the term "anti-Semitism" or offered any thoughts about its sources, she did recognize the unpleasant pattern in her life and reported direct harassment in a matter-of-fact way. In the spring of 1922, following an after-school session with her French teacher, Helen complained that she had to stand "belittlement for I am Jewish." A few weeks later she reported meeting Hop Eldridge, a local Amherst boy, who called her "a female Jew" as he drove away on his bicycle. This made Helen "awfully mad" and caused her to comment in her diary that it was "a cursed world."

But most of the time, Helen's discomfort was generated by feelings of exclusion rather than name calling or taunts. When a song she wrote failed to be published in the *Graphic Board*, the school newspaper, she responded to the rejection note with this quip: "A Jew has no place unless he works hard." And when she longed for the leading role in the prestigious Junior Play, she asked God to give her the part in exchange for "being a Jew": "Yes, God I have been disappointed enough in my life. Make me get in [the] play. Please." Helen failed to get the role she coveted, but she considered herself lucky, given her religion, to get any part at all. Over and over she felt the pain of exclusion in Amherst and admitted to feeling "jealousy" and "hatred" toward "those terrible Christians." A set of troubled interactions with classmates prompted her to write: "After school talked with the girls. I can feel the curse of those Gentiles in my Jewish blood and so I wish I could go to Springfield and live with Tante Edith and go to Springfield High School."

In 1924, when she was seventeen, Helen Landis got her opportunity to attend college and also to enter a larger, more Jewish world. Because Rose (now twenty-four) was working as a dietitian for the Federation of Jewish Charities in Baltimore, Helen went there to live with her sister and attend Goucher College, formerly the Women's College of Baltimore.[18] Although Goucher did not have the panache of Smith or Cornell, it was well regarded, and the sisters' consolidated living arrangements made it possible to pay the tuition and launch Helen on a collegiate career.

Although Helen loved the idea of being a college girl, the experience did little to resolve the anxieties she felt about being Jewish. In fact, the first few years in Baltimore exacerbated her uneasiness because she became profoundly sensitive to social class distinctions both within and outside the Jewish community.

In Baltimore, Helen was exposed to more varied forms of Jewish life: the squalid tenements of East Baltimore with its newly arrived Russian immigrants; the lively social organizations and noisy entertainments of young Jewish working people; and the ample, well-managed homes and private clubs of the city's successful German Jewish elite. Although the house she shared with Rose and two other unmarried Jewish social workers provided her with access to many young Jewish professionals, including a sizable pool of eligible young men in medical and law school, Helen was not terribly happy because she still felt that she did not fit in.

At Goucher, Helen felt like an outsider again, only this time it was worse. Not only was she Jewish, now she had an occasional "flunk slip" to deal with, and she felt poor by comparison with classmates who lived in the dormitories. Helen rarely even got invited there, and when she did, it was notable: "spent some time in the girls' college room—it's nice to be rich, Oh boy!" Helen also felt different because she had no real family, as did the other commuting students, most of whom lived at home with their parents. "I'd love to have a home here [in Baltimore]," she wrote. "Why should my life be so different from the millions of other girls in this world?" Some of the "city girls" did invite Helen for dinner or bridge at their homes, where she got a taste for a more affluent, bourgeois Jewish life.[19] But her pleasure was tempered by her envy and an adolescent tendency toward exaggeration. After a visit to the home of a Goucher friend, Helen wrote: "I felt a sense of jealousy grip me for the people who live in real houses—and go around with their own type. . . . This is a thing I've been deprived of all my life. Something that can never be made up for—not even a case of lost time."

So despite the opportunities Baltimore provided for lively entertainments, frequent dates, and numerous absorbing romances, Helen never felt like a real college girl, although she adopted all the collegiate lingo, such as "darling" and "row-did-dow" or "bummed" and "bunk." Helen's most gnawing concern was whether or not she could afford to continue being a college girl. Although she had saved the required $425 for the first year, she was uncertain as to how and where she would find the money to enroll for the second. This was particularly upsetting in the context of Baltimore, where she met all kinds of young Jewish men and women, some aspiring and preprofessional but many other poor and ignorant, and this forced her to realize how precarious her class status really was. Without college, she would be just an ordinary working girl like those she saw at parties and dances but did not like.

Given her admiration for New England culture and reserve, in Baltimore, Helen became particularly sensitive to the specter of "the kike."[20] Although she never cut herself off from the city's Jewish social clubs and enjoyed occasional Friday evening services at the Reform Synagogue on Eutaw Street, Helen sprinkled her diary with expressions of her distaste for ordinary Jews and their social life. In November 1925 she lamented having wasted "a good day of my life preparing and serving at . . . a true Jewish banquet. What fuss and business over nothing. How those Jews can talk." When Helen went to an event sponsored by the Council of Jewish Women, she came away with little feeling of sisterhood and declared instead: Jewish girls . . . as a type do not agree with me." Her complaint was that they were "loud and flashy"; another time she wrote: "I dislike the average type of Jewish girl. She's so boisterous and flippy." Helen clearly saw herself as different: "the Jews here, I'm not used to them!" she exclaimed after a dance at the Young Men's Hebrew Association. A Phi Delta Epsilon fraternity dance prompted her to detail how she stood out: "Had a darling time. Feel as tho[ugh] I have poise and beauty among those heterogenous Jew girls."

Helen drew pride from her Yankee roots and her allegedly "non-Jewish" looks because they signified assimilation and suggested her status as a college girl. When a student at Johns Hopkins remarked that she "looked Jewish" and asked if she lived in East Baltimore (the Jewish section), Helen was deeply insulted. At this stage in her life the highest compliment anyone could pay her was to say that she did not look or act Jewish. "I slept at Ann Robinson's house," Helen wrote when she was eighteen. "Had a nice time. They said I had lovely skin and looked like a Gentile." In the fall of 1925, Helen was equally delighted when Morris Davidson, an artist who was one of Rose's friends, told her that she was not only "sophisticated for a girl of eighteen" but that she also acted differently from most Jewish girls. "I don't act Jewish," she wrote pointedly and excitedly, underlining Davidson's welcome affirmation of her identity. At another point she stated bluntly: "Revelled in the fact that I am not an average Jewish type." (In effect, Helen prided herself on her ability to "pass" in much the same way that light-skinned African Americans did.)[21]

But Helen had to work in order to remain a college girl, and that was an unpleasant and disappointing reminder of how close she really was to the mass of young Jewish working women. Her sister announced that in her sophomore year she would expect Helen to begin paying $5 a week toward her board, a request that Helen considered "just" but provoked her to ask: "My God, how will I do it?" As a result, at the end of the spring term of 1925, Helen did not go home to Amherst but began to work five days a week as a salesclerk in the lingerie department at Hochschild, Kohn & Company, a flourishing Jewish-owned department store in the heart of Baltimore's shopping district, where she had worked before as a "contingent" just on Saturdays. During the summer, Helen tolerated the work because she was able to combine it with an active social life and frequent jaunts, even during the week, to a cottage on the Middle River, where she could swim and row in the evening after work. Moreover, she was anticipating her fall return to Goucher and a swift conclusion to her stint as an urban working girl.

But on a hot sticky day at the end of August, Helen heard from Rose that she must continue working throughout the month of September, right up until school started, or return to Amherst and go to "Aggie." This turn of fortune took Helen by surprise and became a focus for outbursts of unhappiness and a general moodiness. "[I] realize how much I am ashamed of working when others about me of my intelligence and career don't have to," Helen admittedly candidly. But understanding her resentment did not stop her from deliberately "playing the college girl" at work and belittling the "plain" and "illiterate" working girls who were her colleagues at the store: "I feel right[ly] superior towards the average sales girl. She is ignorant, selfish, and unwilling to help fellow workers." Store policy fueled Helen's distance from the other salesgirls; because she had college credentials, she was paid more for the same work.

Although Helen had some good days at work, in her diary she represented September 1925 as a tragic interlude that entailed great suffering: "Realize how much I hate work and everything in Life. Hate the people around me and the life I am leading." Late in September, when some girls were already back on campus, Helen lamented her class position: "I don't realize [understand] why I have to work when other girls who attend Goucher with me are so wealthy and well-dressed. Why is it my fate to work, to toil, and suffer? What have I done to deserve the miserable lot I have to take? Life—what has it in store for me . . . ? I am told I have a beautiful face and perfect form! I can swim, row, dive to perfection. [Nothing] is beyond my power to do and comprehend, except that I am unhappy." By late September, when there was still no assurance that she could return to Goucher, Helen became extremely nervous and fearful. To convince Rose that she would do anything to remain, Helen promised to be responsible for cleaning the house they shared with two of Rose's friends. Privately, Helen was willing to act as a domestic to ensure that she could be a college girl.

Helen's return to Goucher in October was a great relief, and she looked for assurance that the tribulations of September and her temporary loss of status had had no long-term effect. "Felt as much like a college girl as they did," she pronounced happily after seeing some classmates from the year before. The first week of classes provided Helen with a time to revel in collegiate life and its obvious privileges: "It sure does seem good to be back again among the college friends of mine. These girls and this environment is so different from that of the average working girl. Oh how thankful I am to be among the 'intelligentia' [sic]." Helen repeated this theme many times, as if repetition would solidify her status: "Love to feel like one of the college girls—to sit among them and imbibe the same things and be in their environment. After all I am one of them." College, she said, "elevate[d] [her] feelings and thoughts on the cosmic things in life."

Yet Helen Landis's remaining years at Goucher continued to be marked by emotional oscillations rooted in her feelings of class insecurity rather than absorption in her schoolwork. "I had an inferiority complex all day," she noted as a junior when Goucher seemed threatening and inhospitable; a week later she felt positive about her ability to adapt to the college's tony environment: "Felt very important and acted like one of the Goucher girls." However flexible and successful she was, the Goucher experience generated in Helen a deep awareness of the prerogatives of wealth and social class: "How little one is worth after all if they have no money," she wrote in 1927. With the help of her older sister she began to acquire some of the outward, costly trappings of her collegiate status. In her junior year she had her hair bobbed in what she called a "panjola," and Rose bought her a raccoon coat so that she would feel stylish and truly collegiate.

Even though Helen's diary entries revolved around boyfriends and social anxieties, she did have some meaningful intellectual experiences at Goucher that were critical in shaping her adult life. As a result of readings and discussion in her social science classes, as well as a number of inspiring chapel sermons about the value of social work, the class-conscious young woman in the raccoon coat began to accompany friends who were social workers on their visits to poor families in East Baltimore, exactly the social address she longed to avoid.[22] In 1928, Helen Landis graduated from Goucher with a degree in sociology and became a social worker, living in and working out of the Neighborhood Center, a settlement house in the pushcart section of Philadelphia run by the Federation of Jewish Charities.[23] During the Depression she worked with the Department of Homeless Men and later with the County Relief Board; she also married (a Jewish attorney, Milton Mitchell Bennett) and raised two sons.

In maturity, Helen Landis Bennett became a competent and caring social work professional who empathized with the plight of the poor and also felt a strong identification with Judaism and humanitarian causes. But as an adolescent girl who longed for social acceptance, she was often unhappy, and she articulated in her private diary some of the most painful and intimate aspects of growing up female in the second generation of American Jews. Although her concerns about popularity, autonomy, and identity were (and are) characteristic of most American adolescent girls, these concerns had a particular edge for the daughters of immigrants who lived in a non-Jewish world, such as Amherst, Massachusetts, or Goucher College.

As Helen did the normal developmental work of separating from parents, establishing an individual identity, and mapping a future, she also had to cope with the difficulties of being Jewish and female in a fast-paced society, where sexual mores were in flux, her parents were "greenhorns," and her religious identity was a real liability. Although Helen attributed many of her high school problems to prejudice, she felt relatively secure and happy as long as she remained in Amherst, where there were only a few Jews and she knew them all. But in Baltimore, where she saw the full range of Jewish experience, including the rough, illiterate, and avaricious, she began to internalize some of the worst aspects of popular anti-Semitism. Increasingly, her self-definition and self-esteem rested on her ability to separate herself from the mass of her own people, a pattern often described as Jewish self-hatred.[24]

Because she was a truly modern girl, one who understood the critical linkage between good looks and female success, Helen focused her energies on looking and acting like a "college girl," a status that somehow neutralized both her Judaism and her tenuous class position. By attending Goucher and also looking Gentile, Helen hoped to distance herself from the mass of working-class Jewish girls whose dark hair and eyes, common clothing, and boisterous behavior were a reflection and a reminder of her roots. But Helen's reliance on negative differentiation was not unusual at her stage of life: most adolescents find it easier to articulate what they do not want to be, rather than what they admire or are.

In her diary, Helen Landis represented herself to herself as a girl who was doing something original. Like most young people, she regarded herself as authentic and unique. Of course, in some ways she was: her perspective was shaped by the experience of her particular family, their special location in Amherst, her subsequent move to Baltimore, and her individual psychological makeup. But her personal diary also stands as testimony to the anguish and the rewards of the assimilation process for an entire generation of Jewish women. With its frank admission of envy of others and disgust for her own, Helen captured the pressures experienced by Jewish girls who were both bright and confident enough to pursue higher education in an environment that provided them with enormous new opportunities but failed to welcome them with open arms. For these girls, growing up Jewish required that they cope with a range of normal developmental burdens as well as their difference, difference from their classmates and also from their own mothers, whose old-world origins provided inadequate preparation for raising daughters who were so deeply invested in modernity.[25]

. . .

How young women of the second generation traversed adolescence had real consequence for the kind of mothers they became, which in turn affected the daughters they raised and encouraged to keep diaries in the 1950s. Those who were "outsiders" in their youth, such as Helen Landis, made serious investments in helping their teenage daughters "belong," be popular, and look good in ways that were sanctioned and encouraged by postwar educators, doctors, and beauty experts. This was the first generation of Jewish parents able to buy their daughters unblemished skin (with dermatologic treatments), perfect teeth (with orthodonture), and better looks (with contact lenses).[26] And because of Anne Frank and the legacy of the Holocaust, Jewish mothers in the 1950s probably aided and abetted their daughters' immersion in teenage culture because it seemed so "normal" and they felt so fortunate.

Ultimately, the diaries of Jewish girls in the 1950s stand as a powerful symbol of security and middle-class expectation. Their numbers, compared to the 1920s, and their formulaic content demonstrate how potent the ideals of youth culture had become and how cultural imagery is internalized by young girls as they struggle to define and understand the self in their adolescent years. Although the material circumstances of Jewish life in America had certainly improved, adolescent girls in the 1950s seemed no more able than their mothers to resist powerful imperatives about beauty and feminine behavior. The irony may be that the hard-won economic and social success of postwar Jewry and the legacy of Anne Frank combined to make them even more vulnerable to the seductions of mass culture.

June Sochen

From Sophie Tucker to Barbra Streisand

Jewish Women Entertainers as Reformers

The title of this essay contains words that stand together uneasily. Entertainers are never regarded as reformers, a category reserved for serious political, educational, legal, and cultural activists. Women reformers have always been characterized as sober women who entered the public arena only to better society, to "do good." Similarly, Jewish women reformers are defined as workers for the betterment of the Jewish community's religious and secular institutions. So the combination of Jewish, women, entertainers, and reformers evokes an unusual combination of qualities, precisely the aim of this essay. Also, the women entertainers described herein defy the usual public depictions of Jewish women; in this sense, my analysis breaks with the traditional images of Jewish women presented by Jewish male writers throughout this century.

The following remarks are suggestive and speculative, designed to create a new way of considering the role of Jewish women entertainers and by extension, many women entertainers and Jewish women in American culture. The dual focus of this essay then—the reformer theme coupled with the bawdy personas of most of my examples—alters our perceptions and interpretations of Jewish women. The subjects of this study carry out their mission with humor. They all share the label of social satirists, commentators on the human condition, particularly the woman's condition in society. Indeed, it is humor that gives these Jewish women entertainers their major weapon.

There has been a known tradition of male writers and performers of humor, but women's contributions to the field have been largely ignored until recently.[1] The American humor tradition has included Mark Twain and Will Rogers, with Jewish male humorists such as S. J. Perelman, Saul Bellow, Lenny Bruce, Mort Sahl, and Jerry Seinfeld contributing to the genre. Jews, women and men, have been overrepresented statistically in the field of humor, largely because of their outsider status. This is not to say that all Jews have great senses of humor or that Christian, Hindu, or Muslim Americans cannot be witty and satirical. But it is to say that the striking presence of Jews in comedy suggests that their minority status is an asset for making people laugh.

I would extend the point to underline the fact that Jewish women are a double minority; as both women and Jews in a male-oriented Christian culture, they are painfully aware of their marginal status. As women, they have been acculturated to observe manners and morals closely. The quick-witted, the wickedly funny, and the antic among them put this training to good use. Women, both Jewish and Christian, have been raised, until recently, to be obedient, passive, and deferential. An acerbic, fast-talking woman is seen as dangerous in both religious communities. A performing Jewish woman is a force to be reckoned with—and possibly feared. Jewish culture admires verbal and written talent, though it has been cultivated among men more than among women.

Sophie Tucker, Fanny Brice, Joan Rivers, Barbra Streisand, and Bette Midler, the subjects of this study, represent three generations of Jewish women entertainers who operated as shrewd and funny observers of the battle between the sexes, the double standard, and sexuality. Tucker and Brice belong to the first generation in this century: children of immigrants who became very successful in the new business of show business in urban America. (Both Tucker and Brice were born in the late nineteenth century, the former in 1884 and the latter in 1891.) Rivers occupies the middle generation (born in 1933, she was farther removed from the immigrant experience, though her parents were immigrants), and Streisand and Midler, both born in the 1940s (Streisand in 1942 and Midler in 1945) are the third generation of Jewish women in America.

Three of the entertainers, Tucker, Midler, and Rivers, presented the bawdy perspective, operating on the margins of society, often in seamy venues. Their unique angles of vision question, challenge, and mock social customs and values. Through laughter they make their audience think again about accepted and conventional behaviors. They do not advocate legislation nor do they lead demonstrations, but their *effect* is to raise consciousness, which may lead to changed values and behaviors; by so doing, they act as reformers. Contrary to Christian fear and suspicion about the dangers of sexuality, Judaic values recognize women's and men's sexual natures and both genders' right to sexual expression in marriage. Jewish women bawds stretch the boundaries beyond respectability. They behave in decidedly unladylike ways, offering salacious views on private subjects.

For women to use humor for social purposes is a truly unusual occurrence. Sigmund Freud did not think women had senses of humor, and that point of view seemed to dominate for a long time. Jewish humor has been studied by psychiatrists for a century, following Freud's lead, but it has been a study of male humor and the Jewish condition in various diasporas. The dilemma of

being an outsider in a Christian culture has been a dominant theme in studies
of Jewish humor, but the unexamined assumption has always been that only
men express and analyze that dilemma. To place Jewish women humorists
firmly within the male tradition is to extend the lens and to reconsider
women's roles in public life. Moreover, before Lenny Bruce, Mort Sahl, or
Jackie Mason plied their trade, Sophie Tucker and Fanny Brice had acquired
large audiences. In the nightclubs of the 1950s, there were many red-hot Jewish mamas playing unbeknown to male comics. Joan Rivers began her career
performing in sleazy joints alongside Bruce and Sahl.

Jewish women bawds turn their humor inward as well as on forbidden subjects such as women's sexuality. Their satire is both personal and social. It is
only in America in this century that this phenomenon has occurred. The five
women entertainers-reformers I am discussing all upset social expectations,
reversed sex roles, and behaved in unconventional (at times outrageous) ways.
By using humor as their weapon and tool, they unnerved their opponents and
found the suspicious becoming fans in not too long a period. Joan Rivers has
said: "Comedy should always be on the brink of disaster. Otherwise it is pap,
and who cares?"[2] Though not all of the Jewish women entertainers in this
group performed on the brink of disaster, they all displayed anarchic personas
during their careers and broke the sexual stereotypes.

. . .

In both literature and popular culture, Christian and Jewish men have portrayed
Jewish women according to their values and dreams. Sir Walter Scott, for example, portrayed them as the Eves, the sexy women who enticed innocent men
into sin and vice. As Ellen Schiff has noted, the dark-haired Jewess, the classic
"other," assumes all of the desired but forbidden qualities of Christian women.[3]
In early-twentieth-century America, male Jewish writers and performers replaced this image with the sentimental "Yiddishe Mama" portrait; Sholem
Asch and others lavished warm praise on the vanishing breed of old-fashioned
Jewish mothers. Sophie Tucker sang a song on the same subject for many
years. By the 1930s, playwright Clifford Odets portrayed tougher and more
difficult mothers, and in recent years Jewish male writers have abandoned nostalgia, fondness, and respect for Jewish women and replaced it with the negative Jewish Princess image and the portrait of Jewish Woman as Frigid. None
of these images prepares audiences for the Jewish woman comic and bawd.

The Jewish women comics I am discussing offer a new combination of features, one that merges the qualities of male- and female-based humor. They
complain about their husbands or lovers while also discussing intimate sexual
needs. They were among the first performers to discuss intensely private subject matter in public. Often for the first time, audiences heard the woman's perspective on sexual matters. Traditionally, only men discussed sex in public,

while women's thoughts and feelings on this sensitive subject were unheard and undiscussed in public. Indeed, nineteenth-century people assumed women had no sexual nature and therefore few thoughts on the subject. While Sophie Tucker sentimentalized Yiddishe Mama in her singing, she defied that image in her red-hot routines.

Sophie Tucker and Fanny Brice, first-generation social satirists, presented a womanist perspective in their humor; that is to say, they were not overtly feminist but rather gave audiences the woman's point of view. Tucker qualified as the bawd; Brice provided the gentler comedy and satire. Both made women the subject of their scrutiny, and by so doing they declared women's concerns to be at least equal to men's. In the Ziegfeld Follies and intimate nightclubs, Brice and Tucker respectively looked at women's issues; they sang about and talked about private wishes. In smoky joints during the late 1950s and early 1960s, Joan Rivers crossed the line into rudeness as well as discussion of topics usually reserved for male-only lips and ears. She too gave a woman's point of view without being explicitly feminist. Her ideology was laughter, and she was willing to do anything to achieve it.

Bette Midler's venue, the 1970s concept stage, offered her liberal opportunities to swear out loud, make fun of everything and everyone, and challenge society's gender distinctions. Streisand's humor was gentler and subtler, but it fits into the scheme of social satire. Indeed, these women humorist/performers juxtapose three powerful themes that pervade Jewish culture: a strong interest in social justice, self-deprecatory humor, and a satiric tongue. They all make fun of themselves, of others within their group, and of the larger society. Explicitly and implicitly, they all identified as Jewish. No one and nothing is immune. Lenny Bruce once said that all comics are either predators or prey; it would be assumed that women comics would be prey (the victim role) while men would act as predators. However, within this group of women entertainers, Sophie Tucker behaved like a predator, a decidedly male role, and Fanny Brice played both roles. Streisand, particularly as Fanny in *Funny Girl* was the prey; and Midler, during her 1970s concert days, became the aggressive predator. Rivers could be both prey and predator.

In both capacities the comic examines a particular social problem and comments on it in the role of either victim or attacker. When audiences, for example, heard Fanny Brice sing "Making Breakfast for the One You Love" (she'll make a "beescuit" delighted that he will "reeskit"), she was playing the long-suffering prey, the woman who tries endlessly to please a difficult and demanding lover. Surely, many audience members understood her plight and identified with it. Also, by singing with a decidedly Jewish accent (taught to her by Irving Berlin), she was placing herself firmly within the immigrant Jewish community from whence she came. As a woman she dealt with subject matter that women often hid from public view.

Brice could also be the sharp critic of women's expected behavior. When she sang, "Oy, How I Hate That Fellow Nathan," she warned innocent young women to beware of men who made promises; though he told her the month they would marry, she sang, he neglected to tell her the year.[4] Again, Brice, like the other women comics discussed here, combined a feminist sensibility, which may never have been articulated, with her Jewish common sense. Jewish daughters had to worry about unscrupulous Jewish men just as surely as did Christian women. The context of Fanny Brice's humor, however, was Jewish and woman-centered. Second only to Al Jolson in popularity, Brice surveyed the world in which she lived and wryly commented on what she observed. Pushy and ambitious mothers, puritanical Americans, and devious boyfriends all received her satiric notice.

In earlier times, male moralists, particularly preachers, warned women to be virtuous and cautious of men who made extravagant promises. Assuming their inability to make wise decisions on their own, the patriarchal representatives guided them. Nineteenth-century women novelists like Susannah Rowson issued the same warning to unsuspecting women. In this century, representing new views, particularly the woman's assertive capacities, Sophie Tucker reminded women in her "red-hot mama" songs that "Mamma Goes Where Papa Goes" because otherwise you cannot control men's behavior.[5] Some of Tucker's song titles capture this point: "Make Him Say Please" and "No One Man Is Ever Going to Worry Me" are unambiguously self-confident statements, and Tucker sings them in a no-nonsense manner.[6]

Tucker's songs were gathered from a variety of sources, most notably, African American blues and bawdy songs and traditional Jewish songs. The result was a red-hot mama image grounded in Jewish culture. Sexual and romantic themes dominated the universe of both Tucker and Brice, as this was the world in which they and their compatriots lived. Contrary to later Jewish men's charges that Jewish women were frigid and uninterested in sex, Tucker, particularly, never left the subject alone. Brice's gentler wit focused on romance more than on sex, but her satiric routines reminded immigrant mothers and their daughters to beware of fast-talking men. In her many pieces performed on the Ziegfeld Follies stage in the 1920s, such as "Mrs. Cohen at the Beach," and "Becky Is Back in the Ballet," Brice discussed gossipy mothers and ambitious mothers with no-talent children. Brice touched her audience where they lived when she made gentle fun of pushy mothers who give their children every conceivable lesson, hoping against hope that some talent will emerge. Because she did it with a gentle wit, not a vicious attack, her fans accepted the message with a laugh. Everyone, after all, knew someone else (not them) guilty of that sin.[7]

Brice told her biographer, Norman Katkov: "In anything Jewish I ever did, I wasn't standing apart, making fun of the race. I *was* the race, and what happened to me on the stage is what could happen to them. They identified with me, and then it was all right to get a laugh, because they were laughing at me as well as themselves."[8] Brice understood the importance of identifying with the victims or the objects of the humor so that they could accept the moral of the satire. The comic also shared the failing that she was satirizing. By presenting this double perspective, as both participant and observer, Brice offered her fans a rare vision and one that they could emulate. A frequent criticism of reformers is that they lord it over their "clients"; Brice's humor was not guilty of that offense. Indeed, the Brice style could be seen as the "traditional" feminine concern for others, albeit in a funny vein. Brice's public image displayed an enormously talented woman with a shrewd perspective, a view of a Jewish woman absent in male depictions.

Critic Gilbert Seldes, who adored Fanny Brice, tried to capture the essence of her humor in a 1923 essay. He compared her to Al Jolson but went on to say: "But she has a more delicate mind and a richer humour—qualities which generally destroy vitality altogether, and which only enriches hers. She is first a great farceur."[9] He labeled her a caricaturist and satirist as well. Brice's inimitable ability to evoke a character, a situation, and a dramatic event all contributed to her overall effectiveness. Seldes's remarks suggest that, though Brice's style and persona were firmly rooted in her Jewish environment, her talent surmounted that particular context to give her an audience and a power to affect all peoples.[10]

Fanny Brice performed on the vaudeville stage, particularly in the elaborate setting of the Ziegfeld Follies, which she starred in for many years. Her songs, really minidramatic/comic renderings of various personas and situations, became famous and were constantly requested by her fans. Her "Yiddishe Squaw" (Rosie Rosenstein, who finds herself to be an Indian) and her "Heiland Lassie" demonstrated her versatility and her ecumenical approach to humor. When she created the Vamp character, one of Seldes's favorites, she ended the number with the line: "I may be a bad woman, but I'm awful good company."[11]

Gilbert Seldes's description of a Fanny Brice performance offers later generations of readers an opportunity to dissect the features of a live performance. He was most struck by her style: "For satire it is Fanny's special quality that with the utmost economy of means she always creates the original in the very process of destroying it."[12] This seems to me to be a very accurate and effective characterization of how Brice contributed to her audience's enlightenment. She offers the familiar only to replace it with the new, often audacious alternative. By beginning with the known—and most of Brice's skits dealt with current events—she immediately connected with her audience, only to offer them a different reading of the known material. If she were portraying a burlesque dancer considered scandalous, she found the humor, the silliness, and the humanity beyond the stereotype.

Sophie Tucker's performances were not known for their delicacy. In her autobiography, *Some of These Days*, Tucker wrote of her red-hot mama songs: "I sing to entertain. My 'hot numbers' are all, if you will notice, written around something that is real in the lives of millions of people. They are songs that mean something to everybody who hears them." Tucker went on to claim that, though her songs all discussed sex, they did not speak of vice. Further, she reminded her readers that the songs were all written in the first person. "I've found that audiences always enjoyed it when I make fun of myself in my songs."[13] Like Brice, Tucker acknowledged both her personal and social identity in her songs.

An analysis of a Sophie Tucker song, performed in the intimacy of a nightclub (indeed, Tucker was a pioneer in this new venue), reveals a great deal about her value system. "I Just Couldn't Make Ma Feelings Behave," one of her popular songs, declares an unspoke view in the 1910s and 1920s: that women have sexual feelings, that they have a right to them and, even further, could state them in public. Tucker was a large woman, probably weighing in at 180 pounds by 1916, when she opened at Riesenweber's, a new nightclub in New York; she did not fit society's image of a beautiful, desirable woman. Yet, like her black blues sisters, Tucker sang proudly of her needs and asserted her right to their fulfillment. All women, she implied, of whatever shape, had sexual natures. Besides Tucker, Millie DeLeon, Belle Barth, Belle Barker, Totie Fields, and many others operated within the bawdy comic genre. Contrary to the dominant representations of Jewish women, the bawdy Jewish woman entertainer has had a long history.

Sophie Tucker looked like Mother Earth and sang like a red-hot mama. As already suggested, she followed the lead of Bessie Smith and Ma Rainey and sang lyrics with double entendres and sometimes only single entendres. Tucker knew Smith and often frequented the African American clubs in Harlem and Chicago. She danced the shimmy, like her equally large-hipped sisters in Harlem, and she borrowed and adapted the blues lyrics for her own purposes. Bessie Smith sang "Dirty No-Gooder's Blues," in which she lamented the unfaithfulness of lovers, and Tucker sang "Make It Legal Mr. Segal," in which she turned a similar and potentially tragic situation into a humorous rendering. By using a Jewish name, Mr. Segal, she reminded her audiences that Jewish men made promises that they did not keep, like men of other religions and races.

Sophie Tucker presented a self-confident woman to her loyal nightclub fans all around the country in a career that spanned over sixty years. She, like her contemporary, Fanny Brice, and her successors, taught by example. Her words raised questions about traditional attitudes toward women, but she never preached or advocated other life choices. Rather, when she sang "Nobody Loves a Fat Girl," she sang it mockingly, thus conveying the very opposite impression. "I'm Living Alone and I Like It," by contrast, asserts a little-known view about women in society. Tucker also shared her experience with her audience in the personal setting of the nightclub. One piece of advice attributed to her was "From birth to age 18, a girl needs good parents. From 18–35, she needs good looks. From 35–55, she needs a good personality. From 55 on, she needs good cash."

Like the other popular women entertainers, fans knew Tucker's personal problems. They knew of her three failed marriages and were delighted when she sang: "I Ain't Takin' Orders from No One." They also roared when she declared: "I Am Having More Fun Since I Am Sixty." One of Sophie Tucker's most-asked-for songs, "Mr. Fink," described, in comic rather than blues fashion, how an innocent young woman asks Mr. Fink: "Where's the mink? I let you have on credit what is usually C.O.D." Once again, the cautionary theme is expressed, and women in the audience surely nodded internally, if not externally, at this wise advice. "No One Man Is Ever Going to Worry Me," another Tucker song, also displayed her self-confidence, another departure from the blues tradition.[14]

Sophie Tucker and Fanny Brice sang primarily to Jewish audiences and shared their personal experiences as women. Joan Rivers, by contrast, enjoyed a wider audience for her satiric wit. Born in 1933 in Brooklyn, Rivers was actually two generations younger than Tucker and Brice. Her parents, Meyer and Beatrice Molinsky, had emigrated to the United States from Odessa when they were both teenagers. Meyer became a doctor, a general practitioner who worked long hours, and Beatrice became a doting mother. Rivers has written recently that her mother "was my rock of security, always there for me."[15] Rivers was raised in Larchmont, New York, thus removing her still further from the immigrant culture.

According to Rivers, her parents quarreled frequently over money matters; her mother was extremely ambitious for Joan and her older sister, Barbara. While Barbara fulfilled parental expectations by going to Columbia Law School, Joan insisted on a career in the theater after graduating from Barnard. She worked at various jobs, took acting lessons, performed in seedy Greenwich Village clubs, and discovered that comics earned more than bit players. As she told it, "I humbled myself before sleazy agents, the kind of people who shed their skins every year." One agent, a full-blooded American Indian, Tony Rivers, told her to change her name and she immediately responded, "Okay, how about Joan Rivers?"[16] Rivers's description of those early years captures her irreverent humor: "I worked at a nightclub where you passed the hat and the hat didn't come back, at a club where the cigarette girls sold bullets, and, truly, at a Catskill resort where a man stood beside me translating each line into Yiddish—so the jokes bombed twice."[17] It was an appearance on the Johnny Carson Show in 1965 that became the breakthrough opportunity for her.

Rivers operated in both the prey and predator mode of humor. She mocked her physical attributes, or lack thereof, while also attacking the weaknesses of others. Like Sophie Tucker and Fanny Brice, she used her less than attractive physical appearance to comic advantage. But Rivers was more explicit in her references to breast size and coarser in her language. In Las Vegas and nightclub appearances she told dirty jokes, something Tucker also did but Brice, in the more public and diverse setting of the Follies, would never do. But the circumstances for Rivers in the 1960s and 1970s were decidedly different from those of Tucker and Brice in the early part of the century. Rivers used the energy and the opportunity provided by the "new" feminism of the period to slash and burn all of the stereotypes and all of the forbidden subjects. If female attractiveness was measured by breast size, then Joan Rivers attacked the subject with withering comments, always turning the aggression inward.

Jewish Americans had achieved middle-class status by the 1960s and were better educated that most Americans. The Jewish Princess had replaced both the Yiddishe Mama and the Red Hot Mama in most peoples' consciousness. When Rivers quipped, "I want a Jewish delivery—to be knocked out in the delivery room and wake up at the hairdresser," she satirized both herself and her upper-middle-class Jewish cohort. This was the subject she knew, and though she also broadened her satiric barbs to touch all peoples, she began with the community she knew best. Rivers was a stand-up comic, closer to the Lenny Bruce style than to Tucker and Brice. Fanny Brice was a singer/actress of great accomplishment, whereas Sophie Tucker talked a song. Joan Rivers, in contrast, snapped out her satire, material she had written for herself.[18]

As a social and sexual satirist, Rivers included headlines of the day, the political leaders, and sexual themes in her performances. Her Heidi Abramowitz book deals with the bawdy side, while her jokes about gynecologists bring cheers from feminists. She is usually gentle in her satire about Jewish culture: "A Jewish porno film is made up of one minute of sex and six minutes of guilt." But she is not above exploiting the Jewish American Princess stereotype. When Rivers says that she was gang-rejected in Central Park, she is acting as victim, as an undesirable self-deprecator. Playing on her persona as an outrageous wit, she willingly crosses the line. But again, the object of her humor is herself. She is not making fun of rape so much as declaring her unpopularity by conventional standards of beauty. She also revels in the shock value she elicits in her audience.

By exposing forbidden subjects to public scrutiny in outrageous and tasteless ways, Joan Rivers acts as commentator on social mores. She repels her audiences by saying disgusting and unladylike things in public. Women, Jewish women, and especially bawdy Jewish women are all expected to remain behind closed doors; or if they appear in public, they are expected to behave within accepted conventions. Joan Rivers thrives on breaking those very conventions.

And in so doing she acts as a questioner of society's norms, a subversive, indeed anarchic, force in the universe. These features, it seems to me, qualify her as a reformer. The directions in which she is leading are also clear: break down old expectations about women's sexual thoughts and feelings, recognize human weakness in everyone, and remove all categories of thought from the sacred realm.

Everything is material for the fertile mind of a social satirist. Joan Rivers's willingness to challenge all accepted views makes her a change agent in a society often reluctant to examine long-held assumptions. Joan Rivers has said of her comic persona: "I love that woman up there because she's so common and so vulgar. . . . I do all that for shock value and it really works."[19] Rivers has clearly thought a lot about her role as social satirist. She also has said: "Humor is tasteless. These are tasteless times. . . . Truth is vicious, but why can't we say it? The question is—who is going to tell the emperor he's not wearing clothes? I think that's my job. I am expressing what people think—and they love it."[20]

In some ways, Barbra Streisand is an unlikely candidate for the title of Jewish woman entertainer-reformer; she is each of the adjectives—Jewish and a woman—and she surely is an entertainer and reformer. But because her career has ranged across so many parts of show business, it is hard to restrict her to this label. Streisand is arguably one of the most talented entertainers of the century. Her career has included music and drama—acting, directing, and producing—and her humor has been expressed in the movies and on stage. Recently, Streisand was asked if she planned to run for public office since she had been an active supporter in President Clinton's 1992 presidential campaign. The actress responded by reminding the reporter that she was a filmmaker and that role allowed her to influence more people than politics did.

Streisand's Jewish identity has sometimes been placed stage center, and at other times it has receded into the background. Precisely because she has had such a long and successful career in multiple venues, Streisand's subjects have been far-reaching. But her first major success, the portrayal of Fanny Brice, on stage and in the film *Funny Girl*, offers a nice symmetry; Brice's satiric style is recapitulated for a new generation. But more important for our purposes, it is as Fanny Brice that Streisand establishes her connection with a Jewish character. In subsequent movies, such as *Yentl* and *The Way We Were*, she plays Jewish women as intelligent, curious, and substantial people, a far cry from the male Jewish depictions.

Streisand has demonstrated a zeal for reform right alongside her entertaining ability. And her persona thereby becomes more complicated; her private and public roles interact. Streisand's personal and professional lives have always been written about and discussed by her loyal followers. Her liberal sympathies have become part of the public definition of her; Streisand's willingness to take on controversial film projects is viewed as part of her private interest in bettering the world. In this sense, her movie roles, as actress and director, become reforming roles.

Though space does not allow me the opportunity to analyze all phases of Streisand's prolific career, a reading of the song lyrics in *Funny Girl* offers one piece of evidence of Streisand/Brice as satiric commentator on society's view of women. Though she did not write these songs (Bob Merrill did), Streisand's clear affinity with the material and her later selections of songs attest to her understanding of the cultural values displayed in them. "If a Girl Isn't Pretty" reminds all women of how physical beauty is the chief qualifier in the game of love and life.[21] Streisand as Brice singing lyrics that question America's image of women thereby offers audiences a decidedly complex reading of the multiple layers that make up the persona of an entertainer-reformer.

A major strength of *Funny Girl* is the tension between the clearly talented and self-confident Brice/Streisand character and the cultural expectations of her. "His Love Makes Me Beautiful" is sung mockingly while others keep reminding the heroine, "You Are Woman," and "Find Yourself a Man." Because the message is delivered within a humorous cloak, the audience accepts it willingly. But once again, the point is clear. Talented individuals, even female individuals, have a right to a public career. Streisand's performance as Fanny Brice qualified her as an inheritor of the satiric tradition practiced by Fanny Brice in the 1910s and 1920s.

Streisand's movie roles—particularly in *Up the Sandbox* (1972), a box office failure but a valiant filmic attempt to translate the Anne Roiphe feminist novel to film; *The Way We Were* (1973), in which she plays Jewish radical activist Katie Morosky against the WASP Robert Redford role; *Yentl* (1983), her most explicitly Jewish film, where the issue is woman learning; and *The Prince of Tides* (1992) in which she both directs and plays a Jewish psychiatrist—all qualify as thoughtful efforts to portray women as intellectually formidable, interested and engaged in their society. Except for *Sandbox*, Streisand portrays a *Jewish* woman in American and European culture, a thoughtful and intellectual woman in conflict with patriarchal tradition. Katie Morosky is a Jewish Communist intellectual in 1930s New York and 1950s Hollywood; Yentl is an aspiring rabbinical student in shtetl Europe. In sharp contrast to the one-note Jewish Princess image promulgated by Jewish male writers, Streisand is a one-woman rebuttal.

Barbra Streisand's record albums are so numerous as to defy easy labeling; they offer examples of traditional and unconventional portrayals of women. At times she sings the same song in different styles; Brice's signature song, for example, "My Man," is a case in point. Streisand sings this song earnestly in one rendition, thereby confirming the image of woman as long-suffering victim, and in another treatment she mocks that very attitude. She reprises classic Broadway musical numbers and also sings explicitly feminist lyrics. All in all,

Streisand in *The Way We Were* (1973) as Katie Morosky, the passionate president of her college's Young Communist League. She is about to address a crowd of college students on the evils of Franco. (Copyright © 1973 Columbia Pictures Industries, Inc. Photo courtesy The Museum of Modern Art Film Stills Archive, New York City)

her professional life as singer, producer, director, and star of her own productions offers all women a view of a self-starting, albeit enormously talented, woman. Through both humor and personal example, Barbra Streisand qualifies as a cultural reformer. Her success, based on enormous talent, serves as an inspiration to women to stay the course and pursue a dream.

Bette Midler, who began her career by doing Sophie Tucker songs at the gay Continental Baths in New York City in the early 1960s, exemplifies a Jewish woman entertainer who both resembles her predecessors and enters new territory. Midler was born in Honolulu; she later described her growing up experience in this way: "I was not a hip color. I was white in an all Oriental school. Forget the fact that I was Jewish. They didn't know what that was. Neither did I. I thought it had something to do with boys."[22] Midler's outsider status, combined with her outrageous personality, enabled her to become a comic performer who shocked her audiences with her audacity; in so doing, she raised important social issues. In her concerts, where she could exhibit the full range of her craziness, Midler did a Sophie Tucker medley of songs; swore openly on stage; reminded women that their satisfaction was as important as, if not more important than, a man's; wore mermaid costumes; and wheeled around the stage in a motorized wheelchair.[23]

Midler mocked romance and love while expressing a need for it, nicely capturing the enduring paradox of the woman's condition. In so doing she continued the Tucker–Brice–Rivers–Streisand tradition. Fans could laugh and think about her presentations. On stage she declared: "I am a living work of art," thus continuing the self-confident pose introduced by Sophie Tucker. When Midler turned to the movies, she originally had less success. Her first movie, a drama titled *The Rose*, was well received, but *Jinxed* (1981) was a flop. She recouped with two comedies later in the decade. *Down and Out in Beverly Hills* (1986) and *Ruthless People* (1986) were box office smashes. The following year, she told Barbara Walters: "Everyone is tacky now; I think I'll be royalty."[24]

Just as Joan Rivers tamed her bawdiness for mainstream audiences, so Bette Midler reined in her anarchic humor for the movies, but the twinkle in her eye, the swagger in her walk, and the smirk on her mouth assure her fans that she is still the same unreserved rebel that she was in the early sixties. Her message remains in the same genre as that of her predecessors: women are healthy, thinking creatures with views on sexuality and all other topics of interest to human beings. Midler is safely identified as an unconventional satirist of sexual relations. Her Jewish background, combined with her idiosyncratic personality, assured her a unique perspective. Her conscious identification with Sophie Tucker ensures her connection to the group of Jewish women entertainers-reformers I have described.

. . .

Both Jewish American and American cultures have been enriched by the presence of these women satirists. All of them serve as texts to their audiences; once their reputations were established, audiences *expected* their next performance to add further illustrations of their no-nonsense pose; they were women with minds, bodies, senses of humor, and the spirit to announce those qualities to all who were within hearing range. Perhaps their very presence gave encouragement to audience members—they too could express their opinions, albeit in less outrageous ways. The combination of their personas and the content of their messages offered audiences unpopular views in a popular mode. Why not laugh instead of cry? Sophie Tucker, Fanny Brice, Joan Rivers, Barbra Streisand, and Bette Midler gave their fans much to think and laugh about.

Reformers hope for thoughtful consideration of their proposals. No one received more attentive responses than these women entertainers. They audaciously changed the way women represent themselves in public. Entertainers, especially humorists, have much in common with reformers: both groups discuss social issues and both often challenge social standards. Both groups wish to inform, enlighten, and influence their listeners; both aspire to change their audience's behavior, their minds, and their values. Entertainers wish to convince their listeners that they are worthy of attention, their product is worthy of repeated purchase (whether records, books, or the next performance), and their message is pleasurable and, hopefully, memorable. Reformers seek to educate people to a new point of view and to effect change. They too wish to be approved and hope that their message will effectively change minds and behaviors.

But expanding the definition of reformer to include entertainers involves both audacity and risk. It recognizes that the primary aim of an entertainer is not to educate but to amuse (but are those aims antagonistic to each other?). It acknowledges that the entertainer is the quintessential individualist, whereas the reformer is most often a member of a group. However, a more expansive view of culture and the ways in which it changes requires an inclusion of entertainers into the category of reformers. Change is a complex phenomenon, more difficult to accomplish than traditional reformers and their historian commentators have sometimes thought.

Further, change must occur in multiple arenas to be effective; value, psychic, and behavioral change are not always carefully or closely measured. Moreover, value and behavior change do not occur simultaneously. With the passage of a reform law, reformers and their chroniclers usually close the book on the subject, assuming that the needed change has occurred. However, enforcement, implementation, and follow-through are rarely undertaken, and historians of the same generation do not take a second look. Later generations have the task of revision and reevaluation. By considering all of the complicated interweaving forces and by recognizing the need to measure change from multiple perspectives, cultural reformers-entertainers might be included in such a discussion.

Entertainers become "texts" in American popular culture and therefore are figures that become influential in the popular imagination. Their very beings, in addition to their work, become part of the collective identity they project to the public. Sophie Tucker, for example, presented a very different image of the Jewish woman to early-twentieth-century America. In sharp contrast to the adoring immigrant mother who nurtured her family and sacrificed her personal dreams for the benefit of others, Sophie Tucker projected a bawdy woman absorbed in her own needs. It was Sophie's dreams that concerned her, not those of her family. The text that was Sophie Tucker suggested a very different role for women in urban America. Yet to add to the richness of the mixture, Tucker *looked* like a nurturing immigrant mother, not the sexy femme fatale.

Tucker fans also knew about Sophie's personal love life and her multiple marriages. Her biography and her performance persona merged into one collective whole. Sophie Tucker's career flourished at the same time that male

Jewish writers enshrined the Yiddishe Mama. We must rewrite the literary and cultural histories of this century to include the Jewish women entertainers as extremely visible images of Jewish women. It is only by opening up the lens and including women entertainers that we can revise the restricted and stereotypical image long viewed as the dominant or only one available for Jewish women.

Indeed, it is not surprising that Tucker's persona would not be represented in cultural stereotypes created by Jewish male writers. Tucker left her child in her mother's care so that she could pursue her career, hardly a desirable ideal from the patriarchal perspective. Sophie Tucker was an ambitious entertainer, a careerist who was willing to sacrifice a personal life for her profession, something Jewish male writers might do but would not advocate as desirable behavior for Jewish women. Philip Roth might pursue his sexual interests aggressively and selfishly but could not or would not imagine such a possibility for Jewish women. Understandably, family values, so central to Jewish culture, are not upheld in the life story of Sophie Tucker, but neither are they in the life stories of many male novelists.

Though we can never be sure what effect a performer has on an audience, one measuring stick is popularity. If the fans return again and again to a Sophie Tucker performance, then her message and her persona are having a positive effect on the receivers. Our evidence for success, in addition to attendance figures, salaries, and record sales, is anecdotal, impressionistic, and fragmentary. Nevertheless, it may be in the intimate arena of a nightclub, Tucker's primary venue, that people think seriously about material presented in a comic mode; in this sense, self-redefinition occurs when women in the audience listen to the risqué lyrics of a Tucker song. They do not necessarily leave their families and follow her lead; rather, they think anew about their needs, their husband's strengths and weaknesses, and the virtues and weaknesses of their marriage; and they emerge from the examination healthier and happier women.

It is clear from fan letters, fan magazine literature, and other anecdotal sources that entertainers occupy the minds of many members of their audience. People identify with their favorite stars, they write to them, they applaud their performances, and they empathize with them when they are in trouble. When Fanny Brice sang "My Man" on the stage of the Ziegfeld Follies in 1921, her fans cried and clapped for her, knowing of her troubles with her real-life husband, Nicky Arnstein. They knew that Brice was neither a traditional Jewish wife nor a helpless, dependent female. They also knew that she was a brave professional who performed in the face of personal pain. She was neither a self-pitier nor a carper, thus defying stereotype.

Since the personal lives and the professional roles of many stars intersected, it is not too great a leap, then, to assume that when a favorite Jewish woman comic was satirizing a familiar social subject, audience members

would consider the new material and angle of vision provided by the entertainer and integrate that new perspective into their own lives. The influence
may have been subtle or unconscious, but it nevertheless existed. Further, the
Jewish women entertainers who sing bawdy songs or deliver off-color jokes
are appropriately called reformers because they question forbidden subjects in
public spaces previously reserved for men. They reverse traditional sex roles,
challenge convention, raise doubts, and offer new possibilities for women, new
ways to live, new issues, and new values. Indeed, their very public persona
gives them visibility, power, and influence. Their being in previously unexpected venues for women raises the possibility that other women, under similar or other circumstances, could also venture into new roles and new spaces.

This assertion is also based on the assumption that the greater the variety of
images, values, and opportunities offered to women, the greater the likelihood
for change—the goal of all reformers. Emotional, aesthetic, and psychological
change, as well as intellectual and rational change, could be achieved by observing these Jewish women entertainers. Streisand's rich and exciting career
offers inspiration to multiple generations of aspiring and ambitious Jewish
women. When women are presented with new ideas and options for their lives,
they select those that appeal to them the most, reshape them, and then integrate
the new features into their own sense of self. They rarely adopt the role or style
without personal alteration. When Sophie Tucker sings of how she needs a
man all of the time, women in the nightclub audience smiled knowingly,
laughed uncomfortably or comfortably, and assimilated her perspective;
whether they accepted her point of view or not, they thought about it and compared it to their preexisting viewpoints.

Value change, a very difficult phenomenon to identify and measure, may
not lead immediately or inevitably to behavioral change. It may subtly affect
one's mind-set but not lead to dramatic change in actions. Women did not
leave their husbands in droves after listening to Fanny Brice satirize unfaithful
men; nor did women revolt after hearing Joan Rivers bash inadequate husbands. When Bette Midler made fun of women who always sang the blues because they loved love, her female fans laughed. Internally, they may have had
other reactions. Audiences learn subtle lessons from the stars they watch and
listen to. They look at themselves, their husbands, and their families differently. The very thought, indeed, the very revelatory process of considering the
Brice, Tucker, Midler, and Rivers messages, surely proved to be a liberating
experience for many listeners. The women in the audience achieved some
emotional, psychic, and intellectual distance from their personal situations.

This must be the governing assumption if one believes that performers have
an *effect* on audiences. Fans laughed and clapped at the right places; they left
the show smiling, and they returned the next time the performer was in town.
Presumably, they talked with their companions about the song lyrics they had

just heard and the implications of those words. To see Streisand as a student of the Talmud reminded people that women had intellectual curiosity. For Jewish women to appear in such audacious poses surely received a lot of notice. So while "official" views of Jewish women were often unflattering, masses of Jews, men and women alike, laughed at Joan Rivers, Fanny Brice, Bette Midler, and Sophie Tucker and admired each and every Streisand performance. All audience members could ignore the negative images while supporting the clever and innovative behaviors of their favorite Jewish women stars.

The Jewish women entertainers I have discussed deserve the label of reformer for all of the reasons cited. Their blend of Jewishness, feminine sensibility, and feminist consciousness belied the unidimensional portrait that received popular currency in the last quarter-century. Joan Rivers may have satirized Jewish princesses, but her very words offered liberation from the image. A Jewish woman listening to Rivers could compare her value system to the one satirized, offer an internal monologue of defense or attack, and emerge from the analysis more clear-headed. No one would pigeonhole Bette Midler or Barbra Streisand as a singular image. By noting the long twentieth-century tradition of performing Jewish women and by including them in the public definition of Jewish women, we thereby end the stereotypical perception of that image.

Donald Weber

The Jewish-American World of Gertrude Berg

The Goldbergs on Radio and Television, 1930–1950

In our age of proliferating cable TV channels, it is difficult to imagine a time, especially in the 1930s and 1940s, when people gathered around a lone radio receiver and looked forward, with great anticipation, to the next installment of the continuing saga of a Jewish American family trying to "rise" in their new-world American surroundings. In November 1931, exactly two years after the radio show created by Gertrude Berg (1899–1966) as *The Rise of the Goldbergs* premiered on NBC, a crowd of people in a Chicago neighborhood huddled around a radio between 6:45 and 7 P.M., causing the businessman whose radio drew the audience to lament, "Oi, I won't make a sale for 15 minutes!" If we can believe this anecdote, reported in the Milwaukee *Journal* as "The Goldbergs Go Over in the Ghetto,"[1] it seems that long before the now legendary Tuesday night ritual of (mainly urban) audiences tuning in the manic, zany figure of Milton Berle on their new television sets, Gertrude Berg had already captured the attention of a huge audience of radio listeners.

To suggest how truly staggering Berg's popularity was, during the month of May 1932, the radio show's initial sponsor, Pepsodent toothpaste, reported to Berg that *The Goldbergs* received 3,302 letters, of which 2,838 were complimentary, while only 11 voiced objections.[2] Indeed, the popularity of Berg's radio series family was truly enormous, second only to that of *Amos 'n Andy*, a show *The Goldbergs* followed in most radio markets in the early 1930s (they even shared the same Chicago announcer, Bill Hay). It may also be impossible to recover radio's affective power, at least in the beginning, to generate a cohesive, perhaps even comforting, space for segments of the population. The "new

85

media" of radio, especially "the absurd soap opera," as historian Warren Susman explains in a famous essay, "provid[ed] a huge public with a body of symbols and myths" whose ongoing narrative it could at some level bond with, thus enabling the listener to forge an imagined community—or idealized family, in the case of *The Goldbergs*—in the face of desperate times. "The 1930s was *the* decade of participation and belonging," Susman observes, and at some level radio functioned as a source—and agent—of national identity.[3]

But before the Depression, having returned to her native New York from a sojourn in New Orleans, where her English-born husband, Lewis Berg, had worked as a chemist-engineer in sugar manufacturing, Gertrude Berg began peddling her idea for a radio show about a Jewish family in the process of "Americanization." The show was to be based on characters drawn from her own life and on the weekend skits she had performed years before at the modest Catskill hotel her father owned. The Goldberg family—Mollie (later Molly); her husband, Jake (Gertrude Berg's own father was named Jake); and the children, Samily and Rosily (based on her own children, Cherney and Harriet)—became and perhaps remain the most famous Jewish American family in our popular culture. Interestingly, Berg initially called Mollie "Maltke" and the family "Talnitzky," but she altered the names, explaining in her autobiography, *Molly and Me* (1961), that "Talnitzky was no longer suitable. It was too much, it was trying too hard, and I couldn't take my character seriously. I changed the name to Goldberg because it sounded right."[4] Although the reasoning behind the name change seems somewhat opaque, what does seem apparent is that Berg adjusted the more heavily ethnic-inflected "Maltke Talnitzky" of her original Jewish mother to reflect her own sense of what felt more "appropriate," as she began, starting out in the 1930s, to construct her vision of Jewish American family life.

How can we begin to understand and appreciate Berg's fictional family? Why, for fifteen minutes each day, was the "nation's ear . . . attuned to the conversation of the best-known family in America," as the fan magazine *Radioland* announced in March 1934?[5] Some of the answers to Berg's enormous popularity may be found by examining a variety of cultural discourses that shaped her radio (and later, by 1950) her television imagination in crucial ways.

Perhaps the most helpful approach in the effort to recover the world of Gertrude Berg involves recalling the now relatively obscure early Jewish American dialect comedians and writers who provided a rich yet problematic comedic discourse against which Berg fashioned her characters and their famous habits of ethnic-inflected speech.[6] By paying attention to what might be called *The Goldbergs'* horizon of listener reception, by gauging the *affective* response mailed in from men and women, Jews and Gentiles, from large cities and small towns across the country, elicited by Berg's representation of immigrant family life, we can begin to measure the serial's impact on the culture of

The Goldbergs' radio family, ca. 1932. From left to right, Rosalyn Silver
("Rosie"), James R. Waters ("Jake"), Gertrude Berg ("Mollie"), Alfred
E. Corn ("Sammy"). (Originally published in *The American Hebrew* 131
[October 21, 1932], p. 419. Courtesy of Eddie Brandt's *Saturday
Matinee.*)

the 1930s and 1940s as we chart the shape of Berg's exemplary career in
American popular culture.

In the process, we extract what historian George Lipsitz calls, in a slightly
different context, "the textured layers of immigrant experience" "sedimented"
within "layer[s] of historical knowledge."[7] What, we might ask, is "sedimented" in *The Goldbergs* as cultural text? By listening to or screening the old
shows in the archives can we mine the past only through nostalgia? Or is there

residually embedded in Berg's ethnic art an enabling memory of immigrant life that can speak powerfully to and thus offer a critique of both the culture of its own time as well as our own culture, especially during this moment of fractious identity politics? Before addressing these key issues, let me briefly locate Berg's Mollie and the sources of her famous Yiddish-tinged dialect within Jewish American literary and popular culture.

One suggestive way of entering the ethnic world of Mollie Goldberg begins by comparing the immigrant landscape as constructed by Anzia Yezierska with that fashioned by Berg, for Yezierska's deeply autobiographical fiction of the late teens and early 1920s—virtually contemporaneous with Berg's construction of *The Goldbergs*—offers an important contrast to Berg's portrait of (for the most part) harmonious/sentimentalized ethnic family life. Unlike Yezierska, Berg did not grow up or ever live on the Lower East Side; she was born in Harlem and went to Wadleigh High School and Columbia University. (Yezierska attended Columbia's Teachers College in her early thirties; she met John Dewey, who would eventually inspire her to pursue a writing career). Indeed, a news release from the Jewish Telegraphic Agency in 1930, a year after *The Goldbergs* premiered on the radio waves, notes how "quite removed [Berg is] from the milieu in which she finds her characters";[8] in 1932, Berg admitted that she had been "denied" "Jewish training" as a child.[9] The major influence on her Jewish-immigrant sensibility was her old-world grandfather, who did live downtown and whose reverent awe and respect for American life the faithful granddaughter imbibed.

Unlike Yezierska, who in her own life and in her fiction rebelled against the Old World patriarchal repressions figured in the fathers and who would in 1920 famously reject middle-class family life for a brief career in Hollywood, Berg idolized her "Grandpa Mordecai," whom she listened to extolling the greatness of Columbus (with whom Mordecai, she tells us, was on a first-name basis). "Let anyone say a word against America and Grandpa would get insulted," Berg recounts in the opening pages of her autobiography; "he took it as a personal reflection on his hero and he would say, 'A Klug zu Columbus!' which can be translated roughly as 'What a curse on Columbus—that such a pimple should insult such a man!'"[10]

This vignette is telling for a number of reasons. First, it seems clear that Berg (or her grandfather) either misread or imposed the *opposite* interpretation on the famous immigrant Yiddish curse voiced by those disillusioned with life in the New World. "A Curse upon Columbus!" was a ritual invective uttered from a linguistic space *outside* the American consensus; it heaps scorn on the discoverer of this New World for bringing only woe and generational apostasy upon a once holy people.[11] Instead, Grandpa Mordecai's *un*ironic application of the ghetto curse reveals an uncritical, wholesale embrace of his adopted country/host culture—a stance implicitly aligned with an *alrightnik* perspective, which sees new-world identity as a function of neighborhood and income, an outlook that cannot tolerate the slightest impugning of the "golden land."[12]

Yezierska, however, understood in deep ways the ironies that laced through new-world existence. In her fiction we hear the sad, bitter overtones of immigrant life voiced by her shrill tenement matriarch, Hannah Breineh, who recognizes the tension—and sardonic irony—of the spectacle of American-born, new-world children shamed before their bone-crunching, soup-slurping, Yiddish-speaking, Columbus-cursing immigrant parents. The rising generation is always figured as trapped between two worlds, helpless in a kind of liminal void, overwhelmed with terrific shame in reaction over the parents' boorish manners and mangled speech.

In Yezierska, the strain—and substantial comedy—of this inevitable generational struggle, a struggle that for the most part remains strikingly absent in Berg, is played out at the level of foodways and table manners. In her prize-winning story of 1919, "The Fat of the Land," there is the rich example of Yezierska's vivid immigrant mother, Hannah Breineh, who remains in cultural limbo, alienated from her children's *alrightnik* life-style on Riverside Drive *and* out of place, unhoused back on Delancey Street. Hannah Breineh, Yezierska's narrator tells us, "is starved out for a piece of real eating. . . . 'I'm starving . . . but I can't swallow down their American eating.'" Still, the mother, aware of the boundless ironies inscribed in her historical dilemma, can in the end only laugh the bitter laugh expressive of cultural disjunction and dislocation; she recognizes the ideological weight of the Americanization process—her children's allegiance to host-culture authority, which drives their *inauthentic* new-world quest for manners. With shrewd, profound insight, Hannah Breineh identifies the paradoxical source of filial shame: "'Why should my children shame themselves from me? From where did they get the stuff to work themselves up in the world? . . . it is our choked thoughts and feelings that are flaming up in my children and making them great in America. And yet they shame themselves from me!'"[13]

It was this kind of raw, often bitter shock of recognition on the part of the older generation and—in dialectical response—the often guilt-ridden, shame-ridden reaction in the children that generated the deepest sources of humor—mediating humor—in the early-twentieth-century Jewish American imagination. The humor took many forms and exhibited various modes, from the acting out of "greenhorn" predicaments on the Yiddish stage to Abraham Cahan's great stories about the comedy of acculturation in the late nineteenth century (notably *Yekl* [1896] and "The Imported Bridegroom" [1898]) to the popular genre of "Cohen on the Telephone" monologues of the early twentieth century—heavy-dialect performances on record (a few were filmed as well) that drew on the long tradition of ethnic stereotypes from vaudeville routines to create comedy based on "mis-hearing/mis-readings" of exchanges between a "Jew comic" and his American interlocutor.[14]

Perhaps the richest example of dialect humor may be found in the now obscure parodic sketches of Milt Gross, who achieved a measure of popularity with his collections *Nize Baby* (1926) and *Dunt Esk!!* (1927).[15] Along with Yezierska, Gross is a key figure in accounting for Berg, for it was his style of extreme dialect humor that Berg admitted (in an 1956 interview) working against. Earlier, though, in 1930, she explained that her own representation of Jews issued more generally from a reaction to "Jewish types portrayed on the stage," a tradition of Jewish popular culture that, she confessed, "was very revolting to me."[16]

What must have disgusted Berg about the Milt Gross material was how the mangled Yiddish-English dialect of his characters rendered immigrant family life as unsavory, an endless screaming match between streetwise children and their helpless parents.[17] In light of her grandfather's unalloyed patriotism, Berg also must not have appreciated Gross's wicked parodic send-ups of various American tales and legends: "Cuttsheep from Miles Stendish"; "Sturry from Hurratio Halger"; "Sturry from Reep Wen Weenkle"; "Give a Look is in De Raven" ("Wance oppon a meednight drirry / While I rad a Tebloid chirry—/ 'Pitches Hinnan gatting litty—/ Odder peectures on Page Furr'; / Gredually came a whecking, / Tutt I: 'Feitlebaum is smecking / Goot for notting Isidore! ['] / Smecks heem where de pents is lecking / In de rirr from Isidore. / Wheech hez hepped huft befurr!!").[18]

Gross's collections may also have offended some of his readers made anxious by how awkward (uncivilized?) Jews sound in his English transliterations. That perhaps recognizable overreaction masks what I hear as a deeper, darker world beneath the often brilliant parodies: the raw emotions; the sardonic, mocking humor (which barely contains the father's violent rage); the lure and challenge of street life and of popular culture in general over the authority of the family (the subject, of course, of *The Jazz Singer*); and above all, the *anarchic* potential of Yiddish dialect humor (and probably most dialect humor in general, from Mr. Dooley to Jesse Simple), which explodes American mythologies in the narrative act of parodic retelling. At some level Gross's immigrant landscape is the lowbrow version of Henry Roth's utterly unsentimental, truly brutal portrait of immigrant coming-of-age, *Call It Sleep* (1934), where Yiddish is rendered as a lyrical English between loving mother and terrified son bewildered by the vengeful ravings of his father, who feels himself a failure in America and who takes out his smoldering rage and swelling paranoia on his innocent son.

At the same time, the tones and rhythms of *Dunt Esk* and *Nize Baby* look forward, in their wicked, uncivil puncturing of American popular ideology, to the parodic world of Mel Brooks's "Two Thousand Year-old Man" (along with his wicked, Academy Award–winning 1963 cartoon, *The Critic*, which takes on modern art), to Shelly Berman (e.g., the brilliant 1960 monologue in which he becomes his gruff yet ultimately loving father responding to the son's request for money to study "ecting" in New York, and especially to Lenny Bruce, whose routines are *filled* with Yiddishisms. Bruce's notorious parody of the Lone Ranger and Tonto also seems to me a direct descendant of Gross's Yiddish deconstruction of popular fairy tales).[19] In the case of Henry Roth's often harrowing account of a young boy's journey from home to the street, as well as the arrival of a generation of Jewish-American comics and cultural critics, the power and source of the Yiddish-soaked rhetoric issues from the enabling disjunction enacted by the hyphen, which both separates *and* links immigrant and American identities. It is from within this creative, at times dangerous, imaginative space that the ethnic artist, as liminal being, negotiates both the in-group and the host-culture worlds/spheres, all the while remaining uneasy, unhoused within each.

From this perspective, Gertrude Berg's career in radio and television amounts to a gigantic effort to bridge the space between these dual ethnic and American identities, to soften the jagged edges of alienation through the figure of Molly Goldberg and her special accommodating vision—a vision of a loving family, of interdenominational brotherhood, of middle-class ideals, of *American* life, indebted, it appears, to the *un*ironic faith of her grandfather. Berg's Molly is no Hannah Breineh suffering the abject despair wrought by generational shame or cultural marginality; nor is she a "red-hot mama" like the young Sophie Tucker, who, along with her cohort of early vaudeville entertainers, drew on her ethnic identity to construct a distinctive, often unbuttoned comedy of satire and sexual innuendo. Despite—perhaps because of—its unabashed sentiment, its wholesale embrace of cultural ideals, *The Rise of the Goldbergs*, as the radio series was initially called, offered a soul-inspiring testament to the wonder-working powers of the American way, a daily chapter in the saga of hope and perseverance that struck a profound answering chord in the hearts of her millions of listeners in the 1930s and beyond.

Perhaps we can begin to explain the astonishing popularity of Berg and her show by listening to a sampling of responses drawn from her radio audience, in some cases sent directly to Berg in New York or forwarded to her from the show's first sponsor, the Pepsodent Company in Chicago.

From a woman in Oklahoma City, January 1933:

There is not a single thing about the "Goldbergs" I can find to criticize, for they present life as it should be. The fact that they are Jews does not at all detract from our enjoyment, but rather adds to it. We like the democratic and friendly feeling they have for Jew, Gentile and Catholic. . . . "Molly" is a beautiful character, an example for all wives and mothers, and her philosophy is practical for our every day living. . . . We like their patriotism, their constructive, charitable acts, their sympathy for friends in pleasure or trouble. In fact, we cannot imagine any portrayal of family life more perfect.[20]

From a woman in Maine, December 1932:

My mother and I live here alone. She is 84, still mentally alert, and there's nothing on the radio for her like "The Goldbergs." We never miss the 7:45 appointment unless we are compelled to and then regrets are always expressed. We call it "visiting with the Goldbergs." We have no "better people" within the range of our acquaintance. . . . I continue to marvel at the uniform excellence of the sketches. You seem to draw from a very deep well. . . . I heard of a household in a nearby city where no telephone calls are answered between 7.45 and 8 P.M. because The Goldbergs are on the air. . . . Thank you very much, dear lady, for the clean, wholesome, helpful [like Pepsodent!] entertainment that you send nightly to this household. . . . Truly, the Goldbergs "shine like a good deed in a naughty world." "May they live long and prosper."[21]

Read together, these letters, drawn from a sizable archival sample, convey a rare immediate sense of just how powerful, just how compelling, Berg's construction of the Jewish American family as *American* family proved to be. *The Goldbergs* on radio appears to have truly inspired its listeners and in the process seems (in some cases) to have filled an affective void—the show literally *became* a surrogate family, surrounding households across the country in the 1930s with the familiar sounds of middle-class experience, with the comforting messages of middle-class ideals. If, following Susman, in some sense the cultural moment of the 1930s can be understood as a time when people sought an explanatory, soothing narrative, myth, or ideology to embrace (think of the enormous appeal of that decade's various visionary movements, religious and political), then *The Goldbergs* functioned as an agent of cohesion and, for some, as a utopian dream vision, a redemptive light illuminating how "life should be." The figure of Molly, we might say, inspired faith—and faithful listeners—during an interval of economic doubt and historical uncertainty.

About the overwhelmingly positive reaction to her characters, Berg was genuinely surprised. Potential network executives had originally voiced severe doubts that a radio show about a Jewish family would find a national audience; a 1930 clipping speaks of Berg's "meteoric success in the radio world" as a result of her portrait of Jewish life as "the real article."[22] Though Berg consciously labored to modify the extremely distasteful dialect tones of *Nize Baby*, what is remarkable about the early *Goldbergs* scripts is just *how* heavily ethnic they in fact were. Listen, for example, to a portion from one of Berg's first dialogues:

JAKE: Molly, your soup is feet for a kink.
MOLLY: You mean a president. Ve're in Amerike, not in Europe.

JAKE: Oy, Molly, Molly, soon ve'll be eating from gold plates.
MOLLY: Jake, d'you tink it'll taste better?
JAKE: Soch a question?[23]

This exchange already marks the imaginations of Berg's central characters: Jake (played originally on radio by James G. Waters, the star of *Abie's Irish Rose* on Broadway), always seeking a fuller *material* existence; Molly, always tempering his impulsive, excessive desires with a down-to-earth reality check designed to remind him—and her listeners—about the spiritual costs of acquisition. In its brief distillation of *The Rise of the Goldbergs* for April 29, 1930, the Ottawa *Citizen* told its readers that tonight "Mollie's persistent kindness again melts her husband's heart."[24] Or listen to another very early script (the fifteenth episode, titled "Sammy's Bar Mitzvah," dated February 1930):

MOLLIE: You know, Jake, ull de pipple vhat goes arount saying dat in life is more troubbles den plezzure is ull wrong—I tink so.
JAKE: Bot everybody says so—even de beegest writers.
MOLLIE: Oy, dat's because dey didn't found out de secret.
JAKE: Aha! So you found it, ha?
MOLLIE: Yes, Jake. Dun't leff. Maybe I'm a plain peison, and I dun't ridd vhat de high writers is writing, bot by myself I found out de whull secret.
JAKE: So tell me too.
MOLLIE: You see, Jake, it's true vhat in life is lots of trobbles. Bot de come, dey're here, you go through vid dem, and findished.
JAKE: Nu, so dat's de secret?
MOLLIE: Not yat. Bot de goot tings, de plezzures, is never findished. Dey're ulvays vid you—if not outside, den inside.
JAKE: How's dat?
MOLLIE: Because ull you got to do is cloise your eyes—vhat am I talking?—not even cloise your eyes—unly tink, and ull de nicest fillings, de best experiences in your life is beck again, and even more lovely den before. You can live it ull over again! . . .
JAKE: Your secret can't vork for everybody, Mollie. Maybe unly far drimmers like you.
MOLLIE: Nu, be a drimmer! Dat's de secret, see?[25]

Here is a Yiddish-saturated dialogue designed to address the emotional and psychic needs of its audience less than a year into the Depression. Although it is no doubt difficult to gauge, Mollie's voicing—really revoicing—of the dreamer's unflappable progressivist vision must at some level have reverberated in the hearts and minds of listeners across the country. And if Mollie's rhetoric of dreaming had an impact, its effect may have been connected to her identity as *newly* arrived American visionary, recapitulating the country's innermost ideals of historical optimism and resilient striving (in contrast, say, to the wicked, unforgiving 1930s satires on the American dream of success composed by one of the "high writers," Nathanael West, who, in *A Cool Million* [1934] and *Miss Lonelyhearts* [1933], refused to comfort his generation with *any* hopeful narrative about the future).

Thus, what is "sedimented" at one level in the early radio *Goldbergs* and perhaps was extracted by her *American* listeners—some of whom it seems would adjust, indeed, structure, their lives around a ritual "appointment" with "Mollie"—is a rich deposit of national ideals unearthed by her symbolic-representative status as immigrant dreamer; Mollie, that is, loomed in the popular imagination as the keeper of the dream *through* the visionary agency propelled by her Yiddish inflections. Thus, in utter contrast to (in her view) the degrading ethnic-literary caricatures of Milt Gross, Berg strove (consciously, in my view) to speak in the ideological-mythic tones of the dominant culture by a decidedly *un*parodic process of linguistic incorporation: in the rhetorical world of Molly Goldberg, *drimm* equals *dream.*

At still another sedimented level, *The Goldbergs* mined the memories of its Jewish listeners. Indeed, for some the show assuaged shame anxieties over social marginality and difference; for others its helped release long-suppressed or simply forgotten ethnic feelings. One listener, from Brookville, Indiana, after hearing the Yom Kippur show in October 1935 (Berg would annually broadcast shows concerned with the family's observance of the High Holidays and Passover from the early 1930s on radio through the early 1950s on television), wrote to thank Berg on behalf of the two Jewish families in a town of 2,100 people. It "touched our hearts as it was so real and reminded me of years gone by."[26] A young woman from Los Angeles, responding to the same broadcast, admitted to being "a modern Jew of the younger generation, but [the Yom Kippur show] certainly gave a tug at my heart strings" (she listened to it, she tells Berg, with "her Zeide" [grandfather]).[27] After listening to the Yom Kippur show eight years later, in 1943, a Jewish educator from Cleveland thanked Berg because "this series from your facile pen has done more to *set us Jews right* with the 'goyim' than all the sermons ever preached by the Rabbis"[28] (emphasis in the original). And after the first *Goldbergs* Yom Kippur show aired on television in 1949, a young woman felt moved to respond, "I admire your courage to depict our Jewish life in such a beautiful way."[29]

From the beginning, then, it appears that Berg dislodged in her Jewish American audience a sediment of nostalgia, buried and encrusted by the process of acculturation ("America makes one forget everything," a disillusioned letter-writer to the "Bintel Brief" column of the *Forward* announced in 1908).[30] Almost as if to compensate for her own "lack of Jewish training" (as she had put it) in her private life, Berg redressed the religious balance in art, inserting special shows designed to present Jewish rituals and ways in the warmest, most affecting light. Scanning her massive scrapbook of clippings from the fall of 1933 and the spring of 1934, one senses how important these Yom Kippur and Passover shows were to her; *every* notice of an upcoming broadcast appears to have been saved, some of only a single line or two from the obscurest of newspapers. "Goldbergs Present Special Yom Kippur Program Tonight," announced the Youngstown *Vindicator* (with Cantor David Putterman and the Mechlenberg Boys Choir); it will be "one of the season's most unusual broadcasts," proclaimed the New York *News*.[31] The sheaf of clippings also conveys a palpable sense of how geographically various a market *The Goldbergs* was heard in.

The hallmark of these religious shows, even with the constraints of the fifteen-minute format, was Berg's desire to keep faith with and thus recover a Jewish world that, for some listeners in her audience, had faded from memory; for others, these religious shows stirred a measure of ethnic pride ("set us Jews right"). Following the first year of broadcasts, whose plots narrate the family's rise from the Lower East Side to the Bronx by relating a variety of incidents and occasions in their daily (secular) and religious life—from Mollie's secret saving of pennies in a cookie jar, which "saves the day" for Jake's frustrated business ventures, to "Sammy's Bar Mizvah [*sic*]," Berg sought to inject as much Jewish tradition and culture as could be accommodated by the serial format.[32] Thus, in 1932 she sought the advice of a well-known rabbi about the details of a Jewish marriage ceremony, which she subsequently incorporated on the air;[33] and in June 1933 she transformed *The Goldbergs* into a vehicle of middlebrow culture with a performance of "Sulameth," described by the Chicago *News* as "a popular Jewish opera of sixty years ago." "Gertrude Berg introduces another Jewish novelty" is how the article begins.[34]

Two months earlier, on April 10 and 11, Berg had introduced the "novelty" of Passover to the national airwaves, bracketing, in light of the sacred moment, the regular serial plot concerning (in the words of the announcer) "the release of Henry Fowler and Edith Emmett last Friday."[35] What distinguishes these particular episodes is how they reinscribe the figure of Mollie as agent of familial harmony and reunion, together with the continuing evidence of Berg's faith-keeping design to present Jewish ritual. Thus, in one instance, Mollie secretly sends for Uncle David's (another member of *The Goldbergs* family) daughter all the way from California; the episode concludes with their terse but (I presume) emotional encounter:

DAVID: Florence . . . Florence . . .
FLORENCE: Papa darling . . .
DAVID: Florence . . .

Preparing for the Seder itself, Mollie envisions "vone great big table. . . . Dats how it should be, mein kind . . . everybody at vone table." Berg renders various

Passover songs and rituals via the children, who interrogate each other about the symbolic meaning and use of the ritual foods; there is even a recitation of the Four Questions in Hebrew (followed by their English translation) and a collective rendering of "Dayenu" and other festive songs. Mollie is moved by the chanting of the "Adder-hu" ("Yes, darlink," she tells Rosily," it's de song of freedom"); and David reacts to the sounds of "Hud Gadyo" with nostalgia: "Oh, . . . De foist time I sang dat I vas tree years old."[36]

How did Berg's audience respond to such sentimental confessions? One Jewish listener remarked that he was "sure you proved to many a Jew how impressive the rituals of his religion are," and another Jewish listener was made to feel self-conscious about the public display of religious practice that ought to be kept "for temple service only." In general, though, the Jewish American reception of *The Goldbergs*, especially by various official organizations—guardians and spokesmen for the Jewish middle class—remained enthusiastic throughout the life of the radio series.

To be sure, letters would surface from more observant, more ritually precise listeners over the years: "My dear Mrs. Berg: Shame on you for letting Molly Goldberg pare potatoes on Shabbos," reprimands a woman from Philadelphia in 1934; why did the family attend a "church affair on Friday nite?" asks another listener in December 1933; Mollie chants the wrong Kiddush, according to a woman from Brooklyn, writing in May 1934. One 1934 letter, signed "A 'Goldberg' Enthusiast" from New York, even takes issue with Molly's dialect, which displays the "authentic speech defects of the middle class Jewish woman": since Mrs. Goldberg is so "progressive a person, quick to learn and adapt herself," how can she "show so little improvement in her own grammatical expressions after months—no, years of broadcasting! . . . Please, sirs [the writer has lodged these complaints directly with the radio station], may we ask for just a little better English from the noble lady!"[37]

The request for "better English," of course, misses the point—and the source—of Berg's invention of Molly's signature verbal style, a rhetorical-theatrical *performance* that endeared her to millions. Indeed, *The Goldbergs* almost immediately became something of a cultural *commodity*, especially the figure of Molly, the archetypal Jewish matriarch Berg inhabited for over thirty years. As early as 1932 there seems to be discussion of marketing a "Goldbergs'" puzzle; by 1934, Berg herself began a syndicated column in the Jewish press under the title "Mamatalks," which served out morsels of homey philosophy, written not in Molly's fractured dialect but rather in Berg's own mannered English.

In 1944 Proctor and Gamble sought to put out a "good-will booklet" on the history of *The Goldbergs* show to coincide with a comic strip based on the series that was about to appear in the New York *Post*. Writing her sponsors about the idea for a comic strip, Berg assured Proctor and Gamble that she "would have the final say on what was done" and "would naturally see that characters represented would be in every way lovable and lifelike and would permit no caricatures."[38] The comic strip did indeed begin in the *Post* in June 1944, revisiting the plot of "Mama Saves the Day"; the panels often conclude with a box titled "Molly Says," with a fitting moral tag—for example, "Every day a little is some day a lot."[39] In 1955, after *The Goldbergs* was off television, Berg lent her character to *The Molly Goldberg Cookbook*, which listed recipes based on the individual tastes of her TV family ("Bagels Jake")[40] and even personally marketed her own line of housedresses designed for the "full-figured" woman, making highly advertised appearances at department stores in the Midwest and Northeast.

Indeed, except for a brief interval in the mid-1930s, when Berg wrote and starred in a radio series based on her adolescent life in the Catskills (titled *The House of Glass*), *The Goldbergs* was never off the air. Between 1929 and 1962, Berg remained a major presence in show business, starring in a short-lived (156 performances) Broadway play called *Me and Molly* (1948); a feature film based on the series, titled *Molly* (1951; originally called by Paramount *The Goldbergs*); and then, in the late 1950s, after the TV *Goldbergs* had become *Molly* in 1955, appearing in assorted television dramas (among them *Paris and Mrs. Perlman* and *Mind over Mama*, directed by Sidney Lumet, and *The World of Sholem Aleichem*). She starred in a second Broadway play (*A Majority of One* [1959], with Sir Cedric Hardwicke) and finally, in her last, barely remembered TV show, called *Mrs. G Goes to College* (1961–62), again co-starring Hardwicke.

Like so many popular radio programs and entertainers, *The Goldbergs* moved to television in 1949 and appeared in various formats and on different networks. Although the story of the show's transition from radio to television requires more extended analysis than can be given here,[41] it is significant that Berg probably was the first woman to write, produce, and star in her own TV vehicle. Equally important is how quickly the show changed over time, perhaps adjusting to the transitions in American—especially Jewish American—middle-class life. For example, the earliest television shows more or less borrow directly from the radio series (the radio cast, including Philip Loeb as Papa Jake, became the TV cast); Berg as Molly retains a relatively strong Yiddish accent, but it is not nearly as "heavy," at least in comparison to the first radio scripts.

By the time the family moved from the Bronx to suburban "Haverville" (the "village of the haves," in David Marc's nice formulation)[42] at the beginning of its last year of production (1955), most of the specific Jewish tone and content of *The Goldbergs* had been erased: the show's title had become simply *Molly* (a stage in a steady process of ethnic erasure, from Berg's alter ego "Talnitzky" to "The Rise of Goldberg" to "The Goldbergs" to "Molly" to, by the early

Gertrude Berg as "Molly Goldberg" ca. 1951. (Courtesy of the Gertrude Berg Papers, Syracuse University Library, Department of Special Collections.)

1960s, "Mrs. G" [the *G* stood for "Green"]). Philip Loeb, who had been black-listed in *Red Channels* and removed from the show in 1952, was replaced by an actor whose background didn't conjure a problematic political history;[43] and Molly's speech—the key aspect of her being—became *much* less Yiddish-intonated. In addition, shows inspired by religious holidays in the Jewish calendar (perhaps the hallmark of the radio *Goldbergs*) were displaced by regular, fairly innocuous scripts.

These transformations suggest that by the mid-1950s *The Goldbergs* maintained an unsure, tenuous relation to the new (suburban) world of American middle-class arrival. As powerful television networks replaced individual corporate sponsors as the arbiters of national taste and programming, the world of Molly Goldberg and other "ethnic" families—like the turn-of-the century Scandinavian household on *I Remember Mama* and vaudeville-inspired variety shows like Milton Berle's *Texaco Star Theater* and Sid Caesar's *Show of Shows*—no longer could find an audience. This key transition in American popular culture is best symbolized by the arrival of "ethnically neutral"[44] and often father-centered television, a displacement that lasted, more or less, for twenty years.

The Goldbergs and Gertrude Berg thus remained steadily in the country's imagination for twenty-five years, a remarkable tenure for any work of popular culture. In its radio heyday the show was among the most listened to series in the country. And in light of listener response, Berg's invention of Molly and the various strivings of her immigrant family seem to have elicited deep identification with the public, especially in the 1930s. For its Jewish auditors, *The Goldbergs* constructed a warm, familiar, *heimisch* space that provided the salve of nostalgia against social marginality and difference. Still, we should always remember the cultural counterpoint to Berg's sentimental, harmonious vision of ethnic family life: the shrill universe of alienation and shame and rage, which found expression in the 1920s and 1930s with Milt Gross and Henry Roth and by the late 1950s (the virtual endpoint of Berg's career) became perhaps best represented by the provocative early stories of Philip Roth and the wicked satires of Lenny Bruce. It was against this darker imagination of Jewish life in America that Gertrude Berg created *The Goldbergs.* Each vision has had its audiences; each vision can claim to represent a portion of the truth of Jewish experience in America.

III

Changing Stereotypes:
Jewish Women in Postwar America

Susanne Klingenstein

Sweet Natalie
Herman Wouk's Messenger to the Gentiles

For a recent immigrant to the United States, an invitation to write about the representation of Jewish women in American culture was more difficult to respond to than the editor of this volume may have imagined. Having arrived in Boston in the late 1980s and settled into the narrow embrace of its libraries and academic institutions, I was still unable to tell, almost a decade later, whether American culture outside academe and outside New York City and Los Angeles even took note of the representation of Jewish women or had any perception of them at all. Jewish women did not strike me as a prominent feature of American culture at large.

I could think of one Jewish woman, however, who had entered the homes and hearts of Middle America. She had done so quite ostensibly as a *Jewish* woman, since her fate was intended to exemplify that of the Jews caught in the cataclysm of World War II. She is Natalie Jastrow, an American in her twenties, who is the heroine of Herman Wouk's best-selling novels *The Winds of War* (1971) and *War and Remembrance* (1978). The first volume, covering the events in Europe from the spring of 1939 to the fall of 1941, sold five million copies. An additional two million copies were printed in 1982 to take advantage of renewed interest in the work triggered by the release of the ABC-TV miniseries *The Winds of War* (February 1983), starring Ali MacGraw as Natalie Jastrow. Famous for her role as Jennifer Cavilleri, "an American of Italian descent,"[1] in the movie *Love Story* (1970), MacGraw had also been cast as Brenda Patimkin in the 1968 movie version of Philip Roth's novella "Goodbye, Columbus" (1959). Hence, her face had already been introduced to American consumers as Jewish (or vaguely Mediterranean).[2] Wouk's second volume, *War and Remembrance*, covering the period from Pearl Harbor to Hiroshima, was a less sensational commercial success, but it still sold a respectable two million copies, certainly not all of them to Jews. The subsequent 1988–89 ABC miniseries starred Jane Seymour as Natalie.

Considering the books only, several million Americans had each spent close to one hundred hours ploughing through a fictional version of World War II. They had encountered in their course the story of a secular American Jewish woman caught accidentally in the maw of the Holocaust. Here, then, was a singular chance to bring the representation of a Jewish woman into the homes of Middle America. How had Wouk used this opportunity? How had he reconciled the narrative constraints, which still ruled popular fiction during the 1970s, with the scenes of obscenity and barbarism he would be compelled to narrate if he wanted to live up to his claim "to give a true and full picture" of history?[3] I conjectured that either Wouk would have to violate propriety and expose his heroine to events intolerable to a popular fiction readership of the 1970s or he would have to tinker with history and leave out the reality of what happened in the camps.

I set out to examine these questions with a great deal of naïveté and a large bundle of prejudices about Wouk as the author of popular fiction. Much to my surprise, I discovered that there *was*, in a way, tremendous pleasure to be had from *The Winds of War* and *War and Remembrance*. Imagine yourself whisked through a world on fire on the coattails of five American adventurers, eavesdropping on Roosevelt and Churchill, enjoying (if this is the word) cocktails with Hitler and a banquet with Stalin, while a comprehensive and comprehensible history of World War II is placed in the palm of your hand. The most complicated military strategies and diplomatic maneuvers are spelled out and explained to you in the privacy of your armchair. Suddenly, there is logic to war, good people are in charge of it, and you are their friend. The pleasure of such empowerment is false, of course, because any linear account of World War II flattens reality into untruth and because the events of World War II cannot be made humane or reduced to human scale by showing Roosevelt in his pajamas. As Paul Fussell pointed out in a review, Wouk's war, "unlike [Joseph] Heller's war, or Vonnegut's or Pynchon's, lacks the crucial dimension of the lunatic, the cruel, and the self-destructive."[4]

At the very center of these concerns about the possibility of historic realism in fiction stands the figure of Natalie Jastrow, Wouk's messenger to the Gentiles. She is his major literary device to personalize the Holocaust and to affect the hearts of his fellow Americans. Granting that Wouk's intended effect is important, one is still compelled to ask how well his literary creation squares with historic reality. Taking Wouk seriously—that is, reading his war epic honestly, as an attempt to move and inform his audience—proved a challenging experience. It forced me to reexamine my dismissal of best-sellers and, conversely, my assumptions about the efficacy of high art.

This essay is an uneasy reassessment of Wouk's war epic, based on an analysis of his fictional character Natalie Jastrow. Divided into three parts, the essay begins with a reflection about the need for a new look at Wouk's war novels. It moves on to examine some women characters in literary Holocaust fiction by American Jewish women writers in order to establish a basis of comparison for Wouk's Natalie, and it ends with an evaluation of Natalie's story.

The Narrative Art of Herman Wouk

I first learned about Natalie Jastrow, one of the main protagonists in Herman Wouk's novels *The Winds of War* and *War and Remembrance*, from two physicians, secular Jewish men, whose sources of Jewish identity were the Holocaust and the state of Israel. They spoke earnestly about Wouk's achievement in enticing millions of Americans, who would never pick up a history book in their spare time, into reading a quasi-history of World War II that detailed not only the events in the European and Pacific theaters but also the facts of the Shoah, the systematic destruction of the European Jews.

These physicians were particularly taken with Natalie, "a dark jewel of intellect and loveliness" (*WW*, p. 28), who is trapped in Hitler's net and compelled to share the fate of the European Jews. Natalie, they claimed, is portrayed so realistically and so sympathetically that the reader is forced to identify with her. As she struggles to extricate herself from the ever tightening grip of Hitler's thugs, crisscrossing Europe, being captured and deported to Theresienstadt, and sent to Auschwitz, the reader suffers with her. Through emotional identification with Natalie, the physicians argued, the Shoah becomes a personal experience. Writing for a mass readership, they continued, Wouk made the experience of the Shoah accessible to Jews and non-Jews alike and contributed significantly to the historical education of Americans.

These arguments were familiar to me from the debate surrounding the broadcast of the miniseries *Holocaust* in 1978, when melodrama and sentimentality were justified as vehicles of viewer identification that would painlessly instill millions of people, who would otherwise never learn about Nazi Germany, with some knowledge about the persecution of the Jews and sensitize them to Jewish concerns.[5] Having been born and raised in Germany, I had been caught up in that debate as a nineteen-year-old. I had opposed the broadcasting of *Holocaust* in Germany as an all too easy way of catharsis and atonement. Thirteen years later, living in America and married to the son of a refugee from Nazi Germany, I was still unwilling to concede that the bitter pill of mental exertion, of actually studying the history of World War II in general and of the Shoah in particular had to be sugarcoated with sentimental fiction.

Moreover, I had been trained not only as a historian but as a literary critic. I moved in the rarefied air of Goethe and Thomas Mann, Flaubert and Proust, Jane Austen and James Joyce. And as a specialist in American Jewish literature, I was certainly familiar with the controversy that had erupted around the publication of Wouk's *Marjorie Morningstar* in 1955, the first truly popular American Jewish novel. Stanley Edgar Hyman had summed it all up for me in his 1962 review of Wouk's *Youngblood Hawke:* "Wouk is now a phenomenal merchandising success, sold as a detergent is sold. He can compete with the worst of television because he *is* the worst of television, without the commercials. . . . His readers really are the boobs Hawke describes, so 'starved for an interesting story' that they will ignore the reviews to read him. They are yahoos who hate culture and the mind."[6]

My initial problem with Wouk had been aesthethic, but questions of literary taste were quickly superseded by another concern. I began to wonder how one could trust an author to discharge adequately a task as difficult as narrating the events of the Shoah when his rendition of a scene as simple as the first meeting of a couple destined to fall in love drowns in a medley of clichés and a morass of bad writing. Here, for example, is the first description of Natalie from the perspective of Byron Henry. He is a twenty-year-old American who had been sent by his Columbia fine arts professor to Siena, supposedly to study with Dr. Aaron Jastrow but really to figure out his calling in life. As it turns out, Byron's calling is neither Renaissance art nor church history but the scholar's enticing niece.

She was the first American girl he had spoken to in months; and they were thrown together for many hours every day, just the two of them in the book-lined room. This was reason enough for him to feel attracted to her. But she impressed him, too. Natalie Jastrow talked to her famous uncle as to a mental equal. Her range of knowledge and ideas humiliated Byron, and yet there was nothing bookish about her. Girls in his experience were lightweights, fools for a smile and a bit of flattery. They had doted on him at college, and in Florence too. Byron was something of an Adonis, indolent and not hotly interested; and unlike Warren [Byron's older brother], he had absorbed some of his father's straitlaced ideas. He thought Natalie was a dark jewel of intellect and loveliness, blazing away all unnoticed here in the Italian back hills. As for her indifference to him, it seemed in order. (*WW*, p. 28)

In *The Winds of War* the representation of Natalie recalls the dark lady of American romance fiction. She is the seductively exotic Other, whose precursors include characters like the passionate Cora in Cooper's *The Last of the Mohicans*; the luscious, mad Zenobia in Hawthorne's *Blithedale Romance*; the poisonous Beatrice in his story "Rappaccini's Daughter"; the explicitly Jewish Miriam in Hawthorne's last novel, *The Marble Faun*; and the vicious Madame Merle in Henry James's *Portrait of a Lady*. Aware of this American literary tradition, Wouk refers to *The Winds of War* as "romance" and to *War and Remembrance* as "historical romance" (forewords). Among Wouk's models is Hawthorne, who, in the preface to *The House of the Seven Gables*, had famously defined his quasi-historical novel as a romance. Wouk, of course, is too educated an author not to know that since Hawthorne the term romance, as distinguished, say, from the historical novel, connotes the writer's arrogation of certain liberties.[7] As Laurence Mazzeno pointed out, "writers of romance are usually accorded greater latitude in rearranging historical events and engaging in fantasy than either historians or historical novelists, who claim to offer realistic portraits of people and events, using fictional characters to emphasize the effects of history on everyday people."[8]

Wouk's insistence on having written a romance, although counterpoised by his assertion that "the history in both tales . . . has been presented responsibly and with care" (*WR*, foreword), did not raise my confidence in the adequacy of his "recreation" of the brutal annihilation of the European Jews during World War II. Moreover, Wouk's reputation as the author of fiction for the 1950s mass market simply turned me off.

Two events caused me to reconsider Wouk's achievement. In 1991, Raul Hilberg, author of *The Destruction of the European Jews* (1961), an early seminal work that reconstructed in detail the mechanics of the Shoah, retired from his teaching position at the University of Vermont. In his honor a symposium was convened in Burlington, Vermont, and attended by many of the intellectuals—historians, philosophers, and literary scholars—who had done outstanding work on different aspects of the Shoah. The keynote address at an evening reception was delivered, much to my surprise, by Herman Wouk. I learned then that Wouk had solicited Hilberg's advice during his work on the war novels.

In fact, Wouk's research had been long and extensive. He had begun to outline *The Winds of War* on May 17, 1962, the day his novel *Youngblood Hawke* was published, hoping that his new book would "in a phrase Joseph Conrad used about a Napoleonic novel he never wrote—'throw a rope around' the Hitler era."[9] The task Wouk set himself proved formidable indeed. In 1964, Wouk moved from the Virgin Islands to Washington, D.C., to have easy access to the Library of Congress and the National Archives. In the 1960s, books dealing with more particular aspects of the war in Europe and the Pacific were still relatively rare; therefore, Wouk personally approached historical scholars for information, as well as men who had been military or political players at the time.[10] The result was "an arduous effort to give a true and full picture of a great world battle." Wouk could rightly claim that his representation of history was accurate, his statistics reliable, and "the words and acts of the great personages [either] historical or derived from accounts of their words and deeds in similar situations" (*WW*, foreword).[11]

While my qualms as a historian had been assuaged, my literary snobbery had been nourished. I continued to look down my nose at Wouk's novels because I thought then that sentimental fiction and stone-hard history were incompatible, that bad art could not possibly serve as a vehicle for moral illumination. Conversely, I considered the custodians of high culture to be good people and the individuals most likely to respond to the moral imperative of the Shoah. They were the ones I thought most ready to acknowledge the transformative nature of the Shoah. I naïvely thought them ready to acknowledge that the mind-boggling fact that atrocities of a scale unprecedented in the Western civilized world had been committed by a highly cultured people had to affect in significant ways our assessment of the value, importance, and civilizing power of high art.

Precisely this argument was presented at Harvard's Center for Literary and Cultural Studies by Emily Budick, a professor of American studies at the Hebrew University in Jerusalem. She argued that Lionel Trilling's cultural criticism was "Holocaust inflected" in that way. His suspicion of high modernism and his preference for literary works anchored in the middle class, in the moral constraints of the bourgeois world, Budick claimed, reflected an awareness, touched off by the Shoah, that creativity without moral restraint was easily perverted into mad destructiveness, a notion captured in the biblical term for imagination, *yetser hara*, "evil impulse."[12] Budick argued that Trilling's cautious conservatism in matters of culture and high art had been developed as his response to the Shoah.

The reaction of the seminar participants to Budick's presentation was, quite frankly, shocking. Three objections were raised that concerned not so much her thesis as its premises. First, one woman asked indignantly why Trilling ought to have written with an awareness of the Holocaust, as Budick seemed to imply, "since he gave us so much else to think about." Then someone objected that Americans should not be dealing with the Holocaust; "the Germans should be having this discussion." And finally, a famous critic of poetry took the floor and declared that to expect "Holocaust inflectedness" of American criticism was morally coercive.[13]

The admonition that teachers of literature were to be blind to the lessons of history as they challenged culture's high-minded suppositions about human nature upset me greatly. What was the purpose of high culture if not to alert its consumers to humanity's raw underside and to refine us if that were possible? Yet I began to see that perhaps too great an emphasis on aesthetic perfection warped one's sense of moral responsibility as a teacher and dulled one's sympathies as a *mentsh*. One need only remember, as George Steiner once put it, that "[T. S.] Eliot's uglier touches tend to occur at the heart of very good poetry."[14]

It became clear to me then that the question of Wouk had to be reconsidered. Did it really matter that his characters lacked the psychological complexity of James's Isabel Archer, the philosophic depth of Mann's Adrian Leverkühn, or the aesthetic *rafinesse* of Proust's Charlus if the moral direction into which Natalie Jastrow and Byron Henry "coerce" their readers was right? Did it really matter, as Paul Fussell complained, that Wouk was "unable to conceive an original character or to equip anyone with feelings above the commonplace"?[15]

Given the peculiar response of elite literary critics to an event that should force the custodians of high culture into, at the very least, "painful ways of thinking" (Budick) about the value of their pursuits, it was perhaps not such a bad thing that Wouk's simple goal of educating a mass audience about the horrors of recent history had not been derailed by the aesthetic frills and scruples of high modernism.

The invitation to rethink Wouk's war novels and their impact on an American readership was worth accepting. Very few Jewish women, caught up in the turmoil of the Shoah, had captured the heart of American readers to the degree Natalie Jastrow had. What Arnold Beichman outlined as Wouk's goal, the creation of "stories universal in what they say to the reader, with the characters who play the tale taking on a life of their own and becoming household words,"[16] had clearly been realized for the character of Natalie Jastrow. In the minds of millions of Americans, her "stick figure" (Paul Fussell) came to stand for the suffering of Jewish women in the Shoah. It is reasonable to scrutinize Wouk's representative woman and valuable to compare her with the creations of our more purely literary authors.

Natalie's Literary Backdrop: Women and Holocaust Fiction

The questions that govern my consideration of Natalie Jastrow here are twofold. The first concerns matters of originality and literary stereotype: Given the fact that Wouk's audience is largely non-Jewish, how does Wouk evoke sympathy for a Jewish woman? What are his vehicles of reader identification? Which Jewish features, if any, does he emphasize? The second concerns the issues of genre constraints and content: since the tastes of the popular fiction audience in the 1970s were essentially puritanical and conservative, how could Wouk deal truthfully with the obscene nature of the atrocities committed during the Shoah?

Critics have blamed Wouk for creating characters and a plot that "are purely early 1950s Metro-Goldwyn-Mayer" and have charged that he "thinks, feels and writes as if he were still in the 1940s,"[17] when, in fact, the degree of his explicitness about sex and violence was dictated as much by the comfort level of the pop-fiction readership as by Wouk's own squeamishness. His maudlin romance plot and simplistic character development were deliberate devices to keep his readers glued to the page during a bouncy bus or subway ride after a nine-to-five job. The question remains, however, whether Wouk was also tempted to bend the crass reality of history to the comfort requirements of popular fiction, a genre in which, at least during the 1970s, the preservation of the heroine's life, integrity, and yes, chastity, was still an iron law, to be violated only in the most exceptional circumstances. My guess was that despite his passion for historical accuracy, Wouk would come down on the side of his readers' psychic comfort and peace of mind and that he would not dare to present a world more complicated and cruel than his readers were willing to tolerate. While bringing Natalie close to the unthinkable, he would finally have to preserve, against better historical knowledge, her inviolateness and femininity.

It is important to emphasize that my speculation about Wouk's need to preserve Natalie's physical integrity even in the most extreme circumstances was only conjecture. I had not yet read Wouk, and I resisted doing so because I had no great desire to see the sentimentality of popular culture applied to the Shoah, particularly since there already was a complex and sophisticated Holocaust literature. These differentiated, upsettingly real narratives by American and European writers and memoirists, executed with varying degrees of artistic success, had already demonstrated extensively the immense difficulty of bringing the Shoah into the realm of fiction. Wouk's Natalie would have to contend for credibility with a cast of compelling fictional characters who unfold between them the broad spectrum of Holocaust experience. Women protagonists, in particular, allowed their authors to employ the metaphoric shorthand of literary fiction in illuminating the extraordinary nature of the Shoah.

Childbirth, for instance, often served as the literal and symbolic antithesis to the barbaric destructiveness of the Shoah; and mother-daughter relationships became metaphors for the continuity of life preserved against all odds. A brief survey, anecdotal rather than complete, of some better-known literary works will illuminate how American women writers have used the conjunction of femininity and Shoah. These findings will then serve as a foil for my assessment of Wouk's Natalie. One needs to know what is possible before taking an author to task for falling short of one's literary expectations.

In Norma Rosen's novel *Touching Evil* (1969), set among non-Jews in 1961, childbirth and sexual seduction, traditional metaphors for creativity and knowledge, become conduits of the American heroines' identification with victims of the Shoah. Rosen explained that her protagonists were "two women [who] have been stricken by knowledge of the Holocaust: one [Hattie Mews] through the Eichmann trial, televised daily in the early sixties; the other [Jean Lamb] through reading documents and seeing photographs of the death camps."[18]

Jean Lamb is seduced by her college sociology teacher, who callously transmutes his own shock at the discovery of death camp photographs into the aggression of sexual conquest. "I made my protagonist, at the time of discovery, young—and vulnerable to horror," Rosen declared. "I made the moment of discovery the precise moment of sexual seduction, almost of intercourse itself, so that everything should be open and the appearance of penetration complete."[19] For Jean, the double discovery of Eros and Thanatos, sex and the death camps—Rosen's metaphor for the knowledge of absolute evil—is so traumatic that she vows never to have children. She is befriended, however, by a young pregnant woman, Hattie Mews, who persuades Jean to watch the Eichmann trial with her. Hattie, Rosen wrote, "is overcome by terror, the child in her womb menaced by what has been loosed in the world."[20] The novel, which depicts scenes of cruelty frankly, insists on asking the question "how can we live now," having become witnesses to barbarity in Western culture. But it suggests no answer beyond the low-keyed gesture of mutual assistance that the two women render each other in their distress.

In tone and outlook, Rosen's fiction bears an uncanny resemblance to Ilona Karmel's novel *An Estate of Memory*, published, like Rosen's, in 1969. It is one of the few novels set entirely within the confines of a women's concentration camp. Mutual assistance is crucial to survival, though never uncomplicated or easily rendered because it always involves the utmost danger to the life of the assistant. Karmel, however, who along with her mother and sister had been interned in three different labor camps between 1942 and 1945, had herself received lifesaving help. As Sara Horowitz points out, "Karmel credits her mother's alertness, intelligence, and devotion to her daughters with keeping Ilona and [her sister] Henia alive and together. 'My Mother always knew what to do.' When Ilona was hospitalized with typhus in 1942, her mother—knowing that Jewish patients were often executed—stole her out of the hospital. Another time, Ilona's mother hid her daughters under a mattress during a camp selection (a Nazi euphemism for choosing murder victims), enabling them to escape death."[21]

In her novel, set in a women's labor camp near Kraków, Karmel depicts women in a situation of permanent stress. She describes the social structures and hierarchies that emerge based on physical, psychological, and emotional stamina, adaptability, swiftness, and access to food, clothing, and work. The women congregate in "makeshift camp families—women, young girls, whom loneliness unaccustomed and sudden had brought together."[22] The climactic event of such a makeshift family of four is a secret pregnancy and childbirth. Three women help the pregnant Aurelia, whose name connotes "gold," through her hard time by sharing food, concealing her absence from work, assisting in the delivery, and smuggling the baby out of the camp. The survival of Aurelia's baby is crucial to the preservation of the women's self-worth and emotional sanity. At the same time, it becomes a symbol for the triumph of life over death and of solidarity and dignity, supreme aspects of *mentshlekhkeyt*, over the Nazis' efforts to reduce the Jews to animals. "So the child, carried like a parcel out of the camp, kept growing, until it was big enough to take upon itself the burden of their longing for a proof, for the least sign that out 'in the Freedom' they still mattered."[23]

In 1974, five years after Karmel's complex novel and three years after the publication of *The Winds of War*, a Holocaust romance hit the stands that made the *New York Times* best-seller list. Susan Fromberg Schaeffer's *Anya* is a conventional first-person narrative. Anya grows up in a well-off, assimilated family in Vilna. In the opening sequence she takes the reader through her family's home, recording the wealth and refinement of prewar Jewish life. Anya attends medical school first in Vilna and then in Warsaw, but the German invasion of Poland forces her to return to Vilna, where she is eventually confined with her family (her parents, husband, and daughter) to the ghetto. As the destruction of the European Jews accelerates, Anya is deported to a concentration camp. She describes the pain and degradation endured by the inmates, but she is particularly tortured by the separation from her daughter. Anya manages to escape from the camp, taking advantage of her work privilege and her Aryan looks. She lives through the war, is reunited with her daughter, and begins a new life in America.

Schaeffer's novel reached a much wider audience than either Rosen's or Karmel's. The American romance readership shuddered at being taken inside the camps by a victim but found itself assured by the fact that the narrator's dignity, integrity, and sense of self remained intact. The device Schaeffer used to help Anya preserve her sanity was to instill in her an intense hope to be reunited with her daughter. "Sometimes I think she is all that kept me alive," Anya reflects after the war.[24]

While some survivors testify that hope was indeed the element that kept them going,[25] Anya's intense longing and its fulfillment suffuses Schaeffer's minutely researched plot with a fairy-tale element. The result makes the reader rather uneasy, a feeling that is most evident in Dorothy Bilik's critical assessment, which resorts to paradoxes, simple reversals, and outright platitudes to explain *Anya*. Bilik writes that Schaeffer's "novel of the Holocaust . . . , despite its horrendous subject matter, takes the form of a romance depicting life as it ought to have been. The effect is the opposite of the reductivism of the banality of evil. Instead, by employing the literary conventions and allusions of the fairy tale, twentieth-century evil is rendered more ugly and inexplicable in a fictional context where courageous, admirable characters who live vivid, idealized lives are cruelly and wantonly destroyed."[26]

Anya is in fact less schlocky than Bilik (inadvertently) makes it appear. Schaeffer's depiction of life in the ghetto of Vilna is moving and convincing. The best part of the novel is quite possibly its epilogue. Set in 1973, it presents the ruminations of a fifty-two-year-old Anya about her irreparably damaged life. "It is impossible for me to believe that I cannot accomplish anything; that the film which has recorded the story of my life was spliced one third through to an irrelevant reel by a maniac, that what began in the past will never continue in the future" (pp. 469–70). Forced to give up her career in medicine because her trauma affects her ability to function as a doctor and disappointed in her now adult daughter, who wants to be free of her mother's craving for closeness, Anya is reduced to sitting alone with her wares, "old furniture and antiques" (p. 471), in a corner of somebody else's store.

Anya's fate anticipates the emergence onto the literary scene of the character who has indeed become the household word for survivor trauma, Rosa Lublin. Six years after the publication of *Anya* and two years after the appearance of *War and Remembrance*, the *New Yorker* ran Cynthia Ozicks's story "The Shawl" (1980), which was followed three years later by "Rosa" (1983). Ozick had composed the two stories in 1977 but then locked them away in a drawer because she felt strongly that the Holocaust should not enter the realm of fiction. Eventually, however, the two stories reemerged and were later published together in *The Shawl: A Story and a Novella* (1989), which appeared briefly on the *New York Times* best-seller list. The subtitle, printed only on the dustjacket of the hardcover edition, keeps two fictions separate, and one does well to remember their separateness.

"The Shawl," set in a concentration camp described only in its barest essentials, depicts the interactions of three women: Rosa; her fourteen-year-old niece, Stella; and Rosa's fifteen-month-old daughter, Magda. The story's precise focal point, however, is Rosa's shawl, in which Magda is hidden. Stella craves it for its warmth, protection, and sustenance. The story's climax comes suddenly. "Then Stella took the shawl away and made Magda die."[27] As Rosa stands in the roll-call arena, Magda leaves the barracks in search of the shawl. She is detected and snatched up by a German guard. The climax decelerates to slow motion; the language is polished as if it were conveying a moment of exquisite beauty, while the reader remains hyperconscious of its brutal content. The overall effect is surreal. Here are the last lines of "The Shawl":

All at once Magda was swimming through the air. The whole of Magda traveled through loftiness. She looked like a butterfly touching a silver vine. And the moment Magda's feathered round head and her pencil legs and balloonist belly and zigzag arms splashed against the fence, the steel voices went mad in their growling, urging Rosa to run and run to the spot where Magda had fallen from her flight against the electrified fence; but of course Rosa did not obey them. She only stood, because if she ran they would shoot, and if she tried to pick up the sticks of Magda's body they would shoot, and if she let the wolf's screech ascending now through the ladder of her skeleton break out, they would shoot; so she took Magda's shawl and filled her own mouth with it, stuffed it in and stuffed it in, until she was swallowing up the wolf's screech and tasting the cinnamon and almond depth of Magda's saliva; and Rosa drank Magda's shawl until it dried. (pp. 9–10)

There had been nothing like this in previous American Holocaust fiction. In the elevated style of literary high art, Ozick managed to pinpoint the horrendous nature of Nazi cruelty by focusing on two of the three incidents that broke the spirit of interned Jews. The two occurrences Ozick singles out are the murder of a child and the erosion of solidarity, the turning on each other to assure one's own survival. The third occurrence, witnessing the degradation of a parent, is not made explicit in "The Shawl" but is present in "Rosa." The fact that Ozick realized her intention to formulate the epitome of Nazi barbarism by choosing the image of devastated maternity, of a disrupted mother-daughter relationship, has invited feminist readings and led some critics to see *The Shawl* in relation to some of Ozick's stories that deal with the creative and productive side of the maternal metaphor. But Ozick forcefully resists all interpretations that aim at gendering Holocaust fiction and attempt to make something of her choice of a mother-daughter constellation. "Like it or not," she wrote in 1990, "(and I don't like it either, and feel such matters ought not to be allowed to enter fiction), 'The Shawl' is *about*—no *is* (symbolically)—the Nazi murders. Punkt. No pop psychology. No mothers and daughters. Mothers-and-daughters is NOT my theme, here or elsewhere. I have no biological themes; I am uninterested in biology. (Which doesn't preclude, or contradict, a bemusement with 'heredity.' Or heritage)."[28]

"The Shawl" was a prelude to the story "Rosa," which depicts hauntingly the continuing trauma of survivors, the inconsolable nature of their sorrow. As the story opens, Rosa, now fifty-nine years old, has smashed her secondhand furniture store in New York and moved to Florida. "It was a mad thing to do. In Florida she became a dependent. Her niece in New York sent her money and she lived among the elderly, in a dark hole, a single room in a 'hotel'" (p. 13). In the second, much longer story, the roles are reversed. Stella, "the Angel of Death" (p. 15), becomes the sustainer of Rosa's life. The novella gradually unfolds Rosa's trauma, her continual mourning for Magda, who has turned into an obsession. Rosa brings Magda to life by writing her letters or by cradling her shawl. The refrain of Rosa's life in America is the same as Anya's: "I have not forgotten anything" (p. 470). "Rosa" describes the impossibility of living sanely while being persecuted by the memories of the camps.

In her play *Blue Light*, which premiered at the Bay Street Theater in Sag Harbor, Long Island, on August 12, 1994, Ozick took the story of Rosa and Stella, their suffering from the inability to forget, and pitted their trauma against the brazen denial of the Holocaust by revisionist historians. The outer trappings of Rosa's devastation, such as her loss of femininity when her daughter was killed or her disturbed self-centeredness, reflected, for instance, in her complete indifference to her appearance, lend themselves to theatrical representation, just as the finer literary aspects of *The Shawl*, the subtle play of language and style, do not. Ozick knew, however, that in putting the story of Rosa and Stella on stage "language will be lost."[29]

Yet the central event in Rosa's life, the murder of Magda, is preserved in the play. It is presented on stage in a soliloquy. During her reminiscence, Rosa is bathed in an intense blue light while the rest of the stage is dark. The effect of

Rosa kneeling in an attitude of love and adoration before the shawl lying in front of her on the floor, presumably cradling her baby girl, bears an uncanny resemblance to a great number of nativity scenes displayed in America at Christmastime. And it is precisely this icon of maternity and femininity that Herman Wouk, writing for a largely Gentile audience, cunningly used as a vehicle of reader identification.

Natalie as Maternal Icon

Wouk's double novel unfolds the history of World War II by following the lives of five American Protestants, the Henry family, who find themselves scattered by the winds of war.[30] Victor and Rhoda Henry have a daughter and two sons, Warren and Byron—that is, an American warrior and a European Romantic—who marry appropriately the light and the dark lady (*WW*, p. 378): the "Rhine maiden," Janice Lacouture, and the "dusky Jewess," Natalie Jastrow (*WW*, chap. 26).

Despite Wouk's emphasis on the American perspective, first by choosing the Henrys as his main protagonists and then by structuring the plot "from Pearl Harbor to Hiroshima," it is evident that Wouk's heart is in Europe. He alludes frequently to his literary model, Tolstoy's epos *War and Peace*, which chronicles Napoleon's conquest of Europe (1805–1812), culminating in his invasion of Russia that led to his ultimate defeat. In 1941–1942, Hitler's invasion of the Soviet Union was very much perceived in terms of Napoleon's earlier attempt, and Wouk's fiction cleverly plays with the similarities.[31] Moreover, by choosing Tolstoy's epos as a literary model forty years later, Wouk undermines the exclusiveness of the American theme and emphasizes the importance of the European theater.

Wouk also employs Tolstoy's narrative technique of telling historical events through the lives of fictional characters. The uptight Volkonskys and sensual-chaotic Rostovs correspond quite nicely, although in a somewhat stereotypical way, to the Protestant Henrys and the Jewish Jastrows. This is a somewhat depressing comparison, since Tolstoy's families consist of extraordinary and complex people, while Wouk's characters are hopelessly flat. They are American *types*, and the historical events to which they are exposed overwhelm them as characters. (This is probably why Paul Fussell conceived the idea that the real hero of *War and Remembrance* was the United States Navy.[32] You have to be as big as that to have any weight in Wouk's novel.)

Byron Henry as Andrei Volkonsky is laughable. Yet the comparison may reveal one of the reasons for the incommensurability of Wouk's and Tolstoy's characters. Volkonsky, after all, is Prince Andrei, a late-eighteenth-century Russian noble and heir to a complicated, binding code of honor, courage, patriotism, and moral excellence. To be humanly average meant being a failure as a Russian noble. As an American commoner, Byron Henry is not obligated to be above average except on the battlefield, so as to live up to his ancestor, Patrick Henry.

In true Romantic fashion, Byron falls in love with a somewhat older woman, whose temperament is quite alien to his own nature. Natalie Jastrow's name echoes that of Tolstoy's favorite female character, Natalia Rostova, whose adolescence and fall into romance constitutes the novelistic life force of *War and Peace.* She is the emotional center of the novel. Her transposition into Wouk's war epic signals that the Jewish story is really at the heart of *War and Remembrance.*

Natalie Jastrow is twenty-seven when the war breaks out. She was born on Long Island in 1912, studied at Radcliffe College, and pursued her master's degree at the Sorbonne, working on a thesis titled "Contrasts in the Sociologismic Critique of War: Durkheim's Writings on Germany, 1915–1616, and Tolstoy's Second Epilogue to *War and Peace*, 1869" (*WW*, p. 315). Her thesis topic conveys Wouk's own stance on the limited impact of individuals on the course of history. In Paris she falls in love with Leslie Slote, an American, who does not want to marry her because having a Jewish wife "would be awkward for his career" (*WW*, p. 263) in the foreign service. Natalie, who dropped out of Hebrew school before she was eleven years old and to whom "being a Jew is an accident" (*WW*, pp. 90, 380), is furious and leaves Paris for an extended visit with her uncle Aaron in Siena. There she meets Byron Henry, who was sent to Aaron Jastrow, a writer and historian, by a Columbia professor. Byron falls in love with the tomboyish, independent, unpredictable Natalie, whose attribute is "the lioness" (*WW*, p. 214; *WR*, p. 498), and volunteers to accompany her to Warsaw in August 1939. They are surprised in southern Poland by the German invasion because Natalie had insisted on attending a wedding of her relatives in Medzice, a village near Oświęcim, where Aaron had spent fifteen years as an observant youngster. Helped by a great deal of luck and courage, Byron and Natalie make their way back to the American embassy in Warsaw, where they live through the German siege.

Under stress, Natalie shows herself cheerful, self-confident, and compassionate. Shortly before the fall of the city all foreign nationals are exchanged. Via different routes, Byron and Natalie arrive back in Siena. When Natalie receives a proposal of marriage from Slote in the mail, she discovers that she is in love with Byron, who in turn proposes to her. A letter from her parents calls Natalie home. Her father is ill, and they are concerned that Italy is no longer safe for Jews. Aaron, however, does not want to leave Siena. "I've evolved into a pagan, a materialist, and a hedonist," he says, "and I fell in love with the grandeur of Christianity" (*WW*, p. 272). He does not reveal to his niece that he feels safe in Italy because he converted to Catholicism at the age of twenty-three.[33] Natalie returns home while Byron stays behind as Aaron's assistant.

They meet again in America in May 1940, and Natalie accepts Byron's proposal. She has no compunction about marrying a non-Jew. Being Jewish, she says, "left little trace on my ideas or my conduct. Too little, I guess, we live in a secular age and I am a product of it" (*WW*, p. 380). Wouk has obviously chosen the Jewish type least offensive to his Gentile readers. There is no insistence on Jewish self-preservation, on observance of or compliance with Jewish law; no premium is put on premodern (un-American) Jewish tradition. Instead, the principle of romance rules: *Amor vincit omnia* (love conquers all). Portia is lurking in the wings.

Byron goes off to submarine school, and Natalie rushes back to Italy to persuade her uncle to leave. A foul-up in Aaron's naturalization papers and a lapsed passport create difficulties. In January 1941, Natalie manages to get transportation into Lisbon, where she marries Byron. Natalie is shocked by Lisbon. It is full of desperate Jews waiting for visas. As she strolls through the city, she is thinking of the Inquisition, and for the first time she panics at the thought of being stuck in Europe as a Jew. It is the onset of a remarkable change in Natalie that coincides with the beginning of her pregnancy.

She returns to Italy, where American and Italian officials stonewall her requests for Aaron's papers. On June 22, 1941, the German army invades the Soviet Union. In the wake of the fast-moving front the Einsatzgruppen begin their grisly work. "They had been told," writes Wouk, "that the Jews were Germany's enemies and that the only way to deal with them was to kill every last one of them down to the babes in arms and their mothers" (*WW*, pp. 614–15). We prick up our ears because we know that Natalie is on her way to falling into that category. Her son Louis, conceived in Lisbon, is born in Rome in September 1941.

Three months later, Natalie makes contact with Avram Rabinovitz, who smuggles Jews into Palestine. They meet in St. Peter's at Michelangelo's *Pietà*, the sculpture of a young Jewish mother holding her dead son. Frightened, Natalie agrees to the dangerous trip. She is very upset. "She was nothing and nobody; she had no real identity. . . . She was 'Jewish' but the label meant nothing to her beyond the trouble it caused. . . . The baby was becoming her anchor to life" (*WW*, p. 867–68). She has no inkling that her imprisonment is beginning to rejudaize her.[34] The birth of her son and the Nazis' dominance over Europe have replaced Natalie's freely chosen self by a biological or primary fated identity, that of mother and Jew. At the end of *The Winds of War* we find Natalie in Naples boarding the *Redeemer*, a ship carrying Jews to Palestine. On that soil the features that condemn her to death in Europe would be "redeemed" into assets.

At the opening of *War and Remembrance* we find the tomboyish Natalie of 1939 changed into an "image of Divine Maternity."[35] When Aaron sees Natalie sitting on board the *Redeemer* surrounded by poor Jews and holding the baby perched on her lap, he cries out: "Why, it's the Adoration." Natalie protests that she is no madonna. But Aaron insists: "Typecast, I'd say, for face, figure and racial origin" (*WR*, p. 19). The Adoration, of course, is a hint that in Louis a redeemer is born. He will indeed turn into his mother's savior insofar as hope for his resurrection and reappearance keep her alive in the camps. At this point, Natalie's name reveals its intrinsic significance. It is derived from the Latin word *natalis*, "pertaining to birth," that is, to Christ's birth. Like its variant Noel, Natalie refers to Christmas.

Shortly after the Adoration scene, the Jastrows are picked off the boat by the Gestapo and sent back to Siena. They escape to Elba and arrive in Marseille in September 1942, where they find refuge in an apartment full of Eastern European Jews waiting for visas. The language spoken there is Yiddish, and observance is the unquestioned way of life. Thus, Natalie finds herself lighting Sabbath candles. "It seemed more mannerly to do it than to decline, when Mrs. Mendelson . . . came to tell her the candles were ready" (*WR*, p. 435). The Sabbath meal concludes with a Yiddish lullaby, "Rozhinkes mit Mandlen." Sung over Louis's cradle, it begins to blot out the Adoration. The sweetness of this scene is cloying and its sentimentality barely tolerable. In times of danger, Wouk suggests to his readers, Jews huddle together and remember the ways of their fathers and mothers.

Unexpectedly, Byron appears on the scene. He wants to speed his family out of France by taking the train to Perpignan and from there into Spain. Natalie is terrified. She refuses to go because she knows that the train is controlled by Gestapo men who are good at picking out illegally traveling Jews. Byron is incredulous at his wife's refusal. When he asks her what happened to the courage she displayed in Warsaw, she replies: "We've got Louis now" (*WR*, p. 448). Her fearfulness, however, does not only derive from her justified concern for the child but equally from the abolition of her freedom by the Nazis and her loss of human rights. Thinking about his wife a few months later, Byron reflects: "She had struck him from the start as a sophisticated American all the more alluring for a dusky spice trace of Jewishness. . . . Yet in Marseille she had appeared overpowered, paralyzed by her Jewishness. Byron could not understand" (*WR*, p. 581). At this point the free American and the fated Jew are furthest apart. Natalie's terror as a hunted Jew is completely incomprehensible to Byron. He withdraws in anger and frustration at his "stiff-necked wife" (*WR*, p. 581), thus reviving the old Christian reproach against the Jews, and leaves Marseille. This is an important scene because it allows Wouk to point out the fundamental psychological differences between being free and being endangered and thus to indicate why it won't do to blame the Jews for their destruction, as popular as well as sophisticated intellectual voices have done.

After Byron's departure the Jastrows' fate unfolds with Tolstoyan inevitability. They sojourn in occupied Paris for some time, but by the spring of 1943, Aaron, Natalie, and Louis find themselves incarcerated in the "Prominenten-Lager" Theresienstadt near Prague, a camp for prominent Jews. In mortal danger, Natalie's paralysis vanishes. "She is no more an American Jewess terrified of falling into German talons, and hugging the talisman of her passport for safety. The talisman has failed. The worst has happened. In a strange way she feels freer at heart, and cleaner in her mind. Her whole being has a single focus now: to make it through with Louis, and live" (*WR*, p. 733).

With all options foreclosed and the Enlightenment undone, the Jastrows resign themselves to being Jews. Aaron revives his old religion—he dons *tefillin* and teaches Talmud—and Natalie becomes an underground Zionist. Aaron knows that their conversions to Judaism are mere "mental morphine for the agony of entrapment" (*WR*, p. 855) and at best a "spiritual stiffening [necessary] to survive in the ghetto" (*WR*, p. 825). For her Zionist activities, Natalie is battered by the SS and threatened with sexual abuse and the death of her son. This is the only scene in which we see Natalie humiliated and abused; and even here Wouk makes sure that, while bringing Natalie close to horror, her body (like that of the Virgin Mary) is not physically violated (*WR*, 861–63). That she and Louis remain unharmed while being showered with threats and obscenities (whose vulgar language is among the truly false notes in the book) is Wouk's concession to the constraints of popular fiction.

In July 1944, Natalie pretends to the German officials that Louis has died of typhus and has him smuggled out of Theresienstadt. In late October 1944 she and Aaron are deported to Auschwitz, where the old man is gassed upon arrival. This scene is among the most gruesome and moving in the book. It is extremely well written.[36] Tellingly, Natalie's life is spared and we lose sight of her. Her months in Auschwitz are not described. I think this was a good decision on Wouk's part because it saves him from making further concessions to popular taste, but it does not limit the book's value as popular history.

Natalie survives and is found in the spring of 1945 under an abandoned train coming from the women's camp of Ravensbrück near Buchenwald. "She was not very recognizable, skin and bones" (*WR*, p. 1023). In her terse affidavit she states: "if anything kept me going all these months it was the hope of one day seeing my son again" (*WR*, p. 1026). Louis, officially dead, has indeed disappeared. When Byron discovers him in England, the child is mute. Louis finds his voice again when, after the first frantic embrace, Natalie sings him the lullaby he had learned in Marseille: *Unter Louis' vigele, shtet a klor-waiss tsigele.* On the last page of the book the icon of maternity is restored:

Louis let go of her, sat up smiling on her lap, and tried to sing along in Yiddish, in a faltering hoarse voice, a word here and there

Dos vet zein dein baruf
Rozhinkes mit mandlen. (WR, p. 1028)

This is precisely the lullaby, "her grandmother's cradle-croonings" ("The Shawl," p. 19), that transports Rosa Lublin too back into a world of remembered comfort. Wouk knew exactly what he was doing when he restored Louis to Natalie and to the soothing lullaby. In that way he makes available to the reader the contentment of the song's last line, which Wouk purposely left out in the book, because its sweetness is gone from the survivors' lives: *shluf main yingele, shluf.* The survivors' sleep will always be punctured by nightmares.

A bare reconstruction of Natalie's story may tend to exemplify her bravery and sacrifice and may mask Wouk's shortcomings as a fiction writer. Yet the deficits of his Holocaust narrative emerge quite clearly when it is compared to novels and stories by Karmel, Ozick, or the much younger Rebecca Goldstein. In Wouk's narrative, history becomes unreal. The events of World War II lose their bloody edge and turn into occasions for American adventure and heroism. This effect is in large measure due to the fundamental contradiction that threatens with failure any historic fiction executed by a lesser master than Tolstoy, and it dooms Wouk's epic: It is the contradiction between his insistence on historical accuracy—his scrupulous reconstruction of historical events, such as the Battle of Midway or the tank battle of Kursk—and the obvious improbability that his characters can be in the thick of it all. A writer cannot on the one hand insist on the high realism of context and on the other hand undermine it by the blatant inventedness of his characters. In the readers' minds one will compromise the other.

Tolstoy got around this problem of having his historical reconstruction of Napoleon's invasion of Russia clash with his fictive plot, first, by inventing a huge cast of characters; second, by giving his main protagonists an intellectual depth and psychological complexity that makes the reader forget their inventedness and enables the assumption that such people might indeed have been present at many of the important events in Russian history; and third, by integrating into his novel his pet theory that history is not determined by the strategic decisions of individuals but by the unconscious will of the mass. This theory reduces the stature of the historic personages and makes them compatible—in their overall insignificance—with Tolstoy's invented characters.

Although it is true that the course of most historic events is determined by more or less ordinary human beings, it is also true that once a fiction writer assumes the task of historian, he or she must design characters who can measure up to the narrated events. Such symmetry is necessary in any fiction not written for comic effect. In serious fiction the grandeur of events requires grandeur of character. Unlike Karmel's Tola Ohrenstein, Ozick's Rosa Lublin, or Goldstein's Marta in "The Legacy of Raizel Kadish," ordinary women all, who develop human greatness despite or possibly because of their failures to be hero-ines in impossible situations—Wouk's characters, including Byron and Na-talie, remain small people, too small for the events to which they are exposed.

Natalie, in particular, is confronted with one of the twentieth century's great insanities. But because she has to remain a type with which Middle America can identify, her intellectual and emotional response is of the bland-est, most commonplace kind. Her blandness flattens the extraordinariness of her experience. Because the crazed, brutal, insane world into which Natalie is thrown does not reverberate in her as a character, whatever happens to her ap-pears oddly sanitized. Because nothing affects her as a character, nothing, ulti-mately, affects the reader.

The difference between Wouk's fiction and that of the women writers men-tioned earlier is comparable to the difference between seeing a still from Spiel-berg's movie *Schindler's List* and an actual photograph taken at the time. One such still from *Schindler's List*, the scene of an arrival at a concentration camp, was recently reproduced in *American Theatre*.[37] It is striking for its attention to detail. The environs, the watch tower, train tracks, German uniforms and guns, down to the snow on the ground look strikingly authentic. What gives the still away as inauthentic are the people in it. The approximately two hundred arriv-ing Jews, trudging between the train tracks through the snow past the German guards, can be recognized immediately as actors: the terror of the situation is not reflected in their faces. What is happening to them does not reverberate in their being. The actors try their best, even overdo the body language, but their facial expressions are wrong. That mixture of stunned incredulity, dumbness, mortal terror, and heart-sickening sadness that characterizes the faces of Jews arriving at the ramp cannot be re-created on command. The still, while materi-ally identical with the original scene, appears cleaned up, unthreatening, unreal.

To engage his readers' emotions without having to give Natalie greater depth or firmer contours as an individual, Wouk typecasts her as Madonna and child. By thrusting Louis into Natalie's arms, Wouk counts on evoking the cul-ture's stereotypical response to the mother-and-child figure: As love, inno-cence, and vulnerability incarnate, they are in special need of protection. At the same time, however, a mother is expected to show unexpected courage and resilience when defending her young (a residue of biological reasoning). In the second half of Natalie's story, Wouk exploits her as a maternal icon to ensure the reader's emotional involvement with his character. His reason for doing so lies in his cathartic theory: Only through fear and trembling will his readers understand the injustice done to the Jews and sympathize with them. But as if that were not enough, Wouk deliberately plays with Christian iconography (the Blessed Virgin Mary) to evoke his readers' outrage of the violation of sacred motherhood.[38]

Wouk's reasons for connecting the most prominent Jewish character in his war epic to important types in Gentile culture (the dark lady, the nurturing mother, the bereft Madonna) are obvious: he wants to create a cultural track for reader identification. He reduces the alienness of the Jews by linking his Jewish protagonist to popular cultural icons and so instills his readers with a sense that Jews are like them, that when you prick them, they do indeed bleed. Yet it is questionable whether empathy and understanding evoked in that way are anything more than ephemeral or skin-deep. Wouk's messenger to the Gentiles engages their hearts because she is like them. It would have been better if she had engaged their minds, led them to an intellectual understanding that Jews deserve love and sympathy *as Jews* and that what happened to the Jews was an outrage because it happened to them *as Jews*. Wouk's transformation of his Jewish character into an unexceptional, regular American to make sure his readers tremble with her, undermines the history lesson he wishes to teach. It is easy, because it is in the nature of biology, to love someone who is like oneself; and it is difficult, because unnatural and an achievement of moral culture, to love someone who is different.

Wouk has given his fellow Americans a free ride, allowing them to embark on a sentimental journey and to weep over their own kind. On the other hand, if that is what it takes, as Wouk explained at the symposium in honor of Raul Hilberg, to rivet the Holocaust in the mind of America, then one ought to celebrate his epic as an achievement so far rivaled only by Spielberg's movie *Schindler's List.*

Riv-Ellen Prell

Cinderellas Who (Almost) Never Become Princesses

Subversive Representations of Jewish Women in Postwar Popular Novels

"In a world saturated, perhaps even dominated, by the image it is close to impossible to understand any given interaction without reference to the multitude of mass produced images that often seem like only so much background noise to the real business of social forces."[1]

"It's the nose God gave you," said Aunt Bea.
"The hell with that," said Suzanne.
"So you'll have it fixed," Aunt Bea said after a moment.[2]

The young Jewish woman made her cultural debut as a symbol of American life in the 1950s in Herman Wouk's popular novel *Marjorie Morningstar* and in Philip Roth's critically acclaimed *Goodbye, Columbus*.[3] These beautiful young women became, for their writers and especially for their readers, the embodiment of American Jewish life in postwar New York and the suburbs of the Northeast. They personified the success and excess of that world, which the writers linked to Jews' upward mobility, their changing relationship to work and pleasure, the suburban Jewish family and the synagogue.

Wouk's Marjorie and Roth's Brenda were reference points for American Jewish life for decades. Even as their popularity faded, they were replaced with other images of young American Jewish womanhood. The Jewish American Princess and the cautious but kind Nice Jewish Girl found their way into films, television, popular humor, greeting cards, and novelty books, where they continued to (usually) harshly symbolize the experience of the newly affluent, suburban American Jews.

These women are a persistent feature of popular culture, with appeal for both Jewish and non-Jewish consumers of their image. The very multiplicity of these images leaves open opportunities to "read" them in ways not actually intended, to elaborate on and transform them in order to symbolize a potentially broadened set of meanings; multiple images of the same reality resist simple explanations. Just as the young Jewish woman's image was shaped by men to express their struggles with American Jewish life, so it has been re-shaped by women to resist that very image of Jewish womanhood.

It is not possible to know whether Brenda or Marjorie began as a joke or a stereotype that then appeared in a novel or a short story or perhaps the other way around. However, the multiplicity of these representations illuminates how images purveyed by both men and women may be used for different, if related, ends. It is the subversive and burlesque potential of the image of young Jewish womanhood that I have found in the novels of women authors who cast their protagonists as JAPs (Jewish American Princesses).[4] Between 1973 and 1976, Jewish women wrote at least eight novels about unmarried Jewish women in search of love.

These novels form a series of intertextual dialogues providing a currency in images. One set of novelistic images responded to other images from the mass media, jokes, and novels produced by Jews. The novels written in the 1970s elaborated images constructing Jewish women in one way in order to challenge their basic representation in popular culture. They shared an aesthetic in which women "talked back." The young Jewish woman remained, but these authors elaborated her differently; they rejected her role as a passive embodiment of suburban Jewish success. The novels, which are all funny and poignant, are familiar Jewish writing. Their young woman is a female version of the classic schlemiel—the loser. However, just like the small heroes of Woody Allen and Sholem Aleichem, they subvert the meaning of winning and losing and power and powerlessness.

This "talk back" style was closely linked to each novel's dependence on the central character's "grotesque" body. Each protagonist experienced part or all of her body as misshapen and transgressing socially acceptable norms. The novels construct powerful Jewish women who reconfigure suburban life. They cannot be contained by suburban domesticity in two senses: They cannot get in the door through marriage, and they also cannot find their way there because they resist masculine authority.

This aesthetic in part reflected the rather dramatic changes in Jewish women's lives and hence in the world of suburban Jewish families that began at the end of the 1960s. The partnership that enabled Jewish suburban life—the producer husband and the domestic wife—was undergoing fundamental transformations at this point, and these novels announced the not uncomplicated arrival of a new Jewish woman, family, and culture. The images are used to speak to a moment, which in this case inscribed both early second-wave feminism and the sexual revolution, in order to reimagine American Jewish life and American Jewish women.

The Postwar Prize

Marjorie Morningstar and *Goodbye, Columbus* focused on young Jewish women; however, these novels were fundamentally about relations between Jewish men of different generations. The women—daughters of fathers and wives-to-be—were conduits through which the males transacted their intergenerational relationship. These women were portrayed as prizes that the senior generation bestowed on the junior one. Marjorie and Brenda were the batons passed from one generation to the next in the relay race of American Jewish culture. Neither novel focused on the gory details of father and son entanglements. Rather, through surrogate sons they told tales that pitted American success against disenchantment with it. In both novels younger Jewish men showed no interest in carrying the torch of hard work and economic success. Therefore, each inevitably rejected the women who embodied the reward of enabling lavish consumption for others, the fate of Patimkin and Morgenstern senior. These novels instead portrayed Jewish men refusing both the dance and the partner of American middle-class life.

Herman Wouk's character Noel Airman, an attractive but troubled man of thirty, never succeeds despite his youthful promise. His triumphant failure at law school distinguished his dreams from his father's, a New York judge. But he attributed the flop of his Broadway musical not only to his lack of talent but the constant confidence of Marjorie Morgenstern, the woman ten years his junior whom he loved, resisted, and after three years "seduced." He wrote to her breaking off their affair:

I'm responsible . . . for the fact that Princess Jones was an old-fashioned piece of tripe that closed in five days. You're responsible, however, for my exposing myself and my limitations in such a wretched and crucifying way.

I'm tired of playing the horse to your rider, and I'm throwing you. You're the innocent victim, of course, and I'm the bored old seducer casting you aside. But the fact is, you seduced me as much as I seduced you. If I seduced you to go to bed with me you seduced me to go to work for you. You have ridden me mercilessly. Your left spur has been the American idea of success, and your right spur the Jewish idea of respectability. I have disbelieved in both ideas with all my heart since I was seventeen. Princess Jones was at bottom your big bid for a house in New Rochelle, and for that reason I'm glad it flopped.[5]

This immensely popular postwar novel placed at its core a doomed love affair.[6] Airman refused to enter the respectability of Jewish life with its taint of

Herman Wouk's popular novel *Marjorie Morningstar* was made into a film in 1958. The film's version of the Passover scene captures Wouk's constructions of the tensions in Marjorie's (Natalie Wood) life as a young Jewish woman. Her mother maintains the continuity of Jewish tradition by creating a traditional Seder over which male relatives preside. Noel (Gene Kelly) has broken with Jewish tradition, which he understands as parochial and bourgeois. Marjorie's anxious glance at him suggests that she is torn between these worlds as well. (Copyright © 1969 by Paramount Pictures Corporation. Photo courtesy The Museum of Modern Art Film Stills Archive, New York City)

suburbs, empty synagogue piety, and marriage.[7] In his words, she "rode" him toward the success he wanted and resisted. His anger at his father both fueled and paled in comparison to this deeper rage at providing for Marjorie's wish to create a family and move to the suburbs.

This same anxiety and disenchantment found its place in Philip Roth's *Goodbye, Columbus*. Like Airman, one of Neil Klugman's most pressing concerns was whether the object of his love was just another Jewish woman bound for suburbia in disguise. Both Noel and Neil initially believed that a sexual relationship was proof that their loves were not really simply Jewish "girls" in search of marriage and respectability. Noel's description of the "Shirley" paralleled Neil's musings about the "immortals" and "goddesses" who shared a fate of identical homes, furnishings, hair, and clothes. "Shirleys" and "goddesses" were extremely beautiful, but they were prizes that embodied their own punishment. No matter how they initially appeared, ultimately they demanded their men work, giving up their dreams to enable their families to settle into the comforts of affluence.[8]

Neil resisted these aspirations as a New Jersey public library employee with no plans for his future. But his passionate affair with Brenda Patimkin, daughter of wealthy suburbanites, brought him to the very precipice of the world he rejected.

Both Neil and Noel calculated love in terms of a consistent set of dimensions—lose/win, victory/defeat, resist/seduce—because their passions were inseparable from their fates. Which American dream would they pursue—to supersede their fathers' economic success or to remain free to pursue adventure and art? The men in the senior generation of both novels were manufacturers, occupations involving unrelenting work with no apparent intrinsic value beyond the affluence it brought the family. As these men tasted the sweet fruit of desire and sexuality, they began to lose their autonomy and independence to the taskmaster of hard work. As they lost these women, they won their freedom from fathers and productivity.

Whatever their fate, each refused the middle class by refusing its daughter. They fled the triptych of Jewish life: hard work, personified by the father-producer; the creation of a family, personified by the beautiful, sexual daughter; and the maintenance of Judaism, personified by the mother.[9]

Talking Back

Less than twenty years after *Marjorie Morningstar* and *Goodbye, Columbus* were written, their images resurfaced in eight novels that narrate the lives of seven young woman and one man who "becomes" a woman. The youngest are college age; the oldest are in their twenties. All of them are searching for love and marriage and are frustrated in their pursuit. The writers of the 1970s novels about Jewish women used the persona developed by Roth and Wouk, inverting her in order to subvert her role as the prize. These representations of young Jewish women, along with novelty books and jokes, became a currency with which to negotiate what it meant to be a Jewish man or woman in America.

The source of the novels' comedy is simultaneously the source of their pathos. Rather than beautiful prizes to be bestowed by fathers on stand-in sons, the heroines of these novels are funny, outrageous, ironic women who worry anxiously that they cannot find love without undergoing change.

Within the form of the novel itself rests one of the key elements of these writers' representation of the Jewish woman. She must, in the course of her story, undergo major transformations to achieve her goal, which is marriage. In the novels that portray women setting out for college, Susan Lukas's *Fat Emily*[10] and Louise Rose Blecher's *The Launching of Barbara Fabrikant*,[11] the genre seems straightforward. The protagonists are beginning to separate from their families, to explore their sexual freedom and desires, and to create an independent identity. However, the novels about women approaching their thirtieth year also require them to undergo dramatic changes. What unites all of these women is that to establish an adult identity they must be loved and marry.

Rather than being a normative process, transformation in these novels is a monumental task. Each character is flawed by her failure to attract a Jewish man who will provide home, identity, and the potential for creating a family. The fatal flaw is most often the woman's body; it must either be made smaller, or if it is acceptable, the woman must struggle to keep it from growing too large. The protagonists battle not only fat but noses, which also must be reshaped to be beautiful. What plagues these characters is what Mikhail Bakhtin called "the grotesque body," one that is protruding, unrestrained, and never complete.[12]

In *The Launching of Barbara Fabrikant*, the character describes her 18-year-old body in this way: "At this moment I'm wearing a bra that cuts deep into the skin underneath my breasts whenever I sit down and a 'long line' girdle that pushes the flab up; it feels as though there is a war going on between my bra and my girdle. . . . When you lose in one place you gain in another, and all the bra salesladies and mothers in the world cannot prove differently."[13] This body cannot be masked or liberated. Its grotesque and slapstick dimensions are such that flesh is redistributed at will. Barbara's twenty-five pounds of excess weight define her life.

Emily Howard, the eighteen-year-old college freshman of the novel *Fat Emily*, surveys her body with equal horror. She never looks at herself naked but accidentally catches sight of herself in a mirror after a shower: "Her eyes quickly surveyed the mountainous territory. The flesh appeared to have been thrown on the bone by some careless artisan. The belly sagged as if it had recently produced quintuplets, the breasts hung from the strain of suckling the litter of babies. Every exaggerated curve was emphasized by tiny silvery rivulets torn like strip-mines over the side of a mountain, each one a tribute to her corporeal excess."[14] Emily's mother, unlike Barbara's, does not undertake a constant barrage of reminders that Emily's weight is tied to her failure to find men. She only gently suggests that she "lose a few pounds." But Emily nevertheless experiences the "grotesqueness" of her body.

The never-named protagonist of Sandra Harmon's *A Girl Like Me*[15] does manage to lose weight and transforms her nose through surgery in an effort to climb out of the working class and into the arms of successful men. These transformations are not sufficiently successful. At Westhampton she finds herself surrounded by upper-class women who are thinner still and have smaller breasts. They invite her to play sports that she has never learned. Her body may sexually please her wealthy lover, but she knows that her burned skin and inability to play tennis will keep her a foreigner in the world to which she aspires.

The women of these novels—Gail Parent's protagonist, Sheila Levine,[16] Emily Howard, Barbara Fabrikant, and others—all share bodies that must be changed if they are to find love. Even in the case of a "relatively" normal Jewish woman, there is no freedom from a grotesque body. Florida Burns, the protagonist of Marie Brenner's *Tell Me Everything*[17] works hard to keep her body trim, but she is burdened by what she describes as grotesque breasts: "Breasts. I have a few words to say about big ones. You think you've got problems, well . . . try adding an 'ample bosom' to your list. I'm not just concerned with Edith Lance's custom-made "flattener" fittings, or a monthly swell to honeydew melon size. I'm talking about something much, much more. Nobody looked sillier than a girl with big tits" (p. 29).

A successful gossip columnist in her late twenties, Florida developed her proclivity for humor as a Texas high school student who needed to overcome a body that threatened to doom her to little more than her breasts. She feared then, as she does in her contemporary New York life, that only boys from the working class found large-breasted women attractive, not the success-bound men, who appeared to prefer the flat chests of thin women.

Like their bodies, women's noses demand alteration. They too must be transformed to create attractive and desirable women. Sheila Levine's novelistic suicide note describes 100,000 women looking for husbands in New York, all of whom need their noses and hair straightened. Barbara Fabrikant is the daughter of a rabbi who beams at her face transformed by plastic surgery and proudly declares "she looks like a shikse."[18] Musings on her father's contradictory pleasures, Barbara says, "They want us to sound like the British Royal family and still be proud that we're Jewish, a Jewish heart and a Queen Elizabeth exterior."[19] Barbara's parents urge her to become a "finished" person, to be transformed by changing her body.

Perhaps the most striking nose transformation belongs to Suzanne of Myrna Blythe's novel *Cousin Suzanne.*[20] Suzanne Goldfarb is the wealthy and extraordinarily beautiful cousin of Aileen Walker, the novel's narrator. Suzanne's parents indulge her every desire, worship her beauty, and see no need for her to change. But Suzanne demands the transformation of a nose she comes to understand as grotesque. Her discovery of her grotesqueness is accidental, and it shatters her high school tranquillity. She confronts her cousin who is brought to comfort her.

"Why didn't you tell me I was grotesque?"
"Well—because you're not."

"I AM SO!" She began to cry, great breaking sobs. The night before, when she should have been studying her vocabulary lists, she thought it would be more fun to observe her oval face from a new and different angle. She was quite content with what she saw as usual until she caught an unexpected glimpse of her profile. When with mounting horror she noticed for the first time ever, the sixteenth of an inch mound of flesh that separated the pert nostrils of her nose. A dip, I think it's called, a slight excess of flesh, barely noticeable. In Suzanne's case it was a family characteristic. "It's just grown there—" she insisted, beginning to sob again.

"It's the nose God gave you," said Aunt Bea.

"The hell with that," said Suzanne.

"So you'll have it fixed," Aunt Bea said after a moment.[21]

Both bodies and noses must be transformed from their God-given state to an altered one. The fat daughters of this fiction, for example, have fat mothers. Aileen explains that Suzanne's "dip" is a "family characteristic." But transformations from what "God gave you" are required, nonetheless, to make possible necessities of life—the love that secures suburban households and comfort, children, and a purpose.

One of the most thoughtful reflections on the place of the body in the novel has been advanced by Mikhail Bakhtin, the Russian literary critic. In particular, Bakhtin discussed the role of the "grotesque body" as a way to understand the changing attitudes toward the body in European novels. Bakhtin noted that common biological experiences of pleasure were acceptable in Renaissance novels but became an unacceptable form in later literary works. They excluded the commonplace bodily functions and emphasized control of the body as a "border of closed individuality that does not merge with other bodies and with the world."[22] By contrast, he noted, the grotesque bodies of Renaissance writers, particularly that of François Rabelais—fat, gluttonous, and protruding—undermine the "impenetrable surface that closes and limits the body as a separate and completed phenomenon" (p. 318).

Jewish women's novels depend on a *perceived* grotesqueness, whether it involves one-sixteenth inch of flesh or excess pounds of weight. These women's bodies must be individualized and contained to be made lovable. Indeed, Bakhtin notes that the nose is often crucial to the grotesque body because as an orifice it transgresses the body and may be shown to be detachable from it. The fleshy dip had to be contained as readily as the excess weight.[23]

Clearly, at one level these tales of transforming women are the product of a culture so pathological that it has idealized thinness as the only form of beauty. But Bakhtin's insight on the grotesque body asks us to look further. Why must the Jewish woman shed her features to be reconstituted as desirable? The grotesque body is not "finished," the necessary condition required by Rabbi Fabrikant as he sought to create a Queen Elizabeth exterior for his Jewish daughters. The Jew in the Jewish woman, unconfined by the demands of

American culture, is what is symbolized by the grotesque body. She is imperfect, uncontrollable, and unlovable by her own cultural double, the Jewish male.

In folklore, drama, and comedy the grotesque is exceptionally powerful, transgressing all boundaries. The clown, the trickster, the sexually ambiguous performer, among others, have license to break rules, tell truths, and challenge acceptable norms. In the representations of Jewish women, particularly in these novels, the grotesque is hideous and requires control. The women who succeed do so by controlling their bodies. Barbara Fabrikant loses twenty-five pounds and begins to attract men. Sheila Levine loses thirteen pounds as she sets off to find a husband. Florida Burns exercises her body to control it and follows her mother's advice: "Use your mouth only for talking." But in most cases they all succumb to the desire for food, and their bodies return to their grotesque shapes. These women are untransformable. The 1950s Jewish male feared entrapment in respectability. The 1970s Jewish woman feared that the source of her power—the grotesque body, with its ability to transgress cultural norms—would deprive her of love, trapping her forever in a body given by God and her mother.

The Gaze

The grotesque bodies of these novels are the product of the gaze of others. Mothers, friends, and potential boyfriends determine the right proportion of the body.[24] In fact, what marks all of these works is how often the character narrates herself from the outside looking in. Sheila Levine, in *Sheila Levine Is Dead and Living in New York*, uses the device of the camera repeatedly. She describes herself in this first-person narrative from the perspective of an audience viewing a film. She uses this narrative device for both brutal self-criticism and happy fantasy. Sheila begins her life in New York looking for work in the following vignette:

We open on the exterior of 1650 Broadway, a dirty old building. Pan down to Sheila Levine. She is in a size fourteen black sheath, which is a little too tight so that if one looks closely with the inquiring eye of the camera, one can see exactly where her panty girdle ends. The shot should not be too tight because Miss Levine neglected to shave under her arms this morning.

Well movie lovers, there it is, the Sheila Levine Story. The critics loved it. Sheila Levine was played by Ernest Borgnine.[25]

The novelist does more here than allows Sheila to bare her failures. She reveals them not simply through words but through the lens of a moving camera.

She also uses the lens for "stop-action" shots. In encounters with men at the beach or at her apartment garbage cans she freezes the frame. Sheila steps out of her encounter in real time and fantasizes that this is the moment she finds Love, imagining it as a story she tells her future children. "Daddy and I were taking out the garbage and met for the first time." Each of these fantasies freezes the moment as a potential for love that will resolve her struggles and allow her to become an adult.

Florida Burns is another character whose monologues both narrate and remove her from her own life. She often speaks of herself in the third person, comparing herself either to the people with whom she exercises or those with whom she competes for gossip. But her patter simply allows her to distance herself from her life even as she dominates the novel.

The title of *Fat Emily* is taken from a dream Emily Howard regularly has in which she spins plates dressed as an obese clown for the amusement of children. A ringmaster announces, "And Now, Ladies and Gentlemen, in the center ring, performing her hilarious acts of physical dexterity, the world's greatest plate spinner, FAT EMILY" (p. 79). In an agonizingly detailed dream she moves clumsily, cannot keep all of her plates spinning, and is pulled offstage by a giant hook. Onstage, failing in view of hundreds of people, young and old, she sees herself as the fat clown who is simultaneously too large but not entirely solid.

The self-conscious externalized gaze appears in two novels that differ from the others but in ways that only reinforce these basic messages. The first, Gail Parent's *David Meyer Is a Mother*, is the only novel written about a man—one, however, who is transformed into a "woman" by the book's final pages.[26] David muses on his transformation from a 1950s confident seducer to a 1970s male entirely confused and "mixed up" about the sexes. As a result of cystitis he bleeds regularly—menstrual period–style—keeping him from sex. When his own credit card is rejected, he must use his girlfriend's MasterCard at a restaurant. He finds himself upset if he misses his hair appointment, wants commitment and security from a lover who wants freedom and independence, and finally wants a child. Gail Parent's second novel of the 1970s uses the same type of double narration as in the other works. She writes in the first person but creates a character who sees himself through the eyes of others. David's externalized gaze is embodied in his fantasized feminist tribunal, presided over by Gloria Steinem, a founder of second-wave feminism. David is called upon to justify behavior that was once acceptable and has now become "criminal."

The novel's externalized narrative gaze is all the more interesting because a great many of the characters are engaged in work related to print and electronic media, which by its nature constructs the very types of cultural surfaces that reflect back identities. The media creates images against which individuals often compare themselves. These characters both see themselves through the external gaze and create the alienating gaze of image makers. Florida Burns writes gossip and then gets her own television show. Aileen Walker is a managing editor of a teenage magazine often concerned with gossip. Two characters are screenwriters (the nameless character and David Meyer before he becomes a woman), one for film and one for television. The workplace, like the university, is largely a backdrop to the personal stories of transformation.

The gaze dominates these novels in a final way. Many of them are obsessed by what is communicated by the image of what one wears and how one looks. Who one is reflects, garment by garment and thing by thing, one's success and desirability. Florida Burns, for example, believes that by living at the Dakota building on Central Park in New York she will become the right person, even if she cannot afford a kitchen or sufficient space. Sheila Levine, on the other hand, believes that living in Greenwich Village will provide the same.

Consumption is critical to Rhoda Lerman's *The Girl That He Marries*. Like David Meyer, the novel's main character is not a Jewish woman but nevertheless provides a powerful representation of Jewish womanhood. Stephanie, the book's protagonist, is a Christian art historian who is intrigued with and then wants to marry a Jewish lawyer, Richard. She is failing at her task and turns to a Jewish woman friend for advice. Miriam teaches her how to win a Jewish man by imitating a Jewish Princess. Consumer items become critical in this quest.

Then she burst from the closet. "Here! Are they gorgeous?" Triumphantly, she tossed me an old white T-shirt and a grimy shoulder bag. "See this ratty thing . . . plastic piece of junk. That's my Louis Vuitton bag. The shoulder strap is leather. In the sixties, this bag then cost one hundred and eighty five bucks and the older it is, the longer it looks like you've been rich."

"I don't really like status symbols, Miriam, It's really out of my . . . uh experience."

"Oh sure. That's because you are a status symbol yourself. Listen, now you have your princess uniform. The secret motto of the legion is: attack. But subtly. See? Do their possessions, not them. Mothers attack them. Princesses have a more delicate touch. If he brings you rye bread with seeds, sigh and say you have been lusting for rye bread without seeds, and if he brings you without seeds sigh and say, et cetera. Always an A minus. If you want to marry him, you have to keep him in line."[27]

As David Meyer did not have to be a female to become a Jewish mother, so Stephanie does not have to be Jewish to become a Jewish Princess. These are identities that can be created in service of pursuing love and personal transformation as well as identity. Although Stephanie was herself a status symbol, she could not find marriage, like all the unattractive Jewish women, until she learned to keep Richard off balance, so uncertain that he would finally cling to her.

Clothing, addresses, and objects are important parts of the kits of transformation. What Jewish women own and wear and how they are seen creates a life that precludes love. Inverting the fairy-tale princess, they search for a princely kiss that will liberate them from an imprisoning body and uncertain reality.

Narratives of Class, Gender, and Ethnicity

These 1970s novels explode the proffered prize of postwar American Jewish life. The seductive beauty, thinness, privilege, and self-assurance of Wouk's and Roth's representations of young Jewish womanhood have been transformed by these writers into women who express seething frustration at their inability to become what is expected and their disappointment at love that is never realized. One of the most striking differences between the novels written in the 1970s and the 1950s is that the later ones provide no clear critique of what created these disappointments. The 1950s writers seemed certain that hard work, suburban life, empty Judaism, and alluring young beauty simply could not add up to sufficient reward to follow the senior generation's path. But the angst and disappointments of the 1970s novels are diffuse. Their protagonists learn that the love that promised to be life's prize was not what it appeared. With the exceptions of Emily, who finds "a room of her own" away from family and love, and Florida, who finds love and success, the others remain mired in relationships that hold little promise for the future.

These disappointments with postwar life have been widely documented as the agonies of the American middle class, whose only avenue to success is hard work and constant deferment of pleasure.[28] Elizabeth Long contends that popular novels abandoned themes of the importance of mobility and success by the mid-1950s and turned in the 1970s to themes of personal fulfillment and the loss of a central cultural metaphor.[29] The particular afflictions and contradictions of both American middle-class women and the baby-boom generation have been addressed by a number of scholars.[30] The feminism of the 1970s was a powerful response on the part of women to resolving these contradictions and disappointments. Betty Friedan called this middle-class women's phenomenon "the problem without a name."[31] Women were bored and their skills underutilized as they formed families. Prior to that moment they were expected to be successful and ambitious. As men were disappointed with what productivity yielded, women mourned the loss of the opportunity for work.

These novels, then, might well be read as a comic social realism created by middle-class feminists describing newly liberated sexuality and the challenge of a variety of new freedoms. One reviewer for *Booklist*, for example, characterized *The Girl That He Marries* as "another of those acutely observed and insistently comic novels in the tradition of Jong, Parent, and Drexler."[32] Another reviewer, for *Publishers Weekly*, described the book as follows: "Very much for the same market that loved *Fear of Flying*, this tackles virtually every aspect of the sexual encounter scene and proves that getting what you think you want isn't always the answer."[33] While these mainstream press reviewers recognize the Jewish types that populate the novels—Jewish Mothers and Jewish Princesses, chiefly—they place the novels within a comic feminist genre.

The question is not so much what is "Jewish" about these novels as how do Jewishness, womanhood, and middle-class life become so inextricably bound together to create familiar and powerful markers of 1970s life? How is it that feminist "comic" novels represent Jewish women and their postwar dilemmas as quintessential poignant and funny heroines? If this is a critique of the American middle class, it seems oddly formulated in the language of Jewish women as losers. Their Jewishness, truly an ethnic rather than a religious identity, is simultaneously central and ephemeral. If the disjointed and externalized gaze characterizes virtually all of these works, it is in part linked to that peculiar tension.

The Jewishness of these novels' women rests on their unshakable sense that their own Jewishness must be anchored in the middle class. Many of the fathers in these books are producers, owners, and economic successes. But the world of work is far less elaborated than the family and its various forms of consumption. Barbara Fabrikant's visit to her college roommate's home is the occasion for her to describe the carpet as "Jewish." She tells us that Jewish carpets are works of such comfort that feet disappear into them. Not so "Gentile" carpets, which are never comfortable no matter how wealthy the homeowner might be. In these books men's neckties are Jewish, clothing is Jewish, styles of cleaning up at parties are Jewish, shopping is Jewish, worrying about marriage is Jewish, eating is Jewish, bodies are Jewish, expectations for success and hard work are Jewish, and family interactions are Jewish. In other words, all of these activities in all the novels are glossed as Jewish and can even be appropriated by a non-Jewish woman in pursuit of a Jewish man. By contrast, nothing about the traditional norms of Judaism is apparent other than an occasional ritual or an interaction with a usually insincere rabbi.

The authors, then, reveal the construction of a secular American Jewish culture. Central to its fundamental categories is the need to transform what is given. As Suzanne Goldfarb remarks to her mother's weak insistence that her nose was God-given: "The hell with that." Neckties can be changed, weight can be lost, Vuitton bags can be purchased or given; and yet with all the infinite possibilities for transforming identities, only one of the novels, *Tell Me Everything*, allows for the possibility of love and the formation of a family that will ensure the future. Jewishness is as elusive as love, dominating life, disappearing, and reappearing when one least expects it.

These novels do not consign Jewish life to the synagogue. Jewishness appears where one might least expect it: in gender, in the body, in clothing, and in furnishings. Rather than Jewishness being the backdrop to dilemmas of postwar middle-class life, in these novels it surfaces everywhere and is exceptionally difficult to contain. Ethnic and social class identities are inseparable. Economic success is part of being Jewish, and Jews own certain consumer items. This logic inscribes gender relations in the novels as well: women pursue and men resist. Marriage not only promises love but guarantees achieving or maintaining economic comfort. This connection is troubled.

From the 1950s to the 1970s this logic changed dramatically for the white middle class. As Jews reflected those values, women were no longer defined by their domesticity and voluntarism. With rather extensive educations they reentered the work force, both divorce and intermarriage increased, and expectations changed. The assumptions of who should work and who should consume were put into question. In these novels the fundamental definitions of Jewish womanhood—ability to love, sexuality, and place in the family—are radically questioned, precisely as they parody suburban life.

The search for love, for success, for affluence, and for the possibility of having children are all tied to becoming a woman. That "normal" developmental step is the source of anxiety underlying each work. To capture the love of her Jewish political science professor, Barbara Fabrikant must, at his insistence, wear a gold cross to help him become aroused, which she refuses to do. Stephanie, the non-Jew attempting to become a "Jewish woman," must create such deception and anxiety in her beloved that her final connection to him leaves her completely alienated from her own life and desires. The unnamed woman of *A Girl Like Me* and Emily Howard can each find autonomy but not love. David Meyer can become a mother but abandons work, and Sheila Levine's pleasures are predicated on a promise of suicide.

Only Florida Burns finds love and success. Mike Markman, the object of her desire, is open to love after he loses a fortune and is frightened to tell his father about his bankruptcy. Only then he pursues her, in a gender reversal in which he meets her via an interview, a former ruse of hers. In a chance meeting, Florida describes Markman as her double, as Neil Klugman more warily described himself and Brenda. Florida finds love through affinity; the rest of the characters, in the 1950s and 1970s, both men and women, find only despair within affinity. Both Mike Markman and David Meyer find love through gender reversals that allow the Jewish women they pursue to be highly successful.

These Jewish women, some of whom are neither Jewish nor women, reveal that "Jewish" love, "Jewish" consumption, and "Jewish" success pit men and women in conflict as each circles the other in competition over who is to be the prize, who will create the future, and who will maintain the past. These novels shift the burden of conflict from the easier crisis of intergenerational struggles to the perilous war of the sexes, whose resolution may make attraction, affinity, and love unattainable. The disappointment, anger, frustration, and humor of each of these stories rests not only on the theme of "what is the point of a driven middle-class life?" The books also reveal that the development of a postwar American Jewish culture within the framework of middle-class consumerism made the rejection of that world the rejection of Jewishness itself.[34] The novels reflect the feminist sensibility that creating one's own meaning makes a woman uniquely unsuited to be a man's prize. At the same time, however, in these works of middle-class Jewish life, women deconstruct themselves as prizes but remain entirely uncertain about how to reconstruct themselves as Jewish women. Jewishness and womanhood seem to be realized only in self-narration.

Subversive JAPs

These authors consciously use the image of the Jewish Princess to tell their stories of sexual warfare in postwar life. Characters discuss other literary versions of the princess. Florida Burns defines herself in relation to characters from novels by Nora Ephron and Gail Parent peopled by self-consciously Jewish stereotypes. Several writers refer to Philip Roth and his literary Jewish mother, Sophie Portnoy, often positioning themselves in contrast to her and him. Sheila Levine attributes Jewish men's hatred of Jewish women to what Roth called "Portnoy's Complaint." Stephanie imagines a tribunal in which Richard will be tried for his attachment to another woman. She puts Martin Buber on her side and leaves Philip Roth to Richard. Barbara Fabrikant even describes the color of her father's hair as salt and pepper "like Philip Roth's." These novels are peopled with characters who talk back to literary representations.

In a doubling of reflection, novelistic inventions gaze on themselves through other literary creations in order to give the reader a mirror for still another anxious look. The reader turns to tortured stories of unsuccessful love to "identify" with the wounded on the battlefield of sexual combat. But this is no ordinary war between the sexes. The Jewishness of its combatants transforms the stakes. Jewish love appears to founder on the carpets, neighborhoods, and bodies required by American affluence. A loveless life dooms the future of the Jewish people.

The Jewish Princess representation in the hands of Roth and Wouk, as well as the 1970s authors, tells us that in the Jewish world, which underelaborates communal life and overelaborates images of success and mobility, men and women appear, to use Wouk's image, as the horse and rider of middle-class life. They cannot even agree on who has mounted and who has been ridden. Women refuse to be enslaved as prizes for male success and then are unable to move into new families. Men find freedom only by refusing the formation of the family. Every refusal of these 1970s novels involves choices between pleasure and love, work and love, autonomy and love, and a host of other oppositions. As Wouk and Roth wrote in terms of winning and losing, calculations appropriate to a capitalist society, so these women write of the absence of having (love) within a consumer society.

The novels' protagonists said "no thanks" to the role of prize. Each woman is engaged in a complex and even distorted coming of age, announcing that she is not Sophie Portnoy, she is not Marjorie Morningstar, and she is not confined to the life of the Jewish daughter or wife. These works present women as sexually active with multiple partners. Sometimes their sexuality is motivated by capturing a man, but more often women engage in the chase and indulge their desires. "Grotesque bodies" keep women from love but also reveal their independence, autonomy, and the possibility of pleasure. As classic "losers" these women are funny; their voices control the novels, providing commentaries on contemporary Jewish life, the family, and the impossible dilemmas that beset women. Drawing on familiar styles of Jewish performance—self-effacing, comic, hyperbolic, and iconoclastic—they transform the language of hopelessness into power. These writers not only talk back to Philip Roth and others, they appropriate their writing.

In the 1970s, as master narratives of gender, assimilation, and the family fell apart, these women writers appropriate and reformulate the loser/outsider as a woman bursting out of cultural restraints. Jewish women writers declared themselves capable of narrating lives at the same time that their narratives assert that the future will not be as they imagined it as children. Love, solidity, social class, and Jewishness are all in question, their shapes uncertain and their relationship to one another fractured and cracked open. That uncertainty, with its possibilities as well as its terrors, is condensed into the image of the 1970s Jewish woman.

In the 1970s, Cinderellas rarely became princesses because they wanted to be neither horse nor rider. While waiting for the prince, these Jewish women simply told their stories.[35]

Bonnie Lyons

Faith and Puttermesser
Contrasting Images of Two Jewish Feminists

Grace Paley and Cynthia Ozick, two of the strongest, most distinctive Jewish female writers to emerge in the postwar period, have produced very different bodies of work. Since her first novel, *Trust*, in 1966, Ozick has published novels, novellas, several volumes of stories, and some of the liveliest collections of essays. With her three collections of short stories *(The Little Disturbances of Man, Enormous Changes at the Last Minute*, and *Later the Same Day)*, Paley is acclaimed almost entirely as a short-story writer, although she is also the author of a volume of poetry, *Leaning Forward*. Ozick has been praised as a virtuoso stylist of elegant sentences, a powerful moral thinker, and a writer with passionately embodied ideas. Paley is prized for her infectious humor, the profound social engagement of her work, her increasingly rich approach to storytelling and stories, and most important, her creation of an unmistakable voice.

Despite these significant differences, Paley and Ozick have much in common: together they fill in a large blank area of Jewish American fiction. That is, in spite of their extraordinary strengths and achievements, Bellow, Malamud, and Roth, the three dominant Jewish male writers, have all failed to create memorable female characters or to explore in depth the way the world looks to a female eye.[1] In contrast, and at least partly in response to this absence, one of the major achievements of both Ozick and Paley has been the creation of a number of vivid, complex images of women. Moreover, each of them has created a particularly memorable, convincing female character (in Paley's case, Faith; in Ozick's, Puttermesser) who serves multiple authorial purposes and fulfills multiple aesthetic, religious, and social strategies.

Compared to the female characters created by the dominant American Jewish male writers, Faith and Puttermesser are not only more intensely realized female characters but also representations of women with greater intellectual and spiritual depth; they are less privatized, less willing or able to see themselves as satellites to male suns, as functions of male thoughts and ambitions, or as simple fillers of the biological roles of wife and mother.

A look at their work through the lenses of these central female characters does more than demonstrate the limitations of the female characters created by Bellow, Malamud, and Roth; it also suggests Ozick's and Paley's individual strategies and strengths and illuminates the variety and complexity of possible approaches to being both a Jewish and a feminist writer. That is, both Ozick and Paley are intensely Jewish feminist writers, but their explorations and conceptions of these two key terms, especially as demonstrated through their handling of their principal female characters, Faith and Puttermesser, provide a direct road to the heartland of their fictional domains and also a clarification of the richness of both the Jewish tradition and feminism as thematic centers of meaning for fiction-makers.

While Ozick and Paley are quintessentially Jewish feminist writers, the nature of each writer's Jewishness and feminism is distinctly different. To put their difference as feminists succinctly, Ozick's work embodies the kind of feminism that stresses androgyny and one human ideal, while Paley's work embodies feminism as sexual difference and valorizes the distinctly female. Their different interests in and uses of their Jewish heritage can best be explained by referring to Robert Redfield's critical distinction between the Great Tradition and the Little Tradition that define every culture.[2] The Great Tradition embodies the culture's formal laws, structures, and texts; the Little Tradition, in contrast, expresses itself in the local folkways of the group's beliefs, an oral tradition that remains unsystematized and unidealized, practiced constantly and often unconsciously by ordinary people without external enforcement or interference.

For all Jews the Great Tradition is Hebrew and formal Jewish law and study, and for Jews descended from Eastern Europe the Little Tradition is *Yiddishkeyt*. Although Ozick has written one of the great eulogies for Yiddish, it is the Great Tradition of Judaism, especially Hebrew and the sacred texts, that is the real focus of the Jewish aspects of her work.[3] In contrast, Paley's Jewishness derives from the Little Tradition of *Yiddishkeyt* and in particular from the rich and complicated ethic embodied in the code of *mentschlekhkeyt*, with its validation of the worth of the common person—in her case, the ordinary, specifically female person. I will begin by contrasting their different kinds of feminism and then go on to their different conceptions and uses of their Jewish inheritance.

In a frequently quoted essay in *Art & Ardor*, Ozick identified herself as a classical feminist.[4] Ozick's feminism is the feminism that defines itself as the unfinished business of humanism, stresses the common human elements of experience, attacks the culturally created and reinforced concepts of femininity and masculinity as opposed to biological male and female, and argues for the androgynous ideal of all individuals achieving their own best selves irrespective of gender. Suspicious of ghettoization (whether by others or by oneself) and the resultant diminishment, Ozick has strenuously resisted being categorized as a woman writer. Not surprisingly, one of her early stories, "Virility," satirizes the validity of referring art to its author's gender, describing style as female or male, and associating positive literary value with maleness.[5]

In the three Puttermesser fictions, Ozick creates a female character who identifies herself as a feminist very much like Ozick, and in a recent interview Ozick even refers to Puttermesser as "a kind of alter ego."[6] In the earliest of the three Puttermesser fictions, Ozick definitely places Puttermesser within a feminist framework.[7] Puttermesser's parents, who are obviously and vulgarly in search of a husband for her and who worry that Puttermesser has made herself too educated to please a man, are satisfied for these antifeminist ideas. Likewise, the token hiring of women (like Jews) and the boss's mistaken belief that Puttermesser leaves her job because of the absence of eligible husband material are also held up for ridicule. Most significantly, in two crucial typographically set off paragraphs the narrator announces, "Now if this were an optimistic portrait, exactly here is where Puttermesser's emotional life would begin to grind itself into evidence. Her biography would proceed romantically." Instead, the narrator insists that Puttermesser will not marry and may or may not begin an affair and concludes, "The difficulty with Puttermesser is that she is loyal to certain environments." The word *loyal* suggests Puttermesser's personality characteristic, but more important, it clarifies her conceptual parameters as a character, parameters deriving from Ozick's own stance as a classical feminist.

In the second Puttermesser fiction, Puttermesser longs for a daughter and a link between Xanthippe and Puttermesser's dream daughter Leah is suggested.[8] The novella "Puttermesser Paired" ostensibly describes Puttermesser's late recognition of a desire for a husband, and in fact, Puttermesser considers the idea that her marriage-minded parents may have been right after all.[9] But this thematic exploration of Puttermesser's desire for children and for a husband is not a capitulation to traditional depictions of female characters as primarily biological, sexual beings because this acknowledgment of the biological and sexual side of Puttermesser is never depicted as invalidating her other desires, projects, or interests. There is no implied reductionism, no trivializing of her spiritual or intellectual aspirations. While Xanthippe is in part the fulfillment of Puttermesser's unmet desire for a daughter, she is also the fulfillment of Puttermesser's desire to take a heroic and unprecedented place in Jewish history and, through the golem, to repair the world. Similarly, in "Puttermesser Paired," Puttermesser's desire for marriage is far from a simple biological "call." This is marriage seen as ideal friendship between like-minded people, a mutual relationship between equals that fosters the best of both partners—a perfect classical feminist marriage.

The fact that all three Puttermesser fictions end with the collapse of Puttermesser's aspirations is of course a comment on them as idealized dreams; it also makes the undoing of the character's projects recapitulate the central strategy of "undoing" in the texts themselves and underscores the parallels between character and creator.

In both "Puttermesser and Xanthippe," and "Puttermesser Paired," sex and the body are crucial to the collapse, and Puttermesser's failure to account for the centrality of sexuality and for the limitations and needs of the body gives rise to their destructive power, which defeats Puttermesser's ideal mental constructions—in "Puttermesser and Xanthippe," New York as the new *Gan Eydn*; in "Puttermesser Paired," the re-creation of the ideal George Eliot/George Lewes relationship. In "Puttermesser and Xanthippe," Xanthippe is created after Puttermesser shows more interest in reading than in sex with Morris Rappoport; Xanthippe's voracious sexual appetite later brings down all that has been created. Similarly, in the more directly self-reflexive novella, the failure of the Puttermesser–Rupert marriage is plainly sexual: Rupert cannot or will not consummate the marriage, just as the rejuvenation of George Eliot's aging body through her relationship with the much younger Cross was also short-lived.

Both plots underscore the earth-binding gravity of sex and the body and the danger of weightless ideal mental constructions, such as the dream of a male/female relationship between two disembodied souls. The plot closures are thus Ozick's thematic recognition of the absolute and abstract nature of her classical feminism. That is, the endings of the two fictions embody her recognition that classical feminism is an ideal and that the category of human on which it rests is more abstract than the categories of male or female. Nevertheless, these plots are not a capitulation or a rejection of the classical feminist ideal. While in both cases Puttermesser proves to be an idealistic dreamer, her dreams, like Don Quixote's, have nobility despite her repeated failure to embody them successfully in life.

As Puttermesser is both a reflection and strategic exploration of Ozick's classical feminism, Faith, a character and/or narrator in half of Paley's stories, can be linked with the other major strand of postwar feminism, the feminism that works from a recognition of sexual *difference*, valorizes the stereotypical female virtues, takes a distinctly female world as its center, and sees the world through female eyes. Paley herself has pointed to her recognition of the validity of women's lives as fictional subject matter—her realization that ordinary women's lives were, in her words, "common and important"—as *the* critical impetus to her development as a writer.[10]

The character Faith first appeared in Paley's first collection in the paired stories of "The Used-Boy Raisers" and "A Subject of Childhood," which together are titled "Two Short Sad Stories from a Long and Happy Life."[11] The overall title, with its reversal of the famous Hemingway title, points to this story's oppositional stance toward that quintessentially male text.

The feminist nature of these first Faith stories is far from obvious. For example, in the first of the two stories, Faith comments, "I rarely express my opinion on any serious matter but only live out my destiny, which is to be, until my expiration date, laughingly the servant of man."[12] However, since the opinions the two husbands express are so fatuous, self-serving, and obvious, not expressing any opinion seems almost a sign of moral seriousness. Moreover, in later stories, Faith does come to express serious opinions about moral, social, and political issues; the early story represents a starting point from which the character grows. But even in this early story one of Faith's and Paley's central life strategies is embodied in that word *laughingly*. The ability to transcend the difficulties and failures of the world of events through a humorous attitude toward them is frequently Faith's and the other female characters' strategy, not just for survival but for buoyant affirmation. Moreover, this female life affirmation through laughter contrasts with frequent male despair, for instance, in the last story of her third collection, in which one man tells another, "I too want the opportunity, the freedom to commit suicide when I want to."[13]

Most important, as Faith's traditional embroidery with its sentimental motto "God Bless Our Home" and its "ranch house that nestles in the shade of a cloud and a Norway maple" has nothing to do with her lived realities, so the end of the first Faith story underscores both Faith's distance from her verbally aggressive present and ex-husbands and establishes the value and reality of her world, in which they are finally peripheral.[14] Although the men "set off in pride" at the end of the story, the story's moral judgment of the two men undercuts that triumphant departure.[15] When Faith tells her sons to say good-bye to their father, they ask, "Which one?" She responds, "The real father," and each son chooses a different man. Neither the biological nor the acting father is clearly the real father, and Faith, off to a child-centered day of park, museum, and home-cooked dinner, notes without envy or jealousy that their paths "are not my concern."[16]

The companion story reveals Faith asking herself the "sapping" question, "What is man that woman lies down to adore him?"[17] This story depicts the foolishness and departure of Faith's lover Clifford and concludes with a complex image of mother-son love that brilliantly embodies the depth and complexity of that bond/bind: Tonto sits on her lap, hand on her breast, and Faith concludes as the sun shines on them through the window: "Then through the short fat fingers of my son, interred forever, like a black and white barred king in Alcatraz, my heart lit up in stripes."[18]

Over the years, Faith's point of view has evolved in ways that parallel Paley's own autobiographical statements, although the facts of their lives demonstrably diverge. In part to prevent the naive, direct identification of herself with her character, Paley has recently expanded the role of Faith's female friends, especially Ruthy and Edie. More important, this expanded focus implicitly and explicitly places Faith within a community, embeds her in relatedness with other women in a way that completely contrasts the essential solitariness and abstract quality of Puttermesser as a character. Ozick's Puttermesser fictions point away from the level of fictional representation toward abstract thematic and textual issues, in which Puttermesser becomes less interesting as a character than as a figure in the carpet. That is, Puttermesser is finally a fascinating idea in Ozick's head, her greatest "fictive proposition," to use Philip Roth's formulation. Ozick herself has said, "Very often for me the germ is an idea, and the idea creates the character. . . . the idea comes first."[19] In contrast, Faith seems to exist as "an invented person," to use Paley's own words, a character who grows out of Paley's vision of herself and her friends collectively.[20]

In the recent Faith stories, Paley increasingly focuses on a woman-centered world, the fitting subject matter for the sexual-difference feminist, and celebrates the depth and longevity of female friendships, which so often outlast marriages. Paley's feminism of sexual difference is also expressed through two main strategies: first, reseeing and renaming reality through specifically female eyes and, second, reclaiming and valorizing stereotypical female traits and occupations. As an example of the latter, thickness and weight, stereotypically negative words when used to refer to women, are defiantly positive terms throughout Paley's work. This is not surprising in a writer whose most delightful characters, including Faith herself, describe themselves as fat. In fact, in the dedication of the collection to her daughter and son, Paley says, "without whom my life and literature would be pretty slim."

A single line from one of the recent Faith stories suggests the complex ways that Paley's work derives from and reinforces her vision of the feminism of sexual difference. In "The Expensive Moment," Faith tells Ruth that her love affair with Nick floundered in part because Faith never discussed it with Ruth, so the relationship remained thin. In Faith's words, "I couldn't talk to you about it, so it never got thick enough. I mean woofed and warped."[21] In this one sentence, Paley valorizes thickness, celebrates women as spinners of tales as well as yarn, and implicitly denies the traditionally male virtue of reticence. Hemingway argued that talking either destroys or falsifies lived experience, but in Paley's female world talk enriches and deepens experience, and gossip itself (traditionally considered a female vice) is positive and a pleasure. As Faith tells Ruth, talking is "as good as fucking lots of times. Isn't it?"[22]

Just as Ozick and Paley are very different feminist writers, so their relationship to Judaism and Jewishness is demonstrably contrapuntal, although both of them affirm themselves as Jewish writers, and both their fictions are essentially Jewish, albeit in different ways.

Ozick dates her first feminist impulses to her exclusion from Torah study as a child. This biographical fact is striking in two ways: her initial feminist recognition derives from exclusion from a Jewish world, and this Jewish world is one of texts and textual study. Fourteen years ago, Ozick herself observed that "the synagogue at present" did not speak to her, that she had "no divine shelter other than reading"; in her words: "At the moment print is all my Judaism."[23] Although Ozick has recently argued that the study of texts is a "superimposition of Socratic primacy of intellect upon the Jewish primacy of holiness," many of her best fictions are thematically and formally text-obsessed; and Puttermesser in all three fictions attempts in various ways to return to some original *gan eydn* using texts as her—and Ozick's—time machine.[24]

In the earliest Puttermesser story her most distinguishing characteristic is her obsession with Hebrew grammar: "the permutations of the triple-lettered root elated her."[25] Hebrew language and books are the essence of her Judaism and overtly provide the Jewish equivalent to everything Christian, from buildings to ideas: the triple-lettered Hebrew root is a "trinity"; the idea of Hebrew grammar is "a sort of Vatican" fulfilling her childhood love of the Crotona Park library where she borrowed "a steeple of library books."[26] The only dramatized scene of the story is Puttermesser's visit to Uncle Zindel for a Hebrew lesson. There Zindel "reads" the text of Puttermesser's name, Butterknife, which becomes an essential lesson in Judaism: "Puttermesser, you slice off a piece butter, you cut to live, not to kill. A name of honor, you follow?"[27] Although the narrator subsequently deconstructs the scene by asserting that "the scene with Uncle Zindel did not occur" (i.e., was imaginary only), Puttermesser clings to Zindel as the "single grain of memory"; for, unlike her un-Jewish parents, she finds "America is a blank," and Uncle Zindel, "who knew the holy letters," is "all her ancestry."[28] Moreover, the nonexistent scene is not erased by announcing that it never existed because it continues to exist in the text and in the reader's memory.

"Puttermesser and Xanthippe" is a Jewish text about texts, including Ozick's own earlier Puttermesser story. It is both a musing on and reconstitution of Jewish stories about golems found in "strange old texts," which supposedly Puttermesser had read so often that "she knew certain passages nearly verbatim."[29] Texts of all sorts dominate this text: before the creation of the golem, Puttermesser is reading Plato in bed instead of having sex with her annoyed lover. Immediately preceding the appearance of Xanthippe, Puttermesser is dreaming of an imaginary daughter in high school, memorizing Goethe's *Erlkonig;* and Puttermesser returns to bed carrying Rappoport's *Times*, which is heavy "as a dead child."[30] Puttermesser's and Xanthippe's great creation is a text called the PLAN, and in fact, the entire plan of the story itself is a kind of reiteration and variation of Jewish texts about golems. The unliving Xanthippe is brought to life by a "sharpness of a reading," and what Puttermesser ("whose intellectual passions were pledged to every alphabet") reads is the Hebrew word for God, the Name of Names.[31]

The destruction of the golem is also textual and verbal: when the golem, as predicted, turns against her creator and must be destroyed, the instructions for her destruction are also part of the old texts. To destroy the golem, Puttermesser must reverse the procedures by which she was created, and most crucially she must alter the three letters on her forehead that are the Hebrew word for truth—aleph, mem, tav—by erasing the letter aleph. The remaining letters, mem tav, the narrator explicitly explains for the non-Hebrew reader, spell "met—dead." In the model version of Judea Loew recounted in Ozick's story, the removal of the aleph is simply summarized, but in the fictional present of the story it is (like the nonexistent Uncle Zindel scene) dramatized: the letter is "erased" with a "small blade."[32] This in turn recalls Puttermesser's name (text) as well as the earlier story's lecture (text) on knives. Puttermesser's earlier obsession with sacred tongues and triple-lettered roots ends with periodontal surgery. Her rueful self-knowledge is clear: "the roots of her teeth are exposed . . . and on the lingual side, she is unendingly conscious of her own skeleton."[33]

This witty conversion of Puttermesser's mental obsession with the roots of the sacred tongue of Hebrew to bodily concern about dental roots and a fleshy tongue reinforces the connections between the stories, particularly the shared focus on Jewish texts—with Hebrew in the first story and Jewish texts about golems in the second.

Paley's Jewishness is no less central to her work and to Faith as a character than it is to Ozick and her Puttermesser. Although some of Paley's characters are not Jewish and many of her stories do not deal with Jewish issues or experience, all of Paley's work is deeply Jewish because her voice itself is a distinctly Yiddish-inflected American Jewish voice and because her underlying moral and social vision derives from *Yiddishkeyt*. The fact that Paley's voice itself is a Yiddish-inflected American Jewish voice is crucial since Paley as a writer is tuned to the spoken, not written, word. That is, while Ozick's Puttermesser stories are text-obsessed and keyed to the reading eye, Paley's Faith stories focus instead on the listening ear and the speaking mouth. Paley's oral/aural emphasis and source are apparent in both the highly conversational style of her stories and in her own comments about them. When asked about literary influences on her, Paley often shifts the focus to the influence of the spoken word, "the way people speak in your house, the language they speak, the language of your street and of your time."[34] Saying she writes stories that she needs to hear, Paley has observed, "Whatever I say comes from what I hear. It comes from the speech of my city. But that has to go through my American-Jewish ear."[35] That her stories do in fact go through her "American-

Jewish ear" is clear. The English of some of her characters reflects a Yiddish-knowing tongue, some of her most memorable metaphors derive from Jewish life, and most important, there is an unmistakable Yiddish influence on her style that is felt in word choice, syntax, and ironic phrasing.

From the beginning, Paley has used Faith and Faith stories to explore attitudes to Jews and Judaism. While some of Faith's comments are quite critical, there is an unchanging commitment to the moral values derived from *Yiddishkeyt*; and overall, Faith's own development is toward greater and greater commitment to caring and moral responsibility, the values of *mentschlekhkeyt*. Significantly, Paley's first direct statement about Jewishness appears in the first Faith story. While passively allowing her husband and ex-husband to grumble and complain, Faith finally speaks out during their argument about whether the sons should attend Catholic parochial school, saying that she believes in the Diaspora "not only as a fact but a tenet," that Jews are the chosen people and should remain "a remnant in the basement of world affairs" or "a splinter in the toe of civilizations, a victim to aggravate the conscience."[36]

In contrast, she takes up an anti-Zionist stance against Israel "on technical grounds," saying that once Jews are "huddled together in one little corner of a desert, they're like anyone else: Frenchies, Italians, temporal nationalities," thus suggesting that Zionism will diminish the Diaspora function of Jews as moral witnesses, which is central to *Yiddishkeyt*.[37] Although Faith has clear ideas about what Jews are or should be, she seems ambivalent about whether she identifies herself as a Jew or not. She refers to Jews as "they," not "we," but when asked if she forgot Jerusalem when she married her non-Jewish husbands, she insists, "I never forget a thing."[38] These speeches in the very first Faith story establish the character's idea of Jews having a special moral role and unique place in history. Moreover, these statements about Jews predict Faith's own moral development and Paley's handling of her as a developing character.

In the second volume of stories, Paley explicitly broadens Faith's concerns from private life to large public moral and social issues. In the first paragraphs of "Faith in a Tree," she bewails her manless state and forced captivity tending children; however, at the end of the story, when her older son furiously attacks her and her friends for not defending antiwar demonstrators strongly enough, Faith experiences a critical *t'shuva*, a clear, self-conscious moral turning: "And I think that is exactly when events turned me around, changing my hairdo, my job uptown, my style of living and telling."[39] Moreover, in this story Faith thinks, "If it's truth and honor you want to refine, I think the Jews have some insight. Make no images, imitate no God." She concludes that God, who is "preeminent" in "the graphic arts," should be in charge of beauty and "let man be in charge of Good."[40] This interpretation of the meaning of Jewish tradition stresses human moral responsibility and directly adumbrates her own

development toward *mentschlekhkeyt*. Previously, simply a concerned parent
and friend, Faith here announces her commitment to a broad sense of human
responsibility, her acceptance of the values of *mentschlekhkeyt* in her "style of
living and telling."

In "Friends," in the third Paley collection, Faith directly raises the issue of
the conflict between Orthodox Judaism and feminism by saying, "On the
prism of isms, both of those do have to be looked at together once in a
while."[41] In contrast to this implied criticism of Orthodox Judaism for its antifeminist bias, another story in the same collection once again celebrates Jews
for continuing to be "workers in the muddy basement of history," language that
overtly echoes Faith's early statements about Jews being "a remnant in the
basement of world affairs" in "The Used-Boy Raisers."[42] The work in the
basement is the effort to transform the world to the values of *mentschlekhkeyt*.

Caring and responsibility, the central virtues of *mentschlekhkeyt*, are,
throughout Paley's work, the cardinal virtues for her characters and for the
narrators who speak of themselves self-consciously as narrators. Thus, while
the patriarchal nature of Judaism is called into question and Faith's early statements about Israel are anti-Zionist, from the first stories to the last there is a
consistent moral vision deriving from *Yiddishkeyt*, which valorizes Jews' continuing moral role in history and the values of *mentschlekhkeyt*. Paley, of
course, shares this vision with many male Jewish writers, perhaps most especially with Malamud. But what distinguishes Paley's work is that in her fiction
the little person, *dos kleine menschele*, is most often female because the culture is patriarchal. In patriarchal society, Faith and Paley's other female characters lack great political power or cultural influence, but their attempts to lead
morally aware, socially engaged lives are both celebrated and explored as the
stuff of the fiction.

While Ozick and Paley have both created more complex, interesting female
characters than their male Jewish contemporaries have, and both accurately
define themselves as Jewish feminist writers, their visions are strikingly different in instructive ways. Faith and Puttermesser, their most memorable female
characters, are of particular interest both because of their complex functions in
the fictions and because they are used to embody and explore the moral vision
and worldviews of their authors. The two characters are so different that it is
impossible to imagine them as women meeting. One can mentally move Faith
from her favorite city park, but Puttermesser is, to use Ozick's own word, too
"loyal" to her environment, inseparable from the ornate fictional tapestries in
which she is embedded. The two characters' very names are emblematic of
their contrasts. Faith is the perfect name to embody the deep, wise affirmation
of Paley's vision as well as to nod wryly at Paley's own first name, Grace. In
contrast, Puttermesser (whose name is the source of a mini-lecture about Judaism) may be called Ruth by her mother, but to her creator she is always and

ever Puttermesser. That is, she is called by her last name with the insistence on androgyny of the humanist feminist. More overtly heroic and exceptional in her quests, Puttermesser is also subject to more authorial criticism than the more ordinary Faith, who is pointedly depicted as not very unlike her female friends. Sex, a demonic or at least problematic force for Puttermesser, is a more positive though less powerful force for Faith, who continues crotch-watching right on into middle age. Ozick seems to have taken the image of the Talmudic scholar reverently studying sacred texts (the world from which she was excluded as a female) as the central image of Jews, whereas for Paley, Jews primarily are—or should be—a moral force in history, workers in that muddy basement, moving the world toward *mentschlekhkeyt.*

That contrast reflects another more general one. Ozick as a writer presents her work against a backdrop of other writing, against the world conceived of as a vale of interpretation; for Paley there is a more direct, less mediated relationship to what she calls "the airy rubbly meaty mortal fact of the world."[43] To be a writer like Ozick one must be a great reader; to be a writer like Paley one must be like Paley's first great character and storyteller, the fat Rosie, a self-proclaimed "first-class listener."[44]

Finally, because of their many differences, including their contrasting images of Jewish women, Paley and Ozick suggest an enormous realm of possibility for Jewish women and Jewish women writers and open doors to the treasures of Jewishness and feminism as fictional sources.

IV

Contemporary Jewish Feminists as Image Makers

Sylvia Barack Fishman

Our Mothers and Our Sisters and Our Cousins and Our Aunts

Dialogues and Dynamics in Literature and Film

Women's diversity[1] is seldom more felicitously illustrated than when several female characters interact with each other.[2] Many of the most memorable portrayals of female characters, going all the way back to ancient texts, exist in the context of female-female interaction.[3] The dialogues and dynamics that occur when an isolated female interacts with a variety of male characters are different in kind than when women—friends and mothers and sisters and cousins and aunts—interact with each other. This is not to say that female-female relationships in literature and film are necessarily more significant than male-female relationships, although in some cases they surely are; it is rather to say that female-female relationships, as depicted in literature, often reveal aspects of the women's characters and personalities that are less fully developed when there are no other women in the picture.

Works by contemporary American Jewish writers and filmmakers offer particularly rich examples of the complexity of female-female relationships because the factors of Jewish ethnicity, culture, and religion further underscore and deepen already complicated emotions. Complicated feelings between women about being both Jewish and female are a constant in American Jewish literature from the fiction and memoirs of immigrant authors such as Anzia Yezierska onward.[4] Jewish female characters throughout the twentieth century articulate the fear that their human worth is tainted because of their relationship with other, less than perfect Jewish women. Literature and film produced by American Jews over the past two decades continues to suggest that Jewish women struggle with aspects of themselves and each other specifically as Jewish females. Recent essays by contemporary American Jewish feminists show the persistence of mixed feelings, testifying that many contemporary

American women, including some feminists who are Jews, have absorbed and internalized negative images of the Jewish American woman. Even among "sister" feminists, destructive stereotypes have worked to delegitimate Jewish women, to put them down, silence them, and render them invisible.[5]

This essay explores patterns of female-female interactions in American Jewish literature and film and discusses the tendency of Jewish female characters to measure and evaluate themselves against each other. Its intent is not to deny or diminish the powerful effect of male-female interactions; indeed, female-female interactions are often profoundly shaped by the actions and expectations of men and a male-dominated culture. American Jewish women—and American Jewish characters—often see themselves through the doubly demeaning lenses of scornful American attitudes toward Jewish women and patriarchal Jewish attitudes toward females in general. Some female characters are fortunate enough to have found in male characters supportive and legitimating actions and words.

However, many writers and readers have focused primarily on the male-female interaction and have devoted little artistic or critical attention to the complicated feelings and behaviors that Jewish women experience when they interact with each other. In contrast, this essay illustrates the mixed emotions among Jewish women—admiration and envy, respect and resentment—that are often interlaced, in familial situations, with love and anger and fear. As the essay will show, such warring emotions are found in films as deeply different as *Mirele Efros* (1938), *Goodbye, Columbus* (1969), and *Brighton Beach Memoirs* (1986). Films such as these and fiction written by authors like Anzia Yezierska, Grace Paley, Tillie Olsen, Vivian Gornick, and Rebecca Goldstein demonstrate that when female characters identify with other women, they often react in two opposing ways: at times they model themselves on other women, and at times they reject other women because they believe those women to embody parts of themselves that they find unacceptable. Finally, it argues that, in many works, Jewish female characters ultimately come to terms with other women only when they accept themselves, and they come to terms with themselves only when they accept other women.

These and other works chosen for discussion here are included because the authors, both male and female, depict interactions between women in ways that reveal their emotional and intellectual development, especially as they interact with each other. A brief look at the focus of passages about women in two earlier works can demonstrate the crucial difference between authorial interest in the inner lives of female characters and authorial affection for female characters. An author can be very fond of the women he or she or she writes about, without really caring about what they mean to themselves. A vignette from Alfred Kazin's *A Walker in the City* (1951) focuses on what three female characters mean to the male protagonist of his memoirs—that is, ostensibly his young self. In contrast, the screenplay of Jacob Gordin's 1938 Yiddish film, *Mirele Efros*, focuses on the way two major and two minor female characters compose their own lives and reinvent themselves in light of their interaction with each other.

Here is how the prolific literary critic and author Alfred Kazin, one of the most talented chroniclers of the American Jewish immigrant and second-generation experience, describes his unmarried female cousin and her friends:

> Afterwards we went into the "dining room" and, since we were not particularly ortho-dox, allowed ourselves little pleasures outside the Sabbath rule. . . . The evening was particularly good for me whenever the unmarried cousin who boarded with us had her two closest friends in after supper. . . . They were all dressmakers, like my mother; had work-ed with my mother in the same East Side sweatshops; were all passionately loyal mem-bers of the International Ladies Garment Workers Union; and all were unmarried. . . .
>
> . . . there they were in our own dining room, our cousin and her two friends—women, grown-up women—talking openly of the look on Garbo's face when John Gilbert took her in his arms. . . . arguing my father down on small points of Socialist doctrine. As they sat around the cut-glass bowl on the table—cracking walnuts, ex-pertly peeling the skin off an apple in long even strips, cozily sipping a glass of tea—they crossed their legs in comfort and gave off a deliciously musky fragrance of face powder that instantly framed them for me in all their dark coloring, brilliantly white teeth, and the rosy Russian blouses that swelled and rippled in terraces of embroidery over their opulent breasts.
>
> . . . I was suddenly glad to be a Jew, as these women were Jews—simply and natu-rally glad of those Jewish dressmakers who spoke with enthusiastic familiarity of Sholem Aleichem and Peretz, Gorky and Tolstoy, who glowed at every reminiscence of Nijinsky, of Nazimova in *The Cherry Orchard*, of Pavlova in "The Swan."[6]

Kazin affectionately remembers—and luminously conveys to the reader—the complex symbolism of his adolescent passion for his cousin and her friends. At that stage of his life those vibrant women represent to him the opportunities of American individualism housed in an acceptance of oneself and one's past.

In light of the scorn for Jewish women, often intricately connected with self-hatred, that one finds in the works of many American Jewish male au-thors, Kazin's accomplishments in this portrayal of Jewish women should not be lightly dismissed. Given the long and debilitating history of negative im-ages of Jewish women in American Jewish literature and film, Kazin's affec-tionate picture of a warm circle of Jewish women—not coincidentally linked with his affection for his own Jewish heritage—is a very powerful and uncom-mon combination. Nevertheless, Kazin's portrait offers us no insights to the true nature, the inevitable conflicts and compromises and daring decisions, ex-perienced by the women he describes. We know what they mean to him. We do not know what they meant to themselves.

In contrast, Jacob Gordin's play and 1938 film, *Mirele Efros*, brilliantly explores the psychology of two powerful, intelligent women and the two women who help them each as they struggle for primacy in one domestic family unit. Mirele Efros; her daughter-in-law, Shaindel; her daughter-in-law's mother; and her companion, Machle, demonstrate great personal and moral diversity, although each woman is extremely strong-willed and determined. Gordin is interested not in what these women may symbolize to the men around them but in how they invent themselves and shape their own lives. In Gordin's film, Mirele is a woman who has confronted the most bitter adversity and has triumphed over it. She has built up a business through tireless work, a shrewd understanding of the business world, and unshakable integrity and honesty. Mirele brings misery to herself and her sons, however, by failing to understand human nature. Her lifelong need to dominate others blinds her to what is happening in her own household. When confronted, rather than truly responding and sharing, she simply—and foolishly—gives everything away.

Shaindel is as strong-willed as Mirele, but she is grossly lacking in Mirele's business sense, discipline, and integrity. She does, however, understand people and their motivations much better than does Mirele, and this gives her the upper hand over the Efros family. Shaindel, who resents her mother-in-law's hold over her sons, manipulates herself into power and tries to engineer the estrangement of mother and son. Shaindel's own mother is not nearly as perceptive as her daughter. Ambitious and grasping, she is not only strong-willed but stupidly demanding. Envying the prestige and the possessions of women like Mirele, she has no idea that refinement, not just wealth, is part of what makes them what they are. Vulgar, loud-mouthed women like Shaindel's mother were staple characters on the Yiddish stage, where their presence was often balanced, as in *Mirele Efros*, by making them foils for women far more appealing and dignified.

Ironically, while all of these types of literary and cinematic Jewish women reappeared on the American scene, for a time the typical portrait of the Jewish woman was closer to that of Machle. Quiet and gentle, Machle is selflessly devoted to her friend Mirele. She asks nothing for herself and thinks only of the good of the people around her. Although she lacks Mirele's brilliance, Machle often surpasses her friend in innate understanding of and responsiveness to other human beings. She, not Mirele, is able to put herself into the psychological mind-set of another and to make adjustments and accommodations based on this knowledge of the heart.

Unlike the sensitive and nuanced portrayals of Jewish women in Gordin's *Mirele Efros*, in the decades following his film flatly stereotypical images of Jewish women were promulgated and popularized by novelists, filmmakers, television producers, and other molders of the American imagination. A disproportionately large number of the persons who have brought publicized images of Jewish women are Jewish men, who often seem to be "working out" their own ambivalent feelings toward Judaism. Portrayals of the so-called Jewish

American Princess and of the Jewish mother abound in highly successful books and films by men such as Herman Wouk, Philip Roth, and Woody Allen. The names Marjorie Morningstar and Mrs. Portnoy are synonymous in the popular imagination with negative images of strong Jewish women, and the name Annie Hall evokes the image of the dizzy but delectable non-Jewish female. American Jewish writers at midcentury described controlling mothers and young women whose parents were grooming them to fit into upper-middle-class American norms as they saw them. While some Jewish writers satirize Jewish men as well, depicting a variety of vulgar, aggressive, materialistic Jewish males, their discomfort with Jewish family life is more often channeled into negative depictions of Jewish women.

The publication of Herman Wouk's *Marjorie Morningstar* in 1955 and the release of the film of the same name in 1958 can be seen as watersheds in the public image of American Jewish women, as they were among the first popular books and films to depict the character of the upwardly mobile Jewish daughter and her mother. Within the novel, a bohemian, mediocre dramatist and musician, Noel Airman, whose ambivalent feelings about Jewish life have led him to discard his identifiably Jewish given name of Neal Ehrman, describes what would later be called the "JAP" stereotype to the young and inexperienced Marjorie early in the novel, under the generic name of Shirley. The youthful appearance, lighthearted personality, and ostensible career aspirations of unmarried Jewish women are all a fraud, Airman insists, because they are really pursuing what women have always wanted "and always will—big diamond engagement ring, house in a good neighborhood, furniture, children, well-made clothes, furs." Behind the pretty faces of young Jewish women—all "Shirley"—the images of their mothers—"coarsened, fattened, wrinkled"—come "jutting through," frightening the prospective suitor with a grotesque picture of Jewish womanhood.[7]

Presented with a picture of themselves as despicably materialistic Jewish-mothers-in-training, Jewish female characters learn to dislike their mothers and those aspects of themselves that remind them of their mothers. With uncanny accuracy, Herman Wouk shows the reader how Jewish women absorb and internalize such critiques. As Marjorie Morningstar is finally walking down the aisle to marry a man with whom she shares a reciprocal, mature love relationship, she catches sight of Noel Airman's face. Suddenly, she feels as though someone has slid green theater lights in front of the scene, and she sees her own wedding as her enemies might see it. Rather than observing her own serene joy, her fiancé's profound feeling for her, her parent's exuberant rejoicing—all of which Wouk wrote into the scene as well—Marjorie for a time sees only the ostentatious materialism of the wedding celebration. Noel's attitudes toward "Shirley" alienate Marjorie from herself for a time. She loses sight of the deep inner realities that are shaping her life. Marjorie becomes her own enemy.[8]

Four years later, Philip Roth's *Goodbye, Columbus*[9] presented even more unpleasant pictures of women interacting in an upper-middle-class Jewish family. In the film, perhaps even more explicitly than in the novella, Roth pillories Jewish women as the embodiment of crass materialism, philistinism, and manipulative behavior. Moreover, the three Patimkin women—Brenda, her mother, and her younger sister—are consistently presented within the novella and film as at war with each other. In memorable vignettes, Mrs. Patimkin expresses her hatred and resentment of her blooming eldest daughter, and Brenda expresses her anger and resentment against both her mother and her younger sister, Julie. The envy and competitive spirit that these women exhibit in their relationships with each other is nowhere balanced by any display of affection, kindness, or admiration.

With this film and its preceding story, negative images of the Jewish woman were fixed forever in the American Jewish psyche. Who would want to be a Jewish woman, *Goodbye, Columbus* seemed to ask, if she were spoiled and controlling, if she imagined that any unpleasantness or inconvenience to her could be fixed, if she were totally dependent economically and totally manipulated by her loyalty to her family and their materialistic values despite a shallow veneer of sophistication? The notorious JAP image of the wealthy young Jewish woman lingered and lives on in films such as *The Heartbreak Kid*, *Private Benjamin*, *Dirty Dancing*, and many others.

Jewish mothers were viciously satirized in the post–World War II decades, an epoch when psychiatrists advised women that the only road to feminine fulfillment and happiness was acceptance of a submissive and supportive role, and Jewish male writers often portrayed Jewish women in a distorted mirror image of social norms. In novels such as Roth's *Portnoy's Complaint*,[10] fictional Jewish women tried to conquer their families, and they used food, hygiene, and guilt as weapons of domination. Although fear and loathing of the domineering mother began as a culture-wide trend, it soon became highly associated with the Jewish mother in particular. The Jewish mother, like the Jewish American princess, became a staple of American fiction, film, and humor. The cartoon figure of the omniscient, omnipotent Jewish mother—floating, like the Jewish mother's gigantic, disembodied head in Woody Allen's film *Oedipus Wrecks*—has enjoyed an amazingly long shelf life in the popular imagination. The overbearing Jewish matron, which absorbs the whiny demands and materialism of the JAP as well, endures in films such as *Ruthless People*, *Down and Out in Beverly Hills*, and *Scenes from a Mall*, among others.

Nevertheless, some contemporary male Jewish authors have transcended stereotypes of Jewish women. Neil Simon's *Brighton Beach Memoirs* very effectively focuses on the relationship between two sets of sisters. Simon's play and film comprise one of the most lucid depictions of a secularized traditional Jewish family available to modern audiences. Although references to Jewish

GC·85·4-102

"The classiest affair of the year" is not what Philip Roth's hero of
Goodbye, Columbus experiences when the Patimkin clan marry their son
off in ostentatiously vulgar style; this can all be his, along with beautiful
Brenda Patimkin, in the gilded ghetto of the 1940s upper-middle-class
suburbanized American Jewish world. (Copyright © 1969 by Paramount
Pictures Corporation. Photo courtesy of The Museum of Modern Art
Film Stills Archive, New York City.)

religious ritual are almost totally absent from the film, the values espoused—
and lived by—are almost a textbook presentation of traditional Jewish family
qualities. Both parents in the Jerome family are strong, caring, compassionate
people who see themselves primarily in relationship to their responsibility to
other family members and ultimately to the family unit as an organic whole.
They care for, counsel, and support not only their own children but Mrs.

Jerome's widowed sister and her two daughters as well, almost without complaint. Kate Jerome crisply advises her husband, when he wearily asks, "When do things get any easier?": "When you get seven good hours sleep a night, that's as easy as it gets."

The gendered division of parental attitudes and behaviors in the Jerome family precisely illustrates the way American Jewish families adapted historical Jewish gender roles to American society. Like many American Jews in the late 1930s, Kate and Jack Jerome have thoroughly absorbed the American attitude that it is better for a man to work two jobs, day and night, than for married females to assume paid employment. Because they have assumed responsibility for Kate's widowed sister and her two daughters, Jack Jerome works in the garment industry during the daytime and takes a variety of night jobs.

It is Kate Jerome who confronts the often irritating and sometimes terrifying intricacies of daily life. Tall, lean, pragmatic Kate Jerome has been the responsible and hardworking sibling ever since childhood. She deals with responsibilities that might overwhelm another woman by adhering to two principles: First, she never worries about eventualities but instead deals swiftly and effectively with each day's trials—"I can't deal with boats that haven't landed yet," she declares. Second, she tries to maintain an iron control over every aspect of her household that fate allows her to control.

There are many things Kate Jerome cannot control. She cannot control illness and death. Her brother-in-law, David Morton, died at thirty-six, leaving a timid, asthmatic wife and two young daughters, one of whom has a defective heart. The pretty but frail and disorganized Blanche, whom Kate resented mightily as they grew up, has now once again become her responsibility. Kate cannot control the Depression and its accompanying poverty. Putting dinner for seven hungry people on the table every night is a challenge with their limited budget. Kate is also limited by her own nature, by an emotional restraint or repression that seems almost physical at times. When her son Stanley returns after a long, tense absence, and the viewer knows her to be relieved and joyous, her face shows nothing. Instead, she suddenly declares that she must make a chocolate cake, and she imperiously dispatches Eugene to Gottleib's grocery store for an unheard of luxury—two pounds of sugar.

But behind Kate's dry, controlled exterior glints an affectionate and generous woman. Sitting in the bathroom, talking to her husband Jack as he shaves, she turns a face of pure, adoring love to him. Bullying her two sons, her pleasure in their health and sweetness sometimes breaks through despite herself. And when the boat with a half-dozen more relatives finally lands, she unstintingly offers her own home to them. "We'll put beds in the dining room," she says happily. "I like to eat in the kitchen." She shares a value system with her husband, and they are partners not only in personal affection but also in their care for the family members for whom they believe fate has made them responsible. Their affection for each other is increased by the kindness and generosity each sees his/her spouse showing to other family members.

Neil Simon underscores the theme of sibling rivalry and diversity among female family members by placing an older sibling who has made sacrifices for a younger one in each nuclear family unit. Nora Morton feels angry and unloved because her mother lavishes concern and affection on her sick young sister. She sometimes wishes she were stricken with polio so that her mother would cuddle and pamper her. Nora tries to force her mother to really be a parent and to fully empathize with her. When Blanche seems incapable of the kind of mothering Nora feels she needs, she punitively turns away from her mother in an hour of need. Kate Jerome vividly remembers the dresses she went without and the beatings she absorbed for things the younger Blanche did, and she cannot forgive Blanche for being younger and more indulged. Blanche, on the other hand, is intimidated by her older sister; she both envies and resents Kate's energy and competence. She must learn from her older daughter's struggles for separation and individuation how to confront her own personal strengths and weaknesses.

Relationships between Jewish women have found increasingly nuanced portrayals over the past three decades with the emergence of increasing numbers of female poets, novelists, and screenwriters. Interrelated historical and social trends having to do with both femaleness and Jewishness have come together to give Jewish women psychological permission and economic support to pursue their own unique visions. Some contributory trends include the emergence of feminism and Jewish feminism in the 1960s and 1970s, the discovery that "women's" fiction and films have a paying audience, the rise of ethnic distinctiveness as a societally approved artistic stance, and a new, widespread fascination with religious themes and spirituality.

Works by writers such as Cynthia Ozick, Rebecca Goldstein, Grace Paley, Anne Roiphe, Vivian Gornick, Tova Reich, Sylvia Rothchild, E. M. Broner, Daphne Merkin, Johanna Kaplan, Norma Rosen, Nessa Rapaport, Allegra Goodman, Lynne Sharon Schwartz, and Gloria Goldreich; poetry by Adrienne Rich, Marge Piercey, Irena Klepficz, and Marcia Falk; films shaped by Joan Micklin Silver, Barbra Streisand, Nora Ephron, and Pamela Berger, among many other artists, are presenting to their reading and viewing audiences very different images of Jewish women and the ways in which they relate to each other. They are, to use Adrienne Rich's useful phrase, *revisioning* Jewish women.

These contemporary writers revision the images of Jewish American women not by producing propaganda in the form of heroic, larger-than-life female figures but instead by creating complicated, struggling, multifaceted female characters. They articulate the inner struggles of Jewish women, caught between the demands of mind and body, family and self, science and spiritualism, Judaism and secular Western humanism. They illuminate the strange twists and turns that test and delineate the hearts and lives of human beings, women as well as men. In fiction and films created by Jewish women, women are not accessories to the internal dramas of male characters, as they have been for so much of literary history; their female characters wrestle with their own demons.

Not infrequently, however, the special set of demons that test women and turn women against each other emerge from the stereotypes that men have promulgated about women. One common pattern, which goes back at least to immigrant fiction but is no less common today, depicts a woman whose entire life proceeds in reaction to her mother. Obsessed by the idea that she does not want to repeat her mother's mistakes, the daughter never truly achieves independence from the past. For women who derive from distinctive ethnic groups, especially those with strong hierarchical traditions, such as traditional Jewish, Chinese, and Japanese societies, the stakes in the conflict between mothers and daughters are complicated even beyond their general psychological import. Partially because of the high cultural stakes of the struggle between American Jewish parents and their offspring, in American Jewish literature anger is a freely expressed emotion. Starting with mother-daughter relationships in the literature of Yezierska and Olsen and moving forward to works by Piercy, Gornick, Goldstein, Schwartz, Broner, Chernin, and Roiphe, among others, one repeatedly finds mothers and daughters confronting each other.

A world of such women is evoked in Vivian Gornick's memoir, *Fierce Attachments*, which focuses on thwarted women who turn inward, blighting the lives of subsequent generations of women. The Bronx apartment of the protagonist's youth is a rich and colorful world of women, in which her mother is powerful—and yet bitterly aware that she is removed from the patriarchal power structure of the world of work. The Bronx women send mixed messages about the world of men and work to the protagonist as she grows up: men are longed for, hated, admired, and disdained. Concomitantly, the women's ghetto in the apartment building is both safe and threatening, sometimes shimmering with lesbian overtones, sometimes as claustrophobic as the grave. It partakes of the characteristics of a literary community of women as described by Nina Auerbach, in that it is a kind of matriarchal society that both empowers women yet blocks the progress of young women toward independence and maturity in an outside world that is, finally, both patriarchal and heterosexual.[11]

Gornick's protagonist is obsessed by her mother and by the past partially because her mother withdrew from appropriate nurturing during a pathologically extended period of grieving for her dead husband. As an adolescent, Gornick's protagonist becomes convinced that she can keep her mother alive and functioning only through the sheer strength of her presence and her will. Mothers can withdraw from their daughters for other reasons, as Daphne

Merkin illustrates in her novel *Enchantment*. In Merkin's novel, Hannah Lehman grows up in an affluent German-Jewish Orthodox home on New York's Upper West Side. In contrast with the more familiar stereotype of the "smothering" Jewish mother, Hannah feels that her mother ignores her. Both infatuated with her mother—enchanted—and alienated from her, Hannah finds that all her subsequent relationships are disturbed. Her mother's emotional withdrawal controls Hannah's life just as surely as another mother's direct manipulation.[12]

Mothers can change beyond recognition and seemingly abandon their children for less pathological reasons as well. The sudden escalation of a mother's employment outside the home can be experienced by her children as abandonment; the mother may be perceived as "a different person" from the domestic creature of earlier years. Nora Ephron's film *This Is My Life* presents dramatic career changes as they are experienced by a Jewish single mother, Dottie Engels, and her two daughters. Dottie's meteoric rise as a professional comedienne after sixteen domestic years is exhilarating for her but miserable for her children. "Children are happy when their mother is happy," sagely advises Dottie's agent and first sex partner in years. "No they're not," Dottie says honestly. "Everyone says that, but it's not true. Children are happy when you're there."

Many viewers would recognize as "Jewish" Dottie's personal style and humor. Her daughter begins to find Dottie unacceptably loud and flamboyant. The teenager blames her mother bitterly for what she believes to be selfishness, immaturity, exhibitionism, and inappropriate sexual involvement. It is only when the teenage girl herself becomes involved sexually with a classmate that she is able to evaluate realistically the biological father who abandoned her, her mother, and her sister. She is shocked that her father has remarried a kind but resoundingly nonintellectual, nonhumorous non-Jewish woman; she is angered by the ugly comments he makes about the vibrant and talented Dottie. When her younger sister unwillingly blurts out the comments her father flung at the two little girls when he first left them, a memory she has suppressed, the adolescent daughter is overwhelmed. "He said we would be frigid, like Mom," she remembers. "Frigid means cold in bed. Maybe she was—with him! Who wouldn't be, with him?" Because she herself has come a long way toward womanhood, she is able to understand the enormity of what marriage can mean to a woman whose husband undermines her self-esteem, who despises her for her own best qualities. Woman to woman, she now feels understanding, compassion, and sisterhood for her mother.

In the film each major new scene begins with a voiceover by the elder daughter and then continues in the voice of the mother. The overlapping voices seem to ask, "Whose life is this, anyway?" "This is *my* life," the elder daughter seems to be insisting. "I have talents no one recognizes, I am often shy and awkward, I have a mother who might cause me terminal embarrassment at any moment. And now she's never home. All she seems to care about is herself, and when I need her, she's either not here or she's thinking about something else. She has a responsibility to her children." At the same time, Dottie Engels seems to be saying, "This is *my* life. For sixteen years I was the perfect mother, staying home and taking care of my brood. I had no help, I was alone, and I had talents nobody outside my home recognized. I often felt awkward in new situations. But this is the only life I've got. This is my only opportunity to see how far I can go with the resources I've been given. I have a responsibility to myself."

This Is My Life is one of several in a new genre of films that attempt to honestly confront conflicts in the lives of daughters and mothers, when mothers try to juggle not only conflicting lives but conflicting moral demands as well. When people live together in a family, their lives impinge on each other. No family member can truly say, "This is my life," and imagine that the lives of others are not profoundly affected by his or her decisions and actions. When mothers routinely remained at home to care for children and households, they were sometimes able to mediate between family members and to pick up the pieces when necessary so that one person's self-development didn't create chaos for another. However, films such as *This Is My Life* reflect the social reality that many of today's mothers are themselves pursuing paychecks and/or self-development in careers outside the home. As the film demonstrates, not only are such mothers often not around to pick up the pieces of other people's lives, their own activities sometimes generate anxiety or chaos.

While every daughter is convinced that she thinks she wants to live her own life, literature and films reveal that daughters are less sure of how they ought to relate to their mothers' choices and destinies. Daughters are frequently distressed by the shadow that the mother's fate seems to cast over their own future. For example, daughters in many pieces of recent American Jewish fiction observe their mothers being neglected or abandoned, and their first impulses are to blame the mother for "provoking" mistreatment and to distance themselves from the mother's fate by showing how "different" they are from their mothers. Sometimes the intelligent, ambitious daughter feels that she has more in common with her father than with her mother; it is the father who is the kindred spirit. This alliance between father and daughter can leave the mother feeling displaced and alienated from her daughter's love when the daughter moves beyond the need for simple nurture.[13] In Grace Paley's short story, "Dreamers in a Dead Language," the protagonist identifies strongly with her father until life circumstances thrust gender bonds on her and she finds herself identifying with her mother. Among the many authors who are especially interested in the ways in which women relate to each other as they struggle with life, Paley stands out for her sustained interest and the subtlety of her understanding and portrayals of female friendships.[14]

In some American Jewish fiction, daughters distance themselves from their Jewish mothers and their unwished for characteristics or experiences by marrying or becoming sexually involved with partners overtly quite different than the man who married—and then neglected or abandoned—mother. Anne Roiphe, in *Lovingkindness*, makes the Jewish import of these emotional currents between mother and daughter explicit.[15] Roiphe expands the reactive mother-daughter pattern to three generations: the grandmother, a wealthy, heavily made-up, card-playing, dependent, and conventionally Jewish woman whose husband cheats on her; the mother, Annie, an independent, intellectual, assimilated woman who marries a non-Jew to escape the same fate her mother suffered; and the disturbed granddaughter, Andrea, an emotionally fragile girl who goes from a punk life-style to extreme religiosity in Yeshiva Rachel, a girl's school that educates and indoctrinates "born-again" Jews in Jerusalem, to escape her own mother's values system and behavior.

Even women's ability to love and nurture each other is sometimes feared and demeaned by male characters. In Cynthia Ozick's *The Cannibal Galaxy*, the male protagonist of the novel is convinced that most women are frenzied creatures carried along by hormonal floods. In Brill's view, it is women's very tendency to be relational, to care about and often to define themselves in terms of human relationships, that makes them inferior. Lilt, however, is rational, honest, and direct; Brill decides that any woman with these "masculine" qualities of mind cannot have the same passion for her child as the typical "inferior" maternal type of woman. Brill muses: "It was strange to think she had a child. Profoundly, illimitably, he knew the mothers; she was not like any of them. The unselfconscious inexorable secretion ran in all of them. From morning to night they were hurtled forward by the explosions of their own internal rivers, with their roar of force and pressure. The mothers were rafts on their own instinctual flood. . . . That was why they lived and how; to make a roiling moat around their offspring. . . . they were in the pinch of nature's vise."[16]

Ozick shows the reader that a woman can be both brilliantly logical and passionately maternal, but society is more likely to punish than reward her rich spectrum of talents. A male-authored society is likely to feel much more comfortable dividing human beings into those who are driven by physical or by intellectual impulses and relegating women, by and large, into the first category.

The need that many men have to divide humanity into mind and body, and the destructive ways in which women have internalized these false dichotomies, are a recurring theme in the fiction of Rebecca Goldstein. In Goldstein's novel *The Mind-Body Problem*, the protagonist, Renee Feuer, pursuing a Ph.D. in philosophy at Princeton University, feels that her mother had always viewed her intellectualism as an impediment to happiness.[17] But it is not only Renee's Orthodox mother who delegitimates the integration of female physical and intellectual capacities. Renee's best friend from undergraduate days at

Barnard, a fiercely antireligious physicist named Ava, is convinced that she must make herself both androgynous and ugly to be taken seriously by herself and others as an intellectual.[18]

Squeamishness about one's own female, physical nature, to the point of outright denial, is carried even further in Goldstein's novel *The Dark Sister*, in which the Jewish female protagonist is brilliant and talented but retreats from her own physicalness and looks and behaves like an all-mind golem. A huge, hulking reclusive, almost sexless creature, Hedda (head-a?) has adopted the nom de plume Dunkele, Yiddish for "little dark one," her mother's pet name for her. Goldstein draws the reader into the novel as a collaborator and co-conspirator by making the reader more aware of what is motivating Hedda and her literary creations than is Hedda herself. Hedda suffers from what she recalls as her mother's rejection of her, and she despises the sister Stella, who seems to embody all the physical, flamboyant tendencies that Hedda imagines are lacking in herself. Hedda's mother and her sister—and the pieces of herself—whom she fears and suppresses, hover dangerously over Hedda's life.

Goldstein's fiction often illuminates the way in which women in general and Jewish women in particular can be alienated from each other and from their inner selves and can use their own negative feelings about being females as weapons against each other. Women reject themselves and other women if they feel that they are unacceptably intellectual, artistic, scientific, mystical, violent, angry, or nonmaternal—any of these pieces of themselves can potentially be viewed as "other." When they acknowledge these pieces of themselves, women sometimes feel like "monsters" (as in Adrienne Rich's poem, "Planetarium," in which a female astronomer sees a sky full of female monsters—brilliant, creative women who have been made to feel monstrous because of their talents and their intellectual energy). Women have been manipulated by society to reject intrinsic aspects of their personhood, doing irrevocable damage to each other and to their own mental health and productivity and self-esteem. In different societies the objectional—or monstrous—portions of the female psyche change, but the dynamics of creating and rejecting a "dark sister" remains the same.

Hedda's rejection in her novels of the image of the JAP, the Jewish American princess, seems healthy. Hedda has produced instead a series of novels featuring JAWs—the "Jewish angry woman." Their titles and some details of their action enable Goldstein to satirize not only male misogynist stereotypes but also feminist stereotypes, which are also based in misogyny because they require women to deny aspects of themselves. The protagonists of Hedda's books are "fierce but beautiful JAWs" who appeal not only to feminists but also, unaccountably (to Hedda), to "an untallied number of unregenerate pigs." Thus, Hedda's successful books include *Etta, the Rebbe's Daughter!*; *Hanna, the Husband's Whore!*; *Sara, the Savant's Sister!*; *Mona, the Momzer's*

Mother!; *Minna, the Messiah's Mother-in-Law!*; *Clara, the Corporate Korva!*; *Dora, the Doctor's Daughter!*[19]

Hedda knows that, for Jewish women, an additional layer of potential self-rejection often exists, in which perceptions of monstrousness have a distinctly Jewish flavor. Goldstein's having her protagonist Hedda create a series of Jewish angry women who react to rejection by fighting back may seem to many readers a particularly Jewish female response; one might think, for example, of contemporary Jewish comediennes such as Joan Rivers, Roseanne Barr, and Bette Midler, who have made anger or at least in-your-face assertiveness part of their professional repertoire.

It would be a mistake to gather that conflict is the only relationship between women currently portrayed in female-authored and/or -produced fiction and film. On the contrary, many recent works depict powerful supportive and nurturing female-female relationships. Sylvia Rothchild's *Family Stories for Every Generation* often illuminate the ways in which women's relationships can change and grow, enabling mothers and daughters to reach new levels of understanding. Her portraits of Jewish women are especially moving when they work against the cultural norm of youth worship. One middle-aged daughter has mixed feelings about the inevitable changes that life brings. As she negotiates her mother's kitchen—a scene fraught with emotional import in much Jewish fiction—she realizes that, despite decline, maturity has its rewards. No longer does her own self-respect hang tenuously on her ability to tell her mother what she is doing "wrong." Now that she is a woman of a certain age, she sees that she has enough sense of herself that she no longer needs to correct her aging mother's imperfections.[20]

The aging Jewish woman and her interaction with younger Jewish women is the unexpected subject of some contemporary works; in some, the relationship of women draws heavily on patterns of female interaction gleaned and adapted from the past. One such work is Joan Micklin Silver's *Crossing Delancey*, which focuses on the power of female-female relationships even where male-female romance is involved. Like Jewish female novelists, Jewish female filmmakers often enjoy turning stereotypes on their heads. In *Crossing Delancey*, Silver captures the contemporary societal yearning toward family and stability, juxtaposed with an individualist yearning toward spirituality, spontaneity, and intellectualism, and the way in which women can be caught in the middle. The heroine, named Izzy, is a sensitive, literary, lonely young woman who imagines that literary fame and artistic excellence are the best qualifications in a lover. When Izzy's grandmother and Mrs. Mandlebaum, a Lower East Side matchmaker, arrange a meeting between Izzy and Sam, a gentle young pickle manufacturer, Izzy protests with mighty feminist indignation: "Bohbe, this is not my life. This is a hundred years ago! I have plenty of friends, tremendous women who are doing wonderful things with their lives. I don't need a man to fill my life with meaning."

In *Crossing Delancey* a manipulative grandmother, Bohbe (Reizl Bozyk), and meddling matchmaker (Sylvia Miles), break all contemporary rules of political correctness as they harass Izzy (Amy Irving) into dating the man of their choice. The older generation's tricks—and wisdom—prevail, as Irving discovers that gentle, traditional Sam "the pickle man" really may be the ideal mate for a feminist heroine. (Copyright © 1988 Warner Bros. Inc. Photo courtesy The Museum of Modern Art Film Stills Archive, New York City)

In the brave new world of feminist individualism, exemplified by Jill Clayburgh in *An Unmarried Woman*, this I-don't-need-anybody-but-myself sentiment was the punchline of the entire film. But Izzy's female friends, in contrast, want companionship, community, and family as well as careers. They have discovered that life is complicated and their desires are diverse. One direct, outspoken friend declares openly that she is looking for a sweet, old-fashioned boy. To her, the pickle man looks like the ideal candidate. Another friend tires of waiting for an appropriate husband, has a child out of wedlock, and invites all her friends and family to the traditional *brit milah* (circumcision ceremony).

Izzy is not as much of a feminist as she thinks she is, and she has very little honest insight into her own romantic choices. She is infatuated with a man who looks like the Prince Charming of every nonfeminist fairy tale: a tall, handsome, fair-haired writer, a man whose Aryan lineage is only slightly more striking than his narcissism. Izzy looks to her exotic Prince Charming writer to redeem the dreariness of her life, although she would never admit to this motivation. But the prince's romantic love proves disappointing, shallow, and most exploitative. Sam the pickle man, on the other hand, is a caring, sensitive, nonauthoritarian and nonexploitative male who respects women of all ages— he even does an old lady's windows.

In *Crossing Delancey*, Izzy would never have discovered Sam's tender sexuality, his strength of character, his innate dignity, if her grandmother and an aged matchmaker didn't follow an older, interventionist model of female-female relationships, such as that often exhibited by mothers, nurses, crones, and witches in older literature and folklore. They break all the rules of contemporary relationships by mixing in, by telling Izzy what she should do, by pushing, lying, and manipulating. The aggressive behavior of two Jewish old women leads to the ingenue's ultimate happiness. Thus, the movie not only legitimates the elderly Jewish women—unlikely heroines indeed—it also legitimates historical patterns in the ways in which older and younger women relate to each other.

Fiction and film over the past three decades differs from that of previous eras in the self-consciousness of its focus. Purposively focusing on relational dynamics between women, recent works explore the ways in which women define their lives by competing with and/or nurturing each other, by growing and revising their ways of understanding each other and their relationships. When female characters analyze the ways in which they feel about and relate to each other, these works indicate, they better understand themselves and their feelings about themselves as well.

One of the most touching paradigms of the necessity for Jewish women to accept the other women who give shape to their lives in order that they may accept themselves is found in Lynne Sharon Schwartz's recent novel, *Leaving Brooklyn*. For much of the book, the protagonist, Audrey, is fifteen years old and is having a sexual affair with a Manhattan ophthalmologist to whom her mother has sent her to correct a congenitally wayward eye. Audrey thoroughly enjoys the "voluptuous, atavistic, outrageous, and above all delicate circumstances" that led her to be seduced by an adult caregiver to whom her mother has entrusted her. At the same time, Audrey unfairly blames her mother for being careless, or uncaring, enough to let her eye get damaged in the first place and then careless or uncaring enough to send her to the seductive physician; she also blames her mother for being too staid, conventional, careful, proper— too "Brooklyn"—for Audrey's creative instincts. Audrey rejects and is furious with her mother for being too protective and for not being protective enough.

Audrey imagines—and her affair with the doctor helps her believe—that she is different from her parents and all they seem to represent. However, at the end of the book, Audrey discovers that her parents and their friends have a

fierce and courageous inner life that involves a vibrant, liberal, risk-taking political activism. As her "mother fetched the coffee pot and poured seconds
while they all argued about Roosevelt," Audrey discovers that "there is life in
Brooklyn. Passion. Conflict. Thought. An ample scene for both my eyes."

With this discovery, Audrey is ready to face the fact that the adventurous-
ness she treasures was part of lower-middle-class Jewish Brooklyn before she
was, and that lower-middle-class Jewish Brooklyn will be part of her heritage
forever. This realization frees her to accept herself at last and to pursue her
own destiny with confidence and understanding. She is not freed from conflict
and struggle, for they are a part of life and self. Thus, she comments, "I left
Brooklyn. I leave still, every moment. For no matter how much I leave, it
doesn't leave me." But she is, finally, accepting of and thus true to all the diverse pieces of herself.[21]

Living in a society that stresses separation and individuation and coming
from a tradition that prescribes intense familial relationships, American Jewish
women have often felt that they are receiving very mixed messages indeed.
Fiction and films by contemporary Jewish women writers often present female
protagonists who struggle with these mixed messages. Such characters yearn
for independence yet for closeness to others. They strive for Americanization
yet are drawn to Jewish distinctiveness. As they struggle to make sense of their
lives, they often project pieces of themselves onto the women around them:
thus, we frequently see a female protagonist who believes she can be secular,
free, and urban only if her female relative or friend balances her by being Jewish, burdened, and provincial. When the protagonist can stop resenting other
women for being what they are, when she can cease envisioning other women
as demonized alternative selves, when she can accept the fact that other
women too have (and have a right to have) some qualities to which she herself
aspires, when she can see that she herself has at least occasional leanings toward a less culturally approved life-style, then she is ready to come to terms
with others and herself.

By revisioning reactions to female friends, as well as mothers, sisters,
cousins, and aunts, female characters are enabled to revision, accept, and integrate diverse pieces of themselves. In much contemporary American Jewish
fiction and film, when women come to terms with each other, they come to
terms with the integrity of their own lives. Separation may promise to make
them free, but only relation can make them whole.

Felicia Herman

The Way She *Really* Is
Images of Jews and Women in the
Films of Barbra Streisand

America's newest Graccland has just opened. The new shrine, however, is devoted not to Elvis Presley but rather to a figure who, with the exception of her choice of careers, is in many ways Presley's polar opposite. Hello, Gorgeous!!, a museum/store centrally located in the predominantly gay Castro district of San Francisco, celebrates the career of Barbra Streisand, the liberal, feminist, Jewish actor/singer/director from New York. The museum's creator, Ken Joachim, says that he felt inspired by the notion that his life, especially his oppression as a gay man, was "very parallel" to Streisand's. Streisand's appeal, Joachim suggests, derives not only from her creative talents but also from what journalist Carcy Goldberg describes as "the adversity and prejudice she had faced down from all the people who had said she was not pretty enough or white-bread enough or able enough to succeed."[1]

Even as Joachim was putting the finishing touches on his museum, Streisand was being feted back in New York in a different way. In an exhibition at the Jewish Museum titled "Too Jewish?" wherein contemporary young Jewish artists explored the concept of being "too Jewish" in America, images of Barbra Streisand were in abundance. In *Four Barbras*, for example, artist Deborah Kass repeatedly silkscreened Streisand's profile (with its prominent proboscis) in a parody of Andy Warhol's portrait of Jacqueline Kennedy Onassis. In *Barbra Bush*, Rhonda Lieberman decorated a fake Christmas tree with Barbra Streisand ornaments. Even the cover of the exhibition catalog was festooned with Streisand's image, this time as the yeshiva girl in drag, Yentl.[2] Streisand, the exhibition implied, is the archetypal "too Jewish" American Jew.

Streisand's first film, *Funny Girl* (1968),[3] in which she played comedian Fanny Brice, established what came to be a filmic alter ego for her: the wisecracking, loud-mouthed Jewish—or sometimes unspecified New York "ethnic"—woman.[4] Her emergence in the late 1960s has been called a watershed in Jewish film history, the first time in decades that a Jew appeared on-screen with unapologetically Jewish features, an unchanged Jewish name, and unmistakably "Jewish" mannerisms. Praise resembling that of Rabbi Chaim Seidler-Feller has echoed throughout the American Jewish community from the time of *Funny Girl*'s release until today: "Streisand was a Jew, is a Jew and will always be a Jew. Her sense of self and commitment always drew on her essential Jewishness. Never was there an effort to deny it, and when opportunities arose to affirm, she pursued them."[5]

Jewish feminists have joined in the adulation of Streisand, praising her characters for their strong-willed toughness and their espousal of feminist precepts. Letty Cottin Pogrebin labels Streisand's most famous character type the "Jewish Big Mouth," arguing that it has offered the best image of Jewish women on film screens up to now: "the character of the clever, outspoken Jewish girl has become a film convention that empowers every woman. Most important, films portraying the Ugly Duckling who rises above her appearance have assured girls with big noses and frizzy hair that they too can invent their own kind of terrific and leave Miss America in the dust."[6] Similarly, Anne Roiphe has suggested that "Barbra Streisand made it possible for Jewish girls to feel beautiful,"[7] and Marcy Sheiner, in a recent article in the Jewish feminist periodical *Lilith*, remembers that "in a landscape devoid of young Jewish girls, Barbra Streisand served as a needed reference point that finally validated my looks. . . . [B]y shoving a Jewish girl's face in front of the cameras she was announcing, beneath all the self-deprecation, *I'm here, I'm a bagel, and you're gonna learn to love me.*"[8]

Streisand's ability to be unapologetically Jewish and wildly famous at the same time is due, in large part, to the effects of the countercultural movements of the 1960s and 1970s, which sanctioned overt ethnicity as a form of revolt against the white, male, Anglo-Saxon Protestant ruling elite. Aggressively ethnic figures such as Streisand were accepted as part of the rebellion against the homogenized WASP norm of the 1940s, 1950s, and early 1960s, which had been as hegemonic in film as it had been in society. Streisand's characters appeared not to agree with previous generations of European and American Jews who, John Murray Cuddihy argues, believed that political emancipation was tied to social assimilation, that "access to the political *rights* of the *citoyen* hinge on [their] prior performance of the social *rites* of the *bourgeois*."[9] Instead, Streisand's characters maintain their identity by behaving in a particularly "Jewish," unmannered fashion. They "look Jewish" and "act Jewish," presenting Jewish identity in a positive way and refusing to submit to assimilationist pressures. Similarly, Streisand's nontraditional looks assert that even "If a Girl Isn't Pretty" (the first song in *Funny Girl*), she still deserves happiness. As

Fanny's mother asks, "Is a nose with deviation such a crime against the nation?" The film's answer, of course, is no. This attitude, combined with the characters' frequent and prominent espousal of feminist values, indicates that Streisand's films are intended to serve as criticisms of society's mistreatment of women as well. Her films thus function as a kind of social critique, protesting the mistreatment of Jews and women in mainstream American culture.

Yet the images of Jews and of women that arise from Streisand's films are significantly more complex than Jews and feminists have heretofore assumed. A closer examination of Streisand's most popular films reveals that as critiques of the status quo, they fall prey to several shortcomings.[10] Streisand's films present sentimentalized, reductive views of both Jews and women that neutralize their purported criticism of the hegemony of WASP culture and the predominance of sexism. Because her films are so nearly devoid of Jewish religious content, it is more appropriate to speak about their images of Jewish*ness* than of Juda*ism*. This Jewishness arises out of an idea, popularized in the interwar period in America, that Jewish identity encompassed more than religious observance and could, in fact, exist in the absence of religion. Second-generation American Jews adhered to this ideology religiously, as it were, believing that it was the most "modern" and "progressive" way to be Jewish in America.[11] Streisand's films, then, seem to be attempts to create this Jewishness on-screen, but they fall short even of this. Jewishness in Streisand's films seems confined at the most to a kind of secular liberalism or a "superior" morality that leaves no room for the particularism of Jewish experience, religious, cultural, or otherwise; at the least, Jewishness is equated only with stereotypical "Jewish" features and behaviors: a nose, an accent, a mention of a bagel.[12]

The films also subvert their own feminist messages.[13] They portray Streisand's characters as pure, long-suffering women with whom the audience cannot help but sympathize, thus oversimplifying sexist oppression and denying women their individuality and human complexity. And these are women who simply want to "make it in a man's world"; they do not call for the overthrow of the status quo but rather argue that women can exhibit the qualities that society most values and that it traditionally attributes to men. Though this itself is a kind of feminism, akin to what has been called liberal feminism,[14] the films cannot even sustain this most conservative of the feminist critiques of society. Instead, in each film, the Streisand character's feminism ultimately yields to the more important power of the traditional romance. Her characters suppress their own needs for those of their men and willingly trade in their independence and individuality to "get the guy." In almost every film under discussion here, this strategy ultimately fails: Streisand's characters are almost uniformly punished for their strong-willed behavior and/or for the success that has been the result of that behavior. Rather than celebrating feminism, these films first dilute it and then condemn it.

It is doubtful, of course, that any film seeking to undertake an in-depth treatment of either Jewish identity or feminism would enjoy wild success at the box office—or for that matter, would be produced at all. And Streisand's films have consistently targeted general moviegoing audiences rather than specific religious or political circles. With the possible exception of *Yentl*, they have never claimed to be serious investigations of the meaning of either Jewishness or feminism. Yet this acknowledgment of the power of the mass-media market does not release Streisand's films from criticism, for it is precisely their mass appeal—the powerful influence they exert over popular conceptions of Jews and feminists—that demands a close, rigorous examination of their specific interpretations of these two groups.

This essay focuses on five of Streisand's most popular films: *Funny Girl* (1968), *The Way We Were* (1973), *A Star Is Born* (1976), *The Main Event* (1979), and *Yentl* (1983). These are the films that critics laud most often for their admirable portrayals of Jews and women, and not coincidentally, they also constitute five of Streisand's seven highest-grossing films.[15] Their very popularity implies that these are the films that have made her a cultural icon and the films that audiences have most enjoyed. They seem, therefore, to be the perfect place to begin an exploration of the images of Jews, of women, and of Jewish women that Streisand's films present.[16]

Funny Girl

Streisand's portrayal of Fanny Brice in *Funny Girl*[17] catapulted her to national and eventually to international fame. Part of the reason for the film's and Streisand's success was the actor's seemingly intuitive ability to play Fanny. As producer Ray Stark commented, "the two personalities have come together. I don't know what is Barbra and what is Fannie [*sic*]."[18] And many Jewish women saw Streisand and Fanny as extensions of themselves as well, as Sheiner relates: "In my young mind, the experiences of Fanny Brice, Barbra Streisand and myself merged into one and the same story," the ugly Jewish duckling rebelliously triumphing over those who try to keep her down.[19]

The film chronicles Brice's life from her Henry Street beginnings to her celebrated role in the Ziegfeld Follies. There is no attempt to hide Fanny's ethnicity: the filmmakers employ cultural references to Brice's Jewishness throughout the film, as, for example, when Fanny uses the explanation "I'm a bagel on a plate full of onion rolls" to account for her value in a theatrical world where all the women look alike and none look like her, or when, to cover her uneasiness at Nick Arnstein's sexual advances, she responds with Yiddish-accented quips and the line "What a beast to ruin such a pearl—would a convent take a Jewish girl?"

Fanny's Jewishness, however, is a Jewishness devoid of religion. As one reviewer notes, even the re-creation of Jewish New York lacks religious content: "Push-cart Henry Street where Fanny was born, predominantly Yiddish in the 1910–20 era, in the film—while there were a couple of Yiddish-Hebrew store-signs—was peopled with non-Jews—only one beard, no *yarmulkes, sheitels,* frockcoats, etc. etc."[20] Fanny's Jewishness is also devoid of cultural content—there are no political or intellectual expressions of Jewishness, and for as much as Fanny and the other Jews speak with Yiddish accents, they surely do not seem to speak Yiddish. Instead, *Funny Girl* presents a nostalgic and sentimental view of the Lower East Side; its Henry Street is a sanitized, jovial ethnic utopia. There is no conflict among ethnic groups, and Irish and Jewish immigrants coexist peacefully, even gathering together for the poker game that takes place regularly in Fanny's mother's saloon. (In fact, the Irish women in the crowd are among the first to wish Fanny *mazel tov* when she receives a telegram from Florenz Ziegfeld inviting her to audition for him.)

Rather than acting as a religious or a cultural Jew, Fanny expresses her Jewish identity only through her looks and her ability to entertain. She employs her Jewishness as a vehicle for her comedy; Jewishness becomes reduced to a funny accent, a funny nose, and one-line quips. *Funny Girl*, for all that it has been hailed as a cinematic watershed for Jews, is not *about* Jewishness. The reduction of Jewishness to mostly physical qualities reduces the struggle for acceptance by Jews to the almost banal question of whether society can accept a woman who "looks Jewish" as beautiful. Though both Fanny's success in the film and the popularity of the film itself have been taken by some as a symbol of Jewish acceptance in America, the film so oversimplifies the meaning of Jewish "difference" that the real complexities of Jewish integration remain ignored.

Yet the question of Fanny's acceptance either as a Jew or as a girl who "isn't pretty" is not even the central focus of the film; the real center of the film is the question of whether Fanny's romance with gambler Nick Arnstein will succeed.[21] Fanny's success in her chosen career (despite her physical liabilities) is taken for granted and indeed is even made evident in the film's first scene, which takes place after Fanny has already become famous. Whether her marriage to Nick will succeed, however, remains unanswered until the film's conclusion. Fanny has little control over her relationship with Nick; his actions largely determine the course of their romance. After sweeping Fanny (a naive, poor girl from Henry Street) off her feet with his ruffled shirts and gentlemanliness, he abandons her for a year while he gambles around the world, leaving her to pine for him; when they meet again, he introduces her (still a naïf) to expensive food, lobster, and sex. They marry, but Nick cannot cope with Fanny's fame and resorts to various forms of fiscal malfeasance rather than allow her to help him out of a deepening financial hole.

The climax of the film is also left up to Nick. When Nick returns from a two-year stint in Sing-Sing for his illegal activities, it is he who will decide whether he and Fanny will remain together. Fanny has been waiting for him since the first scene of the film (the rest of the action occurs in flashback), making whatever professional success she may have achieved secondary to the question of whether Nick will take her back. She finally "chooses" to divorce him only after his demeanor indicates that *he* has already decided to divorce *her*. In a theme that recurs throughout most of her films, Streisand's character pays a heavy price for wanting more than the role traditionally allotted to women: she loses the man she loves. And because it is the love affair and not her career that has been the central force of the film, Fanny, at the film's conclusion, is a failure.

Yet critics typically view the last scene of the film, in which Fanny sings the song "My Man" alone on stage, as Fanny's triumphant expression of her faith in herself and in her ability to succeed without Nick. As Joseph Morgenstern writes in a 1970 *Newsweek* cover article on Streisand: "She started small, injured, all trembly-tearful as if there were nothing left to do with an old chestnut about a lovelorn lady. Before the end of the first chorus, however, her funny girl made a decision to sing herself back to life. Her voice soared defiantly, a spirit lost and found in the space of a few bars."[22] Pogrebin agrees with this interpretation: "When her guy is gone, [Fanny] has something left: [her] spectacular career. . . . The point is, when things don't work out [she] still knows who *she* is."[23] The visual clues of the scene add further support: Fanny is alone on stage, lit by a spotlight that makes her look more beautiful than ever, and, in Morgenstern's words, she ends by belting out the song "with the force of a mighty Wurlitzer."[24]

The actual lyrics of the song, however, belie the positive interpretation of *Funny Girl*'s conclusion. "My Man" is a song in which Fanny pledges herself to Nick. Even though he has shamed her, even though he has refused to accept her professional success as important or as a more legitimate way of supporting their family than his gambling, and even though he has, finally, left her, Fanny sings, "Whatever my man is, I am his, forever more." Thus viewers learn that romantic relationships are all-important, that no matter how poorly a man treats a woman, she should stay by his side, and that whatever success a woman may achieve on her own, she must subvert it to her romantic relationships if she wishes them to succeed.

Granted, *Funny Girl* made its appearance before America experienced the real impact of the so-called second wave of feminism. It does, however, establish a precedent for Streisand's later films, which, while purporting to project a feminist bent, prove to be little different in feminist content than her first.

The Way We Were

The Way We Were[25] is one of several Streisand films built around the idea of opposites—Jews and non-Jews—attracting. The film begins in 1944 Manhattan, when Katie Morosky (Streisand) sees Hubbell Gardiner (Robert Redford)

Katie (Streisand) and Hubbell (Redford) in Hubbell's screenwriting days, moments before they find out that their dinner party has been bugged by those looking for Communist sympathizers in Hollywood. Katie's hair is in its straight phase. To their left are Carol Ann (Lois Chiles) and J.J. (Bradford Dillman), friends from college. (Copyright © 1973 Columbia Pictures. Photo courtesy The Museum of Modern Art Film Stills Archive, New York City)

asleep in his Navy uniform at the El Morocco nightclub. Katie has a long flashback to her college days, when Hubbell, a blond, athletic, fraternity-boy WASP, played touch football on the college lawn while she, the frizzy-haired, ardent, Jewish president of the Young Communist League, mimeographed leaflets protesting Franco's role in the Spanish civil war. While he engaged in fraternity pranks, she met with professors. While Hubbell and his friends planned the senior prom, Katie, a waitress, served them sodas.

After the film returns to 1944, Katie and Hubbell become romantically involved and eventually marry. They move to California, where Hubbell works as a screenwriter despite Katie's desire for him to become a novelist. They have a child but divorce soon thereafter because of Hubbell's unwillingness to accept Katie's involvement in fighting the HUAC blacklists and film censorship of the 1950s. Katie then moves back to New York, where she marries a Jew, David Cohen, and becomes involved again in citizen activism, this time for nuclear disarmament.

While many have taken this film as a condemnation of intermarriage,[26] a closer examination of the role of Jewishness in the film forces a new interpretation. In fact, the ways in which Katie is Jewish present few obstacles to intermarriage. Katie's "Jewish" traits could easily be confused with her political leanings; political leftism *is* her religion. In the beginning of the film, Katie is a Communist; later on she becomes a New Deal Democrat, and by the end of the film she has taken on both McCarthy and nuclear proliferation. She never evinces any Jewish religious behavior, nor does the film imply that this behavior occurs off-screen. Pictures of Lenin and then of Roosevelt—rather than Jewish art or religious artifacts—adorn her walls. Katie's Jewishness, the film asserts, *is* her liberal conscience. She is the moral force of the film, ever encouraging Hubbell to act more morally.[27] Though the character of Katie clearly arises from the tradition of American Jews' affiliation with liberal, even radical politics and their view of liberalism as an expression of their Judaism,[28] Katie's political leanings seem to exist in what is otherwise a Jewish vacuum. As the only expression of Katie's Jewishness other than her looks, Katie's political leanings serve merely as an unsubstantiated token for her Jewishness rather than as an accurate reflection of cultural Jewishness.

Because Katie's morality embraces Communism (notoriously antireligious), civil rights (Katie protests the army's censorship of a radio program that denounces the way the army "spits on its Negroes"), and interracial friendship (Katie has her hair styled in Harlem and has friends there), it is a worldview that would encourage, rather than discourage, interfaith marriage. In this view, religious divisions such as prohibitions on intermarriage seem more like "the narrowness of particularism" than anything else.[29]

In a further contradiction of the traditional analysis of the film as anti-intermarriage, Katie's Jewishness—her superior, liberal morality—is precisely what attracts Hubbell to her during their college days. Throughout the film, Hubbell shows admiration for Katie as she demonstrates her outspokenness and moral rectitude. When she speaks at a peace rally on campus, he listens attentively to her speech; when other students ridicule her, he is one of the few people in the crowd who do not laugh. When Hubbell sells his first story, he tells only Katie. When early in the film he tells her, "Go get 'em, Katie," his tone of voice makes it clear that he greatly admires her for being able and willing to do so.

Hubbell never denigrates Katie's Jewishness nor the fact that Katie is Jewish; in fact, not only does Katie's religion present no obstacle to their relationship, but Hubbell's apparent understanding of it allows them to connect and engage in lighthearted banter. For example, when they are married and living in California, Katie works for a publishing company, where she writes plot synopses. To keep herself interested in the work, she writes phony synopses, such as the one she dreams up with Hubbell:

KATIE: *"Shavuous"* exclamation point! . . . *A kibbutz* of Chinese Jews living
           in a rice paddy. She cooks Communist rice patties so he gets the
           idea—
HUBBELL: —of calling them *matzahs*!
KATIE: You read the book!
HUBBELL: Backwards!

Katie and Hubbell's relationship fails not because Katie is a Jew and Hubbell is not but rather because Katie represses her idealism in order to stay with him; and when she finally decides to stand up for what she believes in, Hubbell cannot accept her autonomy. The divorce occurs more for reasons of gender than of religion or ethnicity. As *Funny Girl* does, *The Way We Were* presents a negative view of the success that independent, intelligent and idealistic women like Katie will have in romantic relationships. Though Katie clearly is this type of woman and though she consistently holds the moral high ground in the film, the one aspect of the film in which she has *no* power is in her romantic relationship with Hubbell. As William Taylor's visual analysis of the film shows, the camerawork reinforces this notion by placing her "above" Hubbell in all of their scenes together except the romantic ones. For example, Katie rows the boat when they are on the lake in Central Park, and while unpacking in their beach house, she stands on a ladder while he sits on a chair. The only time Hubbell is "on top" in the film comes "appropriately," according to Taylor, "during Hubbell's performance as 'America the Beautiful'—in lovemaking."[30]

The goal of *The Way We Were* is for Katie to get her man, and to do that she must repress her activism and her ideals. Katie allows Hubbell to determine the course of their relationship and thus the course of her life throughout the film. After marrying him, she loses her independent identity and forgoes her political activities, learning French cooking and looking the part of a wealthy Hollywood screenwriter's wife. Only at the end of the film, after they divorce, does Katie's true nature reassert itself: she demonstrates against nuclear weapons and even stops straightening her hair. Their breakup is hardly a declaration of independence on Katie's part, however. As in *Funny Girl*, the couple separates because the *man* decides it should be so. Here, Hubbell initiates the split by having an affair with his former college girlfriend, Carole Ann (Lois Chiles), thus forcing Katie's hand. "Give up, please," Hubbell pleads when Katie confronts him. "I can't," she protests. And when they meet for the last time, she tells Hubbell that she is only agreeing to give up on their relationship because he has "absolutely forced [her] to." Audiences can only surmise that Katie would have continued to forgo her activism had she been able to stay with Hubbell. He *allows* her to become an activist again by choosing to give her up, thus diminishing her power over her own life.

Finally, because Katie and Hubbell's romance occupies the center of the film, when it fails, so does Katie. By asserting her own identity, she loses Hubbell, who cannot accept a wife who stands up for herself, especially when such behavior might pose a risk to him.[31] And the concluding scene of the film does not at all suggest that Katie's new marriage in any way compensates for the one she has lost: her new husband does not appear at all in the film and thus does not have an opportunity to compete (at least visually) with Hubbell; Katie herself describes her husband only as a good *father;* she does not say whether he is a good *husband.* No man but Hubbell, audiences understand, could be that.

Katie emerges as an unsullied paragon of morality. The film treats her and her political idealism sentimentally, oversimplifying and romanticizing both. Presumably, many people watching the film would not have sympathized with Communism in the 1930s, but Katie's Communism consists only of, as one reviewer writes, "such a bland plea for world peace that no one to the left of Hitler could disagree."[32] When audiences weep over the breakup of Katie and Hubbell, they do so comforted by the feeling that by seeing this film they have "done something": struck a blow for a woman's right to have ideas, for liberal causes, against McCarthyism, and against upper-class WASP apathy. But the film's romanticization of Jewish leftism and of the ease of intermarriage, and the placement of Katie and Hubbell's love affair above all else, detract from the "issues" the film seems to support. Katie may be a woman with ideas, but she is more than willing to forget them to keep Hubbell, and all of Katie's railing against Hubbell's complacency fails to make much of a dent in his life choices. If anything, Hubbell changes Katie much more than she changes him, and Katie is ultimately punished for her ideas by losing Hubbell. The film's "feminist" content is best summarized by Molly Haskell: "Although Katie of *The Way We Were* ends up 'committed' and politically involved, the dominant image—the one we retain—is that of the dynamic but loving wife of the desirable man."[33] Her "pathetic solitude"[34] as she hands out leaflets at the film's conclusion hardly encourages women to follow her example.

A Star Is Born

Although she does not include it in her discussion, Pogrebin's labeling of the Jewish Big Mouth[35] type applies equally well to Streisand's portrayal of Esther Hoffman in the remake of the 1954 film *A Star Is Born.*[36] Esther, as in Pogrebin's description of the other Jewish Big Mouths, also "acts like a person. She lets everyone, especially the men in her life, know who she is and what she thinks. If she wants something, she goes for it. A nonconformist, she won't play her assigned role—either as a Jew or as a Woman."[37]

Esther is a young, struggling singer who is performing at a small bar when washed-up, alcoholic rock star John Norman Howard (another "opposite," Kris Kristofferson) enters. Esther likes to sing vague women's lib–type songs; she is an innocent, gutsy, straightlaced, glib young woman. Meeting John Norman puts her on the fast track to success. When he is booed off the stage at a benefit for Native American causes, he pushes her on to replace him. The crowd loves her, and she becomes an overnight sensation.

John Norman and Esther have a passionate, loving relationship, but their love cannot overcome his despair about both the demise of his own career and the overwhelming success of hers. He finally commits suicide by crashing his car while listening to her music. In a scene seemingly modeled after the finale of *Funny Girl*, the film concludes with Esther alone on stage singing a tribute to her lost love, appearing to triumph over the adversity that fate has dealt her.

Esther's career and life story actually bear a striking resemblance to Streisand's, which is perhaps a reflection of the creative control Streisand exercised over the film as its executive producer. Esther refuses to change her name (as Streisand was repeatedly advised to do), despite advice from people in the music industry. Esther and John Norman have a retreat in the desert (as did Streisand and her then–love interest/coproducer Jon Peters), and Esther's first television special is called *My Name Is Esther* (Streisand's first television special [1965] was *My Name Is Barbra*). The film even makes reference to Streisand's reputation as controlling when, during a difficult point in the rehearsals for *My Name Is Esther*, Esther declares, "I'm not trying to be difficult or anything; I just want to get it right."

Though Esther's name implies that she is Jewish, *A Star Is Born* contains not a single reference to Judaism or even to Jewishness. For example, when Esther and John Norman marry, they do so before a justice of the peace without any comment as to the interfaith nature of the relationship; again, religious and/or ethnic differences present no obstacle to interfaith romance. Proof of Esther's Jewishness comes only from her name, which was changed to "Hoffman" from the 1957 version's "Blodgett" (when Judy Garland played Esther), and from the fact that the film stars Streisand playing a character indisputably modeled on herself.

Despite the lack of overt identification of Esther as a Jew, her implied Jewishness does give her some purchase on moral values similar to those demonstrated by Katie in *The Way We Were*. Esther is clearly the most moral character in *A Star Is Born*, and she seems also to be the only assuredly Jewish one.[38] Esther, like Katie Morosky, is a pure soul with whom the audience cannot help but sympathize. In fact, as Pauline Kael points out, Esther is so pure that not only does she not share any of John Norman's weaknesses—drinking, the "hatred of the audience"—but she also never seems to struggle with any of the conditions of a rock-and-roll life-style that turned John Norman into a "sadomasochistic wreck."[39]

The film ties Esther's "superior" morality to her liberal attitudes, most especially her espousal of feminist values. During her wedding, for example, she alters the vows because "'[o]bey' is out—dawn of a new century and all"; she also wears a man's suit instead of a wedding dress. Her music also makes plain her feminist sympathies: in "Queen Bee," Esther rattles off the names of female leaders from the past who belied the notion that men were the superior sex, and in "Woman in the Moon," she sings about the demise of the old world, where girls were taught not to act too strong, and the birth of a new one guided by more egalitarian principles.

Again, however, the centrality of the romance to the film manages to override Esther's ideological stance. This fact becomes more clear in the last scene of the film (as it did in *Funny Girl* and *The Way We Were*), when Esther comes onstage to sing her torch song medley to John Norman. Esther is introduced, for the first time in her career, as Esther Hoffman *Howard*. Until this point, Esther had not taken John Norman's last name, but this aspect of the finale assures the audience that Esther has learned her lesson. Not only does it imply that Esther realizes (alas, too late) that her husband's name is more important than her own ideals, but it also states clearly that, now that her husband is dead, she will identify herself primarily through her relationship to him.

Although this film does focus more on Esther's career than *Funny Girl* or *The Way We Were* did on Fanny's or Katie's, Esther could not have achieved her stupendous success without John Norman's help. And it is this success that causes their relationship to self-destruct: again, the Streisand character's mate cannot accept her success, and the relationship, as well as Streisand's character, fails.

The Main Event

The Main Event [40] opens with a side view of Barbra Streisand's most discussed physical feature, her nose. The shot widens to reveal Streisand as Hilary "The Nose" Kramer, the head of a major perfume company, Le Nez. It is, as Lester Friedman writes, "a sly visual joke on those who seem obsessed with [Streisand's nose's] size and shape."[41] After years of comments from reviewers and critics about her most prominent facial feature (described, for example, as "prodigious"[42] and likened to "the prow of a ship"[43]), this film turns the tables and uses Streisand's nose to her character's advantage; once the most vilified feature of a Jew's physique, the nose now becomes the Jew's greatest asset.[44]

Early in the film, Hilary's ex-husband and lawyer, David (Paul Sands), informs her that her accountant has stolen all of her money and fled the country. She has only one asset remaining: a run-down boxer named Eddie "Kid Natural" Scanlon (Ryan O'Neal), whom the accountant had been paying *not* to fight. Hilary becomes Eddie's manager, persuading him to fight again and training him to return to the ring. All the while, she learns about life "on the other side of the tracks," and she and Eddie eventually fall in love.

As in *The Way We Were* and *A Star Is Born*, the romance in *The Main Event* depends on the concept of the opposite stereotypes attracting: here, the bright, successful, classy Beverly Hills Jewish business executive versus the lower-class, lazy, non-Jewish, slightly corrupt Long Beach ex-fighter/driving instructor. As Hilary says: "You live in a glove, I wear them" (Eddie's house is shaped like an enormous boxing glove). By giving Eddie the last name of Scanlon, the film also alludes to the conflict between Irish Americans and American Jews,[45] which has a long history in both film and the real world. But the "classic" films of Irish/Jewish relationships—*Private Izzy Murphy* (1926), *Becky Gets a Husband* (1912), and *Abie's Irish Rose* (1928)—usually feature Jewish *men* and Irish *women* falling in love; in fact, most *shiksa* stories rely on this gender combination.[46] *The Main Event*, however, transposes the genders for comedic effect, making Hilary the intelligent Jewish hero and Eddie the mindless, blond, beautiful *shaygetz*.

Hilary's Jewishness does not restrict her from having a romantic relationship with Eddie; as in other films, Streisand's character seems to have no opposition to interfaith relationships. Jewishness, here, has determined the shape of Hilary's nose; it does not, however, influence her dating roster at all. Hilary's Jewishness is but one of many differences between herself and Eddie, but it is difficult to separate what is Jewish about Hilary from what is upper class or female about her.

The Main Event is primarily about the battle between the sexes, and class differences often appear as metaphors for gender differences. Hilary, the upper-class woman, possesses all the trappings of style, taste, and refinement. Eddie, on the other hand, is the stereotype of a "man," as that is understood in popular culture intended for women: he is crass, has no taste and no style, and is always "on the make." (Indeed, his driving school seems more intended to help Eddie meet women than to earn him a living.)

The Main Event relies heavily on traditional stereotypes about class, gender, and ethnicity to make its comedic impact: refinement, progressivism, and taste are the province of the upper class, of women, and, the film implies, of Jews. What remains—boorishness, conservatism, and tackiness—seems to belong to the lower classes, men, and the Irish. Once again, the Streisand character's sophistication is evinced by her liberalism, especially her feminism. Hilary insists that Eddie call her his "cornerperson" rather than his "cornerman," and when he asks her to marry him, she insists on continuing to work and on handling her own finances. Conversely, the film links Eddie's vulgarity and crassness to his disavowal of feminism. He rankles at Hilary's ownership of his contract because she is a woman, and he assumes that she will want him to take the dominant role in their relationship. When Hilary asks, "Who thinks that way anymore?" Eddie answers: "All the guys in my neighborhood."

The alleged challenge to these stereotypes comes in the realm of gender, where the film reverses some male and female stereotypes. For example, Hilary decides that Eddie should capitalize on his good looks in order to draw a larger crowd (especially women) to his fights. When she designs stylish, tight satin boxing shorts for him to wear, he responds: "You treat me like an object—what do you think I am, a girl?" And when, after they have spent a romantic evening together, she refuses to marry him, he feels used, he tells her, like "just another pretty face."

These gender reversals, as well as the play on the *shiksa* story, are used only for comedic effect, however. Because they are not explored in any depth, the film defuses their feminist message. *The Main Event* does not take feminism seriously but instead devalues it, especially when Hilary's desire to control Eddie sabotages his career. At the end of the film she literally throws in the towel to end one of his fights, just to demonstrate her ability to dictate the course of their relationship. As Janet Maslin writes in her review, "The ending of the film tries so confusingly to reconcile Miss Streisand's femininity with her authority that it has her doing the one thing most likely to frustrate her audience."[47]

The Main Event may feel like social criticism—it appears to protest the way women are treated in society and men's feelings about women having more power or money than they do—but it is not. Worse even than oversimplifying feminism, as other films of Streisand's do, it ridicules it. The film dismisses feminism as the frivolous prattling of a few high-powered women like Hilary who want to succeed in a man's world so that they can run (and ruin) men's careers and lives.

Yentl

Streisand's desire to create the film version of *Yentl*[48] began in 1968, when she first read the original story by Isaac Bashevis Singer.[49] Making the film was an intensely personal project for Streisand: like Yentl, whose father dies before the Singer story even begins, Streisand lost her own father when she was only fifteen months old; his death and absence in her life had been a defining factor in her development. Emanuel Streisand, who held a master's degree, worked as a high school English teacher and a part-time Hebrew teacher. His daughter, relegated to a childhood of semipoverty and familial misery after his death, idealized him and, as a logical consequence, idealized what she felt he stood for: knowledge and education. What drew her to Singer's story were Yentl's love for and loss of her educated, religious father and her insatiable desire for learning. This desire leads Yentl to disguise herself as a man to be able to continue at a yeshiva the informal Talmud lessons her father had given her while he was alive.

But Singer's Yentl is a freak of nature: an intelligent and serious woman in a world where women are identified with "silly chatter."[50] She is described as physically freakish: "tall, thin, bony, with small breasts and narrow hips. . . . There was even a slight down on her upper lip."[51] And though Singer's story ostensibly focuses on a Jewish woman who breaks out of the usual role allotted to Jewish women, it does not transform the average woman's role in any way. Instead, Yentl is compared to Beruriah and Yalta, token exceptional women who demonstrated an intelligence comparable to that expected of men. Singer's story is not feminist and can barely be seen as encouraging to women like Yentl: to pursue her illicit passion, Yentl must hide her true self, leave her home, and live in isolation and fear. The story ends with Yentl having to leave the people she loves and spend the rest of her life traveling, alone and in disguise, from yeshiva to yeshiva, always in fear that her secret will be discovered.

Streisand's Yentl, however, is significantly different from Singer's character. Her Yentl is Singer's seen through twentieth-century, American, Jewish, and feminist eyes. Yentl is no longer a freak of nature. Her love for learning is entirely natural, and only society's rules, which prevent her from indulging this love, are unnatural. These rules, Yentl constantly argues (not entirely correctly), are not "written" anywhere, a requirement that, the film implies, would lend them religious authority.[52]

Yentl quenches her thirst for learning at a yeshiva, which she attends dressed as a boy and under the pseudonym of Anshel. She becomes the study partner of Avigdor (Mandy Patinkin), the brightest student in the yeshiva (and the best-looking one, of course), and proves a good match for his intelligence and learning. She soon begins to fall in love with Avigdor; and after Avigdor is forced to give up his own love, Hadass (Amy Irving), Yentl/Anshel marries Hadass to keep Avigdor from leaving town. Yentl expends much energy hiding her true sex from her wife and eventually confesses her secret to Avigdor, at which point he offers to marry her. Knowing that he still loves Hadass, however, and that he will not let her be the kind of woman—learned, studious— that she wants to be, Streisand's Yentl sets off for a "new place, where I hear things are different." Audiences can only assume she means America.

As a film that purports to explore a woman's place in traditional Judaism, *Yentl* is extremely simplistic. First, the film reduces the complex system of Jewish law to single axiom: if it is written, it holds authority. Aside from implying a complete rejection of the authority of *minhag* (custom), this simplification also assumes that there is one single place where Jewish law is "written." Does Yentl follow only the laws in the Torah? What of those in the Talmud? Or later rabbis' commentaries? The *Shulchan Arukh*? The film ignores these questions, allowing the audience to assume that Yentl only has to

Yental (Streisand), disguised as Anshel, discussing Talmud with her study partner, Avigdor (Mandy Patinkin), with whom she has secretly fallen in love. (Copyright © 1983 by Ladbroke Entertainments Limited. Photo courtesy The Museum of Modern Art Film Stills Archive, New York City)

consult a kind of "Big Book of Jewish Law" to prove which laws are written. Moreover, the film implies that those laws that *are* written are liberal and free of sexism. By repeatedly asking "Where is it written?" that women cannot study and never receiving an answer, Yentl implies that "true" Judaism, untainted by misogynist customs, would allow her to be the kind of woman she wants to be.

The film oversimplifies Judaism as well. *Yentl* reduces Judaism to learning, to the exclusion of all other forms of Jewish expression. (The film, therefore, rather than exploring any of the other important legal, liturgical, theological, and social issues facing women in Judaism, can only address their exclusion from study.[53]) Although the film boasts many warm, sepia-toned scenes of men poring over their Talmuds, there is almost no other *religion* in this film that purports to portray what was in reality an extremely traditional community of Jews. No man has sidelocks (though the old men have beards), no one blesses a meal before or after eating it, and women, especially, do not engage in any religious behavior, such as preparing for Shabbat, going to the *mikveh*, or lighting Shabbat candles. And God has no place in *Yentl*. As MaryHeléne

Rosenbaum contends, "Yentl's yeshiva pursuits evidently provide only cerebral stimulation; . . . and her interior life, as expressed in voice-over sung monologues, evinces concern with her relationships with her father, with the beloved fellow student Avigdor, with the innocent young bride and with Yentl's own personhood rather than with the Deity."[54]

Yentl herself demonstrates religious behavior only twice in the film, and both scenes are highly problematic from a traditional religious point of view.[55] First, at her father's funeral, Yentl leads the mourners in the Mourner's Kaddish over her father's grave, something that is forbidden to women in traditional Judaism; the other mourners, though momentarily surprised, respond at the appropriate points in the prayer, implying that traditional Jews would allow Jewish women to do as they pleased if the latter would simply take the initiative. Yentl's other religious experience comes when she is alone in the dark woods on her first night away from home. She lights a candle and kneels by a rock—a sure sign that something strange is about to happen, for Jews almost always pray standing or sitting, and they certainly never kneel. Looking up at the stars, Yentl begins to pray. "God, our heavenly Father / Oh God, and my father, who is also in heaven." Although traditionally, women are exempt from the obligation to recite more of the specific prayers said three times a day, and although they often composed modified versions of those prayers, such as *techinot*, one presumes that they would *not* have been encouraged to model their prayers after the very Christian Lord's Prayer, which begins, "Our Father, who art in Heaven."

Taken together, the lack of scenes of Jewish religion (in a community that was historically *very* religiously observant) and the appropriation of Christian religious symbols and prayers reassures the audience that, truly, Jews are no different from Christians. Surely, the film seems to argue, if Jews were truly accepted by society, they would look and act (and pray) just like everyone else.

Yentl's appropriation of Christian prayers fits in well with the film's overall attitude toward Jewish-Christian relations. In this arena again, *Yentl*'s approach to Jewishness and Judaism is oversimplistic. The film takes place in "Eastern Europe" in 1904, one year after the Kishinev pogrom, in which a mob killed almost fifty Jews and injured hundreds more; this event shocked the Jewish population of the region as well as both Jewish and non-Jewish communities throughout the world. Yet there are no pogroms, no oppression of Jews, and no Christian authorities—either good or bad—in *Yentl*. The greatest oppression Jews face in the film is when Yentl is cheated out of a ride on a cart driven by non-Jews. This absence of persecution leads to some confusion when Yentl takes the boat to America at the end of the film, accompanied by hundreds of other emigrants, for nothing in the film indicates why all those people had chosen to leave Europe (though one doubts that they, like Yentl, left because of sexism).

Yentl, then, stands outside both history and religion.[56] Its shtetls and yeshivas are populated by almost secular Jews who evince scant knowledge of Judaism and of traditional Jewish practice. It crafts a nostalgic shtetl and yeshiva world where Judaism is nothing but a love of books, thereby making "Jewish" life palatable to and simple enough for all audiences to sympathize with and understand. Both Jews and non-Jews can watch the film and imagine that Jewish history was as peaceful, serene, and devoid of oppression as *Yentl* implies and that Jewish integration requires hardly any effort at all on the part of either Jews or non-Jews.

In fact, Yentl's only enemies in the film, ironically enough, are other Jewish women. Even the Jewish men who are allegedly to blame for Yentl's exclusion from study are treated better, shown in the beautifully lit, even glowing scenes of the yeshiva and the synagogue. Only a rather boorish book peddler and the otherwise-adored Avigdor ever actually try to stop Yentl from doing what she wants to do. But the film's other women show a disrespect for those aspects of Judaism that are most valorized in the film, an attitude that stands in stark contrast to Yentl's reverence for those very same things. For example, after the mourning period for her father has ended, a group of women comes to move Yentl out of her house. Aside from a general callousness—one of the women (inaccurately) exclaims to Yentl, "We mourn for ten days only, then it's on with life"—the women also display an unrealistic ignorance and disrespect for Yentl's father's holy books, not even apologizing when they drop one carelessly on the floor. Yentl, conversely, rushes to pick it up, kisses it, and caresses it.

By this point in the film, however, audiences will have already gotten the picture about women. In an earlier scene, when Yentl and her father attend services one day, Yentl sits among several townswomen in the women's balcony. The other women gossip and talk away, oblivious of the religious service below them. The scene ends with a quick cut from the chattering women behind the balcony's bars to Yentl's father's chickens clucking away in a wire cage.[57] The metaphor is painfully obvious.

Yet many feminist critics argue that the film treats women quite well.[58] Streisand herself insists the same: "I . . . felt a responsibility to women. In the character of Hadass, for instance, I didn't want to portray her just as she was in Singer's story. He had a tendency to be misogynistic. I added another element—her intelligence."[59] But even Streisand's example of Hadass is problematic. Yentl decides to teach Hadass Talmud only as a way of distracting her from the fact that they have not yet consummated their marriage. The tactic works: Hadass eventually falls asleep in the middle of one of Yentl's talmudic discursions, having been awake since dawn. In fact, throughout their brief married life, Yentl uses Hadass's education only as an escape from physical intimacy. By the end of the film, although she expresses the hope that Hadass will continue with her studies—"she has great promise," she says—it becomes clear that though Yentl considers other women capable of learning Talmud, she has not sought to change their traditional exclusion from learning in any substantial way.

Instead, to counter misogyny in the Jewish tradition, Yentl *evades* it. She does not consider ways of changing the system for others; she simply makes it work for herself. She dresses like a man and indulges in and appreciates the benefits that go along with being male. In fact, by the end of the film, Yentl has not succeeded in changing any aspect of Judaism's limitation on women's roles. Her protestation of the treatment of women in Judaism is safe because it does not *do* anything: Yentl does not challenge or change her own society but simply escapes to America, which, she believes (or hopes), already boasts the liberal society she refuses to build herself.[60]

Thus *Yentl*, despite its seemingly revolutionary approach to women's place in traditional Judaism, falls short on the important issues it attempts to address. Yentl selfishly seeks her own liberation without taking into account the plight of other women, all the while nurturing a healthy dose of disdain for other women's ignorance and apathy. And she does not seek to transform the system that oppresses women but only calls for allowing "women who are like men" to compete in a man's world. This approach is significantly less threatening than the alternative, which would require the rejection of society's system of hierarchies and, indeed, of much of society itself. Streisand's dedication of the film, which flashes across the screen at the end, is illuminating: "This film is dedicated to my father. . . . And to all our fathers." The omission of "our mothers" is glaring but not surprising, given the film's general romanticization of and admiration for all that has been traditionally male in Judaism.

. . .

Whatever the message of Streisand's films may be, legions of moviegoers seem enraptured by it. At the box office alone, her films have grossed over $277 million.[61] This mass appeal suggests that the images Streisand's films present of Jews and women—and of course, of Jewish women—are those that movie audiences wish to see. Given that the images she presents are those that have been discussed above, why are her films so popular?

As films about Jews, Streisand's films have succeeded because they have seemed to reflect the very image of themselves that many American Jews have tried to promote, an image of "cultural Jewishness" made popular in the interwar period that has continued in some fashion up to the present. As this essay has shown, however, these images only poorly reflect cultural Jewishness, relying instead on reductive stereotypes of Jews and symbols of Jewishness that equate Jewishness at the most with political liberalism and at the least with stereotypes. Yet watching Streisand's films seems to constitute, for many American Jews, an *expression* of Jewish identity, in much the same way that watching TV's *Seinfeld* might be said to. These images of Jews are appealing because they offer an idealistic view of Jews' acceptance into American society: none of these characters seems to suffer as a result of their Jewishness, and in fact, it is Jewishness in its most stereotypical form that becomes these characters' most appealing feature. The idea that Jews could be fully accepted *as Jews* is more important, it seems, than the ways in which these films (and television programs) portray Jewish identity.

As films about women and feminism, Streisand's films seem to reflect the general difficulties Hollywood has had with portraying complex, committed feminists. Though her characters pay lip-service to feminism, the films, in fact, resemble nothing so much as romance novels. Their sentimental treatment of women and their favoring of the romantic relationship over all else, especially over the woman's independence and her career, undermine their own feminist assertions. Yet it seems unlikely that Streisand's films are so successful because audiences believe that women should give up their ideals for romantic success and that no woman's career, even one as successful as Fanny Brice's, should take precedence over her love life. Streisand's characters are not remembered and praised for their ideological capitulation and their almost uniform romantic failures.

Instead, Streisand's characters are usually remembered in the popular imagination as both feisty Jews and feisty women; this is the image that has stayed with audiences, the image that has been praised so often by Jews and feminists. This, too, is the image that led Ken Joachim to create Hello, Gorgeous!! and is the inspiration of the work of so many of the "Too Jewish?" artists. As Janice Radway has shown, this is the kind of image many readers retain of the heroines of romance novels as well. The ideal romance heroine, she demonstrates, is one characterized by independence, intelligence, and a sense of humor.[62] Perhaps, then, as the subjects of Radway's study do with romance novels, audiences use Streisand's films as a way of imagining alternatives for themselves. It seems to be the ideas of what Jews and women *can be* that catch audiences' attention, not the shortcomings in the way both groups are treated on-screen.

Perhaps, therefore, Streisand's films are more properly viewed as only a step in the process of the full integration of Jews and women into mainstream American culture—not the final step but certainly a necessary one. Streisand's lasting legacy may be that her characters have provided a bridge between a filmic world where Jews barely existed and where women were valued only for their looks and their submissiveness and a world yet to come, where both Jews and women are treated with the respect, complexity, and richness they deserve.[63]

Sarah Blacher Cohen

From Critic to Playwright
Fleshing Out Jewish Women in
Contemporary Drama

In 1987, I made the descent into the forbidden realm of make-believe, where one lies to create the semblance of truth. From writing serious analyses of humor in Jewish American literature, I, a professor of English at the University of Albany, State University of New York, did an about-face and created my own irreverent comedy of character, ideas, situation, and language. I gave myself permission to discontinue being the male critic within me, rigidly constructing and deconstructing elaborate theories of knowledge, to become the spontaneous female playwright, eager to flesh out and shape characters that would please many constituencies. In other words, I left off writing complex treatises on sartorial perfection to become that androgynous craftsperson: the Jewish tailor willing to make the pants longer or shorter, the bodices tighter or looser, to please the customers.

The greatest catalyst igniting my playwriting was collaborating on the play *Schlemiel the First* with Nobel Laureate Isaac Bashevis Singer. But collaboration was not control. Isaac was to be the chief playwright; I, the woman, was granted the privilege of being the handmaiden to his male creativity. For two weeks, in a moldy hotel room near his Miami Beach condominium, I awaited his afternoon visitations, when we were to write and rewrite the play together. He napped, yet he permitted me to shape the structure of the play, flesh out the characters, heighten the comedy of the scenes, write new dialogue, and prune out anecdotal materials. For another two weeks he had me stay in an inexpensive New York hotel frequented by "ladies of the night" while I hostessed the play through its rehearsal period. In 1984 the play had a six-week run at New York's Jewish Repertory Theater. The credits read: "Playwright, Isaac Bashevis Singer; Editor for the Stage, Sarah Blacher Cohen."

In 1985 and 1986, I decided not to remain one of the nameless female editors and translators of Singer's literature. Like Sylvia Plath, I did not want to type someone else's letters. I wanted to dig into myself, sift through my experiences, and grapple with my conflicting views of people and events. I wanted to write my own creative works.

Ideas for my own play began percolating in my head during my daily physical therapy swims at the Albany Jewish Center. They came to a boil as I sat in the ladies' locker room, that compressed chamber of life, where I listened to scarred women speak openly about breast surgery, young nubile ones mutter narcissistic fears of growing old, and the elderly mourn the loss of family, friends, and vigor. With their idiosyncratic personalities and unique physical impairments, they became for me the stuff of drama, quirky characters in search of an author.

What happens to these women in the ladies' locker room? In what ways do these bared souls bare their souls? The play I wrote[1] comically explores the connections among the elderly, the disabled, and the young able-bodied women of different nationalities and religions. Through diverse, accented dialogue and varied levels of discourse, the play illustrates the intricate workings of the locker room as a miniature United Nations, with its power plays, strained attempts at negotiation, inevitable compromises and capitulations.

From a Jewish point of view, the locker room companions are, in the words of one reviewer, "a microcosm of Diaspora Jewry—East European, Central European and American. Susan's handicaps place her in a doubly 'marginal' status. Jewish and disabled, she finds kinship as one who 'walks funny' with immigrant Sophie, who 'talks funny' but who 'didn't have no accent' until she moved to America."[2]

First plays tend to be autobiographical, with little distance between dramatist and dramatic personae. My play is no exception. It is based on no historical figure or psychological case study but on my own anatomy and criticism of that anatomy. My leading character, Dr. Susan, is a university English professor in her mid-thirties who suffers from a muscle-nerve disease. Her curiosity about her locker mates, however, prompts her not to dwell on her infirmities but to be outgoing and inquisitive about others. Nonetheless, she complains too much about her inability to do many things. Unlike her real-life prototype, she can't muster enough humor to conceal her self-pity.

However, the play is not only a portrayal of the disabled protagonist's self-pity; it is an expression of the twin poles of her own identity: her academic self and the vibrant Yiddish woman inside her, embodied in the eighty-two-year-old Sophie Gold from Bialystok who functions as the tutor in the play. Amazingly agile and gregarious for her age, she motivates the disabled Jewish American professor to help an able-bodied Gentile woman give birth to her first child. Thus, Sophie, the Yiddish woman in my script, is not the know-nothing, awkward greenhorn. She is the Yiddish life force, whom Cynthia Ozick describes as the "deus ex machina and mentor and historian and explainer and continuer and sardonic merry angel," who enables Dr. Susan to experience "the victories of an imagination courageous enough for happiness," which "hint or teach . . . that happiness is hard and muscular labor. (Like laughter!)"[3] Though Dr. Susan obsesses about the tragic parts of her life, Sophie engages her wit in the humor of verbal retrieval. Through her comic reformulations of the tearful, she succeeds in salvaging the antic from the anguished. In her own way, Sophie is the Yiddish midwife who contributes to the symbolic rebirth of the disabled.

Indeed, for Sally Chasnoff, the director of the Northwestern University production of the play, the "central issues of *The Ladies Locker Room* is disability, or rather the tension between 'dis-abled' and 'differently abled,' and how these perspectives not simply influence but actually determine lives." The play compels us to look at "'disability' as a metaphor for the countless difficulties and limitations of living in the physical body for all of us, as well as a term for special bodily conditions. Are these 'disabilities' products of our psyches, 'just our imaginations,' or are they products of the culture into which we are born, and projected onto us until we finally accept them as our own, or refuse to do so any longer?"[4]

But for me, Sophie is not merely an articulator of a theme. She functions as a superannuated cheerleader for much of the play. Her pep talk is expressed in her old-country language and her immigrant frames of reference, which comically dispel Susan's mounting depression:

> SOPHIE: You know, my dear, carrying a load of worries is like wearing heavy galoshes in the summer. You spend so much time waiting for the snow to fall that you don't enjoy the sunshine. When I worry at night and can't sleep, I wash all the floors on my hands and knees until four in the morning. That takes away all my worries. Listen, when I was in my sixties, the doctor said I had a cancer in the rectum. He wanted to operate, but I wouldn't let him. By eating lentil soup, my rectum I healed myself. That was fifteen years ago and I'm still alive today. So you got to stop worrying the way I did. Throw away those galoshes in the garbage and sit in the sunshine instead.

Dr. Susan, outwardly angry at New York cabbies who tell her "to take an ambulance," is, however, in inner despair over her bad feet and the progressive nature of her disability. From the shtetl world of our mothers, Sophie offers her a remedy from her repository of superstitions and folk medicine:

> SOPHIE: Your feet are not so bad. Just a little crooked here and there and maybe a few sores. Now I'm going to tell you how to take care on your feet. A

very big doctor from Russia showed me what to do. First, he said, you go pishing in the morning, you save it in a big white pot, then you soak your feet there for ten minutes. The healthy chemicals from the pishing go straight into the holes in the feet and heal all the sores. I do this myself three, four times a day. And when you're through soaking your feet, don't wipe 'em. Let 'em dry natural.

SUSAN: But, Sophie, don't your feet stink?

SOPHIE: No it don't stink. Try it. It'll make your feet all better.

SUSAN: But Sophie, the doctor said my feet would get worse.

SOPHIE: Not true. Listen to my doctor, the biggest from Russia. He had three diplomas, five offices, six satchels and his great grandfather was doctor to the Tsar. The Tsar soaked his feet in the pishing and they were much better off.

SUSAN: Too bad the Tsar didn't soak his head in the pishing, then we'd all be better off.

Not only does Sophie get Susan to laugh at her plight, she does not allow her to remain passive in her acceptance of it. A body builder, ahead of her times, she is a Yiddish Jane Fonda aerobics lady: "You gotta exercise the whole body. First, pretend you're a Yiddishe windmill and wave your arms from right to left. Next wave a blue hanky in the air to scare away all the demons. And then walk like a fancy goose and sing the 'Green Cousina,' so you won't think about your feet. When you're all tired out, I'll give you my special massage— like when I squeezed the dough to make *challahs* in Bialystok."

Sophie is the adoring mother Susan never had. She is unconditional in her acceptance of her. In many respects her perpetual love of Susan mitigates Susan's perpetual self-hatred. Sophie says: "You're still a *shayna maidel*. You have a beautiful body, a young-looking face, a healthy head of hair and a little extra fat to keep you warm in winter. You should only take care on yourself. You'll be even more beautiful as you grow older."

The loving Sophie also connects Dr. Susan with the life-sustaining memories of her Yiddish past: the times she was cherished as a young girl singing with the old men of the synagogue on Saturday mornings. But Dr. Susan's mother in the play, representing hypercritical femininity, chastises her for having the loudest voice in the synagogue and for making too much noise walking in with her orthopedic shoes.

SUSAN: *Yismachu, B'malachozechu, Shomrai, Shomrai Shomrai Shabbos, V'korey Oneg Shabbos.*

MOTHER: Don't sing at the top of your lungs. You're too loud for a girl. You're drowning out the men. And you're getting too old to sit with the men. Sit in the women's section and act like a lady. Try not to call attention to yourself . . . with those shoes. Whisper and tiptoe in during the service. Why can't you be like the other girls?

SUSAN: *V'Tahere Libaynu. V'Tahere Libaynu, V'Tahere Libaynu, V'Ovdecho*
         B'Emet.
MOTHER: Oh, there you go again! Didn't I tell you? Keep your voice down.
         You're embarrassing me. People are looking at you.

Sophie tries to counteract the adverse effect of Susan's judgmental mother
by being the affirmative mentor who struggles to convince Susan that she can
be what she wants to be. Sophie makes Susan see that she doesn't have to define her worth by being an actor on the stage. Sophie convinces her she can be
an excellent teacher by acting for her students in the classroom. Susan suddenly realizes that Sophie is right:

SUSAN: My students are a great audience! From my desk chair, my thrust
         stage, I can perform my favorite roles. I'm the Madwomen from Chail-
         lot. "I have my dogs to feed and cats to pet." Or I'm Maura from *Rid-*
         ers to the Sea (in an Irish accent) "They're all gone now. There isn't
         anything more the sea can do to me." Or if I want to be funny, I can be
         Lady Bracknell from *The Importance of Being Earnest.* "A man should
         know everything or nothing. I do not approve of anything which tam-
         pers with natural ignorance." But I'm even more hilarious when I play
         parts not supposed to be comic . . . like my Blanche Du Bois opposite
         a Brooklyn freshman as Stanley Kowalski. "Western Union, take down
         this message! 'In desperate, desperate circumstances! Help me!
         Caught in a trap.'" My accent is so phoney that Tennessee Williams
         must be giggling in his grave. So for a brief span of time, Sophie
         causes me to be the class clown and I forget about my wooden legs.

A far more significant task that Sophie assigns to Susan has to do with the
special delivery of a baby. This assignment causes Susan to remember
painfully a traumatic experience from her past: the directive not to become a
mother, which her officious Viennese neurologist issued to her at age sixteen.

DOCTOR: Susan, you're a pretty girl and I'm sure you must be looking forward
         to having a family some day, but I just don't think it would be ethical
         or fair of you to have children. As you know, your muscle nerve dis-
         ease is both hereditary and degenerative. Would you want your chil-
         dren to have to live your kind of life? Sure, you're alive, but there are
         many things you can't do. Your condition will only get worse. It's
         your life, of course, and you can do what you want with it. Just re-
         member. The percentages are not in your favor. You risk bringing a
         defective human being into the world.

The doctor persuades Susan to perform a mental abortion on herself. Yet
Sophie deters Susan from engaging in such a disastrous act. Rather, she per-

suades her to take charge of Peggy's childbirth in the locker room. Not only is the birthing process filled with Rabelaisian fun and games, it becomes a ritual act of empowerment for the disabled Dr. Susan, as well as a source of female bonding in this "theatrical bath-house." Sophie, Yiddish high priestess, directs the proceedings:

SOPHIE: It's about time. We got to measure Peggy's opening. If the woman's opening is the size of a 2-inch *knish*, the baby's ready to come out. And Peggy's opening is as big as three *knishes* now. Just a few more pushes and the little one's body will come out just as easy. Dr. Susan, help Peggy, push and pant.

SUSAN: Push and pant, push and pant. Oh my God. Here it comes. Here it comes. It's beautiful, just beautiful. This baby is a present from God.

SOPHIE: *Boruch atoh, adoshem eloheynu melech hoolom, ha yetzer nes godol.*

SUSAN: Praised be thou Lord our God, King of the Universe who has created a great miracle! Here Peggy, here is your great miracle.

PEGGY: Come here you little darling. You know, we may name you Susan Sophie, Bubbe Rivke O'Flaherty.

SUSAN: I feel one week old. At your age, Sophie, a successful midwife and a psychiatrist. How do you feel?

SOPHIE: Like it's a big blessing from God—to be old yet to be young. To live to bring a new life into this universe.

SUSAN: And to bring new life into people's lives.

SOPHIE: Come Dr. Susele, let's celebrate. Life, they say, is the biggest bargain. We get it from God for nothing.

SUSAN: For nothing? For everything!

SOPHIE: Yes, for everything. *Siman tov, u mazel tov, u mazel tov v'siman tov/ Siman tov, u mazel tov u mazel tov v'siman tov/ Siman tov, u mazel tov v'siman tov, u mazel tov, y'he la-a-a-nu/ Y'he la nu, y'he la nu u l'chol Yisrael/ Y'he la nu, y'he la nu, u l'chol Yisrael!* (As the song is sung, Sophie and the women dance a spirited *Hora* around mother and child. Susan becomes the most agile she's ever been in her entire life.)

And so I, Sarah Blacher Cohen, professor of English, have given birth to my own literary baby, my fledgling play, *The Ladies Locker Room.* Like a good Jewish mother, I am loath to let go of her and have a life independent of me. Will she thrive and prosper in the world? Will they appreciate her special talents and view her as unique? Will they like her and seek out her company? Will they have good things to say about her or will they malign her? I, who have been in control of her conception, want to be in control of her reception and ultimate fate. In my daydreams I want her to have instant recognition as a masterpiece. I imagine stellar actors vying to play her roles. But as I discover some of her awkwardnesses, I realize, alas, that I am not a divine Thalia, effortlessly fashioning dazzling comedies. Rather I must accept myself as that

Sarah Blacher Cohen with actress Carol Provoncha, who played Sophie
Tucker in *Sophie, Totie and Belle.* (Photo courtesy Sarah Blacher Cohen)

earthbound Jewish tailor, arduously outfitting the baby, mending and remend-
ing her apparel to make her, if not stunning, then at least presentable.

It is probably no coincidence that the protagonist of my next play, *Molly
Picon's Return Engagement*,[5] is Molly herself, who cannot give birth to a baby
and feels diminished because of it. Her childlessness causes her husband,
Jacob Kalich, to infantilize her in life and in many scripts he wrote for her. Instead of creating roles for her as a mature woman, he has her masquerade as
young boys in such hits as the Yiddish Peter Pan, *Yankele*, which she played almost three thousand times, and in the 1936 Yiddish film *Yid'l Mit Fid'l*. The
only time she is a mama is in the Yiddish film *Mamele* (1938), when she is

forty years old and has to portray a twelve-year-old who has to be the mama of the household and bring *mazel* to everyone of the family but herself.

My other kinship with Molly Picon was that she, I, and Grace Paley's protagonist, Shirley,[6] were Jewish girls with loud voices who, I imagine, would have liked to sing with the old men in the synagogue and not be constricted to the refined behavior of the women's section. We would have liked to give full voice to the expression within us and not have to censor ourselves for propriety's sake.

But as a physically challenged woman who "walks funny," I especially admired and envied Molly Picon's physical agility, her talent for being what we term in Yiddish *spritne*. Hence, I highlighted the many instances of her dexterity in the play: her fearless performance of somersaults and cartwheels; her simultaneous singing and walking on a tightrope; her sparkling *ganayvishe oygen*, or "mischievous eyes," to lure the crowds; her scapegrace slapstick routines to keep the audience laughing; and her bouncy delivery of Yiddish songs to encourage group singing. Molly Picon was an effervescent performer from age five well into her eighties. Before her death at ninety-four in April 1992, Molly was the leading star of more than two hundred productions of Second Avenue's Yiddish theater during the 1920s.

Another great achievement of Molly Picon was her versatility, her amazing ability to move successfully from one theatrical world to the next, to make life-long friends of people so unlike herself. In her mid-sixties she appeared on Broadway, achieving her most notable acclaim in a two-season run of *Milk and Honey*, a hit musical. She co-starred with Robert Morley in a London production of *A Majority of One* and was acclaimed by the British critics as well. After *Milk and Honey*, she worked mostly in English-language performances, such as *Paris Is Out* in 1970 and *Something Old, Something New* (later called *The Second Time Around*) in 1977 with Hans Conreid. She appeared in the films *Come Blow Your Horn*, which starred Frank Sinatra, and *For Pete's Sake* with Barbra Streisand.

Though Molly was hailed for her performances as "the female Charlie Chaplin," the "Yiddish Helen Hayes," and a "bean-sized Bernhardt," the most intriguing and most taxing part she plays in *Molly Picon's Return Engagement* is herself in three phases of her life: as a young woman, as a married woman opposite her husband, and as a widow. The play is first a tribute to Molly, the impoverished Philadelphia girl who gives up school to help support her costumiere mother, who encouraged her to enter the theater. Molly tells us: "If I were Louis Picon's son, I would've gotten a classical education and been a scholar. But as the daughter of Clara Picon, costume maker, I became an actress who could be all the things she never was in real life. So in 1915 I left high school to perform in out-of-town vaudeville to support the family." At the same time she persists in perfecting her talent and struggles to advance her career.

She is responsible to others yet is self-reliant. She takes risks, travels to other cities to look for work, and creates opportunities for herself.

Molly's fifty-six-year-old marriage to Jacob Kalich, Galician rabbinical student turned director and scriptwriter of forty of her plays, makes for a great love story. Perhaps because I have enjoyed thirty-two years of a successful professional life and a successful marriage, I have written the play in such a way that Molly has managed to combine an independent fate and love too, that is, a flourishing career of her own and a lifelong commitment to the well-being of Jacob. Yet the relationship is far from idyllic. Because they are each strong-willed individuals, it has its fair share of disappointment, conflict, and rivalry.

Yonkel, as she called him, taught her Yiddish, which she learned quickly, and she performed in a repertory of Yiddish shows that he created solely for her in Europe and America. The audiences and reviewers usually liked her more than his plays. Projecting his disappointment onto her, he became hyper-critical of her work and more dictatorial about her career. As she gained more artistic confidence, she wanted more autonomy in her life. They would have such altercations:

MOLLY: In all the plays you write for me, my characters never grow up. What you like is making a baby of me on stage and mothering me off stage.
YONKEL: No, taking care of you.
MOLLY: You mean controlling me. Telling me when to sleep, what to eat, how to dress, how to behave. But you don't tell me that you love me.
YONKEL: Ah, come on, now. When we met, you were an untrained vaudeville tummler. I groomed you.
MOLLY: What? Was I a horse?
YONKEL: I made you into a star.
MOLLY: Yes, You always did the talking and I did the listening. You made the deals and I performed out there until 2:00 A.M. and had to ask you for taxi money.

They gradually resolved their differences when Yonkel got praise for being an actor on stage and television. He was then more generous in his acceptance of Molly's increasing fame and able to show her more love. And Molly was content for awhile for Yonkel to be in the limelight while she took a leave of absence to decorate their country home, Chez Schmendrick.

With the passing of Yonkel in 1975, Molly, at seventy-seven, wanted to give up her career. She tells us: "Mama gave birth to me on the Lower East Side of New York and Yonkel introduced me to the whole world. . . . When Yonkel died, my leading man for 56 years, I wanted to retreat from the world. Every corner of my life reminded me of him."

But Yonkel, whom she had internalized within her, urged her to perform again and never keep an audience waiting. Even if it were with her last ounce of strength, he urged her to perform. Molly, as widow, did have the strength to present her best and get on with her life. Appearing as phenomenal star and role model before a standing ovation at her Carnegie Hall concert, she persuaded herself to go on: "I found the breath and legs and I sang and danced for a cheering young audience. Yes, Yonkel, if you believe in me, I can do it!" (Molly ends the show singing "Abi Gezunt.")

Thus, Molly, in our memories and in the dramatization of those memories in my play, *Molly Picon's Return Engagement*, continues to be the resilient woman entertainer and the embodiment of the vibrant Yiddish cultural past. The two are inextricably linked.

"In "Yiddish," said the storyteller rabbi, Nachman of Bratslav, "it is easier to break the heart." But according to author Steve Stern, "in the beguiling *Molly Picon's Return Engagement*, in Yiddish it is also easier to make one laugh. Through an affectionate act of theatrical magic the playwright," he claims, "has materialized the pre-eminent laugh-maker and heart-breaker of her day, Molly Picon herself, from among the shades of the vanished Yiddish theater. So vibrantly is the great star resurrected, that those who remember her may forever keep the faith and those who never knew her might become believers."

With *Molly Picon's Return Engagement*, I became an archaeologist of Jewish women entertainers, digging into their past and unearthing vital information about them. By talking to Molly's friends and relatives; by studying Molly's autobiography and her papers, scripts, and letters at the Jewish Historical Archives at Brandeis University; by examining her photographs and sheet music at YIVO and the Yiddish Book Center; and by listening to her recordings from the Workmen's Circle, I received a sense of who she was. My critic's self began to resurrect her as a performer to analyze. But as a playwright, I resurrected the performer in her and in myself, fused both of them, and made them come alive as a character in my play.

I did the same thing with the Jewish performers Sophie Tucker, Totie Fields, and Belle Barth. I had become their greatest fan and was addicted to making them known. As a critic, I wrote about them in my essay "The Unkosher Comediennes: From Sophie Tucker to Joan Rivers" and as a sit-down comedienne did impersonations of them across the country.[7] They came alive as fully fleshed individuals only in the plays with music that Joanne Koch and I wrote about them: *Sophie, Totie and Belle*[8] and the full-length drama about Sophie's life, *Sophie Tucker: Red Hot Yiddishe Mama.*[9]

Why did I single out these three women and choose to breathe theatrical life into them? Sophie Tucker was a secular legend during and after her lifetime, a dynamic entertainer who made a remarkable contribution to American culture during more than fifty years in show business. From her earliest hits in 1915 to her final TV and nightclub appearances in the 1960s, Sophie stood for the women who could manage on her own, an attribute I so desire in my own life.

She was among the first entertainers to advocate independence for women in all areas of life, including sex. In blues songs and in songs about life after forty and life after sixty, Sophie acknowledged that women had desires equal to men and should have equal opportunities for fulfilling them. But the songs she sings in our play, "Red Hot Mama," "Mister Siegal, Make It Legal," and "Myron, You're Not Desirin'," give voice to humorous complaints of women who either get plenty of attention but not enough respect, or respect and marriage but not enough attention. My play's depiction of a Sophie Tucker who, like supposedly liberated women do not get all of their sexual wishes fulfilled, is more lifelike than the supercharged red-hot mama who "can't keep her temperature down."

Similarly, Sophie's desire to be a Yiddishe Mama is not as overpowering as she claims. Her desire to perform in New York is so strong that she leaves her baby son in Hartford to be raised by her mother and sister. Her yearning for a lifelong companion causes her to marry and divorce three exploitive husbands so that she ends up singing, "I'm Living Alone and I like It," but then adds the realistic coda, "I didn't always like it, but you think anyone will pay to hear an old broad complain about living alone?" "So I'm Living Alone and I Like It."

Totie Fields, on the other hand, was the more dependent of the three women entertainers. Though her husband, Georgie, was her bandleader and she had supportive sisters who cared for her two daughters when she was on the road, Totie admires Sophie for her self-reliance and her ability to be successful without a man. The pudgy comedienne is the insecure woman, wanting desperately to be beautiful and paying an exorbitant price to do so. Though she is diabetic, her vanity prods her into having risky cosmetic surgery to eliminate a minute facial blemish. A victim of feminine perfectionism, she develops phlebitis from the surgery, then loses her leg, then her breast from cancer, and ultimately dies of a heart attack at forty-eight.

In the play I inject in Totie large doses of my own humor of wry self-deprecation, which I employ in the acceptance of my body. She complains: "Do you think it is easy pushing fat Jewish feet into thin Italian shoes?" Or she says, "Happiness is finding a library book that's three weeks overdue and that you're not." Or "Happiness is going out to dinner with friends and getting a brown gravy stain on a brown dress." But after Totie's surgery, which caused her to have an artificial leg and long hospital stays that reduced her to 120 pounds, her routine of "fat jokes" was inappropriate.

In the play I devised for her a new brand of prosthetic or missing-parts humor: zany hyperbole to cope with extreme loss:

Believe me the peg leg has its advantages. You don't have to shave it. It never gets varicose veins. It doesn't swell up. . . . But sometimes there are misunderstandings. Yesterday I hear this tapping. A woodpecker. He didn't know. . . . (She strikes a seductive pose.) But Georgie finds me very sexy this way. Plenty of people can screw, but how many can unscrew. Georgie got so excited the other night caressing my thigh, he didn't even notice the splinters. He didn't care that his new pair of polyester slacks were full of snags. He still adores me. And I still adore him—20 years. I guess he's stuck with me—fat or thin, flesh or wood, he doesn't care. That's why they say love is blind. Would anybody else but a blind man say a one-legged, one-breasted dame is beautiful? But that's what Georgie says about me.

Georgie's twenty-year love, like my husband's thirty-two-year love, is there to compensate for the worst misfortunes and enables Totie, like me, to continue performing.

Belle Barth was called the "Hildegard of the Underworld," and "the doyenne of the dirty line." She was born Belle Salzmen in New York's East Harlem area in 1911, appeared in vaudeville in the 1920s and performed at the Catskills, Atlantic City, Las Vegas, and her own Belle Barth Pub in Miami Beach until her death in 1971. Though she wanted to be remembered as a female Victor Borge, she entertained millions with recordings of her ribald comedy routines: "My Next Story Is a Little Risque," and "If I Embarrass You, Tell Your Friends." This coarse vulgarian destroys the illusions of others and has very few about herself. The veteran of five failed marriages, she constantly undercuts Sophie's sentimentality and Totie's bourgeois notions of femininity.

For Belle and I have reached a stage in our lives where we are not afraid to be brazen offenders of the faith, invading the holy sphere of the Jewish male comic and usurping his audience. Employing the humor of camouflaged aggression, we have been bold enough to clash with the code of *edelkeit*, or gentility, observed by respectable Jewish women. And finally, we have been daring enough to violate Judaism's central commandment for women: enforcement of the ritual of *kashrut*—keeping kosher, keeping clean. But we have become creatures of unclean lips with positive results. By infusing the bland with the spicy, the sterile with the racy, and the staid with the forbidden, our foul mouths do not tarnish our life. Belle Barth, MD (*Maven on Dreck*, "Expert on Feces"), and the rest of us add zest to it.

Sophie Tucker, Totie Fields, and Belle Barth, representing different parts of myself, were funny, strong, and independent at a time when women weren't supposed to exhibit any of those traits. They were the unkosher comediennes who broke tradition and flaunted taboos. They were unique voices in the wilderness of "acceptable" comedic performers. With postmenopausal zest, I bring them together on stage in a quirky meeting in the afterlife, where they share songs, anecdotes, routines, and self-discoveries. They compete, argue, and commiserate. Ultimately, they forge a bond of friendship before they do their last number—three women who have used humor to survive sexism, anti-Semitism, and even ageism and by so doing have extended the boundaries of comedy.

As an untamed playwright, I have employed gleeful abandon to make these unorthodox ladies into *vilde chayes* (wild beasts), leaping over the boundaries of Jewish respectability. Yet I have not alienated audiences with their breaches of decency. Rather than offending sensibilities, their big mouths have created an enduring tumult, and their innovative *schmutz* (filth) has left an indelible mark. Meanwhile, as playwright, I am in the process of creating other obstreperous sisters to disturb the peace.

V

**Recovering Religious Role Models:
New Images of Women in Stories and Song**

Gail Twersky Reimer

Eschewing Esther/Embracing Esther
The Changing Representation of
Biblical Heroines

For generations, Jewish women's images of themselves have come from the Bible stories read to them at bedtime or taught to them in religious school. In them, women figure as minor secondary characters, loved for their beauty, revered for their motherhood. Yet these stories have functioned as the Jewish fairy tales of our collective consciousness, influencing the way we think of ourselves and others think of us.

What we remember about Sarah, Rebekah, and Rachel, beautiful girls all, is their yearning for sons. What we remember of the "not as beautiful" Leah is her grief over being unloved. Sarah's jealousy of Hagar and Rachel's envy of Leah leave us with lasting images of women's instability, especially around problems of conception. Sarah's cruel banishment of Hagar and her son Ishmael and Rebekah's deceitful ruse to gain the birthright for Jacob offer us powerful images of the protective Jewish mother who will risk anyone and anything ("Let the curse be upon me," Rebekah tells Jacob) for the sake of her beloved sons. Sarah is also remembered as the ideal homemaker, able to whip up a meal at a moment's notice when Abraham announces the need to entertain unexpected guests; and Rebekah, too, is expert at preparing the foods and delicacies Isaac likes with a speed that astonishes even him.

In the Bible stories of our childhood, obedient women like Ruth and Esther are worthy of praise, and disobedient ones like Lot's wife are turned into pillars of salt. Even public figures like Miriam, the sister of Moses, who leads the women in song as the Israelites cross the Red Sea, must know their place and refrain from challenging men's authority lest they find themselves afflicted with leprosy. Revered for her role as the protective sister, Miriam is also disparaged for her role as the critical and confrontational sister.

Generations of girls whose religious education was limited by tradition and convention have carried these images into adulthood and allowed them to define Jewish character and delineate its possibilities. But in the wake of the reemergence of the women's movement in the late 1960s, women began actively resisting these stereotypes and altering our images of biblical women. Feminist studies of the Bible appeared with increasing frequency in scholarly journals and books in the 1970s alongside new rewritings of Bible stories in books targeted to children and new interpretations of those stories in magazines and essay collections targeted to a general adult audience.

Several recent essays have focused on major trends in recent scholarly readings of biblical women.[1] My intention here is to look at trends in popular readings, in works produced for a general audience. Rewritings of a Bible story in children's books and in popular commentary or interpretation, as Mieke Bal compellingly demonstrates in *Lethal Love*, merit our attention, for they "show the interaction between what our culture teaches its younger members and how adult education reinforces this primary ideological insertion with the justifications of 'reason.'"[2]

Motivated as many of the contemporary popular representations of biblical women are by the quest for relevant and appropriate role models within the tradition, they tend to feature images of women who are independent and assertive, women who are acting rather than acted on. Much of this work, however, reproduces and exaggerates existing images of biblical women, even as it claims value and merit for the women the text seemingly—and the rabbis certainly—scorned. While it successfully reveals (and counters) the patriarchal biases of the biblical text and its subsequent interpreters, it frequently is as reductive and/or tendentious as the previous representations it critiques. The representation of women in much of this work continues to conform to the binary oppositions characteristic of male representation: passive/aggressive, independent/loyal, proud/humble, assertive/self-sacrificing. More disturbingly, this work continues to rely on a male standard of measurement even as it rejects conventional male judgments. Passivity is valued less than assertiveness, loyalty less than independence.

As a case in point, this essay focuses on contemporary representations of women in the Scroll of Esther in the writing of Jewish women over the past three decades. Far better known than Ruth, the only other woman with a biblical book named after her, Esther has the good fortune of being associated with a child-oriented Jewish holiday (Purim). Moreover, cast as she frequently is in Sunday school books and enactments as the biblical Cinderella, the orphan girl chosen for her beauty and modesty to be the wife of the Persian king, Esther readily captures the imagination of young, ambitious Jewish girls like Ella in Sydney Taylor's best-selling children's series, *All of a Kind Family*.

In recent years, Purim has increasingly come to resemble Halloween, with most American Jewish children opting to dress as anything but the characters in the Purim story. Yet just one generation ago little girls looked forward to the holiday of Purim as their annual opportunity to be Queen for a Day. Nearly all the writers included in this essay make reference to their experience as girls when, like Ella, they could imagine nothing more perfect than being Queen Esther.

In one of the earliest essays in contemporary Jewish feminist interpretation of Bible, subsequently reprinted in Elizabeth Koltun's "The Jewish Woman," Mary Gendler recalls: "When I was a child Purim was one of my favorite Jewish holidays. I loved to dress up as Queen Esther in a long, flowing gown, put a sparkling crown on my head, and feel brave and loyal at the thought that I might risk my life for my people."[3] And in one of the most recent essays on Esther, Celina Spiegel, co-editor of *Out of the Garden*, similarly recollects "feeling queenly and beautiful as a young girl when [she] dressed up as Queen Esther for the holiday of Purim."[4]

Not all girls, however, have looked forward to the opportunity of "being" Queen Esther. Michelle Landsberg, speaking in the first documentary film about Jewish feminists, significantly titled *Half the Kingdom*, has a distinctly different memory of childhood Purims.

I remember my indignation and bewilderment about the Purim Story. Everyone loves Purim right? But there was Queen Vashti of whom we know so little. Ahasuerus, king of Persia and Media, demanded that she perform a dance before assembled guests and notables at a banquet. She refused and was dismissed. The Purim story depicts her as a villainess. Then Esther was chosen to be queen in a beauty contest: docile, beautiful, submissive Esther. She was the good one in the story—she saved the Jewish people.

Saving the Jewish people was important but at the same time her whole submissive, secretive, manipulative way of being was the absolute archetype of 1950s womanhood. It repelled me. I thought, "Hey, what was wrong with Vashti? She had dignity. She had self-respect." She said, "I'm not going to dance for you and your pals."

There I was, nine or ten years old, and I thought, "I like Vashti but I'm supposed to hate her. Puzzling."[5]

But if Landsberg's memory of what Esther—and by contrast, Vashti—represented to her as a child is the exception rather than the rule for women of her generation, her images of the two queens have become common fare in recent versions of the Purim story produced for children. Often edited out of children's books altogether, Vashti, when represented in the past, has generally been cast as the haughty, arrogant, and even wicked queen. This image still hovers over some current retellings, even when writers for children consciously try to preserve the simplicity and ambiguity of the original biblical text, which tells us little about Vashti other than that she refused to appear before the king. In Miriam Chaikin's *Esther*, for example, Vashti's act is reported

Vera Rosenberry's line drawings recreate a familiar fairy-tale world of a vain and wicked queen and of a modern young orphan girl. (From *Esther* by Miriam Chaikin, Philadelphia: Jewish Publication Society, 1987)

in a single sentence that echoes the biblical verse. "But Vashti refused to come" is all Chaikin writes.[6] But while the story Chaikin tells offers no particular image of Vashti, thus remaining true to the original text's refusal to pronounce judgment, the Beardsley-like line illustrations by Vera Rosenberry that accompany her text tell an all too familiar story, as they take the young reader directly into the world of vain, wicked queens and modest young orphan children.

Shoshana Silberman, in *The Whole Megillah*, also limits her retelling of Vashti's part in the story to the simple statement: "But Vashti refused."[7] But if we contrast the illustration of Vashti by Katherine Kahn that accompanies her text with the one that accompanies Chaikin's, we observe a noticeable change in Vashti's image. The portrayal of Vashti's defiance and anger is neutralized. It isn't necessarily attractive, but it also doesn't damn the woman. Though Silberman's retelling in words and pictures render Vashti as neither villain nor heroine, the commentary that accompanies her text attempts to not only vindicate Vashti but exalt her. Dismissing the vilification of Vashti as without basis in the text, Silberman continues her commentary by noting that "in fact, feminists think of her as a heroine. Many interpret her refusal to appear at the King's feast as an act of modesty." (That this image of Vashti is equally absent from the biblical text, Silberman tellingly neglects to mention.)

In Katherine Kahn's illustrations for *The Whole Megillah*, Queen Vashti's defiance seems justified by the overbearing and mean-spirited king at her side. The glamorous Esther is granted an independent mind, choosing her own path rather than simply following Mordecai's directions. (Art copyright © 1990 by Katherine Janus Kahn, from *The Whole Megillah* © 1990 by Shoshana Silberman, published by Kar-Ben Copies, Inc., Rockville, Md. Used with permission.)

The paradoxical representation of Vashti as modest but assertive, loyal but disobedient, is developed more fully in Ruth Brin's *The Story of Esther.* In Brin's version Vashti's refusal of the king is motivated by respect for her husband and obedience to Persian law. Brin portrays Vashti as a loyal Persian, committed to the observance of Persian law, and a loyal wife interested in saving her husband from violating the law of his own land. Brin's modest Vashti doesn't simply refuse the king; she first pleads with him to reconsider and rescind his order. The illustration that accompanies the scene that follows shows us a sad and frightened Vashti, quite different from the Vashti that appears in either Miriam Chaikin's book or Shoshana Silberman's: "The guests listened in silence as the king told his messenger that Vashti was to appear, unveiled, before the company of men. Such a thing was unheard of for a Persian lady never appeared unveiled before any man except her husband. Vashti was shocked when she heard the king's command. Rather than obey it, she sent the messenger back to King Ahasuerus, begging him to change his mind. When the king insisted that Vashti appear before him at once, the queen refused. 'Never would I do such a thing,' she cried."[8]

Brin's image of Vashti as a modest, loving, and loyal wife and citizen is meant to counter the rabbinic image of Vashti as a vain and lascivious woman who would have willingly appeared naked before the king had she not discovered marks of leprosy upon her. It also counters conventional stereotypes of loyal wives as submissive ones. Yet Brin's vindication of Vashti ultimately relies on Vashti's conformity to conventional expectations of women.

For Vashti to become a feminist heroine, her refusal had to be represented as a bold and courageous statement of independence rather than as an act of modesty. Variations on the image of Vashti as a woman with a political stance have been appearing with increasing frequency in retellings of the story for children. Often it takes only a single sentence to transform the disobedient queen into a liberated woman. In *Festival of Esther*, for example, Maida Silverman presents Vashti's defiance of the king's order thus: "Vashti did not like to be ordered around as if she were a servant. She refused to obey the king's command."[9] And in Barbara Cohen's retelling of the story in *Here Come the Purim Players!*, the episode is reported with comparable pithiness: "But Vashti was a queen, not an entertainer. She sent back a message: I will not come."[10]

Supporting these new images in children's books is a growing body of popular commentary by Jewish women that represents Vashti as a bold and daring woman who refuses to be treated as an object. Emerging from a profound discomfort with the roles they are expected to play and with the role models typically presented to them for emulation, the writers of these essays comb the Bible for new sources of inspiration and find in Vashti a model of dignity, independence, and nay-saying. Their exaltation of Vashti often leads to a vilification of Esther in ways that unwittingly sustain the traditional polarization of biblical women into the good and the bad. And as we'll see, while presented in the spirit of fusing feminism and Judaism, their exaltation of Vashti reinforces rather than resolves the tensions women often feel between Judaism and feminism.

Mary Gendler paved the way for feminist reevaluation of the Scroll of Esther with her essay "The Restoration of Vashti." Echoing the feelings of many of her contemporaries, Gendler acknowledged that as she grew older, a maturation that significantly coincided with the rebirth of the women's movement, Queen Esther "felt less and less like someone with whom I wanted to identify totally."

Gendler's closing qualifier, "totally," opens the way for more complex and nuanced representations of Esther than the one that dominates her essay. But before such nuanced representations could surface, the restoration of Vashti (significantly, the title of Gendler's piece) was necessary. The traditional polarization of biblical women into the good and bad, the obedient and disobedient, was initially reversed, and only later would it be resisted through a repudiation of the categories themselves.

Gendler's initial retelling of the first part of the tale both lays bare the text's ideology of male dominance and her own ideology of female independence:

Esther becomes queen as the replacement for Vashti, Ahasuerus' first wife. Vashti has been disposed of because of her refusal to display her beauty in front of Ahasuerus and other drunken princes of the land. Ahasuerus had prepared a great feast in order to consolidate his power and display his great wealth. Therefore, when the discussion turned to bragging about whose women were more beautiful, Ahaseurus was ready to display more property, this time his wife. However, unlike jewels and gold, people—even women—will not always allow themselves to be treated as objects. Vashti refused.[11]

The remainder of the retelling includes the traditional representation of Esther as "beautiful and pious" and concludes by describing Esther as initially "frightened" by Mordecai's request that she petition the king to save her people and only later acting more courageously and "indeed" saving the Jews. In the place of a disobedient Vashti stands a rebellious Vashti, and in the place of a brave and courageous Esther stands a courageous but frightened Esther. These new images support Gendler's sociological reading of the scroll, which transforms it from "a story of a close escape from annihilation, a holocaust averted through the defiance and piety of Mordecai and the courage and beauty of Esther" to "a story of female response to patriarchal authority." Read from this latter perspective, Vashti and Esther serve as "models" of how to deal with patriarchal authority. The Bible, Gendler argues, is unambiguous about which model is preferred: "The message comes through loud and clear: women who are bold, direct, aggressive and disobedient are not acceptable; the praiseworthy women are those who are unassuming, quietly persistent and who gain their power through the love they inspire in men. These women live almost vicariously, subordinating their needs and desires to those of others. We have only to look at the stereotyped Jewish Mother to attest to the still-pervasive influence of the Esther-behavior model."[12]

While the message the story traditionally carried is anathema to women trying desperately to break free of the Esther-behavior model, the story, Gendler argues, provides them with an alternative model. In Vashti women can find a "role model for appropriate self-assertion." Following Gendler, Vashti's open defiance of the king (and her subsequent punishment by the king, in deed, and by the rabbis, in word) becomes the dominant motif in numerous feminist readings and renderings of the scroll. And these readings are no less ambiguous than the Bible as to which model for dealing with patriarchal authority is preferred.

As has already been suggested, the transformation of the arrogant and con-

ceited Vashti into a bold, dignified, assertive, and independent woman who refuses to "be treated as an object" takes place at Esther's expense. Once admired for her glamour and courage, her beauty and piety, Esther is rejected as
the prototype of the "ideal Jewish woman," an ideal newly liberated Jewish
women denounced as "restrictive and repressive." Though Gendler concludes
her essay by proposing that "Vashti be reinstated on the throne along with her
sister Esther," her essay effectively deposes Esther, granting the seat of honor
she has occupied throughout Jewish history to the Gentile Queen Vashti who,
like the Jew Mordecai, refuses to debase herself "by submitting to illegitimate
demands."

To promote Vashti rather than Esther as the model for how Jewish women
"ought to be" is not without its problems. While it enables Jewish women to
discover female characters within scriptural tradition with whom they wish to
identify, the female character they are asked to identify with is from outside
the faith; the female character they are discouraged from emulating is the Jewish woman in the tale. The centrality of ethnicity to the tale, as well as the fact
that the drama of which Esther and Vashti are a part revolves around threatened annihilation of the Jewish people, makes ignoring Esther's Jewish identity and imagining both her and Vashti as variations on everywoman a trouble-
some move.

In a recent essay on Esther, included in Buchman and Spiegel's *Out of the
Garden*, Rachel Brownstein recalls the resistance she met when, as a young
Sunday school teacher, she tried to convince her nine- and ten-year-old students that Vashti was a perfectly decent role for girls. "Vashti was not Jewish,
one little girl protested, when we tried, with deliberate subversiveness to talk
her up."[13] These little girls, in their own way, were refusing to choose between
being powerful and beautiful women and being Jewish. Resisting the role of
Vashti was a way of insisting that, at least in Sunday school, young Jewish
girls be given opportunities to admire and personate Jewish heroines.

While presenting an alternative vision of womanhood, efforts at Vashti's
restoration, such as Gendler's and Brownstein's, tend to both maintain the disturbing binary opposition between women that characterizes centuries of interpretive retellings of Bible stories and reify the stereotyped vision of Jewish
womanhood popularized by Chaim Grade earlier in this century and by Herman Wouk and Philip Roth in the postwar decades. Nowhere is this more evident than in Gendler's repeated identifications of Esther with the Jewish
mother. This identification is especially curious, given that Esther is one of the
few biblical heroines who is married without children, whose story is neither
about childbearing nor child rearing. In describing Esther's dramatic solicita-
tion of King Ahasuerus, Gendler writes, "*like a good Jewish mother*, she first
wines and dines him, and only then makes her request." And later in the essay,
as she sums up rabbinic representations of Esther, Gendler observes, "in short,

except for her momentary lapse when Mordecai asks her to petition the king, she is 'perfect,' *a kind of ultimate Jewish mother* who risks her life in order to save her children (the People Israel)."[14]

Rachel Brownstein sets out to read the Purim story against the grain and avoid reproducing "the binary opposition between women that the Hebrew Bible reiterates" but ends up representing even more polarized images of Esther and Vashti than those in Gendler's essay. Initially, she suggests that the stories of Vashti and Esther be read as "parallel tales about people in perilous positions" rather than as oppositional tales: "The stories reflect each other, and the echoes between them suggest another theme of the holiday of Purim . . . the theme that life is a gamble rather than a fair test in which merit prevails."[15]

As she turns the women's stories into "tales about people" and universalizes their specific position in a patriarchal society to "perilous positions," Brownstein removes gender as well as ethnicity as significant categories for interpreting the scroll. With gender and ethnicity out of the picture, she momentarily succeeds in avoiding a polarization of the two women. But no sooner does she turn her attention to how Esther and Vashti behave as women than she unwittingly sets them up in opposition to one another. Brownstein's Vashti is the "queen who dared to say no to being a sex object"; her Esther, on the other hand, "docilely spends months being creamed and groomed and polished to perfection."

For all Brownstein's disdain for it, in her essay the compulsion to binary opposition prevails; if Vashti "was a pretty good queen," it has to follow that Esther was not as good. She inverts the representations of the two queens we are accustomed to but maintains the familiar binary structure of representation. While encouraging a "double crowning," in "Chosen Women," Brownstein chooses one woman over the other, robbing Esther of her crown in order to award one to Vashti.

The paragraph in which Brownstein summarizes the story begins with the statement "Because of her primacy in the Purim story, Esther is sometimes called a heroine, but it is hard to make a very persuasive case for that." The same paragraph concludes with its own series of oppositions: "Where Vashti lost her place by refusing to be the king's guest, Esther charms him by being his hostess. And where Vashti enraged her husband by not revealing her (bodily) charms, Esther's beauty induces the man even to embrace her newly revealed Jewishness."

In the analysis that follows this summary, Brownstein elaborates on why Esther "falls short of being a cause for feminist celebration": "Esther conceals her real name, Hadassah; evidently she has no problem being less than true to herself. There is no evidence that she has ideas of her own: she is the puppet of her wise and good male guardian. She submits without question to the exotic cosmetic treatments and complaisantly exhibits her body to the gaze of evaluating men. Finally her great achievement is to get what she wants by duping her dot-ing husband over dinner, as in an episode of 'I Love Lucy.' "[16]

After this catalog of harsh indictments, it is difficult to take seriously Brownstein's claim that "Queen Esther is by no means an embarrassment to women." Other than the brief description of Esther as "a canny political actor who manages to rule a king," all Brownstein musters in support of her claim is that Esther is not one of "those homey Mothers of Israel who want only sons" and that she is married outside the faith. This odd defense of Esther implies that what saves Esther from being a total embarrassment to women is that she is not "completely Jewish."

It is instructive to contrast Brownstein's retelling of Esther's story with Letty Cottin Pogrebin's in *Deborah, Golda and Me*.[17] Brownstein's Esther comes off as little more than Mordecai's puppet. The only credit she is given is for introducing Mordecai into the palace:

The king announces he will hold a beauty contest, the winner of which will be his new queen. Esther is sent by Mordecai to enter the contest under a false name (evidently so as to conceal her Jewishness). With the other contestants she docilely spends months being creamed and groomed and polished to perfection; finally judged the fairest of them all, she wins and marries the king. Her strategic position very soon proves to be invaluable: the evil courtier Haman is planning to persuade Ahasuerus that the Jews are plotting against him and must be destroyed. Esther introduces Mordecai into the palace and ultimately ensures Haman's destruction during a banquet in her quarters.[18]

Pogrebin, seeking to reclaim her Jewish identity, is eager to "distill the best message" possible from the stories of biblical women. She thus imagines Es-ther as an independent woman of courage who defies convention and risks her life to save her people:

The king called for a bevy of virgins from which to choose a new wife. The winner was Esther, who did not reveal that she was a Hebrew. Once installed as queen, she was able to save her people from the wicked anti-Semite Haman, the royal adviser who had con-vinced King Ahasuerus that Jews were dangerous subversives. When Esther learned of Haman's plan to exterminate her people, she ignored the rule that wives must not bother their husbands or interfere in state business and she successfully petitioned the king to revoke Haman's evil decree and to have the madman killed.[19]

The most obvious difference is the deletion of Mordecai from Pogrebin's account in service of granting Esther agency. Not only does Esther have ideas of her own, she also acts on them. Brownstein, on the other hand, not only in-cludes Mordecai but subtly expands his role to ensure Esther's passivity. Though in the biblical text we read that Esther was taken into the king's palace, Brownstein has Mordecai send Esther to the palace. She also reverses the order of events and has Esther introduce Mordecai into the palace before the banquet at which she cleverly manages Haman's downfall, rather than after. A seemingly minor alteration but one that further reinforces the image of Esther as little more than Mordecai's puppet. Where Pogrebin edits out Mordecai so that Esther's heroism can be appreciated without distraction, Brownstein tries to undercut Esther's heroism at every possible point.

Out of the Garden includes a second essay on Esther by one of the collection's editors, Celina Spiegel. In an interesting and significant variation on other recollections of childhood Purims, Spiegel recalls that as a young girl, though she felt "queenly and beautiful" when dressed up as Queen Esther, she "never quite felt like the hero of the day." "Even as a child," she continues, "I sensed that Esther's guardian-cousin, Mordecai, was the brains behind Esther's success." Troubled by her own experience of the eponymous hero as secondary, Spiegel sets out to reframe the relationship between Esther's heroism and Mordecai's heroism. Through a reading of Esther as satire, she discovers a new way of representing Esther that challenges traditional representations that define her as subordinate. Read within a context in which the sexual nuances of Esther's portrait matter, her heroism becomes both central and controversial. In the pervasive suspicion of women's sexuality common to both the Jewish tradition and American culture, Spiegel finds an explanation for her earlier failure to appreciate Esther's heroism. The affirmation of the erotic at the core of Spiegel's portrayal of Esther is, she recognizes, "not one that many teachers might want to teach uncomprehending children."

Shifting the emphasis from Esther's beauty to Esther's sexuality provides a lively challenge to early feminist views of Esther as a disappointingly conventional virtuous heroine. Spiegel represents Esther's decision to "play her sexuality for all its worth" as far more bold and daring than Vashti's refusal to parade her sexuality. By positing the opening banquet as a saturnalia, Spiegel inverts Vashti's bold act into one of compliance with the spirit of the festivities: "Such a festival in ancient practice, was the one opportunity for every person . . . to speak his or her mind. . . . During this one week . . . Vashti may have her only sanctioned opportunity to disobey the King."[20]

Given the codes of behavior at saturnalia, Vashti's behavior is not "disrespectful or improper." Esther's unbidden appearance before the king, on the other hand, is a clear violation of Persian law, an act she undertakes in full recognition of the danger involved. And while she "breaks the King's law out of her obedience to Mordecai," in delaying her request to the king she "departs from a literal execution of Mordecai's wishes." "Improvising from his script," Esther surpasses Mordecai in "satire's subtle art," proving herself a "master of using time and circumstance to her advantage." With her "shrewd understanding of the stirrings of men" (an understanding Vashti conspicuously lacks), Esther brilliantly manages to win the king's favor, to orchestrate Haman's downfall, and to outperform Mordecai to the last.

Elizabeth Swados pushes the representation of an independent, active, and sexually confident and powerful Esther even harder. Complete justice to Swados's creation demands discussion of the music as well as the lyrics. But for the purposes of this essay, I am treating the libretto of *Bible Women* as a self-contained text that represents Esther in a startlingly new way.

"A meek and gentle Esther," Swados explains in her introductory notes to the libretto of *Bible Women*, "reveals herself to be strong and crafty so she can make the king love her and win her way to power. She is sort of Jewish Wonder Woman."[21] Elsewhere, Swados describes Esther as "a Jewish Mata Hari." Drawing on stereotypes of active, sexual women to represent Esther, Swados simultaneously complicates the meaning of these stereotypes and our image of biblical heroines.

In the cycle of songs dedicated to the story told in the Scroll of Esther, Vashti is represented as an angry, militant feminist. With her constant references to her husband, King Ahasuerus, as "a pig" and "fool," hers is the uncompromising confrontational style frequently associated with the first wave of contemporary feminism. In contrast to Vashti, Esther presents herself in terms of both a typically feminine loving relationship to a man and an independent "masculine" ambition and strength:

> Goodbye Mordecai, uncle, cousin, lover, patriarch,
> I'm off to save the world like Noah with his ark.

In this song, Esther's first in the cycle, images of masculine strength are immediately overwhelmed by ones of feminine strength, turning a contradictory representation of femininity and female sexuality into a complex and complicated one:

> Esther, the invincible, I am braver than Eve.
> I'm a lover like Sheba, with a knife up my sleeve
> . . . .
> I'm a pillar like Delilah, I act sweetly but,
> The moment the sun disappears, I pull out my
> razor and I cut . . .

Esther's invocation of Eve and Delilah to describe her own power is itself an expression of her power. By defining herself in relation to two biblical women who traditionally symbolize evil, deceitfulness, seductiveness, and treachery, Swados's Esther demonstrates her willingness and ability to challenge patriarchal tradition. If Vashti gives voice to women's resistance to the overt oppression of women, Esther gives voice to women's resistance to the covert oppression of negative representations of women. Esther takes possession of two powerful images of women that have been used in the past to foster fear and condemnation of women's sexuality. In her reconstruction of the past, Eve and Delilah become models of heroism rather than of wickedness, women empowered by their sexuality rather than destroyed by it.

Just as the character Esther presents herself in relation to other women, in *Bible Women*, Swados tells Esther's story within the context of several other women's stories. By placing Esther within "a circle of women," Swados radically alters the frame of reference through which we experience Esther. Esther ceases to be wholly defined in terms of her relationship to Mordecai, Ahasuerus, and Haman. Nor is she defined in terms of her difference from Vashti. In Swados's woman-centered reading, Esther takes her place among other heroic biblical women and is experienced in relationship to them. In this company, rather than being submerged in the intensified relationship Swados posits between Esther and Mordecai in the "duet of love and sacrifice," Esther emerges as a woman who embodies the devotion of Ruth, the sensuality of Eve, and the wisdom of Deborah—a woman strong enough to both love and lead.

Significantly, Vashti is also given a place in this company of women, for she too is a proud and independent and courageous biblical woman. Neither Esther's foil nor her opposite, Vashti is represented simply as the bold queen who preceded Esther. Read allegorically, Swados's Vashti and Esther each represent a different stage of feminist politics. In Vashti we recognize the all-consuming anger and indignation that a later generation of feminist heroines, like Esther, moves beyond as they struggle to identify the sources for their own power and then exercise it. Swados's representation of these two women as part of a continuum is a striking departure from the polarization of the two that characterizes most of the works we've examined. Her work makes space for both women, finally accomplishing what Mary Gendler had first proposed in "The Restoration of Vashti"—reinstating Vashti on the throne *along with* Esther.

My essay concludes, in a peculiarly appropriate way, with "Esther Invincible," the title of the Swados song quoted from earlier. For Swados the title is purely descriptive of the character. For me it has deeper resonances. "Esther Invincible" encapsulates a history of twenty-five years of contemporary feminist interpretation of the Scroll of Esther and its eponymous heroine. Subject to a struggle over meaning, to changing understandings of women's heroism, sexuality, and relationships to men, Esther was temporarily eclipsed by Vashti. But she was never fully overcome. In several recent readings of the Scroll, Esther has reclaimed her place as biblical heroine worthy of admiration and emulation by even the most strong-minded of contemporary women. Considerably more complicated and powerful a heroine than either our rabbis imagined or our early feminist readers of the Scroll were able to see, Esther has proved herself, even within the annals of interpretive rereadings, genuinely invincible.

Maida E. Solomon

Claiming Our Questions
Feminism and Judaism in Women's Haggadot

The Song of Questions

Mother, asks the clever daughter,
Who are our mothers?
Who are our ancestors?
What is our history?
Give us our name. Name our genealogy.

Mother, asks the wicked daughter,
If I learn my history, will I not be angry?
Will I not be bitter as Miriam
Who was deprived of her prophecy?

Mother, asks the simple daughter,
If Miriam lies buried in the sand,
Why must we dig up those bones?
Why must we remove her from the sun and stone
Where she belongs?

The one who knows not how to question,
she has no past, she has no present, she can have no future
without knowing her mothers
without knowing her angers
without knowing her questions.
　　　　　　　　—E. M. Broner and Naomi Nimrod,
　　　　　　　　　　The Women's Haggadah

Beginning in the 1970s and growing rapidly since then, an extraordinary grass-roots movement—women rewriting haggadot for Passover—has been taking place throughout the United States. Still mushrooming at a steady pace, this movement and its products reveal the contagious energy of Jewish women

220

who question the patriarchal structure of Judaism. For three thousand years women have lived with contradictions based on a denial of their existence as they celebrated Pesach. For less than thirty years women have been reshaping haggadot to create a Judaism of inclusion rather than exclusion. Women redefining the Festival of Passover—such an upheaval demands examination of the ritual in the light of Judaism, feminism, and Jewish women's lives.

Judaism always has encompassed more than theology; rather it stands for ways of living and cultural traditions. Women's haggadot also reflect the cultural values, the changing roles of women in America, that Jewish women have been integrating into the daily rhythm of their lives. These newly written haggadot and their celebration of Passover spring from the intersection of seemingly conflicting frameworks. Yet this enormous, bottom-up surge of social change is breathing fresh life into Jewish rituals and making Pesach more immediately relevant to the daily lives of Jewish women and men today.

As I search my memory of girlhood seders, I find little awareness of exclusion, nor do many Jewish women with whom I have spoken. We accepted omission as part of the landscape. As women at traditional seders, we quietly assumed our presence in the Passover saga. By doing so in silence, we unconsciously took on the mantle of invisibility cast to us simply because of our femaleness. Feminist theologian Judith Plaskow has spoken of the need to hear silence before transformation can occur, noting that "hearing silence is not easy. A silence so vast tends to fade into the natural order. . . . [At] the great events at Sinai, we do not look for ourselves in the narratives, but assume our presence, peopling the gaps in the text with women's shadowy forms."[1]

In the feminist haggadot women exchange shadowy images for spoken strengths, at last breaking this vast silence. A newly defined Passover functions as a catalyst for growth by acknowledging the unheard silences and the accompanying potential for transformation. A conduit for feminism as well as for a more inclusive Judaism, these new haggadot are reaching an ever widening span of Jewish women, moving beyond even national boundaries.

To understand the dynamics of this ongoing story, I look at the following: the historical interaction between survival and adaptation in Pesach, the stages of development in women's haggadot over three decades, and the elements of women's presence (as women move from victims to resisters) and women's practice (as women engage in Godwrestling and life wrestling) woven into the new haggadot.

Historical Background

Feminist haggadot are closer to Jewish traditions than is usually assumed. Passover has ever intertwined itself with what is necessary for the survival of the religion; therefore, its form has changed at different times in history. As the first ritual of the new religion it celebrated the Jews' escape from Egypt and the new covenant with the exclusive male deity in a family or clan setting, even while it incorporated indigenous spring rituals of the surrounding peoples— the Festival of the Pascal Offering and the Festival of Unleavened Bread. Two centuries later the evolving and more centralized religion dictated that Pesach become a temple-based ritual to guard against "pagan" influences, and only Jewish men were allowed on the Temple grounds. Several centuries later, as the Temple and even the nation came under siege from invading armies, the priests widened the ritual, to make sure that women and children felt some link to it, by permitting each head of household to take home his sacrificial lamb's carcass for a home-based feast.

Early in the Diaspora, the ritual components of Pesach are outlined in the Mishnah, the first written record of Jewish customs, schools of thought, and varied practices, which forms the core of the Talmud. The second-century rabbinical Mishnah authors purposefully created a dialogic and pluralistic central source of wisdom, one that integrated questions and interpretation with directives. In the ninth century, Rabbi Amran drew almost literally from the Mishnah in producing the first haggadah, a written document that families could own and use at the Passover meal. This haggadah has been passed down through the centuries almost word for word. Yet the original Mishnah text had represented a potpourri of religious and folk traditions clustered around some absolutes, with an overall goal of preserving Jewish customs as of old and making Judaism adaptive to the Diaspora. The question/answer format, as well as the multiplicity of answers and variety of traditions in the Mishnah, ensured that this ritual would be acceptable to Jews of differing beliefs as well as adaptable to unknown circumstances. Passover had to be responsive to the paradox that survival in exile posed in its contradictory needs for constancy and change.

"In every generation let each man look on himself as if He came forth out of Egypt." This most fundamental absolute in the ritual is extremely adaptive to whatever hardships Jews have faced in varied circumstances. The directive creates a unique concept of time—to relive the exodus rather than to remember—and transforms the ritual from a memory of the past to an experience in the present. Each spring, Jews must experience the Exodus rather than simply hear of it and, as such, immediately revisualize Egypt as whatever oppression currently exists in their lives. The possibility of liberation through Judaism thus becomes immediately relevant to Jewish people of any era, creating almost an urgency. Passover is often the last ritual to be forsaken in the process of assimilation because of this urgency.

For Jewish feminists in America, this urgency no longer sufficiently rationalizes the contradiction of reliving an experience in which women do not see, hear, nor feel themselves. The Mishnah was written by men and to men, in accordance with the culture and values of its time. The haggadah, its essentials springing from that document and having come through the centuries so intact, not surprisingly omits women consistently, in spirit as well as in letter. "Now we are slaves; next year may we be free men."[2] The Four Sons ask vital questions. The leader of the ceremony is male, the deity is male, the wise rabbis are male. The human hero of the exodus from slavery, although rarely mentioned by name, is male. The Prophet Elijah is male. The biblical references are to male figures. "As it is said: 'And He brought us out from thence, that He might bring us in, to give us the land which He swore unto our fathers'" (Deut. 6:23).[3] The historical narrative describes the slave labor of the men ("their lives bitter with hard service, in mortar and brick . . . and in the field") but not of women.[4] Even in the midst of Blessings Over the Matzah (in the Union Haggadah that I grew up hearing), we read about the "dough of our fathers."[5]

A reference to the Mothers of Israel in a post-seder chant (amid Fathers of Israel, Moses, God, and so on), a mention of women in the context of meal preparations, a token female presence in some Reform haggadot through the lighting of the candles (not a part of the traditional haggadah), even haggadic illustrations of biblical women or women at the seder table—none of these incidents, which can be counted on one hand, can make the haggadah validate the lives of Jewish women and girls. As Jews, yes, the haggadah and the Festival of Passover reach out and touch some deep chord in us—of survival and triumph, of slavery and freedom, of commitment and joyousness—and we respond. As women, if we allow ourselves that consciousness, traditional Passover reaches out toward us and misses. No, that picture is incorrect. The haggadah fundamentally never even points itself in our direction.

With a need to be visible both as Jews and women, feminists of the past three decades have been building new Passover traditions inclusive of women. Although these changes often contradict patriarchal values in Judaism, they nonetheless embody the intersecting traditions and adaptive nature that has ensured Jewish survival. The very process of questioning and rethinking, back and forth, taking delight in dialogue and argument and interpretation—this tradition runs through the marrow of Jewish survival. Women haggadists and seder participants are openly engaging in this tradition of dialogue, reliving rather than merely rereading. Perhaps—if we leave aside gender—the new haggadot are returning to the spirit of the Mishnah goal of adaptation and survival. The new circumstance facing Judaism, in this instance, is feminism.

The Spread of Women's Seders

A brief overview of the spread of women's seders gives a context for examining feminist haggadot. In the early 1970s, the second wave American feminist movement, with its women's buildings and women's centers, spawned the very first women's seders conducted by Jewish women. From these origins, women's haggadot moved out of women's centers and into women's homes as a tremendous explosion of unpublished haggadah writing by individual women took place each year. This almost underground activity continued all through the 1980s in a variety of forms, as many Jewish women created their own relationship to the relevance of the Passover story and ritual. Women haggadists have been building new oral traditions that, in the modern era of communication, take written forms. For these Jewish feminists, writing the haggadah (or rewriting, compiling, or choosing which new text to use) became as much a task of preparation for the seder as making the *charoset*. In the early and mid-1990s the next development in this grassroots chain reaction involved feminist seders returning to community settings, but this time to *Jewish* community settings. A proliferation of Jewish community women's seders with once again newly written women's haggadot is currently taking place and bursting with excitement.

My own association with feminist seders goes back at least fifteen years, predating my textual study of women's haggadot in 1986.[6] As a secular Jew with limited religious background, I found that feminism opened a doorway for me to expand my identity as a Jew, and women's seders became a part of my journey. My own recollections paint one picture of the growth of women's seders over the years.

I remember a seder in 1980. I am a fairly recent East Coast migrant to San Francisco, a lesbian mother with a five-year-old. I join two other single mothers and children, and together we put together traditional foods. Dusty's kitchen table is not big enough, so we create a table on the floor in the living room, and sit on cushions around it. Using a traditional haggadah, we talk about Judaism's incredible sexism yet we affirm the comfort of the familiar Hebrew, the story, the songs, our favorite parts and our memories.

I had never experienced anything like the ease of that Pesach night—an easy preparation; an informality; talking about our grandmothers and mothers, about food, about the dual perspectives of daughters and mothers (as our kids wiggle while waiting for permission to go play); and most of all, the opportunity to express our own selves.

I remember a seder in 1986. Feminist seders with a choice of haggadot have become common now, at least in this city of many hills. This Pesach several women sit at my house surrounded by many women's haggadot (I am in my research phase now). We work our way through the ritual, debating and discussing and questioning the varying attempts to create a Passover ritual satisfying to women. The very process of debate we engage in empowers us as much as the documents in front of us.

We realize, suddenly, that this dialogue is a foundation of Judaism that men have been relishing for many centuries.

I remember a seder in 1987. A group of thirty women associated with Temple Emanu-El (a Reform temple in San Francisco) hold their first women's seder on the last night of Passover, having fulfilled their family obligations at the traditional first-night seder.[7] To this seder they disinvite both husbands and children, they use the *San Diego Women's Haggadah*, and they share in that first awesome rush of self-knowledge.

This seder reminds me of the grassroots power of feminism as well as the increasing reach of Jewish feminism.

I remember a seder in 1989. I go down the peninsula to Stanford, invited by Mary and John to their Pesach. What a wonderful mixed group at this seemingly traditional nuclear family seder—family and friends, heterosexual and lesbian, women and men, old and young. They use *The Egalitarian Haggadah* (written by feminist Aviva Cantor) as has been their practice for some years. The leadership of this seder is a shared venture, rather than paternally dictated.

I wonder what it would be like to be a daughter or a son knowing only this tradition. Would I carry different images of women and men with me as I entered the world of adulthood?

I remember a seder in 1991. Having returned to the East Coast, I am invited to a seder of lesbian friends who have shared Pesach for ten years. Rotating houses each year, whoever hosts the seder invites additional guests. It is multi-generational—some of the couples have had babies during the decade, and my mother is also invited. She eagerly attends, and her views are sought. This seder takes place on either the first or the second night, as women's needs to be with their own families as well as their created community produce varying schedules. These women re-create their own haggadah each (or every other) year, "cut and pasted" from women's haggadot circulating around the country.

This creation through compilation, the *Boston Rotating Seder Lesbian Haggadah*, is not uncommon. I marvel at the resourceful networking of women.

The Evolution of Women's Haggadot

In the early 1970s, before I had begun my own journey toward Jewish feminism, other feminists who were Jewish began reshaping the haggadah to speak of the struggle for freedom from their perspective. It is important to note that they were part of a larger wave of people who were putting on paper new versions of the Passover story of freedom.[8] Arthur Waskow's *The Freedom Seder*, written in 1969 but stemming from the "moment of agony at Passover 1968 when Martin Luther King had just been killed,"[9] is a well-known "liberation" haggadah, which evolved five versions and fifteen years later into *The Rainbow Seder.* The new surge of haggadah writing can be linked not only to the civil rights movement but to other progressive, left movements of the 1960s and 1970s. Inevitably, similar to the birth of the second wave of feminism, Jewish women in these progressive movements were not satisfied even with the liberation haggadot and responded by writing their own.

As early as 1971, a group of Jewish women in Portland, Oregon, wrote a haggadah that "told of the freedom-minded midwives who were the first to resist the Pharaoh's murderous edicts."[10] The *Rice-Paper Haggadah*, as it was informally known, made its way to Jewish feminists in New York and was described in "This Year in Brooklyn: A Seder to Celebrate Ourselves," a 1976 story in *Off Our Backs*.[11] Already one can see the pattern of haggadot moving around the country and, through word-of-mouth and feminist publications, sending ripples out into a broad and varied community.

Jewish women in California also produced haggadot in the early 1970s. In 1974, seven women met at the Los Angeles Women's Building to create a new Passover ritual, which evolved into *Women's Passover Seder—1977*, a haggadah later circulated among women. Co-author Anna Rubin described feeling "tremendously exhilarated and a little awed by our task. We felt like pioneers in a new land and yet linked to thousands of generations of Jewish women."[12] A year earlier, in northern California, a group of women gathered for Passover and used *Pesach Haggadah: A Statement of Joyous Liberation—Women's Seder, Berkeley, California, 5733–1973*. While many of its sources were recent haggadot of the left, this haggadah's female co-authors proclaimed, "The Jewish Women's Movement is just beginning; we are its matriarchs and the only hope for its future."[13] Early haggadot like these were more grounded in feminism and American women's history than in any extensive knowledge of Judaism. They combined feminist culture and history with a largely traditional haggadic exodus tale and traditional Hebrew prayers.

The feminist haggadah of the 1970s with the most far-reaching influence and circulation is one clearly and strongly based in Judaic research as well as in a commitment to Jewish women's experiences and knowledge. In March 1977, *Ms.* published "A Woman's Passover Haggadah and Other Revisionist Documents" by E. M. Broner and Naomi Nimrod. (In the next decade, this haggadah also informally found its way from one Jewish woman to another as stapled pages titled "The Stolen Legacy"; in 1994 it was formally published as *The Women's Haggadah*.) Broner has described how she and Nimrod came to research and write this haggadah in Israel in 1975. Producing both Hebrew and English versions, they each used the new text at seders the following year in their New York and Haifa homes.[14] In the United States, women from around the country immediately borrowed from its powerful words and images, taking them as given but also as a springboard to create their own tellings over the next decade.

In addition to the women's haggadot, the decade of the 1980s saw a flood of research and writing about Jewish women as a result of the broad Jewish feminist movement and the field of women's studies. This new knowledge made its way into the feminist haggadot, which took on breadth as Jewish documents. Haggadah writers learned and wrote about Jewish women whom many had not known existed. Haggadot of the 1980s drew from a multiplicity of sources to include Jewish history and lore, biblical women, World War II resistance fighters, pre-Judaism goddesses, current issues in the Middle East, and Jewish literature and poetry. A continuing outburst of writing, creating, compiling, and sharing—one heard of it all over the country if tuned into Jewish feminist circuits—took many forms at many seders. Most of the writing was unpublished.

The Content of Women's Haggadot

What makes these haggadot different from those used traditionally? In all other haggadot, we know what to expect. Why must we look twice at the ones written by women? Can we ever lean back and know what will come next?

Despite enormous differences from the traditional haggadah, women's haggadot utilize the Mishnah guidelines, which provide a comforting sense of constancy. If one looks at the Mishnah checklist (see note 15), the essentials—with "blessing" defined broadly—are for the most part present in almost all feminist haggadot.[15] These documents give the blessings, ask the questions, retell the exodus from Egypt, link redemption with freedom—within their own definitions. True, some haggadot omit or shorten the Psalms of Praise. However, all are still responding to the urgency of the exodus story.

"In Judaism memory is not simply a given but a religious obligation."[16] Judith Plaskow speaks of "living memory," and Martin Buber wrote of a community based on memory. Each feminist haggadist grapples with the paradox of Judaism: Passover participants do not remember and memorialize, they relive, but women have all lived with the unspeakable contradiction of not being included in either the memory or the reliving. No longer is this so, as feminist haggadot revise the traditional words. For example, "In every generation it is the duty of a woman to consider herself as if she came forth out of Egypt"; or "It is the duty of all Jews to consider themselves . . ."; or "each Jew should regard her or himself as though she or he personally went forth from Mitzrayim." Judaism's circular concept of time thus becomes a strong force pushing women to rediscover the past and to rewrite the haggadah.

This force produced a range of haggadot, with those on the extreme end of the continuum testing the limits of understanding even for some Jewish feminists. An anti-Zionist haggadah enabled me to understand more fully the challenge that a feminist haggadah might present to a traditional Jew. *Haggadah for Revolutionaries—An Initial Attempt*, a self-published haggadah from 1986 states "*This Passover or the next I will never be in Jerusalem. The Jordan flows* between me and the land I never remember anyone promising me."[17] In another vein, *Di Vilda Chais Haggadah* in 1981 speaks of pre-Judaism goddesses and implies that the word for the Jewish prayer, Kaddish, is actually a derivative of Ashtarte, one of the many names for the Goddess. Following another tradition, that of secularism, Judith Stein's 1984 *A New Haggadah: A Jewish Lesbian Seder* removes all references to any divinity from the service.[18] Yet each of these haggadot followed the Mishnah guidelines in creating a Passover seder.

One has to be impressed with the flexibility of the Mishnah outline for the seder. Women's haggadot that attempted to integrate appreciation for the Goddess, atheism, or an anti-Zionist stance with Passover were small in number, but these Jewish women authors felt their right and need as Jews to celebrate Passover in a way relevant to their sense of oppression and freedom. Indeed, the second-century rabbis did succeed in creating a framework that allows Jews to find and articulate a Judaism integral to their lives. Feminists have revived the radicalism of the Mishnah's approach to Pesach and have revitalized the Jewish tradition of dialogue and debate by approaching the haggadah as a responsive and adaptive document. As women make the dicta of the past relevant to a present that envisions equality, they uphold Judaism's approach to survival and paradox. Understanding this fundamental role of paradox and dialogue allows us to see whatever may discomfort us in a women's haggadah as yet another form of emerging paradox.

No two haggadot resolve or articulate the paradoxes posed for women by Judaism in exactly the same way, as can be seen in two of the most influential haggadot—Broner and Nimrod's *The Women's Haggadah* and the *San Diego Women's Haggadah*. Although they use some similar images and historical information, these haggadot represent two different strains. The *San Diego Women's Haggadah* attempts to find balance with the traditional haggadah, and is still "thankful for the Ten Commandments" while also cognizant of the need to articulate the "special part women have played in Jewish liberation."[19] Broner and Nimrod try to create a consistently nonpatriarchal ritual, structured around a council of elders and daughters asking and answering questions about their legacy as women and daring to speak of anger and pain. Broner and Nimrod move beyond anger, just as the *San Diego Women's Haggadah* moves beyond accommodation. Each articulates a different emphasis. Take, for example, their presentations of Beruriah.

In 1977, Broner and Nimrod were apparently the first to include the second-century Talmudist Beruriah within a haggadah. Four years later, the *San Diego Women's Haggadah* also told the story,

We turn now to Beruriah. *Mother, we ask, why do we taste this bitterness and keep it fresh in our mouths? . . .* It is told of Beruriah that she rebuked her husband when he prayed for the death of certain evil persons. "God seeks the eradication of sin, not sinners," she said, and exhorted her husband to pray for the sinners to give up their evil ways. Her incisive mind sometimes led her to reply sharply and she was known for her quick retorts.

"My life," explains Beruriah, . . . "has been both sweet and bitter. The sweetness . . . flows from the Torah . . . The bitterness . . . scholars considered my degree of learning to be astonishing for a woman. . . . these learned men never realized that any woman, given the same opportunity, might have become my equal . . . or theirs.

Be reminded at this celebration of freedom, that freedom must be won again by every generation."[20]

Broner and Nimrod, however, narrated the horrific end of this learned woman's life as well as her achievements. Rabbi Meir (Beruriah's husband) tested his wife by arranging for a man to seduce her; after several attempts the man succeeded, and shame drove Beruriah to suicide.

Ima Shalom asks, "Who are the guilty? The woman who yields to temptation, or the man who created the situation in order to test her? Beruriah was dishonored in death, but no dishonor befell her husband or seducer."

The niece of Ima Shalom asks, "And why would such an unlikely story of a virtuous and learned woman be told?"

Because women's learning is anathema. If women read books, soon they will write books. And the heroes and plots will change. If women read Torah, they will write the unsung songs and name the nameless women.[21]

The *San Diego Women's Haggadah* delivers the message that women are men's intellectual equals and that the battle for such recognition continues today; Broner and Nimrod name the danger that women's learning brings to a male culture and question the intertwining of guilt with a double standard.

Rather than choosing between one haggadah and another, numerous women have pieced and patched together their own unique texts. These may be called the "compiled" haggadot. The *Boston Rotating Seder Lesbian Haggadah* borrows a description of Deborah from the *San Diego Women's Haggadah*:

Mother, we ask, *Why is this night different from all other nights? Why do we celebrate a women's Seder?*

Deborah, judge and prophetess, "who arose a mother of Israel" [Judges 5:7], considers this question carefully. . . . This is the reply Deborah gives to our first question:

"They called me a judge in Israel. They called me a woman of great and rare distinction, a mother of my nation. And yet when they came to me for advice, to draw on that wisdom and compassion of which they were in such awe, they made me leave my home and sit outside. For in their eyes all women were the same, weak and wanton, not to be trusted alone in the company of men."

We celebrate a women's Seder tonight so that we are free to be ourselves, not afraid that our actions will be misjudged or misinterpreted, considered bold or unwomanly.[22]

It also included "The Song of Questions" from Broner and Nimrod. Such blending is utterly characteristic of this mode, increasing the reach of images, philosophies, and political themes while still leaving infinite room for each user to form her own experience of reliving the Exodus.

With the wealth of haggadot created in the 1980s and continuing into the 1990s, it makes sense to consider any single characteristic of a women's haggadah as part of a fluid and changing whole, as well as a unit in itself. Two currents run through this process of change, the *presence* and *practice* of women. The presence of women refers to the visibility of specific women within the story. The practice of women refers to the articulation of woman's perspectives within the story. While each haggadah voices its own mix of these elements, a selection of textual examples illuminates the scope of resistance to patriarchal Judaism.

The Presence of Women

From being absolutely absent in the traditional haggadah, women's presence has gone to the other end of the spectrum in many feminist haggadot. Women enter the haggadah everywhere—in the questions, in the answers, in the narration, in the plagues, in the *dayenu* (and *lo dayenu*), in the blessings, in the dedications, in new liturgy.[23] Distinct aspects of women's presence in the haggadot might be named: biblical women, learned women, competent women, heroic women, and fighting women.

We are Biblical women linked to the Exodus tale

Midwives were acknowledged in the Talmud: "For the sake of righteous women we were delivered from Egypt"[24] but were not named at traditional seders. In women's haggadot they step forward as the "women who took the first daring step of defiance which led to our redemption from Egypt. . . . Two Hebrew midwives, Shifra and Puah . . . refused to kill the babies . . . their moral courage." We also hear of Yochaved, who "opposed Pharaoh's decree, risking not only her son's life but her own,"[25] and of the unnamed daughter of Pharaoh who "reached beyond class and station to rescue a child from death. The rabbis call her 'Batya,' daughter of God, for her action. Together these two women [Batya and Yocheved] nurtured this child. Did these two mothers know one another's true identity? Did they know that all liberation requires cooperation?"[26]

Miriam is recognized in many ways, becoming the lost but now found woman hero of the Exodus tale. In some haggadot, her life is seen as an early example of the lethal double standard and clear silencing of women: Why was only Miriam and not Aaron punished by Moses for questioning his words? Why did she have to die such a terrible death, alone with leprosy?[27]

More common are the actions of Miriam recorded in the Bible as good deeds. With great wisdom, the girl Miriam advises her father that the men should not divorce their wives as a response to Pharaoh's decree to kill all sons, "and Amran listened to his daughter."[28] She takes part in "the defiance . . . that enabled Moses to survive the slaughter," she watches over him as he is rescued from the river, she arranges for his Hebrew nurse (his mother), and later as "all gave thanks for having crossed the Red Sea in safety . . . Miriam, the Prophet, who foretold the birth of Moses, 'took a tambourine in her hand, and all the women went out after her with tambourines and with dances'" (Exod 15:20).[29] Many haggadot "open the door" for Miriam as well as or instead of Elijah. "We are told that Miriam the prophetess visits every house where a woman's seder is being held. We open the door to welcome her. Eagerly we await her arrival. As we think of Miriam, we admire her unusual strength and courage, and give honor to the great leader."[30] At some seders, water instead of wine is used to fill the glass in honor of Miriam's well.[31]

We are Biblical women from other eras deserving of recognition

Biblical women, doers and thinkers, make themselves visible even if not a part of the Exodus.

Had God given us our matriarchs, Sarah, Rebekah, Rachel and Leah, and not our judges, wise women, and prophets, *Dayenu!*
  Had God given us our judges, wise women, and prophets, Devorah, Miriam, Hannah and Hulda, and not our Talmudic sages, *Dayenu!*[32]

Or one might read of Ruth and Naomi, Tamar, Lilith, Dinah, and "Hagar, founder of a great nation."[33]

Even, more significant, many women's haggadot also express respect for the women of the Bible whose names and stories we do not know. "Journey to Freedom—Ma'yan Haggadah" (1995) declares,

צֵא וּלְמָד, t'zei u'lmad, the tradition tells, "Go and learn." Learn about Jacob . . .
  The Torah says that 70 souls went down with Jacob to escape the famine in Canaan. Seventy—a favorite Biblical number. Who knows 70? We know 70: 70 are the sons of Jacob and the sons of his sons.
  But the daughters and the daughters of the daughters? Are we named? Are we counted? No. And the mothers: Rachel, Leah, Bilhah, and Zilpah—they aren't counted in the 70 either.
  And where is Dinah when the family goes down to Egypt? The one daughter of Jacob whose name we know isn't counted either. Where did she seek refuge after her

rape by Shechem? Did she build a new life? Did she have children? Are they counted among the 70? Not if they were daughters.

No women were counted among the 70 who went down to Egypt, nor among the 600,000 who came out 430 years later . . .

Our coming out of Egypt begins with the telling of these missing stories. צֵא וּלְמָד, t'zei u'lmad, we must go and learn the story as it has been recorded. And then, צֵא וּלְמָד, t'zei u'lmad, we must go and teach the stories that have not yet been told.[34]

We are learned and competent women in Jewish history

In the 1980s and 1990s the naming and telling of historical Jewish women grew exponentially. Sometimes women are listed by name and birth, sometimes individuals are described by a sentence, other times with a page-long story—all depending on the format and emphasis of the haggadah.

In addition to talmudic scholars such as Beruriah, one might hear of Hassidic "rebbetzins," such as nineteenth-century Chana Rochel of the Ukraine (also known as "Maiden of Ludmir"), who studied Kabbala and became a teacher of men and women, young and old. She had her own shul for several years, but under pressure from rabbinic authorities, she emigrated to Israel in 1858, where she again attracted throngs of followers.[35]

Or, earlier in history, one might read of the Marrano businesswoman, Beatrice de Luna, later known as Dona Gracia of Constantinople. This sixteenth-century woman was a trader in wool, pepper, and grain, with her own fleet of ships, and a patron of Jewish arts and charities.

Or one might hear of many other women not known to Jewish women today.

From victim to resister, we are heroic and fighting women

I need to know about the women, and that many Jews fought back, as they could, Jewish women among them. . . . About the women who fought inside the camps. Say their names.

Rosa Robota; Esther, Ella, and Regina, all hanged for crucial parts in the Auschwits resistance . . . or Sala . . . or Mala Zimetbaum, the "Runner" or . . .[36]

Regardless of gender, postwar haggadot have acknowledged the Holocaust at Pesach. The feminist haggadot honor women who fight back, particularly women who resisted the horrors of the Holocaust. Just hearing women's names, such as those above from an early women's haggadah, or those included in a more recent haggadah—Sonia Madeisker, a founder of the Vilna underground; Leonie Kazibrodski, an arms smuggler in Poland; Frumka Plotnicka, a resistance organizer; Vitke Kempner, of the Jewish partisans of Vilna[37]—empowers listeners and honors the deeds of these women. Sometimes a haggadah goes into more depth about a specific woman or tells a story about a particular group of girls and women who were heroic. A South African women's haggadah reprints Marsha Greenbaum's description of Pesach inside Ochenzahl Langenhoren, a concentration camp for women.[38] The links between survival, Passover, and women cannot be more clearly demonstrated.

Other types of resistance also have found their way into the haggadah pages, including workers, mothers, and political activists. *Journey to Freedom Haggadah* describes women in recent years carrying the Sefer Torah to the Kotel (the Wall) in Jerusalem where women have not been permitted to pray since the Temple was originally built,

In a traditional seder, we tell the story of sages . . . gathered at B'nai B'rak . . . Tonight we remember the subversive courage of our own teachers of our own generation.

It is told of Rabbis Deborah Brin and Helene Ferris; Dr. Phyllis Chessler and Blu Greenberg; Rivka Haut and Francine Klagsbrun; Professors . . . that they carried a *Sefer Torah* to the Kotel.

And they were so intent on praying together, Conservative women with Reform, Orthodox with Reconstructionist, so engrossed in the blending of separate voices and traditions . . . that they ignored the curses from behind the *mehitza.* They ignored the angry hands at their sleeves and ugly words in their ears.

They formed a circle around the *Torah* and read from it . . . *Higi'a z'man.* It is time . . . *Raboteinu, achyoteinu. Our rabbis and sisters . . . Higi'az'man.*[39]

The Practice of Women

In addition to the presence of women who have or are resisting patriarchal forms of domination, the practice of women has entered the seder. Women's haggadot wrestle with questions of everyday life and divinity. Through God-wrestling, women engage in the creation of new prayers, new ways of naming the divinity and of degenderizing the service. Through life wrestling, women engage in the creation of a new body of haggadic literature.

Life Wrestling

Not only are women writing of and thus reclaiming heroic women. As ordinary women, haggadah writers are giving voice to what *they* personally see and hear and feel as *they* relive the Exodus. A *New Haggadah: A Jewish Lesbian Seder* includes Janet Berkenfield's lyrical ode "To Her Grandchild." The grandmother tells the story of crossing the sea not as a miracle but as a nightmare. The children cried, the wind blew too hard, and the mud was too thick. A listener feels the urgency with which everyone worked to help the children and move the animals, and then one feels the horror of recognition, seeing the Egyptians drowning among the reeds:

> young boys in their uniforms
> now wrapped around their pale frightened faces
> Sarah, my neighbor, saw her owner's son
> and I, a palace guard who helped me pack
> and gave me food for the journey.
> Everyone saw a face they knew
> and such wailing then! It went on and on
> grief and fear, we were so tired,
> where was Moses, when would he take us home?
> Then, gradually, through the crying,
> Miriam's thin sweet voice
> trembling, her tune spun in the air
> and floated over us.
> It was a quieting song,
> one we used to sing to our animals in Egypt,
> and now she sang it to us
> like a shepherd to her frightened goats . . .[40]

A grandmother's sensibility of the occasion articulates women's experiences on an everyday level. This viewpoint can be found in many original writings now filling women's haggadot. Merle Feld's "We All Stood Together,"[41] seen in many 1990s haggadot, communicates a similar sensibility. "My brother and I were at Sinai" begins the poem, which tells how he kept a journal but the female narrator was too busy holding babies to have her hands free to write. "As time passes" the narrator can only retain a feeling for what happened, and what are feelings but "just sounds / the vowel barking of a mute," whereas her brother "is so sure of what he heard / after all he's got a record of it." The poem ends with a vision, "If we remembered it together / we could recreate holy time / sparks flying." Again, the everyday reality of women but here coupled with a possible future through connection between women and men.

Besides poetry, the new haggadot include short prose pieces that can be seen as women's midrashim. As with midrashim, the stories evoke emotion and elicit questions. A story may come from biblical or life sources or take the form of a fable. "Liberation Times Three" from the *San Diego Women's Haggadah* asks what liberation is for women in the context of women's past hardships;[42] "Two Sisters" from *Project Kesher Haggadah* poses a dialectic between integrity and rebellion;[43] and the Alef Haggadah articulates age-old questions about responsibility and freedom, drawing from the teachings of Hillel.[44] *Journey to Freedom Haggadah* and *Project Kesher Haggadah* are just two of the haggadot speaking of the orange on the seder plate as a new Pesach symbol of women's place "at the center of Jewish life and practice."[45] Extremely varied and rich, this new body of haggadic literature—"her-stories," female heroes, poetry, songs, and midrashim—springs from the experience and practice of women.

Godwrestling

Godwrestling is the other aspect of women's practice, involving women in ongoing theological and philosophical dialogue. In various ways, women haggadists have confronted questions of gender, language, prayer, and divinity. No consistent mode yet exists or will in the near future. Women's haggadot need at least the equivalent thousand years that the "male" haggadah had before finding a common approach, or perhaps such conformity will not be an end goal.

Changes in gender and language not related to divinity may be the most uniform area of change within women's haggadot, although various solutions are utilized. All women's haggadot employ some means of degenderizing the service. All reject the Four Sons, some switching to Daughters, some to children or Jews or persons. None retain the Youngest Son to ask the four Questions.

Where possible, many haggadot use gender-neutral pronouns. Some may use the feminine; others alternate female and male. Not only has the reclining father/patriarch disappeared from the head of the seder table, but generally, no specified "Leader-of-the-Seder" has replaced him. Certain responsive pattern readings may have a "leader," but this does not function as a substitute for the patriarch's authority. Overall, women's haggadot promote a collective rather than hierarchical approach to the seder.

Prayer and divinity in women's haggadot pose deeper challenges, partly because changing gender in Hebrew is more complex linguistically than in English.[46] "Shekinah" was known to represent a feminine side of God and has become the most common choice as an alternative to the male "Adonai." The lack of a sophisticated knowledge of Hebrew in many 1980s unpublished haggadot led frequently to a Hebrew-English split in which the traditional Hebrew prayer was written with either "Shekinah" or "Adonai" but accompanied by an English version that was not a direct translation and thus could degenderize freely. During the 1990s, feminist Hebraic scholars have been creating a new body of prayer, religious language, and liturgy that women haggadists can now draw on. Just as the 1980s haggadot were able to bring the history of Jewish women to women's seders, 1990s haggadot introduce new Hebrew language and prayer created by feminist liturgists.[47]

For example, the *Journey to Freedom Haggadah* discusses the blessings in its opening, so that one understands how בְּרוּכָה אַתְּ יָהּ אֱלֹהֵינוּ רוּחַ הָעוֹלָם *B'rucha At*

Ya, Eloheinu Ruach ha'Olam . . . You are Blessed, Our God, Spirit of the World"[48] was developed. After this explanation, both the traditional and new Hebrew formats of prayers with English translations are used throughout this haggadah. *The Dancing with Miriam Haggadah* translates the same Hebrew formulation into "Let us bless Yah, Divine presence, Life's Breath of the universe,"[49] and does not reproduce the traditional prayers. More cautious haggadot put a "Shekinah" prayer, properly worded in Hebrew, at the start of the haggadah and simply use the "Adonai" prayers throughout the service.

Each haggadah resolves this divine paradox differently, yet most haggadists choose not to use a female pronoun for God in English, whatever the Hebrew is. They will find neutral references instead—"ruler" or "divine force" rather than "Lord" or "He," "universe" rather than "kingdom." The varied choices can be surprising, as in *The Santa Cruz Haggadah* (1991) written by Karen G. R. Roekard to bring the evolving consciousness of "psycho-spiritualism" to others. This haggadah refers to the masculine "HASHEM" throughout. It degenderizes prayers and language but overall does not seem particularly concerned about women—until an unexpected English passage states, "And She stood up for our forebearers and for us."[50] Apparently, for Roekard, a door of changing consciousness is opening on the gender of God. However, for many Jewish women, the concept of a bi-gender God would probably be a big enough change in consciousness.

The 1990s and Beyond

The desire for self-definition is reaching a broader base of Jewish women in the mid-1990s than in earlier decades. In addition to the ongoing formulation of women's haggadot, a new tradition of community seders for women is evolving and producing another generation of feminist haggadists. Written to be used on the seventh night of Pesach in a setting with women rather than with family, the *San Diego Women's Haggadah* was clearly a forerunner of the 1990s community seders, which take place on varying dates but not on a traditional Passover night. While some feminists might question whether patriarchal Judaism has deflected the force of Jewish feminism by the separation of women's presence and practice from the "real" seder, a close look at this new development in women's haggadot suggests just the opposite. The haggadah is becoming a conduit of feminism for Jewish women from many backgrounds.

All over the country a rush of changing consciousness is taking place through these community seders with their newly created haggadot. In Los Angeles the American Jewish Congress started a Feminist Center in 1991, and each year since has hosted a women's seder and written new versions of the text *And We Were All There: A Feminist Passover Haggadah*. In New York

"Ma'yan: The Jewish Women's Project," a program of the Jewish Community Center of the Upper West Side, began in 1993. In its first two years, women wrote two haggadot, *From Slavery to Freedom—From Darkness to Light* in 1994 and, using different and original material, *Journey to Freedom* in 1995.[51] In only their second year of existence, Ma'yan had to hold three seders to accommodate close to six hundred women. For Pesach 1997, they prepared for an expected, 1,100 women to attend these women's seders and use the newly published *The Journey Continues—Ma'yan Passover Haggadah*. In Palo Alto, Elaine Poise and Rebecca Schwartz organized a community seder in 1994. By its second year, 230 women attended and used the second edition (all original writing) of *The Dancing with Miriam Haggadah*. From that seder, a Rosh Chodesh group formed, with a core group of women meeting once a month and seventy-five women on a mailing list. "Out of the seder came a women's community that did not exist before."[52]

The 1994 Ma'yan seder became the spark igniting a community women's seder coalition in Westchester County, New York. An editorial committee of nineteen women (including rabbis and cantors) from synagogues across the Jewish spectrum jointly wrote their first haggadah and in 1995 held their first county women's seder, in which more than two hundred women participated. Written by and for Orthodox, Conservative, and Reform women, *In Every Generation Haggadah* talks of its own process in creating a haggadah that would "cut across the boundaries of . . . affiliation in order to speak to the shared knowledge and experiences" and of how they had to give "up a little on the outer edges of where they personally stood in order to find a firm ground for as many women as possible."[53] The haggadah keeps traditional prayers but incorporates the presence and practice of women. It contains an "Additional Readings" section with feminist poems by Jewish women and an excerpt from Ellen M. Umansky's "Reclaiming the Covenant: A Jewish Feminist's Search for Meaning": "[I]t is my obligation as a Jew to help create a Judaism that is meaningful for my generation. Three thousand years ago, Moses stood at Mt. Sinai and received the Ten Commandments from God. When he came down the mountain and saw the Israelites worshipping a golden calf, he broke the tablets in anger. Perhaps he did so not only to warn us against idolatry but also to make it clear that not even God's words are irrevocably carved in stone."[54] This model of integrating the old with the new, balancing traditional values with radical concepts and working collectively with those of differing beliefs might be a model useful to a larger feminist movement or to the branches of Judaism.

The 1990s women's community haggadot tend to be written by groups of women, some new to the task of creating a haggadah, some experienced. The seders resulting from their efforts are just as much the result of research and intense dialogue as the home-based feminist seders were and are still today. These 1990s desktop-published documents look and feel like more finished products than their predecessors did. They also tend to name individual authors of the varied original writings included. Feminist haggadic literature increases each year.

Not competing for Passover nights widens the reach of the women's community seders to the traditional Jewish community, where a broad spectrum of middle-class Jewish women seem hungry for women's seders and haggadot. A feminist consciousness touches large numbers of Jewish women through these events. This consciousness also extends to wider issues than those of women, often visible in the naming of the plagues or the *dayenus*. "When we live in a world where sexual preferences, racial, religious, and ethnic differences are accepted without prejudice—Dayenu."[55] The women's community seders are definitely rooted in the same grass-roots movement that began in the 1970s, even if the balance between social justice issues and women's voices within Judaism has changed in form. The 1990s haggadot are, like the women's haggadot of previous decades, part of a dialectical process of change rather than an end product. No one knows exactly what the next decade will bring.

As this process of change continues to fuel itself, haggadot in the United States are becoming a force of change for women in other parts of the world. In 1989, a small group of Jewish women from Illinois named themselves Project Kesher and extended the boundaries of Jewish feminism as they worked to empower Russian Jewish women in the former Soviet Union (FSU). At a 1994 international conference for Jewish women in Kiev, organized by Project Kesher, three hundred women came together from New Zealand, South Africa, Jerusalem, England, the United States, and Germany as well as from the Ukraine.[56] At this conference, Project Kesher conceived of a Global Seder as an experience that would encourage community for Jewish women in their home countries. The result, *Project Kesher Haggadah*, used in a 1995 Global Seder around the world, propelled this movement of women rewriting haggadot for Passover onto an international level.

Project Kesher organizers were clear in their goal of being a catalyst of empowerment to Jewish women in other countries, although not making the false assumption of knowing what women in those other countries need or want.[57] *Kesher* means "connection" in Hebrew, and these feminists are attempting to build a connection based on respect for autonomy. The American women blended original and compiled writings into a succinct haggadah and sent it as a model to women in the other countries as well as to groups of women in the United States. They gave women in each country a stimulus to create their own haggadot and seders.[58] In each country a different haggadah was developed, but all were used in the spirit of a global seder simultaneously on the same day. In the FSU for example, Russian Jewish women used a Conservative haggadah and added from the *Project Kesher Haggadah* the Four Daughters, the Global Women's prayer, and the orange on the seder plate.

In South Africa (where 90 percent of the Jewish population is Orthodox), the Union of Jewish Women felt that they had to write their own haggadah in order to make it acceptable to their membership. Over 400 women attended four community women's seders in four locations in the country, including 250 women in Johannesburg. The South African women did not name their text a haggadah but *A Celebration of Jewish Women's Freedom*. It begins by explaining the meaning of "haggada," and ends with a historical fable about a young woman who becomes a sacred vessel for a blank "haggada." The young woman is briefly surrounded by foremothers and political activists, from biblical women to South African Jewish women who fought apartheid, and then is given the challenge of accepting full spiritual responsibility for herself and for the planet. It articulates that the young women must be each other's teachers as they find their "own pathway through halakha and tradition."[59] This celebratory document uses traditional Jewish prayers and thoroughly researched and historically oriented material about Jewish women of the past. In the middle of the document is a seder menu: thus, South African Orthodox women are combining Jewish traditions with feminist sensibilities.

The potential for self-empowerment in Jewish women's lives through this grassroots intersection of feminism and Judaism takes my breath away. *Project Kesher Haggadah*'s "Four Daughters," retained in each of the thirty-seven global seders, summarize well the three decades of women's haggadot with their questions and particularly the Fourth Daughter, who "never asked the question—for in questioning, her life was endangered and her voice silenced by oppression and fear. To the fourth daughter, we offer process: of asking, learning, feeling, and experimenting to find her voice. She can then ask the questions for her generation and those who follow."[60]

Jewish feminism is not simply giving "the one who never asked" a story of Passover to substitute for the traditional haggadah. Rather, through the presence and practice of women in haggadot, it is giving tools to Jewish women. *Project Kesher Haggadah*'s Fourth Daughter and Broner and Nimrod's "The Song of Questions" each make clear the vital function of questions in defining self and forging change.

Most fundamentally, Passover and feminism together give women the opportunity to redefine, to challenge and to make changes within Judaism and beyond. The questions may change over time depending on social conditions both within and outside Judaism, but once started, this questioning contains its own life force. With many twists and turns, an unstoppable current is gaining momentum each year. Knowing our mothers, knowing our angers, knowing our questions—women stake out a future based on inclusion rather than exclusion—as Jews, as women, and as human beings. What began as a movement for change by those on the margins is now becoming the practice of those much closer to the mainstream of Judaism—what does this shift mean? Will

Jewish feminists eventually question only the gender balance within Judaism while ignoring larger questions? Or will they continue to raise questions that challenge many layers of privilege functioning not only within but outside of Judaism? The future remains an unknown but the asking of questions clearly spreads a seed of potential, a possibility of change in that which has always been.

Women's Haggadot

Schwartz, Fayla, Susie Coliver, and Elaine Ayela. *Pesach Haggadah: A Statement of Joyous Liberation—Women's Seder, Berkeley, California, 5733-1973.* Berkeley, Cal.: Authors, 1973.

"This Year in Brooklyn: A Seder to Celebrate Ourselves." *Off Our Backs* 3, no. 8 (May 1973): 15–18.

Flashman, Sherry, and Margaret Fuller Sablove. *The Feminist Seder.* Np.: Authors, 1976.

Rubin, Anna, et al. *Women's Passover Seder—1977.* Los Angeles, Cal.: Authors, 1977. Based on haggadah originating from 1974 seder at the Women's Building of Los Angeles.

Broner, E. M., and Naomi Nimrod. "A Women's Haggadah and Other Revisionist Rituals." *Ms.* (April 19, 1977): 53–56.

———. *The Stolen Legacy: A Women's Haggadah.* New York: Authors. Changing versions circulated by hand during the 1980s, excerpts already published in *Ms.* article.

Class R299, Indiana University—The Jewish Woman. *Women's Voices: Passover Haggadah.* Bloomington, Ind.: Authors, 1978.

Rosen, Lynn, et al. *A Woman's Haggadah—Pesach—Season of Liberation.* Minneapolis, Minn.: Authors, 1979.

Zones, Jane Sprague, ed. *San Diego Women's Haggadah.* San Diego: Women's Institute for Continuing Jewish Education, 1980.

———. *San Diego Women's Haggadah—Second Edition.* San Diego: Women's Institute for Continuing Education, 1986.

Di Vilda Chais Haggadah. New York: Author (unknown), 1981.

Cantor, Aviva. *The Egalitarian Hagada.* Cathedral Station, New York: Beruriah Books, 1982.

Passover Celebration Haggadah. San Francisco, Cal.: Author (unknown), 1982.

Linden, Ruth, and Alice Prussin, eds. *Haggadah for Passover.* San Francisco, Cal.: Authors, 1984.

Miriam's Timbrel. *A Women's Haggadah: Oberlin College 1984.* Oberlin, Ohio: Authors, 1984.

Stein, Judith A. *A New Haggadah: A Jewish Lesbian Seder.* Cambridge, Mass.: Bobbeh Meisehs Press, April 1984 [Nisan 5744]).

Comerchero, Sarah. *A Passover Haggadah: The Alef.* San Francisco, Cal.: Author, 1985.

Haggadah (for revolutionaries): An Initial Attempt. San Francisco, Cal.: Author (unknown), 1986.

Twin Cities Women's Minyan. *Women's Passover Seder.* Minnesota: Authors, 1989.

Roekard, Karen G. R. *The Santa Cruz Haggadah: A Passover Haggadah, Coloring Book, and Journal for the Evolving Consciousness.* Capitola, Cal.: The Hineni Consciousness Press, 1991.

Broner, E. M., with Naomi Nimrod. *The Women's Haggadah.* San Francisco, Cal.: Harper San Francisco, 1993. This haggadah is based closely on earlier versions of *The Stolen Legacy.*

Tilchin, Maida. *The Boston Rotating Seder Lesbian Haggadah.* Somerville, Mass.: Author, 1994.

And We Were All There—A Feminist Passover Haggadah. Los Angeles, Cal.: American Jewish Congress Feminist Center, 1994.

Ma'yan: The Jewish Women's Project. *From Slavery to Freedom, From Darkness to Light—4 Nisan 5754, March 16, 1994.* New York: The JCC of the Upper West Side, 1994.

———. *Journey to Freedom—Nisan 5755, April 1995.* New York: The JCC of the Upper West Side, 1995.

———. *The Journey Continues—Ma'yan Passover Haggadah.* Woodstock, Vt.: Jewish Lights, 1997.

Project Kesher Haggadah—Global Women's Seder. Evanston, Ill.: Project Kesher, 1995.

A Celebration of Jewish Women's Freedom—Pesach 1995. South Africa: The Union of Jewish Women of South Africa, 1995.

In Every Generation—A Passover Haggadah for the Westchester Women's Seder—4 Nisan, 5755 / April 4, 1995. Westchester County, New York: The American Jewish Committee and the UM-YWHA of Mid-Westchester, 1995.

Moise, Elaine, and Rebecca Schwartz. *The Dancing with Miriam Haggadah—A Jewish Women's Celebration of Passover.* Palo Alto, Cal.: Rikudel Miriam, 1995.

Epilogue:
Jewish Women on Television
Too Jewish or Not Enough?

In the catalog for *Too Jewish? Challenging Traditional Identities*, the provocative exhibit that opened at the Jewish Museum in New York in 1996, curator Norman Kleeblatt cited the problematic nature of Jews' self-representation in contemporary art. According to Kleeblatt, Jewish artists in postwar America viewed their identities through a more paradoxical lens than did other racial, ethnic, and marginalized cultural groups who sought to promote the positive aspects of their communities even while criticizing negative attributes. Compared to those other groups, Jewish artists almost entirely avoided the subject of their Jewishness: "Through the process of assimilation and under the formalist hegemony of postwar modernism, many Jewish artists, writers, performers, and theater, film, and television producers—like many other successful Jews—lost their culturally distinctive voices. Admission into the mainstream had required the shedding of that very ethnic and cultural specificity upon which the new identity-centered art is based."[1]

When, only recently, Jewish artists did come to represent Jewishness in their work, they were more likely to portray Jewish aspirations and achievements through images that exaggerated the middle-class, assimilationist values with which they had grown up than to acknowledge a specifically Jewish communal past, whether rooted in immigrant forebears, the Holocaust, or Israel. *Too Jewish*, for example, is filled with representations of nose jobs, hair straightenings, name changes, Chanel menorahs, indoor electric Sukkahs, Jewish Princess tiaras, and more.

Along with the erasure noted by Kleeblatt, *Too Jewish?* emphasizes exaggeration and caricature as major aspects of the representation of Jewish identity in contemporary visual art. Jewish artists' simultaneous embarrassment and pride about Jews' success in mainstream America have led to ethnic amnesia on the one hand and, on the other, despite these artists' recent interest in locating themselves within their tradition, to satire and critique.

Representations of Jewish women in popular culture mirror patterns of avant-garde art; erasure and exaggeration remain the dominant characteristics of the treatment of Jewish women in film and in what is probably the most accessible of all the popular visual media, television. In the almost fifty-year history of television, images of Jewish women, especially in leading roles, have been all too rare. When they are present, they are usually overblown caricatures and pejorative stereotypes that misrepresent the life-styles and attitudes of real women.

With the departure of *The Goldbergs* from television in 1955 after a six-year run, Jewish women virtually disappeared from the small screen for almost twenty years. Then came Rhoda Morgenstern, the wisecracking best friend and sidekick of the character Mary Richards in *The Mary Tyler Moore Show*. Sassy and self-deprecating, Rhoda constantly fought against the constraints of her situation—whether her self-perceived unattractiveness, her envy of Mary's perkiness, or the meddling of her parents, who wanted her married off. Played by the non-Jewish Valerie Harper, *Rhoda* premiered in 1974 as a spin-off from Moore's show. Although it was up against popular Monday night football, *Rhoda* won its time slot. In a mere eight weeks, Rhoda was married off to a non-Jew, played by David Groh (fifty million viewers were said to have watched the wedding). Although the program continued to showcase Rhoda's Jewishness and that of her very ethnic Jewish sister, Brenda (played by Julie Kavner), Rhoda somehow seemed less appealing as a married woman than as a feisty, angst-ridden single one. Soon the show was canceled.[2]

With the demise of *Rhoda* came another long absence for Jewish women on the TV screen. With the exception of occasional characters—for example, the mother and grandmother on the critically acclaimed but short-lived *Brooklyn Bridge*—there were few women characters who were identifiably Jewish and none in a leading role for almost another two decades. Compare this to the male Jewish characters on television series in recent years, both comedies and drama: Paul Buchman (Paul Reiser) in *Mad About You*, Jerry Seinfeld in *Seinfeld*, Miles Silverberg (Grant Shaud) in *Murphy Brown*, Richard Lewis in *Anything but Love*, Jackie Mason in *Chicken Soup*, Michael Steadman (Ken Olin) in *thirtysomething*, Stuart Markowitz (Michael Tucker) in *L.A. Law*, Joel Fleischman (Rob Morrow) in *Northern Exposure*, Marshall Brightman (Joshua Rifkind) in *Marshall Chronicles*, and Jim Eisenberg (Alan Arkin), in *A Year in the Life*.

Then, in 1993, came *The Nanny*, a show about a thirty-something, Queens-born former salesgirl who finds a position as a nanny to three children of a British theatrical producer. Written and produced by Fran Drescher, who plays

Rhoda (Valerie Harper, left) and her sister Brenda (Julie Kavner) with their television mother (Nancy Walker). Although Rhoda's wedding to a non-Jew (David Groh) was watched by millions of viewers, the character seemed less appealing as a wife than as a feisty single woman, and the show was canceled. (Copyright CBS-TV. Photo courtesy The Kobal Collection)

the title character, and her husband, Peter Marc Jacobson, the show has become an unexpected hit. Often at the top of the Nielsen charts, it has attracted a national and even international following (many Israelis are fans); Drescher was nominated for an Emmy for her performance, and there are "Nanny" dolls, "Nanny" fashions, and "Nanny" home pages. Drescher's autobiography, *Enter Whining*, which aptly describes her TV character, has become a best-seller as well.[3]

The show's success is predicated on the premise of culture clash; it pits blue-blood English against blue-collar Jewish. The upper-class Maxwell Sheffield, the debonair, widowed theatrical producer; his three children; the butler, Niles; and uppity female associate, C.C. Babcock, face off against Fran Fine, the nanny from Queens. Although Fran's Jewishness is not essential to the plot, which requires only that the uneducated, lower-class lass wind up teaching her social betters, aspects of the character's Jewish background are featured in most episodes. From the nasal whine, to Yiddish words, to the

The nanny (Fran Drescher) and her mother (Renee Taylor) standing behind a table full of food at a wedding. Drescher is wearing an outlandish pink bridesmaid dress; her mother is in the usual tasteless ensemble wrapped with a blue boa. The mother is holding a plate full of food (also as usual). (Copyright © 1993 CBS Inc. Photo courtesy The Kobal Collection)

nanny's Jewish female desires—like getting married, preferably to a nice Jewish doctor—and certainly, shopping ("My first words," says the nanny, were "Can I take it back if I wore it?"), mannerisms that are identified as Jewish along with Jewish Princess stereotypes fill the air. The contrast—the key to the show's slim plot device—is between the nanny's authenticity, which, however coarse and ostentatious, is a product of her ethnic, supposedly lower-class origins, and the sterility of the British upper class and their hangers-on.

This is not, however, a Pygmalion story. Mr. Sheffield does not try to improve the nanny, nor is she interested in making herself over. Satisfied with herself as is, the nanny lacks only a man: her crush on her boss and his never fully acknowledged attraction for her drives the show. After Mr. Sheffield, in fact, any husband would do, though a Jewish one is clearly preferred.

Neither is the show an updated *Upstairs, Downstairs*, for there is little that divides the so-called servants—the butler and the nanny—from the Sheffields and C.C., except perhaps the servants' greater capacity for humor. And although Fran's family and her Jewish milieu serve as a foil to the Sheffield's posh world, they are never presented as morally superior.

Jewishness is, then, an attitude, a phrase, even a set of clothes—glitzy, gaudy, and ornate. It is a shtick, a framing device that sets the heroine apart from the others in the cast. But it is an artificial, exaggerated Jewishness, drawn from anomalous images and negative stereotypes—Jewish women's self-centered and encompassing desires for money, men, and food—that are long out of date and mainly fictional in origin.

How an exaggerated Jewishness provides the central image and dramatic device of the show is exemplified in an episode aired in April 1996, on which the nanny is dating the young cantor of her mother's synagogue. When the star of Mr. Sheffield's forthcoming Broadway musical falls ill, he taps the cantor to play the lead. "God has sent us a nice Jewish boy," Mr. Sheffield intones. But Fran's mother, Sylvia (played by Renee Taylor), is deeply agitated that no one in her temple will talk to her because they blame her for the loss of their cantor. Sylvia threatens her daughter that she will get even: "Our God is not a merciful God," she warns. With that, locusts appear and there is lightning and thunder. Overlooking the disturbances, Fran's eye falls on an advertising circular on the hallway table. "Oh my God, I missed the Loehmann's yearly clearance," she wails. "God, why are you doing this to me?"

In the final scene of the episode, Fran, dressed in a hot pink miniskirted suit, and her mother, in a loud yellow one, enter their temple and take seats in the last row. "We've been exiled to Siberia," Fran moans as her mother takes out a bacon-lettuce-and-tomato sandwich. "At temple?" Fran asks incredulously. "Nobody can see us here," Sylvia replies. "I can [even] throw a luau."

Fran's discomfort increases when she sees her friend Debby, proudly sporting an engagement ring, seated a few rows ahead. Envious, she asks what she ever did to God to deserve such neglect. Remembering that she scammed five hundred dollars from an airline, Fran goes up to the rabbi to contribute the airline's check to the temple. Immediately, her luck changes. Debby is overheard in a dispute with her fiancé and returns the ring, while another congregant tells Sylvia that she can be first for the front-row seats she no longer needs for the High Holidays. Thankful, Fran and her mother bow their heads: "Find her a doctor," the mother prays. "Find me a doctor," Fran says simultaneously.

Here, not only Jewishness but Judaism as a religion is portrayed stereotypically and negatively. The Jewish God is vengeful, the synagogue is a place for lavish and competitive display, and prayer itself is merely a means for special pleading regarding dating and marriage. The violation of religious norms apparent in eating a sandwich during a service (the running joke has Mrs. Fine an out-of-control eater at all times) is exaggerated by having the sandwich be bacon, lettuce, and tomato; even Reform Jews, which presumably the Fines are, might well balk at taking pork into the sanctuary.

In using Jewishness as the setting for humor, few episodes have gone as far as this one in their disregard for the ethical and moral seriousness of the Jewish religion. Sometimes, as in "The Kibbutz," first aired in December 1995, a Jewish environment is presented as attractive and appealing. In this show, Fran wants Mr. Sheffield to permit his sixteen-year-old daughter, Maggie, to go to a kibbutz in Israel for her school break, but Mr. Sheffield does not want to send her alone. In a flashback, Fran recalls losing her virginity to a handsome sabra on the same kibbutz when she was younger. The show ends with Maggie, accompanied by her father and the nanny, picking fruit on the kibbutz, where she too meets a handsome stranger. Although exotic and foreign, the kibbutz is cleverly used as a plot device, and viewers are at least introduced, although rather haphazardly, to the notion of Jewish collective farming.

Episodes with Jewish settings are exceptions, however. For the most part, the nanny's Jewishness lies in her inflection, her whine, her Yiddishisms, her mania for shopping and for men, and her Jewish family. Like Fran, they are authentics, whether her gaudily overdressed, canasta-playing mother or her chain-smoking Grandma Yetta. But, like Fran, these relatives are without taste and refinement, even without manners, as in "A Fine Family Feud," shown in October 1995, when Fran's Aunt Freta (played by Lainie Kazan) and her sister, Fran's mother, carry on a long-standing feud by throwing cream pies down each other's bare bosoms at a Sweet Sixteen party in a nightclub. It is a vulgar display.

Yet *The Nanny* has called forth admiration and approval, as well as disgust: One critic cites Drescher as the "only reigning Jewish actress on television with the chutzpah to celebrate her ethnic 'otherness.'"[4] What many find likeable in the show are the nanny's cleverness, honesty, sense of pride, and warmth. Not infrequently resorting to manipulation (like her model, Lucille Ball in *I Love*

Lucy), Fran Drescher as the nanny always outsmarts her dramatic antagonists, whomever they may be, because of her innate shrewdness, a genuine concern for others, and the folk wisdom apparently imparted from her heritage. This is perhaps the most accurate aspect of her Jewish characterization. Historically, relatively few Jewish women, whether adolescents or thirty-year-olds, consciously chose to become nannies or other live-in domestics; those who moved up from the lower to middle classes more likely worked in garment factories, retail stores, and classrooms. While the nanny's unabashed materialism may not have been foreign to young Jewish women throughout the twentieth century, it was often combined with concerns about the conditions of daily life and a collective consciousness unusual among both ethnic and native-born workers for its depth and inclusiveness.

The incongruity of the Jewish nanny provides a large part of the show's appeal. Much as Gertrude Berg as immigrant matriarch in a 1950s suburb had become anachronistic, so the premise of *The Nanny* does not fit its time—if indeed the characters fit any era. Viewers' recognition not only of the cultural dissonance between the nanny and the Sheffields but the nanny's employment in such an occupation to begin with enhances the show's humor.

Other aspects of the show are decidedly less funny. The nanny's grasping materialism, her limited interests and anti-intellectualism, her family's and her own vulgar dress and manners—all of these denigrate women and Jews. Despite the nanny's warmth, wit, and honesty, including the breezy sexuality she openly flaunts, she remains the kind of coarse, greedy, and selfish Jew that any anti-Semite might envision. Like Woody Allen's Hasidic rabbi that he conjures in the imagination of the character he plays in *Annie Hall*, the exaggerated qualities of Drescher's Nanny Fine make her a Jewish nightmare, not a dream about which Jews or women may be proud.

Television also has embraced the image of the exaggerated, stereotypical Jewish mother. In a recent article, *New York Times* television critic John J. O'Connor noted that in contrast to warm and nurturing Black mothers and other ethnic types, television seemed "curiously partial to neurotically overprotective, brash and often garish mothers of the unmistakably Jewish persuasion." "Sure, caricature is endemic to prime time," he acknowledges. "But why do Jewish mothers seem to have a monopoly on its more extreme forms? . . . Too many Jewish mothers, it seems to this puzzled goy, become props for humor that often teeters on outright ridicule or even occasional cruelty."[5]

As examples, O'Connor cites Paul Reiser's "take-charge" mother in *Mad About You* and the "growling" mother of the character George Costanza (played by Jason Alexander) in *Seinfeld*. (O'Connor assumes the Costanzas are Jewish, presumably because of their patterns of speech and mannerisms, although their name suggests Italian origins. In fact, the ethnicity of the family is never clarified.) He observes that the obnoxious, "loud-and-brassy" Jewish mother is as likely to appear on Tracey Ullman comedy hours and other special programming as on network TV.

Manipulative, self-indulgent, demanding, and overprotective, the objectified Jewish media mother, reduced to a single clichéd essence, seems not fully human. In fact, television's most extreme Jewish-type mother, *Star Trek: The Next Generation*'s Lwaxana Troi isn't human, but Betazoid, an alien being endowed not only with the gift of telepathy but with many less endearing traits as well. Lwaxana is overdressed, overbearing, altogether a nudge. While she and Fran Fine share warmth, earthy sexuality and a nuts-and-bolts practicality about human (and alien) affairs, they are nonetheless essentially portrayed as bad female jokes. In her stylishness and breeding, Lwaxana is surely worlds apart from the crassness of Fran Fine's television mother, Sylvia, but the two attempt to dominate their daughters' lives (and marry them off) in similar ways. Although Lwaxana is not scripted as specifically Jewish, many viewers tend for these reasons to classify her as a "Jewish mother."

Television does not know what to make of Jewish women. In the absence of well-worn stereotypes, depictions of Jewish women fade to gray. Melissa, Michael Steadman's cousin in the now defunct *thirtysomething*, as played by Melanie Mayron retained a modicum of Jewishness, although at the cost of being shown as too neurotic and unstable to have viable relationships. Another exception was the half-Jewish character Andrea Zuckerman in *Beverly Hills 90210*; Jewish-looking, although played by a non-Jewish actress, the somewhat nerdy Andrea, while often peripheral to the group, is respected for her intelligence. In one episode, when she pledges for a sorority that doesn't admit Jews and is warned by the president to take off her Jewish star and hide her ethnicity, Andrea withdraws in disgust, moving the president, who has denied her own Jewishness, to own up to who she really is. Eventually, Andrea marries a Chicano and has a baby; she accompanies him when he goes East to Yale, and what will become of Andrea's ambitions is unclear.

Although several other female characters on current shows appear Jewish, the markers of ethnicity are not explicit. On *Friends*, the characters Ross and Monica Geller are presumably Jewish. But the smart, funny, and insecure Ross (David Schwimmer) seems more Jewish than his china-doll-like sister Monica (Courteney Cox). According to executive co-producer David Crane, Ross is in fact "half Jewish because Elliot Gould is his father, but Christina Picker (as Ross's mother) sure is not." Crane notes that the show's Rachel Greene (Jennifer Aniston) is Jewish because her father is played by Ron Leibman (an authentic Jewish ethnic like Gould). Yet the character's mother, like Monica's, is played by a non-Jewish actress (Marlo Thomas). When the sitcom began its run in 1995, Rachel broke off an engagement to Barry the dentist and chose to work for a living rather than live off her rich father or a potential wealthy husband. Her quest for financial autonomy and personal authenticity is nothing short of heroic, but in the strange, ironic universe of sitcoms, it also seems to render her less Jewish. Crane admits that Rachel's Jewishness is "not an aspect we've done much with." According to a *Lilith* writer, the fact that neither Monica nor Rachel appears Jewish may relate less to non-Jewish mothers and more to the fact that the women are "too thin, too sexy, and too struggling in their nondescript professions to be considered Jewish." Perhaps even more important, neither is shown to have any Jewish interests or affiliations.[6]

Friends does feature two unambiguously Jewish female characters. The first is Chandler's sometime girlfriend Janice, nasal, crass, and overdressed. Janice may look and sound like Fran Fine, but she lacks the nanny's integrity; after stealing Chandler's heart, she betrays him by returning to her former husband, the mattress salesman. And if Janice is a nanny manqué, Mrs. Geller belongs in the pantheon of overbearing Jewish mothers, whose chief occupation is worrying about why their daughters aren't married. At least Fran Fine and her mother get along (most of the time); Monica and Mrs. Geller are like oil and water.

A more positive image is that of Debbie Buchman, Paul's sister on *Mad About You*. Yet Debbie's proud lesbianism is more openly flaunted than her Jewishness. Like Monica Geller, Debbie is Jewish primarily in relation to the demeanor and manners of the main star rather than her own inherent characteristics. Mrs. Buchman in particular is concerned about her daughter's lesbianism, but her anxieties are somewhat allayed by the fact that Debbie's girlfriend is a doctor! Neither parent shows much concern about Paul's decidedly non-Jewish wife, Jamie, played by Helen Hunt.[7]

Not only in *Mad About You* but in such shows as *Northern Exposure*, *L.A. Law*, *thirtysomething*, *Murphy Brown*, and *Seinfeld*, Jewish men date or marry non-Jewish women; only rarely is a specifically Jewish woman portrayed romantically on such shows. Consider Elaine, the former girlfriend of Dr. Joel Fleischman on *Northern Exposure*, who appears in one episode to free Fleischman from the constraints of his New York past (his Jewishness?), enabling him to bond with the down-to-earth, Catholic-school-educated pilot Maggie.

Another aspect to this Jewish woman disappearing act is the use of Jewish actresses for non-Jewish roles: Roseanne as a working-class woman in *Roseanne*; Rhea Pearlman's Italian waitresses, first in *Cheers*, more recently in *Pearl*; Bea Arthur's Irish Maude Finlay in the 1970s hit series, *Maude*. Such casting raises fascinating questions involving the seeming universalism of Jewish looks if not Jewish traits (is it true, as Mel Brooks once suggested, that everyone, including Native Americans, is really Jewish?) but also speaks to the lack of specifically Jewish roles for Jewish actresses. If she had waited for a role as a Jewish woman, Bea Arthur once commented, she would have remained unemployed.

As this survey suggests, Jewish women characters on television rarely demonstrate the full range of human characteristics—intelligence, generosity, ambition, striving, achievement, conflict—that truly represent contemporary Jewish women's lives; these qualities are more likely to be present in dramas and comedies with non-Jewish heroines. And relatively few Jewish women appear on television as they do in real life—as writers, journalists, teachers, doctors, lawyers, mayors, senators, and judges. Yet the writers, producers, and directors of these shows are often Jewish; indeed, they sometimes are Jewish women. Marketplace considerations play a vital role in the fact that despite their own high profiles in the media, they have collaborated to erase or exaggerate the more varied activities of Jewish women in the real world.

Yet it is noteworthy that in the world of contemporary television, creative and marketing teams apparently find Jewish men's personas more appealing to popular audiences than those of Jewish women. While there were relatively few Jewish characters in television's first forty years—most scripts were "de-Jewished" or "midwestized," as one executive put it—Jewish male characters have been a fixture of prime time in recent years.[8] The presence of such Jewishly identified characters differs from earlier television shows, in which the star's background was deliberately left hazy—for example, George Burns's and Jack Benny's comedy hours; *Taxi*, with Judd Hirsch; *Barney Miller*, with Hal Linden; and *Quincy, M.E.*, with Jack Klugman. (Recall, too, that *The Dick Van Dyke Show*, written and directed by Carl Reiner, starred Dick Van Dyke because Reiner was "too Jewish" to play himself on the air. Instead, he played the comedian Alan Brady—an Irishman!)

The emergence of the newer crop of unmistakably Jewish (male) characters may be a product of the success of many recent Black shows and perhaps, too, of the growing self-confidence of Jews in top positions in the networks and production companies. While television still remains a vehicle for the "great drama of American assimilation," as cultural critic Todd Gitlin puts it, these executives may be more willing to imagine that characters like themselves are of interest to mass audiences and less defensive about real or perceived charges that Jews are too powerful in the media, which once led them to shy away from presenting Jewish plots or characters.[9]

The same considerations apparently do not hold for Jewish female characters, who appear primarily as stereotypes—like Nanny Fine or Mike Meyers's *Saturday Night Live* character, Linda Richman, certain conduits to easy laughs—or who are so universalized that their ethnicity, like that of the new sugar-coated mass-marketed bagel, is unrecognizable. These characters and the shows they are in often *are* funny. Yet in their negative aspects they approximate the kind of anti-Semitic and misogynst characteristics of much Jewish Princess/Jewish mother humor. Audiences who accept the characterizations as truthful, although exaggerated, will have a warped sense of the potentialities of Jewish women; such false perspectives are most dangerous for young Jewish women who may also confuse the stereotypes with reality, engendering negative self-images and even self-hatred.[10] The limited range of the Jewish female characters on television reflects a failure of imagination. There is no reason that mainstream audiences cannot respond to images of Jewish women as both ethnic and American, distinctive yet representative, intelligent and caring, as easily as they do to other smart and sassy female characters or to Jewish men on-screen. There are models from the media, like Izzy in *Crossing Delancey*, as well as many real-life professionals—teachers, lawyers, doctors, and activists of all kinds—who can point the way.

Ethnicity need not be subsumed by distinctions that are egregiously false and absurd, nor need it be erased in the drive to present characters who are racially, religiously, and ethnically indistinct. In homogenizing or exaggerating the portrayal of Jewish women, television silences the diverse voices of real women and renders their authentic experiences invisible. Moreover, in portraying Jewish men almost invariably in relationships with non-Jewish women, TV shows foster the notions that Jewish women are undesirable and unattractive, and that Jews only rarely, if ever, become romantically involved with each other.

The inclusion of viable characters and situations that provide a fair range of the multiple ethnicities of American life without resorting to simplistic exaggeration is the challenge of the future, both for creative artists, writers, and executives and for all of us, the audiences who by their responses can encourage image makers to take greater risks.[11]

Notes

J. Antler, Introduction

1. Catharine Stimpson, "Female Insubordination and the Text," in *Women in Culture and Politics: A Century of Change,* Bloomington: Indiana University Press, 1986 ed. Judith Friedlander, Blanche Wiesen Cook, Alice Kessler-Harris, and Carroll Smith-Rosenberg (Bloomington: Indiana University Press, 1986), pp. 165–69.
2. See, for example, Susan A. Glenn, *Daughters of the Shtetl: Life and Labor in the Immigrant Generation* (Ithaca, N.Y.: Cornell University Press, 1990).
3. Naomi W. Cohen, *Jews in Christian America: The Pursuit of Religious Equality* (New York: Oxford University Press, 1992), p. 123.
4. Louis Harap, *In the Mainstream: The Jewish Presence in Twentieth-Century American Literature, 1950s–1980s* (New York: Greenwood Press, 1987), p. 21.
5. Harap, *In the Mainstream,* p. 23.
6. Marya Mannes, "A Dissent," *Saturday Review* 22 (February 1969): 39.
7. See, for example, Sylvia Barack Fishman, *A Breath of Life: Feminism in the American Jewish Community* (New York: The Free Press, 1993), and National Commission on Jewish Women, *Voices for Change: Future Directions for American Jewish Women* (Waltham, Mass.: Brandeis University and Hadassah, 1995).
8. On contemporary Jewish women's religious explorations, see, for example, Fishman, *A Breath of Life*; Lynn Davidman and Shelley Tenebaum, eds., *Feminist Perspectives on Jewish Studies* (New Haven, Conn.: Yale University Press, 1994), and T. M. Rudavsky, ed., *Gender and Judaism: The Transformation of Tradition* (New York: New York University Press, 1995).

J. Burstein, Translating Immigrant Women

1. In "Gender and the Immigrant Jewish Experience in the United States" (in *Jewish Women in Historical Perspective*, ed. Judith Baskin [Detroit: Wayne State University Press, 1994], pp. 222–42), Paula E. Hyman observes that "East European Jewish culture offered women contradictory messages" (p. 224). One ought to note that these are Ashkenazic Jews, not Sephardim: Jews from the European rather than the Oriental or Middle Eastern diaspora.
2. According to Charlotte Baum, Paula Hyman, and Sonya Michel, *The Jewish Woman in America* (New York: New American Library, 1976), pp. 3–16; Susan A. Glenn, *Daughters of the Shtetl: Life and Labor in the Immigrant Generation* (Ithaca, N.Y.: Cornell University Press, 1990), p. 8; Sydney Stahl Weinberg, *The World of Our Mothers: The Lives of Jewish Immigrant Women* (New York: Schocken, 1988), pp. 6, 9, 14.
3. Weinberg, in *The World of Our Mothers*, says that

> although the great majority of men worked, helping to earn a livelihood was frequently considered a woman's job and an extension of her work in the

home. This meant that working for money was not a source of shame for Jewish women as it would be among cultures where a man's status depended upon his ability to support his family. Throughout most of preindustrial Europe, non-Jewish women also shared this burden with their husbands, but only among the Jews of Eastern Europe was it accepted practice that some women would provide the sole means of support. (p. 6)

4. Glenn, *Daughters of the Shtetl*, p. 8.
5. Other potentially toughening discordances would include the cultural image of the Jewish woman as both "inherently close to the physical, material world," and also "endowed with an exceptional capacity for moral persuasion" (Baum et al., *Jewish Woman*, p. 12).
6. Glenn, *Daughters*, p. 77; Weinberg, *World of Our Mothers*, p. 54.
7. Glenn, *Daughters of the Shtetl*, p. 14.
8. Weinberg, *World of Our Mothers*, pp. 36, 38, 45, 74.
9. Glenn, *Daughters of the Shtetl*, p. 81.
10. Ibid., p. 118.
11. "Learning to Listen: Interview Techniques and Analyses," in *Women's Words*, ed. Sherna Gluck and Daphne Patai (New York: Routledge, 1991), p. 11.
12. Jessica Benjamin, "The Alienation of Desire: Women's Masochism and Ideal Love," in *Psychoanalysis and Women*, ed. Judith L. Alpert (Hillsdale, N.J.: Analytic Press, 1986), p. 122.
13. "Feminist Criticism in the Wilderness," in *New Feminist Criticism* (New York: Pantheon, 1985), pp. 261–62.
14. Antin, *The Promised Land* (1912; reprint, Salem, N.H.: Ayer, 1987), p. xix.
15. Antin, *Promised Land* [Antin's emphasis].
16. Werner Sollors, *Beyond Ethnicity* (New York: Oxford University Press, 1986), pp. 32–33.
17. Antin, *Promised Land*, p. 147.
18. Benjamin, "The Alienation of Desire," p. 121.
19. Jessica Benjamin, *The Bonds of Love* (New York: Pantheon, 1988), p. 12.
20. Benjamin, *Bonds of Love*, pp. 21–24, 31–44.
21. But cf. Andrew Heinze (*Adapting to Abundance* [New York: Columbia University Press, 1990]), who argues that Jewish immigrant women were unlike their Irish, Italian, and German counterparts in that they were "endowed . . . with great authority to run the household economy" (p. 108). Their "control over domestic consumption," Heinze believes, dignified their position in the family and the culture (p. 109).
22. Antin, *Promised Land*, p. 64.
23. Ibid., p. 247.
24. Ibid., p. 246.
25. Ibid., p. 5.
26. But cf. Sollors, *Beyond Ethnicity*, p. 45, who recognizes this excess but interprets it differently. Diane Lichtenstein (*Writing Their Nations: The Tradition of Nineteenth Century American Jewish Women Writers* [Bloomington: Indiana University Press, 1992]) describes in several earlier writers the strenuous effort to define

themselves as Americans and the "anxiety of displacement" that accompanied their efforts" (pp. 97–99).

27. Antin, *Promised Land*, p. 18.
28. Carol Schoen, *Anzia Yezierska* (Boston: Twayne, 1982), p. 15; Ralda Meyerson Sullivan, "Anzia Yezierska, an American Writer" (Ph.D. diss, University of California at Berkeley, 1975), p. 60.
29. Thomas Ferraro, *Ethnic Passages: Literary Immigrants in Twentieth Century America* (Chicago: University of Chicago Press, 1993), p. 76.
30. Benjamin, *Bonds*, p. 100.
31. Anzia Yezierska, *Bread Givers* (New York: Persea Books, 1975), pp. 11–12, 248.
32. In this respect he reflects the norm, rather than the exception. Weinberg, *World of Our Mothers*, reports that fathers were less likely than mothers to encourage their daughters toward an education, and Susan Glenn, *Daughters*, notes that the lack of male encouragement for women's efforts reflected "the status anxieties of immigrant men": as Jewish men experienced the downward social mobility common to immigrants, "women became the victims of men's efforts to assert, or perhaps reclaim, their masculine dignity" (p. 116).
33. Benjamin, *Bonds of Love*, p. 86.
34. Critics suspect that Yezierska's protagonists need mostly "the nourishment to be received from traditional patriarchal culture" (Elizabeth Ammons, *Conflicting Stories: American Women Writers at the Turn into the Twentieth Century* [New York: Oxford, University Press, 1991], p. 165). But in both the early novel, *Bread Givers* (pp. 296–97), and the late memoir (*Red Ribbon on a White Horse* [New York: Scribners, 1950], pp. 216–18) protagonists recognize that the culture of their fathers will not validate women as subjects.
35. Yezierska, *Red Ribbon on a White Horse*, p. 108.
36. Louise Levitas Henriksen, *Anzia Yezierska: A Writer's Life* (New Brunswick, N.J.: Rutgers University Press, 1988), p. 269; Mary V. Dearborn, *Love in the Promised Land: The Story of Anzia Yezierska and John Dewey* (New York: Free Press, 1988), p. 108.
37. Yezierska, *All I Could Never Be* (New York: Brewer, Warren, and Putnam, 1932), pp. 208–9.
38. Yezierska, *Salome*, p. 25.
39. Yezierska, *Red Ribbon on a White Horse*, p. 108.
40. See, for example, memoirs by Rose Cohen, *Out of the Shadow* (New York: Doran, 1918); Lucy Robbins Lang, *Tomorrow Is Beautiful* (New York: Macmillan, 1948); and Elizabeth Hasanovitz, *One of Them* (Boston: Houghton, 1918).
41. Emma Goldman, *Living My Life* (1931; reprint, New York: New American Library, 1977), p. 61.
42. Goldman, *Living My Life*, pp. 22, 117.
43. Ibid., pp. 59–60, 66, 67.
44. Quoted in Candace Serena Falk, *Love, Anarchy, and Emma Goldman* (New Brunswick, N.J.: Rutgers University Press, 1990), p. 121.
45. Alice Wexler (*Emma Goldman: An Intimate Life* [New York: Pantheon, 1984]) describes the complex and sometimes ambivalent roots of Goldman's work for birth control (p. 210).

46. Falk, *Love, Anarchy, and Emma Goldman*, p. 175.
47. Goldman, *Living My Life*, p. 27; Falk, *Love, Anarchy, and Emma Goldman*, pp. 11–12.
48. But Wexler gives to Johann Most, Goldman's earliest male mentor, credit for teaching Goldman her early rhetorical style (*Emma Goldman*, p. 53).
49. Wexler argues that Goldman's public persona may have been her most original creation (*Emma Goldman*, p. xviii).
50. Herbert Liebowitz, *Fabricating Lives: Explorations in American Autobiography* (New York: Knopf, 1989), p. 165.
51. Falk, *Love, Anarchy, and Emma Goldman*, p. 224.
52. Ibid., p. 5.
53. Ibid., p. 224.
54. Ibid., p. 97.
55. Ibid., p. 175.
56. Leibowitz, *Fabricating Lives*, pp. 157, 168.
57. Kate Simon, *Bronx Primitive* (New York: Harper, 1982), pp. 4–5.
58. Ibid., p. 17.
59. Ibid.
60. Kate Simon, *A Wider World* (New York: Harper, 1986), p. 64.
61. Ibid., p. 48.
62. Ibid.
63. Ibid., p. 6.
64. Simon, *A Wider World*, p. 142.
65. Simon, *Bronx Primitive*, 178.
66. Ibid., pp. 123, 125, 159, 160.
67. Ibid., p. 178.
68. Kate Simon, *Etchings in a Hourglass* (New York: Harper, 1990), p. 9.
69. Simon, *A Wider World*, pp. 44, 48.
70. Ibid., pp. 71–72.
71. Simon, *Etchings in a Hourglass*, p. 11.
72. Ibid., p. 238.
73. Simon, *A Wider World*, p. 186.
74. "Metissage, Emancipation, and Female Textuality in Two Francophone Writers, in *Life/Lines*, ed. Bella Brodzki and Celeste Schenck (Ithaca, N.Y.: Cornell University Press, 1988), p. 262.
75. *Feminine Fictions: Revisiting the Postmodern* (New York: Routledge, 1989), p. 11.
76. "Split at the Root," in *Nice Jewish Girls: A Lesbian Anthology*, ed. Evelyn Torton Beck (1982; reprint, Boston: Beacon, 1990), p. 90.
77. Judith Plaskow, *Standing Again at Sinai: Judaism from a Feminist Perspective* (San Francisco: Harper and Row, 1990), pp. ix–x.

S. P. Rivo, Projected Images

1. Scholars are paying increasing attention to early films, which often contain precious historical evidence; nevertheless, there is a surprising paucity of research fo-

cusing on the actual film images of women, specifically Jewish women. Frequently shot on location in the slum districts of the big cities, the films offer rare ethnographic footage of the architecture and environs: Jewish neighborhoods, the local populace, daily activities of work and leisure. These primary documents are invaluable to examine the portrayals of ethnicity and gender in film.

Two recent books have proved especially helpful in focusing scholars' attention on the analytic possibilities of these films as documents. Kevin Brownlow's *Behind the Mask of Innocence: Sex, Violence, Prejudice, Crime: Films of Social Conscience in the Silent Era* (Berkeley and Los Angeles: University of California, 1990) undertakes a detailed study of silent features, including many Jewish theme films. *Bridge of Light: Yiddish Film between Two Worlds* (New York: Museum of Modern Art and Schocken Press, 1991; Philadelphia: Temple University Press, 1995) by scholar and journalist J. Hoberman is a long awaited comprehensive study of Yiddish cinema that provides valuable new source material. In addition to these studies, two important volumes published in the 1980s focus exclusively on Jews in American film: Lester D. Friedman, *Hollywood's Image of the Jew* (New York: Frederick Unger, 1982); and Patricia Erens, *The Jew in American Cinema* (Bloomington: Indiana University Press, 1984). Both books are comprehensive surveys that catalog for the first time every title referable to Jewish images in American film. While Friedman and Erens viewed many of the film prints available at the time, their conclusions relied primarily on written documents because of the unavailability of or impossibility of obtaining prints of many of the films.

2. Motion picture film was invented in 1889, and by April 23, 1896, the United States had witnessed its first public projection at Koster and Bial's Music Hall in New York City. For ten years, films were shown alongside live acts in vaudeville houses, until the first nickelodeons appeared in 1905. In 1908 the Edison Company made 13,100 projection machines and millions of feet of film for an estimated 10,000 theaters with a $40 million investment (*Scientific American*, February 27, 1909).

3. According to Lester Friedman, *Hollywood's Image*, approximately 230 films made between 1900 and 1929 featured clearly discernible Jewish characters, a figure much greater than the number of films featuring other ethnic types (p. 9).

4. Thomas Alva Edison was a close friend of Henry Ford, who publicly proclaimed his dislike of the Hebrew race.

5. *Biograph Bulletin*, March 28, 1908, cited in Tom Gunning *Outsiders as Insiders: Jews and the History of American Silent Film* (Waltham, Mass.: National Center for Jewish Film, 1985), p. 8.

6. Later made into a Yiddish film, *Unfortunate Bride*, in 1926.

7. Hoberman, *Bridge of Light*, p. 27.

8. See Jenna Weiszmann Joselit, *Our Gang: Jewish Crime and the New York Jewish Community 1900–1940* (Bloomington: Indiana University Press, 1983).

9. George Ethelbert Walsh, "Moving Picture Drama for the Multitudes," *Independent* 64 (February 6, 1908): 306–10.

10. Brownlow, *Behind the Mask*, p. 374.

11. Robert Allen, "Motion Picture Exhibition in Manhattan, 1906–1912. Beyond the Nickelodeon," *Cinema Journal* 18 (spring 1979): 4.

12. A contemporary reviewer wrote: "The effect of this new form of pictorial drama on the public is without parallel in modern history, for it more graphically illustrates the panorama of life than the photographs and texts of the daily newspaper and intrudes upon the legitimate theater through the actual dramatization of plays that have had a good run . . . attracting thousands who never go to the theaters and particularly appealing to children. In poorer sections of the cities where the innumerable foreigners congregate, the so-called nickelodeon has held preeminent sway for the last year." Walsh, "Moving Picture Drama for the Multitudes," p. 110.

13. John P. Roche, *The Quest for the Dream: The Development of Civil Rights and Human Relations in Modern America* (New York: Macmillan, 1963), pp. 92–93.

14. Gary Carey, "The Long, Long Road to Brenda Patimkin," *National Jewish Monthly*, October 1971.

15. The film *Humoresque* was recently discovered, preserved, and restored by the UCLA film archive.

16. Erens, *Jew in American Cinema*, p. 78.

17. Harry A. Potamkin, *The Compound Cinema* (New York: Teacher's College Press, 1977), pp. 367–68.

18. Brownlow, *Behind the Mask*, pp. 390–91.

19. Ibid., p. 392.

20. Anzia Yezierska, *Hungry Hearts* (New York: Persea Books, 1985).

21. The film was originally released with German intertitles in Europe and premiered in New York in 1924 with Yiddish and English intertitles. According to *Variety*, the film played for quite some time in New York City.

22. Tom Gunning, *Outsiders as Insiders: Jews and the History of American Silent Film* (Waltham, Mass.: National Center for Jewish Film, 1986), p. 13.

23. In these comedies the Jewish male characters are involved with non-Jewish women. The portrayals of Jewish women are insignificant.

24. *Surrender* (1927) focuses on the European experience and thus is not included here.

25. The silent version of this film is lost, but a sound remake, *Unfortunate Bride* (1932), has been restored.

26. Friedman, *Hollywood's Image*, p. 57 and Appendix I (1920s and 1930s list of titles).

27. Film dialogue as quoted in Erens, *Jews in American Cinema*, p. 87.

28. Ibid., p. 131.

29. Ibid., p. 132.

30. Film dialogue as quoted in Hoberman, *Bridge of Light*, p. 165.

J. J. Brumberg, The "Me" of Me

1. The diary of Sandra Rubin (pseudonym), b. 1939, in the collection of the author.

2. This dynamic—the interplay of the biological, psychological, and cultural—is central to the history of female adolescence described in my forthcoming book *The Body Project: An Intimate History of American Girls* (New York, forthcoming). I am particularly interested in how relatively fixed developmental impera-

tives, such as the biological processes of adolescent development, are shaped by different social and cultural settings.

3. Adolescent girls in the United States first began to keep diaries in large numbers as part of the evangelical revivals associated with the Second Great Awakening. For a history of trends in girls and diary keeping, see Joan Jacobs Brumberg, "Dear Diary: Continuity and Change in the Voices of Adolescent Girls" (Gannett Lecture, Rochester Institute of Technology, Rochester, N.Y., January 1993). On American girls and diary keeping at the end of the nineteenth century, see Jane Hunter, "Inscribing the Self in the Heart of the Family: Girlhood and Diaries in Late Victorian America," *American Quarterly* 44 (March 1992): 51–81.

4. For an excellent description of the history of American Jews in the period preceding, see Henry L. Feingold, *A Time for Searching: Entering the Mainstream, 1920–1945* (Baltimore: Johns Hopkins University Press, 1992).

5. The growth of the personal diary industry is reflected in Thomas's *Register of American Manufacturers* for the years 1910–1960. In the 1950s the largest supplier probably was the Samuel Ward Manufacturing Company in Boston. Over 70 percent of the commercial diaries that I have read, by girls in the 1950s, were produced by this company.

6. *The Diary of a Young Girl*, written by Anne Frank, appeared in Dutch in 1947 and in Germany and France in 1950. In the United States the first printing was sold out on the first day, and 50,000 copies were sold within a week. See *Publishers Weekly*, June 5, 1952; August 2, 1952. Popular coverage of the Anne Frank story developed again in 1957 when the movie, produced by Twentieth Century–Fox, appeared.

7. See *Publishers Weekly* for the 1950s. According to Alice Payne Hackett and James Henry Burke, *80 Years of Best Sellers, 1895–1975* (New York: R.R. Bowker Co., 1977), *The Diary of a Young Girl* had sold over 5 million copies by 1975 making it fifty-ninth in the list of best-sellers.

8. Diary of Ruth Teischmann (pseudonym), b. 1946, entry for September 26, 1959, Schlesinger Library, Radcliffe College, Cambridge, Mass.

9. Unpublished diary of Lynn Saul, b. 1945, entry for October 1960, in the collection of the author.

10. See Wini Breines, *Young, White and Miserable: Growing Up Female in the 1950s* (Boston: Beacon Press, 1992).

11. Beginning in the 1920s, American Jewish girls went to college in disproportionately higher numbers than did other ethnic groups, but only in the post–World War II era did the percentage of Jewish women in college approximate or exceed 50 percent of the eligible age group. On the history of Jewish girls in college, see Ruth Sapinsky, "The Jewish Girl at College (1916)," reprinted in Jacob Marcus Rader, ed., *The American Jewish Women, 1654–1980* (Cincinnati: American Jewish Archives, 1981); Bernard J. Weiss, ed., *American Education and the European Immigrant, 1840–1940* (Urbana: University of Illinois Press, 1982), pp. 46–55; Abraham Lavender, "Studies of Jewish College Students," *Jewish Social Studies* 39 (winter–spring 1977), pp. 37–175; Alfred Jospe, "Jewish College Students in the United States," in *The American Jewish Yearbook*, ed. Morris Fine and Milton Himmelfarb (New York, 1964), pp. 131–45. See also Sydney Stahl Weinberg, *The*

World of Our Mothers: The Lives of Jewish Immigrant Women (Chapel Hill: University of North Carolina Press, 1988), p. 175.

12. This is my own story and another reason that I gave this essay the title "The 'Me' of Me." On the effect of the Depression on adolescents and young adults, see Glen Elder, *Children of the Great Depression* (Chicago: University of Chicago Press, 1974).

13. See, for example, Herman Wouk, *Marjorie Morningstar* (Garden City, N.Y.: Doubleday, 1955); Philip Roth, *Letting Go* (New York: Random House, 1962); and *Portnoy's Complaint* (New York: Random House, 1969).

14. All of the quotations that follow are from the manuscript diaries, 1922–27, of Helen Landis, now in the possession of the author. There were actually ten children born to Sarah Browdy Laprovitz; Lewis died at his bris in 1906, and Florence died of rheumatic fever at age eleven, when Helen was eight. For an interesting account of growing up in Amherst as the son of immigrants, see Edward Landis, "An Immigrant Boyhood in Amherst, 1904–28," in *Essays on Amherst's History* (Amherst, Mass.: Vista Trust, 1978), pp. 270–80.

15. What Isaac Landis and others did not realize, however, was that name changes were often transparent in America and that some educational institutions, such as Harvard, ferreted out students with Jewish origins by asking on preliminary admission forms if the applicant's father had ever changed his name. See "What Was Your Father's Name," *Nation* 115 (October 4, 1922): p. 332.

16. Ibid.

17. The synagogue was in Springfield, Massachusetts, the home of Helen's father's younger brother. Springfield had a sizable Jewish community in the 1920s, a synagogue, and kosher restaurants.

18. Goucher was founded in 1885 by the Baltimore Conference of the Methodist Episcopal Church. See Anna Heubeck Knipp and Thaddeus P. Thomas, *The History of Goucher College* (Baltimore: Goucher College, 1938).

19. Almost all of the Jewish students at Goucher were commuters in this era; as of 1910 there were only seventeen Jewish graduates of the Women's College of Baltimore. See Isidor Blum, *The Jews of Baltimore* (Baltimore: Historical Review Publishing Co., 1910), p. 55.

20. For a definition, see H. L. Mencken, *The American Language*, 4th ed. (New York, 1960), p. 295. It is relevant to note that Mencken lived in Baltimore and probably heard the same vocabulary as Helen Landis. Baltimore was a city whose Jewish population had long been divided into Uptown (German) and Downtown (Russian) Jews; Henrietta Szold initiated the first night schools and Americanization efforts for the Russian Jewish immigration, beginning in the 1880s and continuing unabated well into the 1910s and even early 1920s. See Blum, *The Jews of Baltimore;* Naomi Kellman, *The Beginnings of Jewish Charities in Baltimore* (Baltimore: Jewish Historical Society of Maryland, 1970); and Issac M. Fein, *The Making of an American Jewish Community: The History of Baltimore Jewry from 1773 to 1920* (Philadelphia, 1971).

21. Passing is a theme in fiction by Nella Larson, James Weldon Johnson, William Dean Howells, and Mark Twain. For discussions of passing among African Americans, see Joel Williamson, *New People: Miscegenation and Mulattoes in the*

United States (New York: Free Press, 1986); Juda Bennett, *The Passing Figure: Racial Confusion in Modern America* (New York: Peter Lang, 1996); and Cheryl Wall, "Passing for What? Aspects of Identity in Nella Larsen's Novels," *Black American Literature Forum* XX (Spring–Summer, 1988).

22. Sociology was extremely popular in American colleges and universities in the 1920s; see Dorothy Ross, *The Origins of American Social Science* (Cambridge: Cambridge University Press, 1991). Helen took classes in "social origins" and "social theory," among others.

23. On the history of women in social work, see Penina Glazer and Miriam Slater, *Unequal Colleagues: The Entrance of Women into the Professions, 1890–1940* (New Brunswick, N.J.: Rutgers University Press, 1987).

24. See, for example, Sander Gilman, *Jewish Self Hatred: Antisemitism and the Hidden Language of the Jews* (Baltimore: Johns Hopkins University Press, 1986).

25. This is a theme in Weinberg, *World of Our Mothers*, as well as in the fiction of Anzia Yezierska.

26. On middle-class investments in the skin, teeth, and beauty of adolescent daughters, see Brumberg, *The Body Project*, chapter 3.

J. Sochen, Jewish Women Entertainers as Reformers

1. There have been a number of new collections of women's humor, including *Women's Comic Visions*, which I edited (Detroit: Wayne State University Press, 1991). The most recent collection is Gail Finney's edited *Look Who's Laughing: Gender and Comedy* (Langhorne, Pa.: Gordon and Breach, 1994).

2. Quoted in Richard Meryman, "Can We Talk? Why Joan Rivers Can't Stop," *McCalls*, September 1983, p. 64.

3. Ellen Schiff's essay on Jewish women in drama discusses this subject; see "What Kind of Way Is That for Nice Jewish Girls to Act? Images of Jewish Women in Modern American Drama," in *American Jewish History* Vol. 70 (September 1980): 106–18.

4. One of Fanny Brice's most popular records, containing her well-known skits, was *Fanny Brice/Helen Morgan* (RCA Victor, Vintage Series, LPV-561, 1969).

5. The primary sources for Sophie Tucker's work and life comes from her autobiography, *Some of These Days* (New York: Doubleday Doran & Co., 1945) and Jane R. Westerfield, "An Investigation of the Life Styles and Performance of Three Singer-Comediennes of American Vaudeville: Eva Tanguay, Nora Bayes and Sophie Tucker" (Ph.D. diss., Ball State University, Muncie, Ind., 1987). Lewis Erenberg's *Steppin' Out* (Westport, Conn.: Greenwood, 1981) is also a very helpful source.

6. Tucker's popular records that I heard are *Sophie Tucker: Some of These Days* (Pelican Records, LP 133), *Cabaret Days* (Mercury MG 20046), and *Sophie Tucker: Her Latest and Greatest Spicy Songs* (Mercury, MG 20073).

7. Both "Becky Is Back in the Ballet" and "Mrs. Cohen at the Beach" are on *Fanny Brice/Helen Morgan* (see n. 4).

8. Norman Katkov, *The Fabulous Fanny: The Story of Fanny Brice* (New York: Alfred A. Knopf, 1953), p. 205.

9. Gilbert Seldes, "The Daemonic in the American Theatre," in *The Seven Lively Arts* (New York: Harper & Bros., 1924), p. 306.

10. In my essay "From the Particular to the Universal: Sophie Tucker and Fanny Brice," in *From Hester Street to Hollywood*, ed. Sarah Blacher Cohen (Bloomington: Indiana University Press, 1988), I discuss this concept in greater depth.

11. Seldes, "Daemonic," p. 308.

12. Ibid.

13. Tucker, *Some of These Days*, p. 96.

14. The following record contains the lyrics for all of the titles cited: *Sophie Tucker: Her Latest and Greatest Spicy Songs* (Mercury, MG 20073).

15. Joan Rivers, *Still Talking* (New York: Random House, 1991), p. 24.

16. Ibid, p. 26.

17. Ibid.

18. Among the many articles on Joan Rivers, Lee Israel, "Joan Rivers and How She Got That Way," *Ms.*, October 1984, pp. 109–14, is one of the best.

19. On Joan Rivers, see also Meryman, "Can We Talk?," pp. 63–64.

20. *Funny Girl* was first produced on Broadway in 1964 with Streisand in the original cast. She later reprised the role for the movie version and won the 1968 Academy Award for her performance.

22. Quoted in Clair Safran, "Who Is Bette Midler and Why Are They Saying Those Terrible Things About Her?," *Redbook*, August 1975, p. 57.

23. A video of a Midler concert in the early 1980s provided the material for this paragraph.

24. From the taped video of the interview.

D. Weber, The Jewish-American World of Gertrude Berg

This essay is dedicated to Barbara Weber.

1. All the materials relating to the career of Gertrude Berg and *The Goldbergs*, including radio and TV scripts, newspaper clippings, manuscript letters, and relatively obscure printed material by and about Gertrude Berg are drawn from The Gertrude Berg Papers, George Arents Research Library, Syracuse University.

2. W. W. Templin to Berg, June 17, 1932, Correspondence scrapbook 1, 1931–32, Berg Papers.

3. Warren I. Susman, "The Culture of the Thirties," in Susman, *Culture as History: The Transformation of American Society in the Twentieth Century* (New York: Pantheon, 1984), p. 160.

4. Gertrude Berg, *Molly and Me: The Memoirs of Gertrude Berg* (New York: McGraw-Hill, 1961), p. 177.

5. Printed materials, Box 2, Berg Papers.

6. Like *Amos 'n Andy*, *The Goldbergs*—especially Molly—became famous for malaprop pronouncements, although as George Lipsitz explains, there is a huge difference between our laughing *at* Kingfish's "I'se regusted," which became something of a national phrase, and our laughing *with* Molly's mangling of the language. See George Lipsitz, "The Meaning of Memory: Family, Class, and Ethnicity in Early

Network Television," in *Time Passages: Collective Memory and American Popular Culture* (Minneapolis: University of Minnesota Press, 1990), pp. 39–75.

7. Lipsitz, "The Meaning of Memory," p. 48.

8. Correspondence scrapbook 1931–32, Berg Papers.

9. Published materials, Box 5, Berg Papers.

10. Berg, *Molly and Me*, pp. 3–4.

11. Immigrant Jews were not the only ethnic group to feel the ironies of their new-world condition. In his coming-of-age memoir, Leonard Covello speaks of his mother's kitchen table, "which was covered by an oilcloth with a picture of Columbus setting foot on American soil. More than once my father glared at this oilcloth and poured a malediction on Columbus and his great discovery." Cited in Elizabeth Ewen, *Immigrant Women in the Land of Dollars: Life and Culture on the Lower East Side, 1890–1925* (New York: Monthly Review Press, 1985), p. 137.

12. In her own life, Berg's residential odyssey surpassed any of Yezierska's self-satisfied *alrightnik* characters along Riverside Drive: in the early 1930s, during the Depression, Berg lived first on West 99th Street, then on Central Park West, and finally (in substantial luxury by the early 1940s), on Park Avenue. Later in her career a number of photo-op stories about Berg appeared, showing her shopping on the Lower East Side and talking to the shopkeepers, drawing crowds as she gleaned material for her scripts. See, for example, a profile of Berg published in *Tune In*, March 1943, which includes pictures of Berg both at her country house in Bedford, New York, and on Hester Street, "gather[ing] some local color for her program" (Published Materials, Box 3, Berg Papers).

By contrast, Yezierska, at the end of her life, was virtually unknown, moving around the city from one ramshackle apartment to the next. Information on Yezierska may be found in Mary V. Dearborn, *Love in the Promised Land: The Story of Anzia Yezierska and John Dewey* (New York: Free Press, 1988), and Louise Levitas Henriksen, *Anzia Yezierska: A Writer's Life* (New Brunswick, N.J.: Rutgers University Press, 1988). Henriksen, a journalist in her own right, is Yezierska's daughter.

13. Anzia Yezierska, "The Fat of the Land," in *Hungry Hearts and Other Stories* (1920; reprint, New York: Persea Books, 1985), pp. 218, 219.

14. This and other routines are transcribed by Michael G. Corenthal in *Cohen on the Telephone: A History of Jewish Recorded Humor and Popular Music, 1892–1942* (Milwaukee, Wisc.: Yesterday's Memories, 1984), p. 53. This rich collection contains a discography of (now obscure) recorded monologues along with information on popular songs and entertainers.

15. Milt Gross was a cartoonist for the *Sunday World* when he began a humor column called "Down the Dumbwaiter" in 1924. To judge from reviews of his books, his ethnic sketches had a substantial following in the late 1920s. See, for example, Robert Littell, "Nize Baby," *New Republic* 47 (June 9, 1926): 93–94. "The Jewish East Side speaks through Milt Gross," according to Ernest Sutherland Bates, "American Folk-Lore," *Saturday Review of Literature* 2 (July 10, 1926): 914.

16. Joan Jaffe, "This Is Molly Speaking of the Rise of the Goldbergs," Correspondence scrapbook 1, 1931–32, Berg Papers.

17. It is likely that middle-class, more assimilated (German) Jews in the 1920s bris-

tled over Gross's style of humor, perhaps embarrassed by the exaggerated reminder of how their parents may have talked; in this respect the (presumed) negative reaction to Gross anticipates the Black middle class's sensitive reaction to *Amos 'n Andy*, especially when the radio show made the transition (as did *The Goldbergs*) to television. The debate over *Amos 'n Andy*'s reception among middle-class Blacks is chronicled in Melvin Patrick Ely, *The Adventures of Amos 'n Andy: A Social History of an American Phenomenon* (New York: Free Press, 1991). Ely is thorough but for the most part unimaginative in his reading of the series. (There is no reference to *The Goldbergs.*)

18. Milt Gross, *Dunt Esk!!* (New York: George H. Doran, 1927), pp. 9, 206, 219, 229.

19. Maria Damon speaks of "the modernist tradition of Jewish performance art of stand-up comedy" in her brilliant "Talking Yiddish at the Boundaries," *Cultural Studies* 5 (1991): 20.

20. Correspondence 1931–32, Berg Papers.

21. Ibid.

22. Scrapbook 1, 1930, Berg Papers.

23. Berg, *Molly and Me*, p. 179.

24. Scrapbook 1, 1930, Berg Papers.

25. Radio and TV Scripts, 1930, Berg Papers.

26. The show in question is *The House of Glass*, a serial that Berg wrote briefly between long runs of *The Goldbergs*. *The House of Glass* concerned life revolving around a modest resort hotel in the Catskills, modeled on the similar hotel operated by Berg's own father.

27. Correspondence scrapbook 1935, Berg Papers.

28. Correspondence scrapbook 1943, Berg Papers.

29. Correspondence scrapbook 1949, Berg Papers.

30. Isaac Metzker, *A Bintel Brief: Sixty Years of Letters from the Lower East Side to the Jewish Daily Forward* (New York: Balantine Books, 1971), p. 76.

31. Correspondence scrapbooks 1933 and 1934, Berg Papers.

32. These radio serial plots of 1929–30 were transformed by Berg into a collection of short stories, printed with slightly less Yiddish inflection than in the original radio scripts. See Gertrude Berg, *The Rise of the Goldbergs* (New York: Barse & Co., 1931). The collection includes an introduction by Eddie Cantor.

33. "I am glad to help in any little way that I can," wrote Rabbi David de Sola Pool of the Spanish and Portuguese Synagogue in New York, after providing a detailed synopsis of a Jewish marriage ceremony, "because I believe that you are doing more for better understanding and good will of an interdenominational and interracial character than all the organized movements." Rabbi David de Sola Pool to Gertrude Berg, June 8, 1932, Correspondence Scrapbook 1932, Berg Papers.

34. General scrapbook 1933, Berg Papers.

35. Radio and TV Scripts, 1933, Berg Papers.

36. Radio and TV Scripts, 1933 (Episode 593, "The 'Seder' at the Neighborhood Club House"), Berg Papers.

37. Correspondence scrapbooks 1933 and 1934, Berg Papers.

38. Correspondence scrapbook 1944, Berg Papers.

39. Ibid.

40. Molly Goldberg [Gertrude Berg], *The Molly Goldberg Cookbook* (Garden City, N.Y.: Doubleday, 1955), p. 192. Other recipes include "Fried Herring a La William Shakespeare" (p. 16) and "Challah a La Molly" (p. 193).

41. I discuss the cultural meaning of these various transitions in "Memory and Repression in Early Ethnic Television: The Example of Gertrude Berg and *The Goldbergs*," in *The Other Fifties: Interrogating Midcentury American Icons*, ed. Joel Foreman (Champaign–Urbana: University of Illinois Press, 1997), pp. 144–67.

42. David Marc, *Comic Visions: Television Comedy and American Culture* (Boston: Unwin Hyman, 1989), p. 51.

43. The Loeb affair demands separate treatment. Berg herself argued that Loeb be kept on the show. Unable to support himself as an actor, Loeb committed suicide in September 1955. As a kind of private memorial, Berg kept a huge scrapbook of clippings and articles relating to the Loeb case.

44. Lipsitz, "The Meaning of Memory," p. 72.

S. Klingenstein, Sweet Natalie

1. Erich Segal, *Love Story* (New York: Signet, 1970), p. 4.

2. Nevertheless, she was perceived as a complete miscast. Cf. James Wolcott, "Windy," *New York* 16 (7 February 1983): 76–77.

3. Herman Wouk, *The Winds of War* (Boston: Little, Brown, 1971), preface. Further references are to this edition and are cited in the text as *WW*. Herman Wouk, *War and Remembrance* (Boston: Little, Brown, 1978); all references are to this edition and are cited in the text as *WR*.

4. Paul Fussell, "War and Remembrance," *New Republic* 179 (14 October 1978): 32.

5. The best rebuttal of this argument is still Ruth Wisse, "The Anxious American Jew," *Commentary* 66 (September 1978): 47–50.

6. Stanley Edgar Hyman, "Some Questions about Herman Wouk," *Standards: A Chronicle of Books of Our Time* (New York: Horizon Press, 1966), p. 71. The critical reception of *Marjorie Morningstar* is summed up in Arnold Beichman, *Herman Wouk: The Novelist as Social Historian* (New Brunswick, N.J.: Transaction Books, 1984), pp. 51–58; and in Laurence W. Mazzeno, *Herman Wouk* (New York: Twayne Publishers, 1994), pp. 62–65.

7. "When a writer calls his work a Romance," Hawthorne declared in the preface to *The House of the Seven Gables*,

> it need hardly be observed that he wishes to claim a certain latitude, both as to its fashion and material, which he would not have felt himself entitled to assume, had he professed to be writing a Novel. The latter form of composition is presumed to aim at a very minute fidelity, not merely to the possible, but to the probable and ordinary course of man's experience. The former—while, as a work of art, it must rigidly subject itself to laws, and while it sins unpardonably so far as it may swerve aside from the truth of the human heart—has fairly a right to present that truth under circumstances, to a great extent, of the writer's own choosing or creation. (Nathaniel Hawthorne, *The*

House of the Seven Gables and The Snow Image and Other Twice Told Tales [Boston: Houghton Mifflin, 1883], p. 13).

8. Mazzeno, *Herman Wouk*, p. 77; cf. also Mazzeno's brief analysis in "The Historical Novel," *Critical Survey of Long Fiction*, English Language Authors (Englewood Cliffs, N.J.: Salem Press, 1983), pp. 3150–56.

9. Herman Wouk as quoted in Beichman, *Wouk: The Novelist*, p. 17.

10. Beichman, *Wouk: The Novelist*, p. 82.

11. None of the reviewers took issue with Wouk's historiography. See, for example, Fussell, "War and Remembrance," pp. 32–33; Geoffrey Norman, "Wouk on War," *Esquire Magazine* 90 (5 December 1978): 96. The critical response to *WW* and *WR* is summed up in Beichman, *Wouk: The Novelist*, pp. 88–89, and in Mazzeno, *Wouk*, pp. 91–98.

12. Cf. Gen. 6:5 and Gen. 8:21.

13. Discussion in response to Emily Budick's paper "The Holocaust and the Construction of Modern American Literary Criticism: The Case of Lionel Trilling," presented in the Seminar on American Literature at the Center for Literary and Cultural Studies, Harvard University, February 1992.

14. George Steiner, letter to the *Listener*, 29 April 1971, quoted in Christopher Ricks, *T. S. Eliot and Prejudice* (London: Faber and Faber, 1988), p. 28.

15. Fussell, "War and Remembrance," p. 32.

16. Beichman, *Wouk: The Novelist*, p. 1.

17. Fussell, "War and Remembrance," p. 32; Melvin Maddocks, "Wouk at War in Slow Motion," *Life*, 26 November 1971, p. 16.

18. Norma Rosen, "The Second Life of Holocaust Imagery," in *Accidents of Influence: Writing as a Woman and a Jew in America* (Albany: State University of New York Press, 1992), p. 49.

19. Rosen, *Accidents*, p. 10.

20. Rosen, "Notes Toward a Holocaust Fiction" (1990), in *Accidents*, p. 105.

21. Sara R. Horowitz, "Ilona Karmel," in *Jewish American Women Writers: A Bio-Bibliographical and Critical Sourcebook*, ed. Ann R. Shapiro (Westport, Conn.: Greenwood Press, 1994), p. 147.

22. Ilona Karmel, *An Estate of Memory* (Boston: Houghton Mifflin, 1969), p. 7.

23. Ibid., p. 277.

24. Susan Fromberg Schaeffer, *Anya: A Novel* (New York: Macmillan, 1974), p. 471.

25. This is even announced in the title of a survivor narrative by Ruth Elias, *Die Hoffnung erhielt mich am Leben: Mein Weg von Theresienstadt und Auschwitz nach Israel* (Hope kept me alive: My journey from Theresienstadt and Auschwitz to Israel) (Munich: Piper Verlag, 1988).

26. Dorothy Bilik, "Susan Fromberg Schaeffer," in Shapiro, *Jewish American Women Writers*, p. 371.

27. Cynthia Ozick, *The Shawl* (New York: Knopf, 1989), p. 6.

28. Cynthia Ozick, letter to author, February 1990. A successful rescue of a toddler daughter by her mother is the theme of a poem in Irena Klepfisz's "Bashert," collected in *A Few Words in the Mother Tongue: Poems Selected and New, 1971–1990* (Portland, Oregon: Eight Mountain Press, 1990), 187–89. Excerpts from the

poem were reprinted as "Poland, 1944," in Faye Moskowitz, ed., *Her Face in the Mirror: Jewish Women on Mothers and Daughters* (Boston: Beacon Press, 1994), pp. 105–7.

29. Cynthia Ozick, quoted in Bruce Weber, "On Stage, and Off," *New York Times*, 9 September 1994. See also Joyce Antler, "The Americanization of the Holocaust," *American Theatre* 12 (February 1995): 16–20, 69. A revised version of the play premiered under the title *The Shawl* at the Jewish Repertory Theater in New York on 11 June 1996, starring Dianne Wiest as Rosa.

30. "In Manila I said to Byron that we've become a family of tumbleweeds. That's the truth, and lately the winds of war have been blowing us all around the world" (Victor Henry in a letter to his wife Rhoda on 12 December 1941 [*WW*, p. 881]).

31. In March 1942, roughly nine months after Hitler invaded the Soviet Union, Simon and Schuster published a new edition of Tolstoy's *War and Peace*. In his foreword to the novel, Clifton Fadiman wrote:

> It is impossible to reread *War and Peace* in the Year of Death 1942 without being constantly reminded of the fact that history can at times be sensationally repetitious. . . . It is understood . . . that the obvious parallels between the Napoleonic campaigns of 1805 and 1812 as described by Tolstoy and the Nazi campaign of 1941–42 are good only as if of today. . . . It is interesting, however, to indicate as of this date the curious, the almost thrilling similarities between the history of Hitler and the history of Napoleon, the link being furnished by what seems to be a constant in European history—the character and geographical setting of the Russian people. (Leo Tolstoy, *War and Peace*, trans. Louise and Aylmer Maude, with a Foreword by Clifton Fadiman [New York: Simon and Schuster, 1942], xxxix)

The similarities between *War and Peace* and Wouk's war novels were first perceived by Zhang Yidong, "Two Panoramas about Great Wars," *Journal of Popular Culture* 19 (summer 1985): 57–63.

32. Fussell, "War and Remembrance," p. 32.

33. Wouk modeled the character of Aaron Jastrow on Bernard Berenson, an art historian and connoisseur who had settled in Florence in 1900. Berenson, whose name Wouk drops at strategic points (*WW*, pp. 26, 267), survived the war in Italy by sheer luck. In Aaron Jastrow, Wouk brings Berenson's biography more in line with the usual experience of the Jews in Europe, demonstrating that neither baptism nor the intellectual mastery of the Christian tradition offered any protection from the brutality of the Nazi persecution. Aaron Jastrow, whose best-selling book *A Jew's Jesus* buys him a villa in Siena (*WW*, p. 27), is in love with Italy, its Christian history, and its Renaissance art, and blind to the rich harvest of modern anti-Semitism that, so Wouk's argument implies, sprang up from the seed of Christianity.

34. We observe that in Natalie's reaction to Aaron, who does not want to go to Palestine—"a hellhole," he calls it, "a desert full of flies, Arabs, and disease" (*WW*, p. 818). In his distress, he confesses that he is safe in Italy because he is really a Catholic and that this might make it possible for them to find refuge in the Vatican.

Hearing that, Natalie "felt a small involuntary stirring of disdain for her uncle" (*WW*, p. 870).

35. The formulation is that of Hawthorne, who wrote: "Had there been a Papist among the crowd of Puritans, he might have seen in this beautiful woman . . . with the infant at her bosom, an object to remind him of the image of Divine Maternity . . . that sacred image of sinless motherhood, whose infant was to redeem the world" (*The Scarlet Letter*, Library of America [New York: Vintage Books, 1990], p. 52).

36. I should note here that Wouk focused the narration of the physical extinction of the Jews, with the exception of Aaron's death, on one person, a man—Aaron's nephew, Berel Jastrow. Berel experiences every form of harassment, pain, and brutality the Nazis had in store, escaping finally from his crematorium detail in a death camp into the woods outside Prague, where he joins the partisans. Berel's hasty burial in a shallow grave concludes *War and Remembrance*. The disclaimer Wouk inexplicably adds at the end—"it is only a story of course"—has always struck me as false; and the Hezekiel-inspired purple prose prophecy with which Wouk chooses to end his narrative of the Shoah is quite bad:

> In a shallow, hastily dug grave in the wood outside Prague, Berel Jastrow's bones lie unmarked, like so many bones all over Europe. And so this story ends.
> It is only a story, of course. Berel Jastrow was never born and never existed. He was a parable. In truth his bones stretch from the French coast to the Urals, dry bones of a murdered giant. And in truth a marvelous thing happens; his story does not end there, for the bones stand up and take on flesh. God breathes spirit into the bones, and Berel Jastrow turns eastward and goes home. In the glare, the great and terrible light of this happening, God seems to signal that the story of the rest of us need not end, and that the new light can prove a troubled dawn. (*WW*, p. 1038)

37. Antler, "Americanization," p. 16.

38. It is interesting that Byron, like Mary's husband, Joseph, really has no role as a father in Wouk's epic. Although readers might be tempted to think that Louis is only half Jewish, Wouk inscribes into his narrative the Jewish view that any child born of a Jewish mother is Jewish. There is no such thing as half or quarter Jewish in rabbinic law. The use of the Yiddish lullaby, *Rozhinkes mit mandlen*, reduces Byron's role even further. In the song's frame narrative the widow Bas-tsion (daughter of Zion) sits alone in the corner of a room in a Jewish house of worship, rocking her only son. Hence, when Natalie sings this song to Louis, the Gentile father is written out of the Jewish bond between mother and son.

R.-E. Prell, Cinderellas Who (Almost) Never Become Princesses

1. Suzanna Walters, *Lives Together Worlds Apart: Mothers and Daughters in Popular Culture* (Berkeley: University of California Press, 1992), p. 4.
2. Myrna Blythe, *Cousin Suzanne* (New York: Mason/Charter, 1975), pp. 36–37.
3. Herman Wouk's *Marjorie Morningstar* (New York: Doubleday and Co., 1955) and

Philip Roth's Brenda Patimkin of *Goodbye, Columbus* (1959; reprint, Boston: Houghton Miflin, 1989) have been the subject of Jewish feminist critiques for decades now, first and foremost in Charlotte Baum, Paula Hyman, and Sonya Michel, *The Jewish Woman in America* (New York: New American Library, 1975).

4. The JAP stereotype has been analyzed in Riv-Ellen Prell, "Why Jewish Princesses Don't Sweat: Desire and Consumption in Postwar American Jewish Culture," in *People of the Body: Jews and Judaism from an Embodied Perspective*, ed. Howard Eilberg-Schwartz (New York: SUNY Press, 1992), pp. 329–59; also see Baum et al., *The Jewish Woman in America*.

5. Wouk, *Marjorie Morningstar*, pp. 429–30. New Rochelle is a suburb of New York City.

6. Wouk's book was among the ten top sellers of the year. In her analysis of the year's best-selling books, Elizabeth Long argues that *Marjorie Morningstar* can be read as tragic. Children go astray because of an overly rapid climb up the social ladder by parents. The children are left placeless. For Long, the book signals the beginning of a more "complex understanding of social mobility," which is apparent in themes of best-sellers by the end of the 1950s. Elizabeth Long, *The American Dream and the Popular Novel* (New York: Routledge and Kegan Paul, 1989), p. 90.

7. Wouk self-consciously chose for Noel an anglicized version of the Yiddish cultural "type," the *Luftsmensch*, who cannot support his family or make a steady living.

8. Barbara Ehrenreich suggests that this was a perspective articulated in *Playboy* and other publications during this period. Women were blamed for their economic dependence on men at a time when only men were expected to work. See Barbara Ehrenreich, *The Hearts of Men: American Men and the Flight from Commitment* (New York: Anchor Books, 1983).

9. Both stories associate Judaism with the mother, her membership in Jewish organizations, and her concern for her daughter's endogamous marriage. Mrs. Patimkin is portrayed as particularly vacuous. When Neil mentions Martin Buber, she can only think to ask what his denomination is. These novels grew in tandem with the comic Jewish mother explored in Prell, "Rage and Representation," in *Uncertain Terms: Negotiating Gender in American Culture*, ed. Faye Ginsberg and Anna Lownhaup Tsing (Boston: Beacon Press, 1990), and G. Rothbell, "The Jewish Mother: Social Construction of a Popular Image," in *The Jewish Family: Myths and Realities*, ed. Steven Cohen and Paula Hyman (New York: Holmes and Meier, 1986), pp. 118–30. Sons, then, refuse both fathers and mothers through their daughters.

10. Susan Lukas, *Fat Emily* (New York: Stein and Day, 1974).

11. Louise Rose Blecher, *The Launching of Barbara Fabrikant* (New York: David McKay, 1974).

12. M. M. Bakhtin, *Rabelais and His World*, trans. Helen Tsivolsky (Cambridge, Mass: M.I.T. Press, 1968).

13. Bleacher, *Launching*, p. 37.

14. Lukas, *Fat Emily*, p. 78.

15. Sandra Harmon, *A Girl Like Me* (New York: Dutton, 1975).

16. Gail Parent, *Sheila Levine Is Dead and Living in New York* (New York: G. P. Putnam's Sons, 1972).

17. Marie Brenner, *Tell Me Everything* (New York: Dutton, 1976).

18. Blecher, *Launching*, p. 11.

19. Ibid.

20. Blythe, *Cousin Suzanne*.

21. Ibid., pp. 36–37.

22. Bakhtin, *Rabelais*, p. 321.

23. See the discussion of the Jewish nose in Europe in Sander Gilman, *The Jew's Body* (New York: Routledge, 1991), pp. 169–93.

24. Feminist scholarship, particularly in media studies, has offered a sophisticated analysis of how the camera constructs women in twentieth-century U.S. culture. The extent to which women can see as well as be seen is raised by this scholarship as well. These novels predate that scholarship but share with it as a consciousness of women as objects rather than subjects. The device of the gaze in these works, including the camera, appear to heighten self-consciousness and distance the narrator from herself. The gaze often incorporates the point of view of the other, the source of love. In this sense these novels are like other forms of media that feminist scholars examined in film and television criticism. See Theresa De Lauretis, *Alice Doesn't: Feminism, Semiotics, Cinema* (Bloomington: Indiana University Press, 1984). For an analysis of the gaze and race, see bell hooks, *Black Looks: Race and Representation* (Boston: South End Press, 1992).

25. Parent, *Shelia Levine*, pp. 49–50.

26. Gail Parent, *David Meyer Is a Mother* (New York: Harper & Row, 1976).

27. Rhoda Lerman, *The Girl That He Marries* (New York: Holt, Rinehart and Winston, 1976), pp. 127–28.

28. Barbara Ehrenreich, *Fear of Falling: The Inner Life of the Middle Class* (New York, Pantheon Books, 1989).

29. Long, *The American Dream*, p. 120.

30. Some good examples are Winifred Breines, *Young, White and Miserable* (Boston: Beacon, 1992); Walters, *Lives Together*; Elaine Tyler May, *Homeward Bound: Families in the Cold War Era* (New York: Basic Books, 1989).

31. Betty Friedan, *The Feminine Mystique* (New York: Dell Publishing, 1963).

32. "Review of *The Girl That He Marries*," *Booklist* 72 (May 1976): 1242.

33. "Forecasts," *Publishers Weekly* (May 1976), p. 55.

34. Deborah Dash Moore, *At Home in America: Second Generation New York Jews* (New York: Columbia University Press, 1981), notes that second-generation Jews also conflated their Jewishness with the markings of American respectability, like furniture.

35. I wish to acknowledge my appreciation to Joyce Antler and Howard Eilberg-Schwartz for very helpful readings of a previous version of this paper. I also appreciate the comments of colleagues who heard this paper in an American studies seminar at the University of Minnesota. I especially appreciate the very perceptive reading by Jason Loviglio, who taught me that there is a great deal more to novels than appears to someone trained in the social sciences. His own understanding of literature and the 1970s fundamentally shaped my readings of these novels. I am quite sure that none of my generous readers would entirely agree with this version, but their insights were crucial.

B. Lyons, Faith and Puttermesser

1. The critical literature on these writers is too voluminous to note, but for example, some critics have argued that Malamud's fiction is entirely hostile toward women. In "Women in Bernard Malamud's Fiction," *Studies in American Jewish Fiction* 3 (1983): 138–50, Barbara Koenig Quart argues that there is revulsion that "suggests fear or hostility toward women's physicality, or sexuality, especially evident in the earlier work" (p. 140); and in "Mirrors, Windows and Peeping Toms: *A New Life* and *Dubin's Lives*," *Studies in American Jewish Fiction* 3 (1983): 151–65, Chiara Briganti observes that all Malamud's female figures "share a common shallowness" and are "unidimensional characters who are never confronted with the responsibility of a choice" (p. 163).

2. Robert Redfield, *The Little Community and Peasant Society and Culture* (Chicago: University of Chicago Press, 1960). In *Number Our Days* (New York: Simon and Schuster, 1978), Barbara Myerhoff fruitfully applies Redfield's distinction between the Great Tradition and the Little Tradition to Jewish culture (pp. 256–57).

3. Cynthia Ozick, "Toward a New Yiddish," *Art & Ardor* (New York: E. P. Dutton, 1984), pp. 151–71.

4. Cynthia Ozick, "Literature and the Politics of Sex: A Dissent," *Art & Ardor*, pp. 233–37.

5. Cynthia Ozick, "Virility," in *The Pagan Rabbi and Other Stories* (New York: Schocken Books, 1976), pp. 219–70.

6. Eleanor Wachtel, *Writers & Company* (New York: Harcourt Brace, 1994), p. 4.

7. Cynthia Ozick, "Puttermesser: Her Work History, Her Ancestry, Her Afterlife," in *Levitation: Five Fictions* (New York: Alfred A. Knopf, 1988), pp. 21–38.

8. Cynthia Ozick, "Puttermesser and Xanthippe," in *Levitation: Five Fictions*, pp. 75–158.

9. Cynthia Ozick, "Puttermesser Paired," *New Yorker*, 8 (October 1990): 40–75.

10. Joan Lidoff, "Clearing Her Throat: An Interview with Grace Paley," *Shenandoah* 32 (1981): 6–7.

11. Grace Paley, "Two Short Sad Stories from a Long and Happy Life," in *The Little Disturbances of Man* (New York: Doubleday, 1959), pp. 127–45.

12. Ibid., p. 132.

13. Grace Paley, "Listening," in *Later the Same Day* (New York: Farrar, Straus & Giroux, 1985), p. 202.

14. Paley, "Two Short Sad Stories," p. 128.

15. Ibid., p. 134.

16. Ibid.

17. Ibid., p. 143.

18. Ibid., p. 145.

19. Wachtel, *Writers & Company*, pp. 11–12.

20. Lidoff, "Clearing Her Throat," p. 10.

21. Grace Paley, "The Expensive Moment," in *Later the Same Day* (New York: Farrar Straus & Giroux, 1985), p. 190.

22. Ibid., p. 180.

23. Ozick, "Toward a New Yiddish," p. 157.
24. Cynthia Ozick, "Bialik's Hint," in *Metaphor & Memory: Essays* (New York: Alfred A. Knopf, 1989), p. 236.
25. Ozick, "Puttermesser: Her Work History," p. 23.
26. Ibid., pp. 23, 32.
27. Ibid., pp. 34–35.
28. Ibid., p. 36.
29. Ozick, "Puttermesser and Xanthippe," p. 99.
30. Ibid., p. 92.
31. Ibid., p. 95.
32. Ibid., p. 157.
33. Ibid., p. 158.
34. Maya Friedler, "An Interview with Grace Paley," *Story Quarterly* 13 (1981): 33.
35. Kathleen Hulley, "Interview with Grace Paley," *Delta* 14 (May 1982): 19.
36. Paley, "The Used-Boy Raisers," in *The Little Disturbances*, pp. 131–32.
37. Ibid., p. 132.
38. Ibid.
39. Grace Paley, "Faith in a Tree," in *Enormous Changes at the Last Minute* (New York: Farrar, Straus and Giroux, 1985), pp. 99–100.
40. Ibid., p. 89.
41. Paley, "Friends," in *Later the Same Day*, p. 81.
42. Paley, "The Used-Boy Raisers," p. 132.
43. Grace Paley, "Introduction: Thinking about Barbara Deming," in Barbara Deming, *Prisons That Could Not Hold* (San Francisco: Spinsters Ink, 1985), p. 2.
44. Paley, "Goodbye and Good Luck," in *The Little Disturbances*, p. 14.

S. B. Fishman, Our Mothers and Our Sisters and Our Cousins and Our Aunts

1. For differing assessments as to the critical importance of gender, see Carol Tavris, *The Mismeasure of Women* (New York: Simon & Schuster, 1992); Carol Gilligan, *In a Different Voice: Psychological Theory and Women's Development* (Cambridge, Mass.: Harvard University Press, 1982); Carolyn Heilbrun, *Reinventing Womanhood* (New York: Norton, 1982).
2. Observers disagree as to what extent differing factors influence psychological development. Gender is critical, but considered alone it provides only a partial explanation of the mystery of human personality. In addition, birth order; the response of parents to the particular child; changing emotional, economic, social, cultural, or religious conditions within the family unit; and not least, the basic genetic package each child brings with her/him—each has an important impact. A fascination with such variations within gender groups informs the works of many great writers who have created female characters with striking variations in personality, ambitions, and passions. Given three daughters, Shakespeare suggested, a father may participate in raising a Goneril, a Regan, and a Cordelia. Yiddish writer Sholem Aleichem gave his Tevye the Dairyman half a dozen daughters, each of whom was a very different kind of human being.

3. Readers have a more complete and vivid sense of some biblical female characters, for example, because of conversations between Sarah and Hagar, between Rachel and Leah, and between Ruth and Naomi, than because of conversations between Sarah and Abraham, Rachel and Jacob, and Ruth and Boaz.

4. See especially Anzia Yezierska, "Children of Loneliness," in *The Open Cage* (reprint, New York: Persea Books, 1991), pp. 145–63, in which a young woman feels as though her mother, through the immigrant woman's own personal ignorance, is somehow "pulling me backward by the hair into the darkness of past ages."

5. Writer Andrea Dworkin, for example, confesses that she deliberately keeps "quiet at meetings more than I should because I don't like feeling singled out as the Jew with the words. . . . now, in the Women's Movement, I am made to feel self-conscious about being an intellectual." Publisher Gloria Greenfield recounts similar slurs: "I'm called a bourgeois Jewish intellectual. Bourgeois! My parents are Russian immigrants. neither of them went to high school. My mother is a janitor; my father works as a cabdriver and a hospital worker." Cited by Letty Cottin Pogebrin, "Anti-Semitism in the Women's Movement: A Jewish Feminist Disturbing Account," *Ms.*, June 1982, pp. 145–49.

6. Alfred Kazin, *A Walker in the City* (1951), quoted in Steven J. Rubin, ed., *Writing Our Lives: Autobiographies of American Jews, 1890–1990* (Philadelphia and New York: Jewish Publication Society, 1991), pp. 134–37.

7. Herman Wouk, *Marjorie Morningstar* (New York: Pocket Books, 1955), pp. 228–30.

8. Ibid., pp. 744–46.

9. Philip Roth, *Goodbye, Columbus and Five Short Stories* (1959; reprint, Boston: Houghton Mifflin Co., 1989).

10. Philip Roth, *Portnoy's Complaint* (New York: Fawcett Crest/Ballantine Books, 1969).

11. Nina Auerbach, *Communities of Women: An Idea in Fiction* (Cambridge, Mass.: Harvard University Press, 1978).

12. Daphne Merkin, *Enchantment* (San Diego and New York: Harcourt, 1986).

13. Thus, in E. M. Broner's novel *Her Mothers* (Bloomington: Indiana University Press, 1985), Beatrix, the protagonist, for years makes her mother feel as though she is unworthy of Beatrix's friendship and regard. Beatrix's mother is acutely aware of the way her daughter snubs her, as she complains: "You had your father sign your report card; when you told about your day, about your night, you looked at your father; when you spoke of foreign affairs, money affairs, travel affairs you looked at your father." Because Beatrix is a mother as well as a daughter, she learns through her own experience how great a gift is the reconciliation of a daughter's embrace, pp. 142, 116.

14. Grace Paley, "Dreamers in a Dead Language," in *Later the Same Day* (New York: Farrar, Strauss and Giroux, 1985).

15. Anne Richardson Roiphe, *Lovingkindness* (New York: Summit Books, 1987).

16. Cynthia Ozick, *The Cannibal Galaxy* (New York: Alfred A. Knopf, 1983), pp. 64, 101.

17. Renee's mother "had greeted each announcement of my educational plans with

'Nu, Renee, is this going to help you find a husband?' so that the consequence of all my academic honors, Phi Beta Kappa, summa cum laude, scholarships, fellowships, prizes, was only a deepening sense of guilty failure." When Renee calls to tell her mother that she has become engaged to a world-famous mathematician, her mother uses this happy occasion to strip Renee even further: "You should be very proud, Renee, that such a man should love you. Of course, I know you're not just any girl. Who should know if not me? This is why God gave you such good brains, so that you could make such a man like this love you." Rebecca Goldstein, *The Mind-Body Problem* (New York: Dell, 1983), pp. 67–70.

18. Ava believes femininity cancels out intellectual brilliance:

> And you know this uglification is intentional. . . . I don't really want to look pretty. I don't want to look feminine. You know why? Because feminine is dumb. . . . Look around at the women in academia, the women who make their living from their brains—especially those in so-called masculine disciplines like math and physics, to take two random examples. They all feel it too. They're telling you with the way they look and dress, the way they hold themselves and speak: feminine is dumb. You've got to stamp out all traces of girlishness if you want to be taken seriously by the others, but more importantly by yourself. . . . You just can't be a cunt with intelligence. . . . We've all swallowed it. I tell you, I think it would be an act of feminist heroism, an assertion of true liberation from the chauvinist myth, to wear eyeliner and mascara. If I ever saw a female physicist dress to kill and wearing eye makeup, I'd be impressed. But it won't be me." (Goldstein, *Mind-Body*, pp. 216–17)

19. Rebecca Goldstein, *The Dark Sister* (New York: Viking Penguin, 1991), p. 222.
20. Sylvia Rothchild, *Family Stories for Every Generation* (Detroit: Wayne State University Press, 1989).
21. Lynne Sharon Schwartz, *Leaving Brooklyn* (New York: Penguin Books, 1988), pp. 142–43.

F. Herman, The Way She *Really* Is

1. Carey Goldberg, "Barbra, Gorgeous! You Have a Shrine!" *New York Times*, 12 May 1996, sec. 1.
2. Michael Kimmelman, "Too Jewish? Artists Ponder," *New York Times*, 8 March 1996, sec. 3.
3. Actually, *Hello, Dolly!* was completed before *Funny Girl*, but because of contractual problems arising from the fact that the stage version of *Hello, Dolly!* (starring Carol Channing) was still running on Broadway, the release of the film *Hello Dolly!* was delayed until 1969.
4. Streisand has played this kind of character in almost all of her films, including *Hello, Dolly!* (1969), *The Owl and the Pussycat* (1970), *On a Clear Day You Can See Forever* (1970), *What's Up, Doc?* (1972), *The Way We Were* (1973), *For Pete's*

Sake (1974), *Funny Lady* (1975), *A Star Is Born* (1976), *The Main Event* (1979), *Nuts* (1987), and *The Prince of Tides* (1991).

5. Quoted in Calev Ben-David, "The Way She Is," *Jerusalem Report*, 2 June 1994, p. 43. Ben-David himself refers to Streisand as the "Jackie Robinson of female Jewish performers." See also, for example, Lester D. Friedman, *The Jewish Image in American Film* (Secaucus, N.J.: Citadel Press, 1987). Streisand not only appears in but also usually graces the covers of other books on Jews in film or "great" American Jews. See, for example, Elinor and Robert Slater, *Great Jewish Women* (Middle Village, N.Y.: Jonathan David, 1994).

6. Letty Cottin Pogrebin, *Deborah, Golda and Me: Being Female and Jewish in America* (New York: Doubleday, 1991), p. 267. Pogrebin contrasts Streisand's "Jewish Big Mouth" with more negative (and more prevalent) character types such as the frigid, materialistic Jewish American Princess and the overbearing, even castrating, Jewish Mother.

7. Quoted in Ben-David, "The Way She Is," p. 42.

8. Marcy Sheiner, "Maybe I Could Be—Like Barbra—GAWJUS!" *Lilith* 21 (spring 1996): 10–12. Italics in original.

9. John Murray Cuddihy, *The Ordeal of Civility: Freud, Marx, Lévi-Strauss, and the Jewish Struggle with Modernity*, 2nd ed. (Boston: Beacon Press, 1987), p. 189.

10. My thinking on this topic has been greatly influenced by James Baldwin's essay "Everybody's Protest Novel," in *Critical Essays on Harriet Beecher Stowe*, ed. Elizabeth Ammons (Boston: G. K. Hall & Co., 1980), pp. 92–101 (reprinted from *Partisan Review* 16 [June 1949], 578–85). Two other interesting essays that touch on Baldwin's arguments but focus on film are Sanford Pinsker, "Spike Lee: Protest, Literary Tradition, and the Individual Filmmaker," *Midwest Quarterly* 35 (autumn 1993): 63–76, and Gerald Early, "The Color Purple as Everybody's Protest Art," *Antioch Review* 44 (summer 1986): 261–75. I have also benefited from Ann Douglas's critique of sentimentalism in nineteenth-century literature for women, *The Feminization of American Culture* (1977; reprint, New York: Anchor Books, 1988), as well as Jane Tompkins's arguments about the *power* of sentimentality in nineteenth-century literature written by women (Jane Tompkins, *Sensational Designs: The Cultural Work of American Fiction 1790–1860* [New York: Oxford University Press, 1985]).

11. See especially Henry L. Feingold, *A Time for Searching: Entering the Mainstream, 1920–1945* (Baltimore: Johns Hopkins University Press, 1922), chap. 7, and Nathan Glazer, *American Judaism*, 2nd ed. (Chicago: University of Chicago Press, 1989), chap. 6.

12. I am using *liberal* here as Glazer defines it: "preference for experiments and new departures rather than cautious adherence to the established order; greater freedom in action for the individual rather than greater state restraint; rights for minority religions, minority political views, and minority social groups rather than acceptance of a traditional order that gave preference to a previously established religion or to charter social groups." Nathan Glazer, "The Anomalous Liberalism of American Jews," in *The Americanization of the Jews*, ed. Robert M. Seltzer and Norman J. Cohen (New York: New York University Press, 1995), pp. 134–35.

13. The definition of the term *feminism*, of course, is hotly contested. I use the term

broadly to mean the struggle for women to achieve full equality with men in all aspects of life. Achieving this goal will require, I believe, both the deconstruction of the terms *male* and *female* and an end to the privileging of all that is "male."

14. See Rosemary Tong, *Feminist Thought: A Comprehensive Introduction* (Boulder, Colo., and San Francisco: Westview Press, 1989).

15. The other two are *The Prince of Tides* and *What's Up, Doc?*.

16. The five films discussed here present remarkably similar images of Jews, women, and Jewish women, despite the fact that each film had a different creator. The question of who is responsible for these images (directors, writers, even Streisand herself) will not be addressed here, however, since I am less concerned with determining the origins of these images than with assessing their message and impact.

17. William Wyler, dir., *Funny Girl*, Columbia, 1968.

18. Quoted in Vincent Canby, "Stark Is Basking in 'Funny Girl' Sun," *New York Times*, 19 September 1968.

19. Sheiner, "Maybe I Could Be," p. 11.

20. Terrys T. Olender, "Films," *American Zionist* 59 (December 1968): 32.

21. This was a conscious decision on the part of the film's producer, Ray Stark. Not only is Stark married to Brice's only child, Frances, but Nick Arnstein was still alive at the time the musical play was written and reportedly threatened legal action if he was maligned in any way. The film also ignores aspects of Brice's life that were less than pleasant and that would have detracted from the central romance between Nick and Fanny. For example, no mention is made of Brice's first, short-lived marriage (at age eighteen) to Frank White, a barber from Albany. See Herbert G. Goldman, *Fanny Brice: The Original Funny Girl* (New York: Oxford University Press, 1992).

22. Joseph Morgenstern, "Superstar: The Streisand Story" *Newseek*, 5 January 1970, p. 37.

23. Pogrebin, *Deborah*, p. 269.

24. Morgenstern, "Superstar," p. 37.

25. Sydney Pollack, dir., *The Way We Were*, Columbia, 1973.

26. See, for example, Barry Gross, "No Victim, She: Barbra Streisand and the Movie Jew," *Journal of Ethnic Studies* 3 (spring 1975): 28–40; and Friedman, *Jewish Image*, p. 202.

27. I thank Andrea Most for this insight.

28. Feingold discusses the notion that political liberalism was an expression of Jewish religious values in *A Time for Searching*, p. 194–97. Cf. Jerold S. Auerbach, *Rabbis and Lawyers: The Journey from Torah to Constitution* (Bloomington: Indiana University Press, 1990), chap. 3. Auerbach argues that it is inaccurate to trace the roots of liberalism to the biblical notion of prophetic justice.

29. Stephen J. Whitfield uses this term in an essay on the ways in which movies represent the best example of American Jews' desire to assimilate into American society, especially through intermarriage. "Movies in America as Paradigms of Accommodation," in *The Americanization of the Jews*, ed. Robert M. Seltzer and Norman J. Cohen (New York: New York University Press, 1995), p. 83.

30. William R. Taylor, *Sydney Pollack* (Boston: Twayne, 1981), pp. 55–56.

31. In contrast, in the last scene of the film, when Katie and Hubbell meet again on a

New York street, Hubbell is with the kind of woman he can handle: a standard American beauty who remains entirely silent during this crucial scene.

32. Stephen Farber, "Time for Hollywood to Stop Playing It Safe," *New York Times*, 4 November 1973, sec. 2.

33. Molly Haskell, "What Makes Streisand Queen of the Box Office?" *New York Times*, 9 March 1975, sec. 2.

34. I thank Thomas Doherty for this phrase.

35. Pogrebin, *Deborah*, p. 267.

36. Frank Pierson, dir., *A Star Is Born*, Warner Brothers–First Artists, 1976. The 1954 film in itself a remake of the 1937 original, which starred Janet Gaynor and Fredric March.

37. Pogrebin, *Deborah*, p. 260.

38. Notably, however, her agent's name is the Jewish-sounding "Brian Wexler" (played by Jewish director Paul Mazursky), and he is the only character who can come close to matching Esther's moral behavior.

39. Pauline Kael, review of *A Star Is Born*, in *When the Lights Go Down* (New York: Holt, Rinehart and Winston, 1980), p. 244.

40. Howard Zieff, dir., *The Main Event*, Warner Brothers–First Artists, 1979.

41. Friedman, *The Jewish Image*, p. 79.

42. Jules Arbose, "London Loves Brooklyn's Barbra," *New York Times*, 24 April 1966.

43. Camille Paglia, "The Way She Was," *New Republic* (18–25 July 1994): 22.

44. On Jewish noses, see Sander Gilman, *The Jew's Body* (New York and London: Routledge, 1991).

45. See, for example, Jonathan D. Sarna, "The Jews of Boston in Historical Perspective," in *The Jews of Boston*, ed. Jonathan D. Sarna and Ellen Smith (Boston: Combined Jewish Philanthropies of Greater Boston, 1995), pp. 1–20.

46. For filmic examples of this story see, for example, *The Heartbreak Kid* (1972) and virtually every Woody Allen film. The story appears in much American Jewish fiction as well, especially in the generation of writers that includes Philip Roth and Herman Wouk.

47. Janet Maslin, "Critic's Notebook: The Screenwriters' Story," *New York Times*, 22 June 1979, sec. 3.

48. Barbra Streisand, dir., *Yentl*, MGM/UA, 1983.

49. Aside from directing and starring in *Yentl*, Streisand also served as the film's producer and co-wrote the screenplay.

50. Isaac Bashevis Singer, "Yentl the Yeshiva Boy," in *Collected Stories*, ed. Isaac Bashevis Singer (London: Penguin Books, 1984), p. 163.

51. Singer, "Yentl," p. 149.

52. Sylvia Barack Fishman argues that though the sources "tended to be negative" on the issue of women's education, it was possible for "exceptional" women to learn Jewish texts (*A Breath of Life: Feminism in the American Jewish Community* [New York: Free Press, 1993], 181–88). However, there are enough examples of passages that frown on women's learning to negate Yentl's claim that prohibitions are not written.

53. For more thorough examinations of the problems confronting women in Judaism,

see, for example, Rachel Biale, *Women and Jewish Law: An Exploration of Women's Issues in Halakhic Sources* (New York: Schocken Books, 1984); Blu Greenberg, *On Women and Judaism: A View from Tradition* (Philadelphia: Jewish Publication Society of America, 1981); Susannah Heschel, ed., *On Being a Jewish Feminist: A Reader* (New York: Schocken Books, 1983); Elizabeth Koltun, ed., *The Jewish Woman: New Perspectives* (New York: Schocken Books, 1976); and Judith Plaskow, *Standing Again at Sinai: Judaism from a Feminist Perspective* (San Francisco: HarperCollins, 1990).

54. MaryHeléne Rosenbaum, "Streisand's *Yentl:* Enjoyable Escapism," *Christian Century*, 7 March 1984, p. 255.

55. There is a third scene that takes place in a synagogue, but Yentl herself does not pray in this scene; she only watches her father pray as she sits upstairs in the women's balcony.

56. See Early's claim that the very ahistoricity of *The Color Purple* is a large part of its appeal to both blacks and whites ("The Color Purple as Everybody's Protest Art," pp. 265–67).

57. As mentioned above, Singer's story also treats women this way, but it is unclear why Streisand chose to be faithful to his misogyny when she altered so many other important parts of the story, such as the ending and the overall portrayal of Yentl.

58. See Pauline Kael, review of *Yentl*, in *For Keeps* (New York: Dutton, 1994), pp. 1015–20; Gloria Steinem, *"Yentl," Ms.*, February 1984, p. 32; Ally Acker, "Arts: Women behind the Camera," *Ms.*, March–April 1992, pp. 64–67; and Allison Fernley and Paula Maloof, *"Yentl," Film Quarterly* 3 (spring, 1985): 38–46.

59. Quoted in Acker, "Arts," p. 65.

60. Only Hadass may be somewhat changed by the end of the film, but it seems more likely that she will revert to her old self soon after Yentl's departure. One can hardly assume that her studies will continue with Avigdor, her new husband, who told Yentl (with whose talmudic brilliance he was well familiar) after he found out she was a woman: "You still want to study? . . . You don't need to anymore; I'll do the thinking. . . . I want you to be a real woman." Yentl has to leave Avigdor to become the kind of woman she wants to be. One doubts that Avigdor's ideas about women studying Talmud have changed much by having known her, and one must be pessimistic about Haddass's chances of continuing her talmudic studies.

61. Waldman, *Barbra Streisand Scrapbook*, p. 154.

62. Janice Radway, *Reading the Romance: Women, Patriarchy, and Popular Literature* (1984; reprint, Chapel Hill: University of North Carolina Press, 1991), p. 77. Among these readers, ideal heroines were chosen for their "unusual intelligence and extraordinarily fiery disposition[s]" (p. 123). Radway concludes, much as Tompkins does about the sentimental literature of the nineteenth century, that "[r]omance reading supplements the avenues traditionally open to women for emotional gratification by supplying them vicariously with the attention and nurturance they do not get enough of in the round of day-to-day existence. It countervaluates because the story opposes the female values of love and personal interaction to the male values of competition and public achievement and, at least in ideal romances, demonstrates the triumph of the former over the latter" (Radway, p. 212; see also Tompkins, *Sensational Designs*, p. 145.)

63. I owe a large debt of appreciation to many teachers and friends who offered insightful comments on earlier versions of this paper. I would especially like to thank Stephen J. Whitfield, Joyce Antler, Jonathan D. Sarna, and Sylvia Barack Fishman, my parents, and my good friends and best critics, Andrea Most, Rona Sheramy, and David Ben-Ur.

S. B. Cohen, From Critic to Playwright

1. The fledgling play *The Ladies Locker Room* was appreciated by audiences around the country: San Diego's Gaslamp Theater, St. Louis Cultural Arts Center, Northwestern University Theater, New York State Writers Institute, the Jewish Centers of Chicago. It received the prize for the best creative work in the College of Arts and Humanities of the University at Albany in 1992 and is published by Syracuse University Press in my anthology, *Making a Scene: The Contemporary Drama of Jewish American Women* (1997).
2. Robert A. Cohn, "Humor Triumphs over Despair in *Ladies Locker Room,*" *St. Louis Jewish Light*, May 30, 1990.
3. Cynthia Ozick, letter to author, December 5, 1988.
4. Program notes, *The Ladies Locker Room*, Northwestern University production, April 10–14, 1991.
5. In 1994, I received a grant from the University at Albany, SUNY, to write a new play with music, *Molly Picon's Return Engagement.* It has been performed before standing-room-only audiences at Syracuse University; Hopewell Junction, New York; Highland Park; Boca Raton; Milwaukee; Chicago; Toronto; Atlanta; Washington, D.C.; the Berkshires; Costa Mesa, California; Miami Beach; and Albany, where it raised $7,500 as a benefit to help preserve Yiddish culture, virtually destroyed in the Holocaust. It was a featured attraction at the Long Island Jewish Cultural Arts Fair and was chosen as a special event at the 1995 Modern Language Association convention in Chicago. In 1996–97 it was performed in Minneapolis; Palo Alto, California; Cleveland, Cincinnati and Columbus, Ohio; Grand Rapids, Michigan; Utica, Newburgh, and Queens, New York; Silver Spring, Maryland, and at the Philadelphia Academy of Music.
6. Grace Paley, "The Loudest Voice," *The Little Disturbances of Man* (New York: Penguin, 1985), pp. 53–64.
7. In Sarah Blacher Cohen, *Jewish Wry: Essays on Jewish Humor* (Bloomington: Indiana University Press, 1987), pp. 105–24.
8. *Sophie, Totie and Belle* ran for three months in Philadelphia in 1992, and for six months it played to sold-out houses in Miami Beach and Boca Raton, Florida. In 1996 the play had a successful revival in Queens; Metuchen, New Jersey; and West Palm Beach, Florida.
9. *Sophie Tucker: Red Hot Yiddishe Mama*, had its debut at Mount Holyoke College and at the Jewish Museum of Miami in 1995. It was sponsored in 1996 by the Jewish Theater of the Berkshires for a successful run in the summer and fall at the Lenox Town Hall. In 1997 it was performed in Hartford and in Albany.

G. T. Reimer, Eschewing Esther/Embracing Esther

1. See Tikva Frymer-Kensky, "The Bible and Women's Studies," in *Feminist Perspectives on Jewish Studies*, ed. Lynn Davidman and Shelly Tenenbaum (New Haven, Conn.: Yale University Press, 1994), pp. 16–39, and Susan Niditch, "Portrayals of Women in the Hebrew Bible," in *Jewish Women in Historical Perspective*, ed. Judith R. Baskin (Detroit: Wayne State University Press, 1991), pp. 25–42.
2. Mieke Bal, *Lethal Love: Feminist Literary Readings of Biblical Love Stories* (Bloomington: Indiana University Press, 1987), p. 37.
3. Mary Gendler, "The Restoration of Vashti," in *The Jewish Woman: New Perspectives*, ed. Elizabeth Koltun (New York: Schocken Books, 1976), p. 241.
4. Celina Spiegel, "The World Remade: The Book of Esther," in *Out of the Garden: Women Writers on the Bible*, ed. Christina Buchman and Celina Spiegel (New York: Fawcett Columbine, 1994), p. 191.
5. Michelle Landsberg in *Half the Kingdom: Seven Jewish Feminists*, ed. Francine Zuckerman (Montreal: Vehicule Press, 1992), pp. 61–62.
6. Miriam Chaikin, *Esther* (Philadelphia: Jewish Publication Society, 1987).
7. Shoshana Silberman, *The Whole Megillah* (Rockville, Md.: Kar-Ben Copies, 1990).
8. Ruth F. Brin, *The Story of Esther* (Minneapolis: Lerner Publications, 1976).
9. Maida Silverman, *Festival of Esther: The Story of Purim* (New York: Simon and Schuster, 1989).
10. Barbara Cohen, *Here Come the Purim Players!* (New York: Lothrop, Lee & Shepard Books).
11. Gendler, "Restoration," p. 241.
12. Ibid., p. 245.
13. Rachel M. Brownstein, "Chosen Women," in *Out of the Garden: Women Writers on the Bible*, ed. Christina Buchman and Celina Spiegel (New York: Fawcett Columbine, 1994), pp. 180–90.
14. Gendler, "Restoration," p. 245; my emphasis.
15. Brownstein, "Chosen Women," pp. 186–87.
16. Ibid.
17. Letty Cottin Pogrebin, *Deborah, Golda, and Me: Being Female and Jewish in America* (New York: Crown, 1991), p. 135.
18. Brownstein, "Chosen Women," p. 186.
19. Pogrebin, *Deborah*, p. 135.
20. Spiegel, "World Remade," p. 194.
21. Elizabeth Swados, *Bible Women* (CD) (New York: Swados Enterprises, 1995).

M. E. Solomon, Claiming Our Questions

1. Judith Plaskow. *Standing Again at Sinai: Judaism from a Feminist Perspective* (New York: HarperCollins, 1990), p. 1.
2. Rabbi Nathan Goldberg, *Passover Haggadah* (Hoboken, N.J.: Ktav Publishing

House, 1949); rev. ed. by Asher Scharfstein (1993), p. 8. The following page number refers to both editions. It is encouraging to note that the 1993 edition of this widely used Conservative haggadah, while still traditionally male, does contain some new English translations of the Hebrew texts. For example, it now uses the more inclusive words, "next year may we be free."

3. Ibid., p. 49.
4. Ibid., p. 8.
5. Ibid., p. 49.
6. Maida E. Solomon, "The New Haggadahs: Feminism as a Force within Judaism" (Master's thesis, San Francisco State University, 1987).
7. On April 20, 1987, a women's seder was held at the Reform Temple Emanu-El in San Francisco; Jane Sprague Zones's *San Diego Women's Haggadah*, 2nd ed. (San Diego, Calif.: Women's Institute for Continuing Education, 1980), was used during the seder.
8. One causal factor in the new haggadah texts is the increasing ease of writing in the twentieth century. Passover has long included the interjection of current topics relevant to participants but always as an oral tradition. Now oral tradition has transformed itself into an informal "written" tradition yet still with the changing characteristics of an oral tradition.
9. Arthur Waskow, introduction to *The Shalom Seders: Three Haggadahs Compiled by the New Jewish Agenda* (New York: Adama Books, 1984), p. 8.
10. Ibid., p. 10.
11. "This Year in Brooklyn: A Seder to Celebrate Ourselves." *Off Our Backs* 3 (May 1973): 15–18.
12. Anna Rubin et al., *Women's Passover Seder—1977* (Los Angeles: Authors, 1977), p. 1.
13. Fayla Schwartz et al., *Pesach Haggadah: A Statement of Joyous Liberation—Women's Seder, Berkeley, California, 5733–1973* (Berkeley, Calif. Authors, 1973), p. 8.
14. E. M. Broner with Naomi Nimrod, *The Women's Haggadah* (San Francisco: Harper San Francisco, 1993). For more in-depth description of the twenty-year evolution of this Haggadah, see E. M. Broner, *The Telling: The Story of a Group of Jewish Women Who Journey to Spirituality through Community and Ceremony* (San Francisco: Harper San Francisco, 1993). Also for another voice describing the evolution of this women's seder, see Letty Cottin Pogrebin, *Deborah, Golda, and Me: Being Female and Jewish in America* (New York: Crown, 1991), pp. 119–27.
15. The second-century Mishnah contains the first written descriptions of Passover, marking its move from an oral to a written tradition and from a temple-based to a diasporic culture. I have come to think of this outline as a checklist, remarkably familiar. It made clear that the ritual was to start with the kiddush (blessing announcing the sanctity of the day), that blessings were to be said over cups of wine during ritual, that questions were to be asked by a child (male), that a response to the questions would include a description of Exodus and commentary describing why that description is still relevant to all Jews, that certain foods and symbols be used and explained, that the Hallel Psalms 113–18) be said or sung, that the services end with a specific closing prayer.

16. Judith Plaskow, "Standing at Mt. Sinai: Re-Thinking the Torah" (paper presented at the Bunting Institute, Radcliff College, Cambridge, Mass., 1986).

17. *Haggadah (for Revolutionaries): An Initial Attempt* (San Francisco: Author [unkown], 1986), p. 7.

18. Judith A. Stein, *A New Haggadah: A Jewish Lesbian Seder* (Cambridge, Mass.: Bobbeh Meisehs Press, 1984). In the secular tradition, it is interesting to note that the early Socialist founders of kibbutzim also wrote haggadot in which all spiritual elements were removed but that otherwise followed the Mishnah guidelines in form. For a brief description, see Philip Goodman, ed., *The Passover Anthology* (Philadelphia: Jewish Publication Society of America, 1961), pp. 83–84.

19. Zones, *San Diego Women's Haggadah*, p. 1.

20. Ibid., p. 16.

21. Broner and Nimrod, *Women's Haggadah*, pp. 40–41.

22. Zones, *San Diego Women's Haggadah*, pp. 14–15. Also cited in Maida Tilchen, ed., *Boston Rotating Seder Lesbian Haggadah* (Somerville, Mass.: Author, 1994), p. 2.

23. Most often, the original Exodus story is retained in women's haggadot. The new text is either blended into the old or appears in a separate mode. Many feminist haggadists retain an appreciation of the biblical narration.

24. Rashi, *Talmud*, Pesachim 108b, cited in Miriam's Timbrel, *A Women's Haggadah: Oberlin College 1984* (Oberlin, Ohio: Authors, 1984), p. 13. Also cited in Zones, *San Diego Women's Haggadah*, p. 34.

25. *In Every Generation: A Passover Haggadah for the Westchester Women's Seder* (Westchester County, N.Y.: American Jewish Committee and YM-YWHA of Mid-Westchester, 1995), p. 13.

26. *And We Were All There: A Feminist Passover Haggadah* (Los Angeles: American Jewish Congress Feminist Center, 1994), p. 23.

27. Broner and Nimrod, *Women's Haggadah*, pp. 31–33.

28. Ibid., p. 28.

29. Ruth Linden and Alice Prussin, eds., *Haggadah for Passover* (San Francisco: Authors, 1983), p. 6.

30. Zones, *San Diego Women's Haggadah*, p. 71.

31. Ma'yan: The Jewish Women's Project, *Journey to Freedom: Nisan 5755, April 1995* (New York: JCC of the Upper West Side, 1995): "According to the *midrash*, when the Israelites made their way through the desert, Miriam's wells served as way stations for them. Our people stopped and were refreshed by the clear, cold waters. Many centuries after Miriam's death, the rabbis of Tzfat still searched for Miriam's famed well, believing that those who drank from it would be granted eternal life" (p. 26). For more information on the symbolism of Miriam's well, see Penina Adelman, *Miriam's Well: Rituals for Jewish Women around the Year* (Cincinnati: Hebrew Union College Press, 1992).

32. *And We Were All There*, p. 18.

33. *Project Kesher Haggadah: Global Women's Seder* (Evanston, Ill.: Project Kesher, 1995), p. 12.

34. Ma'yan, *Journey to Freedom*, p. 13.

35. *A Celebration of Jewish Women's Freedom: Pesach 1995* (South Africa: Union of Jewish Women of South Africa, 1995), pp. 12–13.

36. *Di Vilda Chais Haggadah* (New York: Author [unknown], 1981), p. 25.
37. Ma'yan: The Jewish Women's Project, *From Slavery to Freedom, From Darkness to Light—4 Nisan 5754, March 16, 1994* (New York: JCC of the Upper West Side, 1994), p. 19.
38. *A Celebration of Jewish Women's Freedom*, p. 20.
39. Ma'yan, *Journey to Freedom*, p. 13.
40. Stein, *A New Haggadah*, pp. 9–10.
41. Ma'yan, *From Slavery to Freedom*, p. 17. Also, *In Every Generation*, p. 37.
42. Zones, *San Diego Women's Haggadah*, p. 32.
43. *Project Kesher Haggadah*, p. 4.
44. Sarah Comerchero, *A Passover Haggadah: The Alef* (San Francisco: Author, 1985), p. 14.
45. *Project Kesher Haggadah*, p. 17. Also, Ma'yan, *From Slavery to Freedom*, p. iii: "Some 25 years ago . . . in Florida . . . Professor Susannah Heschel . . . spoke at a synagogue about women as teachers and students of *Torah* . . . and rabbis . . . a man . . . shouted 'A woman belongs on the *bimah* (pulpit) as much as bread belongs on the seder plate.' Professor Heschel responded . . . The teachings of women do not violate the tradition, but renew it. Women bring to the *bimah* what an orange would bring to the seder plate: transformation, not transgression.'" (Both the 1994 and 1995 Ma'yan haggadot and Project Kesher cite as a source for the story about Heschel: Arthur Waskow, *A Pathfinder for ALEPH* [Philadelphia: Alliance for Jewish Renewal].

    Also, see Susan Fielding's "A Crust of Bread at the Seder Table" in Miriam's Timbrel, *A Women's Haggadah: Oberlin College 1984* (Oberlin, Ohio), pp. 25–26. Fielding tells a similar midrash but one that names a crust of bread symbolizing the role of lesbians with Judaism. In Rebecca Alpert's *Bread on the Seder Plate: Jewish Lesbians and the Transformation of Tradition* (New York: Columbia University Press, 1997), further research dates the crust of bread on the seder plate to lesbian haggadot of the late 1970s.
46. See Ma'yan, *Journey to Freedom*, pp. i–ii. Also Elaine Moise and Rebecca Schwartz, *The Dancing with Miriam Haggadah: A Jewish Women's Celebration of Passover* (Palo Alto, Calif.: Rikudel Miriam, 1995), pp. xiii–xx. Both ritual documents, often true of 1990s haggadot, include commentary on the restructuring of the prayers in Hebrew, an interesting challenge both because Judaism has specified language requirements for its prayers and because a neuter gender is not an option with Hebrew.
47. Marcia Falk is one of the current leaders in this movement to rewrite liturgy in Hebrew. Jewish women in earlier centuries have created prayers (not for Passover); see Tracy Guren Klirs, ed., *The Merit of Our Mothers: A Bilingual Anthology of Jewish Women's Prayers* (Cincinnati: Hebrew Union College Press, 1992). For a brief overview, see Moise and Schwartz, *Dancing with Miriam Haggadah*, preface.
48. Ma'yan, *Journey to Freedom*, p. ii.
49. Moise and Schwartz, *Dancing with Miriam Haggadah*, pp. xix–xx. *Yah* forms the first two letters for the four-letter name of the divinity that is not pronounceable by Jews. It is also familiar in Hebrew through the word *Halleluyah* (Praise *Yah!*).

50. Karen G. R. Roekard, *The Santa Cruz Haggadah: A Passover Haggadah, Coloring Book, and Journal for the Evolving Consciousness* (Capitola, Calif.: Hineni Consciousness Press, 1991), p. 29.

51. The Jewish Community Center on the Upper West Side in New York is the parent organization of Ma'yan.

52. Elaine Poise, co-author of *The Dancing with Miriam Haggadah*, interview with author, August 6, 1995.

53. *In Every Generation.*

54. Ibid., p. 38.

55. Ibid., p. 21.

56. Karen Gershon, executive director, Project Kesher, interview with author, July 31, 1995.

57. Project Kesher did not know of women's seders springing from indigenous Jewish women's sources outside the United States and Canada.

58. Kesher representatives were occasionally present during pre-Pesach discussions about the Kesher Haggadah in various countries. Thus, for example, we learn that Russian women considered the whole feminist Haggadah a "Western agenda" and did not see themselves as oppressed. However, each group in the FSE loved the symbolism of the orange on the seder plate. At one seder, women even cheered as the orange was placed there.

59. *A Celebration of Jewish Women's Freedom*, p. 27.

60. *Project Kesher Haggadah*, p. 11.

J. Antler, Epilogue

1. Norman Kleeblatt, "'Passing' into Multiculturalism," in *Too Jewish? Challenging Traditional Identities* (New Brunswick, N.J.: Rutgers University Press, 1996), pp. 4–5.

2. I am indebted to Marlene Adler Marks for this discussion of *Rhoda*. Also see Risa Whitney Gordon, "On Television, Jewish Women Get the Short End of the Script," *Jewish Exponent*, May 7, 1993; Susan Kaplan, "From 'Seinfeld' to 'Chicago Hope': Jewish Men Are Everywhere, But the Few Jewish Women on Television Perpetuate Negative Stereotypes," *Forward*, November 29, 1996; and Michael Medved, "Is Hollywood Too Jewish?" in *Moment* 21 (August 31, 1996), p. 36.

3. Fran Drescher, *Enter Whining* (New York: HarperCollins, 1996). Also see Drescher, *The Wit and Wisdom of "The Nanny": Fran's Guide to Life, Love, and Shopping* (New York: Avon, 1995). Drescher also did a cartoon Christmas special, "Oy to the World."

4. Drescher claims that she insisted on a Jewish nanny despite CBS executives' preference for an Italian character. Robin Cembalist, "Big Hair, Short Skirts—and High Culture," *Forward*, February 14, 1997.

5. John J. O'Connor, "This Jewish Mom Dominates TV, Too," *New York Times*, October 14, 1993.

6. Nora Lee Mandel, "Who's Jewish on *Friends*," *Lilith* 21 (Summer 1996), p. 6.

Also see Natalie Weinstein, "Is Seinfeld Jewish? Experts Seek Cultural Definition," *Northern California Jewish Bulletin,* May 24, 1996.

7. *Relativity*, which debuted during the 1997 season, also featured an explicitly Jewish female character, Rhonda (Lisa Epstein), the older sister of the male lead (whose girlfriend is Gentile).

8. Todd Gitlin, *Inside Prime Time*, cited in John J. O'Connor, "TV View," *New York Times*, July 15, 1990.

9. Ibid.

10. Among the many wide-ranging accounts on negative images of Jews, see Linda Nochlin and Tamar Garb, eds., *The Jew in the Text: Modernity and the Construction of Identity* (London: Thames and Hudson, 1995) and Sander L. Gilman, *Jewish Self-Hatred: Anti-Semitism and the Hidden Language of the Jews* (Baltimore: Johns Hopkins University Press, 1986).

11. I would like to thank Lauren and Rachel Antler, Phyllis Deutsch, Marlene Adler Marks, Jonathan Sarna, and Mara Fein for their helpful comments on this epilogue.

Notes on Contributors

Joyce Antler is the Samuel Lane Professor of American Jewish History and Culture at Brandeis University and Chair of the American Studies Department. She is the author of *The Journey Home: Jewish Women and the American Century* (1997), *Lucy Sprague Mitchell: The Making of A Modern Woman* (1987), and other works on American history, and has edited *America and I: Short Stories by American Jewish Women Writers* (1990) and co-edited *The Challenge of Feminist Biography* (1992) and *Changing Education: Women as Radicals and Conservators* (1990).

Joan Jacobs Brumberg is Stephen H. Weiss Presidential Fellow and Professor at Cornell University, where she teaches history, human development, and women's studies. She is the author of numerous articles and books about the history of adolescent girls, including the award-winning *Fasting Girls: The Emergence of Anorexia Nervosa as a Modern Disease* (1988) and *The Body Project: An Intimate History of American Girls* (1997).

Janet Burstein, Professor of English at Drew University, teaches both Victorian literature and American Jewish literature. She has published in *Victorian Studies*, *American Literature*, and *Studies in American Jewish Literature*. Her book on American Jewish women's stories, *Writing Mothers, Writing Daughters*, was published in 1996. She is working now on writers of the 1920s and 1930s.

Sarah Blacher Cohen, Professor of English at the University of Albany, State University of New York, is the author of *Saul Bellow's Enigmatic Laughter* (1974) and *Cynthia Ozick's Comic Art: From Levity to Liturgy* (1994). She is the editor of *Comic Relief: Humor in Contemporary American Literature* (1978); *From Hester Street to Hollywood: The Jewish-American Stage and Screen* (1983); *Jewish Wry: Essays on Jewish Humor* (1987); and the anthology *Making a Scene: The Contemporary Drama of Jewish-American Women* (1997). As a playwright she has written *The Ladies Locker Room, Molly Picon's Return Engagement*, and *The Old System*, based on Saul Bellow's short story. She has collaborated on *Schlemiel the First* with Isaac Bashevis Singer and co-written *Sophie, Totie and Belle, Sophie Tucker: Red Hot Yiddishe Mama*, and *Soul Sisters* with Joanne Koch.

Sylvia Barack Fishman is Assistant Professor of Contemporary Jewish Life in the Department of Near Eastern and Judaic Studies at Brandeis University; she also serves as Associate Director of the International Research Institute on Jewish Women at Brandeis. She is the author of *A Breath of Life: Feminism in the American Jewish Community* (1993) and editor of *Follow My Footprints: Changing Images of Women in American Jewish Fiction* (1992). The author of dozens of articles on the sociology of American Jewry and on American Jewish literature, she is currently at work on a book entitled *American Jewish Lifestyles in Cultural Context*, based on the 1990 National Jewish Population Survey.

Felicia Herman is a Ph.D. candidate in Near Eastern and Judaic Studies. She received her M.A. degree in Jewish Women's Studies from Brandeis University and her B.A. degree from Wellesley College. She is currently writing a dissertation on the history of synagogue sisterhoods in the United States from the 1887 to the present.

Susanne Klingenstein is Associate Professor of Writing and Humanistic Studies at the Massachusetts Institute of Technology. She is the author of *Jews in the American Academy, 1900–1940* (1991) and the forthcoming *Enlarging America: The Cultural Work of Jewish Literary Scholars, 1930–1990* (1998). She has contributed articles about American Jewish literature and culture to professional journals.

Bonnie Lyons is Professor of English at the University of Texas in San Antonio. She is the author of *Henry Roth: The Man and His Work* as well as numerous articles on American Jewish literature. Her book of interviews with contemporary fiction writers (co-author Bill Oliver) will be published next year. She is currently at work on a book of interviews with contemporary playwrights.

Riv-Ellen Prell, an anthropologist, is Associate Professor of American Studies at the University of Minnesota and also teaches in Jewish Studies and Women's Studies. She is the author of *Prayer and Community: The Havurah in American Judaism* (1989) and co-editor, with the Personal Narratives Group, of *Interpreting Women's Lives: Personal Narratives and Feminist Theory* (1989). Her book *Fighting to Become Americans: Jewish Women and Men in Conflict in the Twentieth Century* will be published in 1998. Her research is about issues of gender and class in twentieth-century American Jewish life.

Gail Twersky Reimer is founder and director of the Jewish Women's Archives. She is co-editor, with Judith Kates, of *Reading Ruth: Women Reclaim a Sacred Story* (1994) and the forthcoming *Beginning Anew: A Women's Companion to the High Holy Days*.

Sharon Pucker Rivo is co-founder and executive director of the National Center for Jewish Film. She is Adjunct Associate Professor in the Department of Near East and Judaic Studies at Brandeis University.

June Sochen is Professor of History and Women's Studies at Northeastern Illinois University in Chicago. Her specialties include U.S. women's history, intellectual and cultural history, and the history of U.S. Jews. Her most recent publications include *Mae West: She Who Laughs Lasts* (1992) and *Women's Comic Visions* (1991).

Maida E. Solomon lives in Somerville, Massachusetts, and commutes to Vermont, where she teaches Psychology and Women's Studies in the Adult Degree Program at Norwich University. She has been a Visiting Scholar at the Schlesinger Library, Radcliffe College, and at Brandeis University Women's Studies Program and is currently working on a book of memoirs about and historical essays by her mother. She comes from a long tradition of women talking back and moving forward.

Donald Weber is Professor of English and American Studies at Mount Holyoke College and the author of *Rhetoric and History in Revolutionary New England* (1988). The essay in this volume is part of a work in progress on comparative ethnic expression in America, 1880–1960, titled "Table Manners and Civility."

Index